Zen Terror in
Prewar Japan

Inoue Nisshō in 1953 at sixty-six years of age. The Buddhist phrase, penned by Inoue, at the bottom left of the photo, reads, "Kill one [that] many may live."

Zen Terror in Prewar Japan

Portrait of an Assassin

Brian Daizen Victoria

Foreword by James Mark Shields

ROWMAN & LITTLEFIELD
Lanham • Boulder • New York • London

Published by Rowman & Littlefield
An imprint of The Rowman & Littlefield Publishing Group, Inc.
4501 Forbes Boulevard, Suite 200, Lanham, Maryland 20706
www.rowman.com

6 Tinworth Street, London SE11 5AL, United Kingdom

British Library Cataloguing in Publication Information Available

Library of Congress Control Number: 2019950639

ISBN 978-1-5381-3166-4 (cloth : alk. paper)
ISBN 978-1-5381-3167-1 (electronic)

∞™ The paper used in this publication meets the minimum requirements of American
National Standard for Information Sciences—Permanence of Paper for Printed Library
Materials, ANSI/NISO Z39.48-1992.

Dedicated to the victims of
religious terrorism everywhere

"There exists a subterranean world where pathological fantasies disguised as ideas are churned out by crooks and half-educated fanatics for the benefit of the ignorant and superstitious. There are times when this underworld emerges from the depths and suddenly fascinates, captures, and dominates multitudes of usually sane and responsible people, who thereupon take leave of sanity and responsibility. And it occasionally happens that this underworld becomes a political power and changes the course of history."

—Norman Cohn, *Warrant for Genocide*

"Positive thinkers and public relations officers for the faiths would repudiate this notion or evade the fact. They want religion to be nothing but godspel, good news. Apologists for the faiths usually minimize the distress that can come with religion or that religion can produce. You will not read about the destructive element in religious impulses in the advertisements for the church of your choice. Yet if the pursuit of truth is still to be cherished as a foundational theme in the academy, one must note the feature of religion that keeps it on the front page and on prime time: it kills."

—Martin Marty, University of Chicago

"Zen has no special doctrine or philosophy, no set of concepts or intellectual formulas, except that it tries to release one from the bondage of birth and death, by means of certain intuitive modes of understanding peculiar to itself. It is, therefore, extremely flexible in adapting itself to almost any philosophy and moral doctrine as long as its intuitive teaching is not interfered with. It may be found wedded to anarchism or fascism, communism or democracy, atheism or idealism, or any political or economic dogmatism. It is, however, generally animated with a certain revolutionary spirit, and when things come to a deadlock—as they do when we are overloaded with conventionalism, formalism, and other cognate isms—Zen asserts itself and proves to be a destructive force."

—D. T. Suzuki, *Zen and Japanese Culture*

"Under conditions of tyranny it is far easier to act than to think."

—Hannah Arendt

"Religious faith without a strong role for critical reason readily falls into fanaticism."

—Gary Gutting, University of Notre Dame

"In world history, few things have proven more destructive than religion in the service of aggression."

—Gary Leupp, Tufts University

"The easiest way to gain control of a population is to carry out acts of terror. [The public] will clamor for such laws if their personal security is threatened."

—Joseph Stalin

"Terrorism is the best political weapon, for nothing drives people harder than a fear of sudden death."

—Adolf Hitler

Contents

Acknowledgments

Let me begin by expressing my appreciation to those individuals who helped make this book possible. First and foremost is Herbert Bix, author of the Pulitzer Prize–winning book *Hirohito and the Making of Modern Japan*. Many students of modern Japan, including me, had long suspected that Emperor Hirohito's wartime role was far more important than his popular image as a powerless puppet of Japan's military leaders. It was not, however, until the appearance of Bix's meticulously researched book that the active role Emperor Hirohito played in directing Japanese aggression from the 1930s onward became clear. I am indeed fortunate that Bix not only reviewed portions of the manuscript but kindly allowed me to incorporate elements of his research into the second chapter of this book. Nevertheless, the history-related comments and conclusions contained herein are mine and mine alone.

I also wish to acknowledge the support I received from Buddhist scholars Richard Gombrich, Peter Harvey, Damien Keown, and Jacqueline Stone. Each of them offered constructive criticisms of my writing, hopefully leading me to increased accuracy, better reasoning, and sounder conclusions. Once again, however, I take full responsibility for the book's contents.

Let me also express my appreciation to one of the main members of Inoue Nisshō's terrorist band, Yotsumoto Yoshitaka, whom I interviewed at the age of ninety-three. In addition, Wada Nichiyū, the late abbot of the Buddhist temple Inoue once headed, Risshō Gokokudō (Temple to Protect the Nation [by] Establishing the True [Dharma]), also cooperated with this study. Still further, I interviewed Inoue's daughter Ryō (aka Ryōko) in order to provide a more intimate view of my subject. All of these interviews were made possible due to the invaluable assistance of my partner, Aimee Tsujimoto, who also introduced me to Tanaka Satoshi, my guide at the time I visited Inoue Nisshō's birthplace in Kawaba village, Gumma prefecture.

Last but not least, let me also express my deep appreciation to Don Cohon, who kindly reviewed and commented most helpfully on early drafts of the manuscript, as well as to those unknown reviewers who offered valuable suggestions for its improvement. I am also grateful to my ever-so-patient editors, Susan McEachern and Mark Selden, at Rowman & Littlefield. While a book carries the name of an author, and sometimes coauthors, it is made possible by the efforts of literally thousands of contributors, known and unknown, past and present.

I am grateful to them all.

Foreword

James Mark Shields, Bucknell University

It has been just over two decades since the publication of Brian Victoria's *Zen at War* (1997). Rarely has an academic publication had such an impact, and one that, let me be clear, went well beyond the realm of scholarly debate—though it did inspire plenty of that, too. More than one of Japanese Buddhism's venerable (and frequently inscrutable) institutions was compelled to respond to the charges brought by Victoria, and more often than not, the response was a recognition of the validity of his claims and admission of their own complicity in the nationalism and militarism of early to mid-twentieth-century Japan. On a personal level, I am fairly sure I was not the only young scholar whose eyes were opened by *Zen at War*, as well as by the subsequent *Zen War Stories* (2002), to the ways that modern forms of Buddhism, and not only Zen, could be used as political ideology, often to deleterious effect. My own intellectual path shifted from a vague interest in comparative religious ethics to the history and analysis of Buddhist political movements in Japan from the Meiji Restoration of 1868 to the present. Victoria's books challenged me in particular to wonder about the other side of the coin: i.e., those (fewer) Buddhists who *resisted* the dominant economic and political ideologies of the twentieth century.

In *Zen Terror in Prewar Japan*, Victoria turns his attention to the involvement of Zen Buddhism in the volatile politics of the Taishō and early Shōwa periods, including the decades leading up to and the years immediately following the Second World War. Whereas *Zen at War* aimed at a comprehensive overview, this book focuses on one man, Inoue Nisshō (1887–1967), a fascinating and colorful figure who, despite his own personal and professional struggles, managed to hobnob in high circles and, according to Victoria, may be seen as a central player in the destabilization of early twentieth-century Japanese democracy. Indeed, given Inoue's involvement in various key events in the tumultuous decades leading up to the end of the war, it is a surprise that no one has written a full-length study of his life in English before now—perhaps this can be attributed to the rather dismissive evaluations of Inoue's competence noted by postwar commentators. Here, Victoria effectively uses Inoue as a means to raise deeper questions regarding the interconnections of Buddhism, Zen, war, violence, terror, and the fragility of democracy in 1920s–1930s Japan.

To provide the reader with some additional context, I will briefly reflect on the life and work of Inoue Nisshō in relation to my own research and publications over the past decade, in which I have attempted to understand the lives, actions, and ideas of the (decidedly few) Japanese Buddhist individuals and groups that challenged the sociopolitical and economic winds of the first three decades of the twentieth century. Perhaps the most significant of these figures was Seno'o Girō (1890–1961), an exact contemporary who functions as Inoue's religious and political *doppelgänger*, or alter ego. A young man of late Meiji inspired by various streams of competing ideas—including Buddhism—Seno'o entered the Nichiren sect priesthood at the age of twenty-six, but he soon became involved in the Nichirenist (J., *Nichirenshugi*) movement established several decades previously by Tanaka Chigaku (1861–1939). While rooted in the teachings of sect founder Nichiren (1222–1282), Tanaka sought in his lay-oriented movement a more socially and politically engaged form of Buddhist practice, one that was also highly skeptical of the institution of monasticism.

By the 1890s, under Tanaka's charismatic leadership, Nichirenism had taken on a profoundly nationalistic hue, combining elements of Nichiren's ideas on protecting the nation with the emerging imperialist or *kokutai* ideology now associated with "State Shinto." Seno'o turned his attention to the work of another significant teacher in the Nichirenist movement, Honda Nisshō (1867–1931), who had recently published his own interpretation of the classic Mahāyāna Buddhist text known as the *Lotus Sutra* (which has influenced virtually every East Asian Buddhist sect, including Zen). Though less overtly political than Tanaka in his quest for "world unification" (J., *sekai tōitsu*) under the *Lotus Sutra*, Honda looked for a unification of all Buddhist sects and, also like Tanaka, questioned the traditional division between monastic and lay Buddhism. Finally, he sought a solution to the deepening class rifts (and social unrest) occasioned by the unbridled capitalism of the age. These ideas appealed to Seno'o. He began to attend weekly meetings of Honda's Tōitsudan (Unification Group, founded in 1896) and, after an encouraging meeting with Honda in May 1918, dedicated himself to working for Nichirenist ideals as a layman under Honda's mentorship.

At this point, however, hints of dissatisfaction with his chosen course, and specifically with the more overtly conservative and nationalist ideals and practices of the Nichirenist movement, were beginning to surface. One historical event that had a lasting effect on Seno'o's thought—and played no small role in instigating his turn toward left-wing politics—was the Great Kantō earthquake of September 1, 1923. This double tragedy of a massive quake and ensuing fire, which devastated the city of Tokyo and caused the death of over 140,000 Japanese, drove home for Seno'o the Buddhist doctrine of impermanence and the brute reality of (material) suffering in this world. At about the same time, Seno'o began to entertain serious doubts about the justice of the capitalist system, and he began to consider socialism as a practical foundation for his thoughts on social and religious reform. This turn seems to have been prompted by his increasing contact (and sympathy) with both tenant farmers and factory workers. Although Seno'o's turn to Marxist socialism represented a move away from the specific right-wing political leanings of Nichirenism, it could also be understood as a differential extension of the shared insights of Tanaka and Honda (and Inoue, despite his Zen leanings) with regard to the fusion of religion and politics.

The divergent trajectories of Seno'o and Inoue from the 1920s are perhaps best encapsulated in their respective interpretations of the East Asian Buddhist phrase, *issatsu tashō*—literally, "kill one to save the many," with textual origins in the *Yogācārabhūmi* and *Mahāparinirvāna-sūtra*. Whereas Inoue appears to have understood this in a literal sense, by which it could act as justification for the assassinations carried out by his Blood Oath Corps, Seno'o understood the phrase metaphorically, as a spiritual admonition to overcome one's own weakness and ignorance in order to more fully serve society. (This is strikingly reminiscent of the contemporary discussion within Islam over divergent interpretations of the term *jihad*.) In short, while Seno'o interpreted the phrase as a derivative of the classic Buddhist precept against the taking of life, Inoue understood it in terms of the classical Mahāyāna (and *Lotus Sutra*) teaching of *upaya* or "skillful means" and thus as grounds for breaking even the most fundamental precepts in times of great urgency. To add a layer of tragic irony to this contrast, when Seno'o was arrested and charged with treason in December 1936, a central aspect of the state's "evidence" against him was his frequent use of *issatsu tashō*—which, no doubt due to the 1932 Blood Oath Corps Incident, was interpreted by the state police as a "terrorist" catchphrase.

Zen Terror in Prewar Japan makes a nice "bookend" to the author's earlier works, *Zen at War* (1997) and *Zen War Stories* (2002). Just as these two works opened up important issues that extend well beyond Japanese or Buddhist Studies, so too does *Zen Terror in Prewar Japan*. This book is primarily about the impact of certain elements of Zen Buddhist thought (as an "enabling mechanism") on "right-wing" violence in Japan in the decades leading up to the Second World War. Secondarily, it provides a detailed account of the life and work of Inoue Nisshō, a central, if largely unrecognized player in several key movements and events of the period. This book fills an important gap in our understanding of the period between the 1920s and 1940s by outlining the links between "right-wing" organizations, political elites, and certain religious ideas. Though firmly rooted in historical analysis, *Zen Terror in Prewar Japan* is much more than simply an autobiography or even a historical study. Rather, it should be read as a work of engaged, Buddhist criticism.

Preface

This book is the conclusion of my three-part study on the close, supportive relationship that existed between the Zen school in Japan, both Sōtō and Rinzai sects, and modern Japanese imperialism and its domestic corollary, a totalitarian society in the 1930s and 1940s. The first volume in the study was *Zen at War* and the second *Zen War Stories*.[1] While *Zen at War* was a broad introduction to the topic, *Zen War Stories* took a deeper look at the wartime teachings and actions of selected Zen masters and lay practitioners. This volume, however, examines what is in some ways an even more shocking phenomenon—Zen's involvement in domestic acts of terror in prewar Japan. As this book will demonstrate, Zen involvement in a series of terrorist acts in the 1930s directly contributed to depriving the Japanese people of a voice in their country's affairs—with disastrous results.

REACTIONS TO THE FIRST TWO VOLUMES

Mark Twain once said, "The glory which is built upon a lie soon becomes a most unpleasant incumbrance. . . . How easy it is to make people believe a lie, and how hard it is to undo that work again!"[2] I am reminded of this truism in light of the reactions to my first two books on Zen's strong, even fanatical, embrace of modern Japanese imperialism. Many Western readers, myself among them, have long cherished the belief that Buddhism in general, and Zen in particular, is the peace-loving, and *peace-practicing*, faith they were originally attracted to.

I first arrived in Japan in the fall of 1961 as a conscientious objector to all wars. As such, I was required to fulfill two years of alternate service duty by "promoting international understanding" through teaching English at Aoyama Gakuin University, a Methodist-founded school in Tokyo. Curious about my new home, one of the first books I read was D. T. Suzuki's *Zen and Japanese Culture*. In the book's early pages, Suzuki wrote: "Whatever form Buddhism takes in different countries where it flourishes it is a religion of compassion, and in its varied history it has never been found engaged in warlike activities."[3] Wow, I remember thinking, unlike Christianity with its medieval Crusades and "holy wars," here was a faith that not only "talked the talk" but actually "walked the walk" of peace!

Many years later, after having become a Zen priest in the Sōtō Zen sect, I was shocked to learn how very naïve I had been. At the same time, I knew I was not the only Westerner laboring under this misapprehension. Thus, I felt compelled to write my first two books, both of which revealed just how deeply flawed Suzuki's claims were. In effect, this "man of Zen," as Suzuki was widely known, was little more than a sophisticated, English-speaking version of his fellow Zen leaders, who became adept at hiding his longstanding war-affirming stance from Western readers. This is not to deny, however, the scholarly contributions he made to his generation of Buddhist studies.

Unsurprisingly, *Zen at War* sent shock waves through Zen circles in the West. One pained reader cried out, "What the hell went wrong?" A few even stated they were abandoning Buddhism, or at least Zen, although that decision was never my intention. By far the most vocal reactions were a series of emotional protests and denials from readers, coupled with not a few ad hominem attacks. Readers charged, for example, that my translations of Suzuki's war-related writings, or those of well-known Zen masters, were taken out of context or exaggerated, or simply mistranslated.[4]

This third book, linking Zen to acts of domestic terrorism in prewar Japan, is likely to be greeted even more critically by Western Zen adherents, for it further discredits their claim to have had the "true Buddha Dharma" transmitted to them by their Japanese masters. They are confronted with the question of their own authenticity, or at least the authenticity of their teachings, when their Japanese spiritual fathers or grandfathers were complicit in Japanese aggression throughout Asia and beyond.

Nearly twenty years have elapsed since the appearance of the first two books in this trilogy, and it is clear that even now many, though not all, Western Zen adherents don't want to hear, let alone consider, the implications my research has for their own teaching and practice. By contrast, the responses in Japan have been far more thoughtful. For example, following the 2001 publication of *Zen at War* in Japanese, and citing my book as one of the catalysts, officials of two major branches of the Rinzai Zen sect, as well as the lay-oriented Sanbō-kyōdan, issued formal apologies for their sect's wartime complicity.[5] These apologies, though long in coming, joined those of other traditional Japanese Buddhist sects, for all of them had supported the war effort.

SEXUAL SCANDALS

Sadly, until recently, something similar could be said regarding the unwillingness of Western Zen practitioners to confront the sexual abuse that has taken place at numerous Zen centers in the West. Needless to say, this is hardly a uniquely Zen phenomenon, for Tibetan Buddhist groups have been shown to suffer from the same malady. Nor is sexual abuse a uniquely Buddhist problem, as vividly demonstrated by the Roman Catholic Church in recent years. What they all share in common is a deep-seated unwillingness to confront this problem.

In the case of Zen centers, a series of denial mechanisms was invoked for years, even decades, to dismiss the very existence of such abuse, based on the conviction that allegedly "enlightened" Zen masters, whether Japanese or Western, simply couldn't or wouldn't act in such a deeply hurtful manner. In some instances, senior male disciples either turned a blind eye to the abuse or went so far as to claim that sexual abuse at the hands of a Zen master was beneficial to the spiritual advancement of the abused women. In the process, the voices of the victims were either silenced or marginalized by the Zen communities of which they were a part.

Like the Roman Catholic Church, albeit on a far smaller scale, Zen communities in the West have finally demonstrated willingness to honestly confront the issue of sexual abuse in their midst. This willingness is certainly to be welcomed since it is only in doing so that a recurrence of past abuses can be prevented and a better, safer future ensured. Significantly, one major mechanism put in place to prevent a repetition of sexual abuse is the creation of written guidelines concerning sex between Zen teachers and their students. Without enforcement, however, the guidelines mean little.

In traditional Buddhism of whatever tradition, there have always been strict rules, or precepts, governing every aspect of male and female clerics' lives. There are also increasingly severe penalties, including expulsion from the community, for anyone who breaks these rules. In Japan, however, the Buddhist precepts were gradually relaxed (or disregarded) over the centuries to the point that today they effectively no longer exist in Japan's traditional Buddhist sects, Zen included. That sexual abuse has happened over so many years in Western Zen circles only underscores one of the main points made in my books, which is that the Zen school in Japan long ago abandoned key aspects of Buddhist morality. In addition to clerical sexual abuse (which in Japan is usually hushed up), something similar can be said regarding the Zen school's relationship to violence, including everything from warfare to domestic terrorism.

TWO MAJOR EXCEPTIONS

Happily, there were two notable exceptions to the studied indifference, and often hostility, displayed by Western Zen adherents in the years following the 1997 appearance of *Zen at War*. The first exception was John Daido Loori (1931–2009), late abbot of Zen Mountain Monastery. He wrote the following endorsement for the book's back cover: "*Zen at War* is a wake-up call for all Buddhists. Victoria has shown in a passionate and well-documented way that Buddhism is not immune to the kinds of distortions that have been used throughout history by virtually all of the world's religions to justify so-called holy war."

The second exception was Robert Aitken (1917–2010), late head of the Honolulu Diamond Sangha. His endorsement read: "In this carefully documented study, Brian Victoria exposes the incredible intellectual dishonesty of Japanese Buddhists who perverted their religion into a jingoistic doctrine of support for the emperor and imperial expansion during the period 1868–1945. Good job! We must face this dark side of our heritage squarely."

I was both impressed and grateful that these two American Zen leaders were willing to write endorsements, especially as both men had trained under Zen Masters Nakagawa Sōen and Yasutani Haku'un, both of whom I demonstrated had been staunch supporters of Japanese aggression during the Asia-Pacific War. Not only did Yasutani support aggression abroad, but he was also an anti-Semite and misogynist.[6] For example, in 1943, Yasutani Haku'un wrote, "Of course one should kill, killing as many as possible. One should, fighting hard, kill everyone in the enemy army. The reason for this is that in order to carry [Buddhist] compassion through to perfection it is necessary to assist good and punish evil."[7] As for Jews, Yasutani wrote, "We must be aware of the demonic teachings of the Jews who assert things like [the existence of] equality in the phenomenal world, thereby disturbing public order in our nation's society and destroying [governmental] control."[8] Yasutani also claimed that women should strictly adhere to their patriarchy-ordained gender roles: "Men should fulfill the Way of men, while women fulfill the Way of women, making absolutely sure there is not the slightest confusion between their respective roles."[9]

On the one hand, in light of sentiments like these, it is difficult to see how knowledgeable Zen practitioners like Loori and Aitken could have remained uncritical of men like Yasutani once their wartime statements came to light. On the other hand, in the heavily Confucian-influenced, hierarchical world of Japanese Zen, criticizing one's teacher remains, even now, unheard of. One reason the Japanese version of *Zen at War* had such a strong impact in Japan was because I dared to "name names." Although most of Japan's major Zen sects and subsects have now issued apologies for their war support, none of these apologies identified, let alone criticized, even a single wartime Zen master *by name* for his bellicose statements.

Sadly, Robert Aitken's support for my research was not destined to endure. Shortly before the publication of *Zen at War*, Aitken sent me an email requesting the deletion of statements from the book that offended him. Specifically, he referred to the book's last two sentences: "Thanks to missionary activities of numerous postwar and small numbers of prewar Zen leaders like Yasutani, it can be argued that modern-day variations of Imperial Way [prowar] Zen and soldier Zen are now to be found in the West as well as in Japan, although often without the support or knowledge of their Western adherents. As these Zen variations settle into their new home in the West, the critical question is simply this: Will the doctrine of the unity of Zen and the sword, with all this implies historically, settle in with them?"[10]

What Aitken found offensive was the suggestion that the war-affirming sentiments of Japanese Zen leaders might possibly be present in Western Zen. It is true that at the time I wrote the offending sentences I had no concrete evidence to prove the doctrine of "the unity of Zen and the sword" was present in the United States, let alone the West as a whole, with the exception of some martial arts teachers. Yet the intent of my warning was to alert Western practitioners to this possibility. For that reason, I was unwilling to make the requested deletions, and my correspondence with Aitken came to an end.

ZEN ON THE WESTERN BATTLEFIELD

Inasmuch as my warning was mostly theoretical initially, it came as something of a shock when I later discovered that Zen meditation (*zazen*) was actually being used as part of mental training for American soldiers in Iraq. A video posted on YouTube showed Lt. (now Capt.) Thomas Dyer, the first Zen-affiliated Buddhist chaplain in the United States Army, providing meditation instruction to soldiers serving with the 278th Armored Cavalry Regiment stationed at Camp Taji. In preparation for fighting on the battlefield, many of the meditating soldiers were dressed in BDUs (Battle Dress Uniforms), some still wearing their combat boots. Lt. Dyer explained the purpose of meditation as follows: "It is better to be at peace than not to be at peace. It is better to be clear in the mind than to be confused. It is better to be happy than sad. It is better to be disciplined and sit to give your body time to heal than to stay on this wheel of grasping and running. So with that Buddhism can say to the whole world, start with meditation."[11] In a March 2012 YouTube video, Capt. Dyer explained the relationship of Zen to Buddhism as follows:

> Primarily Buddhism is a methodology of transforming the mind. The mind has flux in it or movement, past and future fantasy, which causes us not to interact deeply with life. So Buddhism has a methodology, a teaching and a practice of meditation to help one concentrate in the present moment to experience reality as it is. . . . Zen practice is to be awake in the present moment both in sitting and then walking throughout the day. So the idea is that enlightenment will come from just being purely aware of the present moment in the present moment.[12]

Clearly, neither of these two explanations seems war-affirming, let alone "blood-thirsty." At worst, Dyer's initial comments, stating that meditation is a way to be "at peace," "clear in the mind," and "happy not sad," may be criticized as turning meditation into a form of ersatz pop psychology that no one could object to. Likewise, what could possibly be wrong with saying that the purpose of Zen practice is to be "awake in the present moment"?

Needless to say, Dyer was aware that Buddhist soldiers on the battlefield may, at any moment, be ordered into combat. However, instead of viewing combat as resulting in death and destruction, he claimed soldiers were "protecting what's beautiful and right":

> Buddhist soldiers have to deal with issues of livelihood: How do I view myself as a Buddhist and a soldier who carries a weapon? . . . I have developed procedures that help

them see themselves as a force for good in the world, protecting what's beautiful and right. It allows them to promote happiness and reduce suffering in the world. I try to teach those things to Buddhist soldiers.[13]

When placed in context, however, the problematic nature of these comments becomes apparent, especially when one considers the role of chaplains in the military. As an Associated Press article noted, "As American troops cope with life—and death—on a faraway battlefield, military chaplains cope with them, offering prayers, comfort and spiritual advice to keep the American military machine running."[14] In the Iraq video, many of the meditating soldiers were dressed for battle, meaning they could be ordered on a mission at a moment's notice, a mission that might well involve killing those Iraqis identified as the enemy. This is despite the fact that the invasion of Iraq has been shown to have been predicated entirely on falsehoods, with Iraqis and the Iraqi government posing no threat whatsoever to the United States and its citizens.

Thus, when invading American Buddhist soldiers were ordered to kill Iraqis, they were, thanks to their practice of meditation, able to do so while being "at peace," "clear in the mind," and "happy not sad." Furthermore, they were to kill "concentrate[d] in the present moment," believing themselves to be "a force for good in the world." Who knows? According to Dyer, they might even become enlightened inasmuch as he claimed "enlightenment will come from just being purely aware of the present moment in the present moment." In light of these comments, we can understand the claim made centuries ago by the famous Rinzai Zen Master Hakuin Ekaku (1686–1769): "The warrior can accomplish in one month what it takes the monk a year to do."[15]

Nor should it be thought that Dyer is alone in his efforts to promote the unity of Zen and the sword within the United States military. A second example occurred in connection with the dedication of the "Vast Refuge Dharma Hall" at the Air Force Academy in Colorado Springs in October 2007. This facility was the result of a request made in 2004 by a graduate of the academy's first class of 1959, Wiley Burch. Burch, now a Buddhist priest affiliated with the Hollow Bones Rinzai Zen sect, requested that a multipurpose room in the lower level of the Cadet Chapel be transformed into a Buddhist hall. At the hall's dedication, Burch said:

> I understood there was a possibility of a place for Buddhism in the military. I understand the culture very well, and I understand the diversity of it. From that place, rather than being hard and coming in against, I came in willing to accept all. That's a Buddhist teaching, not to set yourself up against things so much as to just be, we say, like clouds and like water, just flow. . . . Without compassion, war is nothing but criminal activity. It is necessary sometimes to take life, but we never take it for granted.[16]

Once again, these words seem relatively innocuous until they are put in context. These Air Force Academy cadets are learning that Buddhism means being "willing to accept all." They are learning they shouldn't set themselves against anything, but literally, like clouds and water, they should "just flow." Upon graduation, these cadets will become commissioned officers, having taken an oath to obey the orders of their military superiors. For those who become future bomber pilots, bombardiers, and nuclear missile operators, this means that in the event they are ordered to drop their hydrogen bombs, or fire their nuclear armed missiles, they will, as good Zen Buddhists, "accept all," bringing on a nuclear winter that may well result in the extinction of all human life on this planet—out of their compassion.

COMPASSIONATE TERRORISM

As readers will soon realize, the word *compassion* is key to understanding the acts of domestic, Zen-related terror in prewar Japan. At the time of the Russo-Japanese War of 1904–1905, the famous Rinzai Zen Master Nantembō (1839–1925) told his disciple Army General Nogi Maresuke (1849–1912), "There is no *Bodhisattva* practice superior to the compassionate taking of life."[17] Heartened by this teaching, Nogi took his master's words to the battlefield in his fight against Tsarist troops. Like Nogi, the Zen terrorists in this book also believed they were acting compassionately. They claimed it was an act of compassion to kill those corrupt politicians and financial leaders they held responsible for Japan's societal woes.

It can be argued there is a quantum leap between killing the designated enemies of one's country and killing one's fellow countrymen, no matter how "corrupt" they might be. The major difference is, of course, that in the case of killing foreign enemies, soldiers typically do so with the encouragement and full support of their government. In fact, the greater the number of enemy killed, the greater "heroes" soldiers are held to be. On the other hand, to refuse to kill a designated foe is to risk being labeled a traitor, imprisoned, and even executed.

Domestic terrorists, on the other hand, are vehemently opposed by their government, their acts of violence regarded as contemptible and completely unjustifiable. Given this, how could the Zen-related terrorists described in this book have possibly viewed their murderous acts as "compassionate"? Were they no more than crazed fanatics? Were they a demented Zen Buddhist version of today's ISIL? While it is tempting to view the men featured in this book that way, as we have seen, the identity of "Zen and the sword" has already moved seamlessly, and largely unopposed, from Japan to the West. If Japanese Zen practitioners could become domestic terrorists, justifying their actions as "compassionate killing," is it unthinkable that such a phenomenon might be repeated in the West? This, together with many other questions, will be explored in this book.

1

Introduction

The Christian Crusaders of the eleventh to thirteenth centuries fortunate enough to make it back to their European homelands brought with them tales of exotic lands, peopled by veiled women and mighty warriors on magnificent steeds. In particular, they told of a fearsome group of men known as the *Hashshashin*, thought to be derived from the Arabic *hashishi*, meaning "hashish users." While, in light of their Muslim faith, historians question their use of hashish, it is certain that these men engaged in and regarded the use of assassination as a sacred religious duty.

Properly speaking, the men were a subgroup or sect of Muslim Shi'ites known as Nizari Isma'ilites. Significantly, this sect had come into existence in the late eleventh century not to fight Christian Crusaders but to silently and unexpectedly strike down (i.e., assassinate) those Muslim generals and statesmen who did not share their religious ideals. Although largely a spent force by the mid-thirteenth century, this sect is today regarded as a minor heresy in the Muslim world. In the West, however, the word *assassin* came to mean someone who murders a politically important person either for hire or from hatred or other motives.

While the religious connection to assassination has all but disappeared from Western consciousness, the same cannot be said for the religious link to "terrorism." In fact, in the aftermath of the 9/11 attack, let alone the rise of the "Islamic State" (ISIL), the link between religion and terrorism has become nearly inextricable. Symbolized by the terrorists' frequent battle cry, "Allāhu Akbar" (God is [the] greatest!), the religion referred to is almost exclusively Islam or at least "Islamic extremism."

However, as this book demonstrates, terrorist acts also played a very important role in pre–World War II Japan. This time, however, the religious motivation, where it existed, was Buddhist, not Muslim. And this time the terrorists, on at least three occasions, would be associated with the Zen school of Buddhism, including both the Sōtō and Rinzai sects.

DEFINITION OF TERRORISM

Before proceeding further, it is important to understand what is meant by "terrorism," even while recognizing there is no universally accepted definition for this contentious term.[1] Nevertheless, there are definitions of terrorism that have gained wide acceptance. The operating definition of terrorism in this book is taken from United Nations Security Council Resolution 1566 of October 2004. Terrorism is identified in this resolution as "criminal acts, including against civilians, committed with the intent to cause death or serious bodily injury, or taking of hostages, with the purpose to provoke a state of terror in the general public or in a group of persons or particular persons, intimidate a population or compel a government or an international organization to do or to abstain from doing any act."[2]

Today, in an era of IEDs, car bombs, and suicide bombers, it is popularly assumed that terrorism exists almost exclusively "to provoke a state of terror in the general public or in a group of persons or particular persons." However, it must not be forgotten that terrorism can also be directed at "compelling a government or an international organization to do or to abstain from doing any act." In fact, historically speaking, the roots of terrorism lie in the latter, for it is first and foremost a *tactic* employed, typically by the weak, to place pressure on the powerful, especially governments, to do the terrorists' bidding. The terrorist acts referred to in this book are of this kind.

A good argument can be made that terrorism by the weak, typically substate actors, is but one form of terrorism. For example, full-scale warfare conducted by the militaries of states can also be understood as a form of terrorism. Such wars are fought with the goal of forcing enemy government(s) to do or abstain from whatever the winning side considers to be in its national interests. Seen in this light, the use of any form of violence, even domestic spousal abuse, is yet another form of terrorism. These forms of terrorism, however, are not the topic of this book.

It is important to note that in Japan prior to the Meiji Revolution of 1868 politically motivated killing, apart from large-scale warfare, can best be identified as simply assassination (J., *ansatsu*) rather than terrorism. The difference between the two is that the goal in traditional Japan was to kill one or more political rivals, typically feudal lords, in order to enhance one's own political power, independent of any larger ideological purpose. Needless to say, neither Buddhism nor Zen played significant roles in such assassinations. The *ninja* spies who have so captured the Western imagination may in fact be rightfully considered Japan's first professional assassins, though they were more typically spies.

With Japan's emergence into the modern world via the Meiji Restoration, conflicts between competing ideologies became an important ingredient in the political landscape. While capitalism became the dominant economic ideology (up to the present day), it would be challenged at various times by varieties of anarchism, socialism, and Marxism, not to mention Western liberalism. As this occurred, assassinations were no longer simply about eliminating political rivals, but they became vehicles for achieving larger and more far-reaching ideological goals extending to major social revolutions.

It was thus that assassinations morphed into, or became a part of, terrorist acts, acts directed toward the establishment of a new social compact. In this book, while the word *assassination* is still employed to describe the killing of specific individuals, these assassinations are collectively considered to be terrorist acts in that they were part of movements directed toward larger political goals. Thus, the assassinations and violence preceding and accompanying the establishment of the Meiji Restoration of 1868 can be considered the harbinger of modern terrorism in Japan. This helps to explain why the terrorist acts described in this book were directed toward the creation of yet another Meiji-like restoration, only this time called a "Shōwa Restoration," the details of which will be introduced in following chapters.

FOCUS ON INOUE NISSHŌ

A second major feature of this book is its primary focus on the life and thought of Inoue Nisshō (1887–1967), one of a number of terrorist leaders active in prewar Japan. Inoue was selected for a number of reasons, beginning with the fact that thanks to his own substantive writings, including a detailed biography, we know more about him than almost any other terrorist of his era. Additionally, Inoue details his relationship to religion, in this case Zen Buddhism, and the important role it played in both his spiritual life and the creation and training of his terrorist band. What is particularly surprising about this relationship is that in the postwar era Inoue became known in both Japanese and Western scholarship as a "Nichiren sect priest" not the Zen-trained layman that he was. Why this error was made, and its relevance to understanding Inoue's terrorist acts, will become clear in what follows.

One of the main goals of this book is to move beyond the popular stereotypes of "terrorists" as men (and sometimes women) who are "pure evil," filled with nothing but fanatical religious hatred and destructiveness. Instead, terrorists are presented as fellow human beings who in many respects were once not all that different from the rest of us. However, to do this I have adopted somewhat of an unusual stance in that the initial chapters of this book introduce Inoue's words and actions as he himself described them. The same holds true for Inoue's Rinzai Zen master, Yamamoto Gempō, and others with whom Inoue interacted.

In adopting this stance, I have been guided by what is known as the "life-history method." Briefly, the life-history method uses life story—whether in the form of oral history, personal narrative, autobiography, or biography—as a primary source for the study of history and culture. Life stories capture the relation between the individual and society, the local and the national, the past and present, and the public and private experience. Critically, life-history research is, of necessity, concerned with ethics and power relationships, and with the potential for advocacy and empowerment.

The life-history method is particularly relevant to this book because, in the case of terrorism, it is essential to research the factors that underlie a terrorist group's origins, leader(s), grievances, and demands. This method also facilitates understanding of how "normal people" can become involved in conflict and organizations that are designated as "terrorist bands." More importantly, and as will be discussed further in the epilogue, such insights may help others intervene more effectively to prevent future acts of terrorism, especially by reaching out more effectively to those who are tempted to become terrorists.

In addition, I find the life-history method also contributes to rectifying a telling criticism of existing research on terrorism, that is, the overall lack of studies based on primary data. For understandable reasons, those engaged in studying terrorism have been either reluctant or unable to spend much time "talking to terrorists." In his 2008 survey of the literature, Andrew Silke reported that systematic interviews had been used to secure primary data in "only 1 percent of research reports."[3]

Given this, I believe it is imperative to gain more access to the feelings, perceptions, and thoughts of terrorists. With the emergence and spread of "homegrown terrorism" throughout the world, the reasons for doing so have never been stronger. If we are to understand why someone, especially the young, becomes a terrorist, we need a better grasp of what sociologists call their "definition of the situation." Admittedly, the information we acquire from talking (or listening) to terrorists is subject to distortion, not least of all by what the terrorists choose to share (or hide). Additionally, the small number of individuals with whom we are able to interact poses problems for generalizing findings. Nevertheless, if we wish to increase the validity of our insights, there can be no substitute for listening to terrorists, even when we find their thoughts repugnant.

NORMAN COHN'S INSIGHT

Keeping this in mind, readers will recall the following words from Norman Cohn:

> There exists a subterranean world where pathological fantasies disguised as ideas are churned out by crooks and half-educated fanatics for the benefit of the ignorant and superstitious. There are times when this underworld emerges from the depths and suddenly fascinates, captures, and dominates multitudes of usually sane and responsible people, who thereupon take leave of sanity and responsibility. And it occasionally happens that this underworld becomes a political power and changes the course of history.[4]

As readers will soon realize, these words perfectly describe the terrorists discussed in this book, beginning with Zen-trained layman Inoue Nisshō, head of a terrorist band. However, there is only one way to truly understand the "subterranean world" Inoue and his band members inhabited, that is, by entering that world, by walking in their footsteps. Thus, readers are invited to become modern-day "Alices" sliding down the rabbit hole in Lewis Carroll's *Alice's Adventures in Wonderland* to meet the wide assortment of characters living there. Like a modern-day March Hare, Inoue serves as our "guide" to this world. As Alice hypothesized, "The March Hare will be much the most interesting, and perhaps as this is May it won't be raving mad—at least not so mad as it was in March."[5]

Just how "mad" Inoue was in March, May, or any other month in his long life is left for readers to decide. For my part, I am convinced that, like Alice, readers will find Inoue's tumultous, adventure-filled, and spiritually challenged life "much the most interesting." In accord with the life-history method, my role in the initial chapters is that of an amanuensis, ensuring the descriptions of Inoue and his terrorist band's activities accurately portray those provided by the principals themselves. Toward this end, many direct quotes by Inoue and his band members are included to allow readers to encounter, albeit in translated form, their raw, unfiltered voices. The accompanying prose narratives are also based on materials they provided without adding any judgements or opinions on my part. However, when Inoue and his band's comments reference personalities, incidents and Buddhist teachings with which the Western reader may be unfamiliar, I have added additional purely explanatory information, preferably in the text but sometimes in footnotes.

As Cohn noted, the underworld described in this book sometimes emerges from the depths and fascinates multitudes of usually sane and responsible people, large numbers of the Japanese public in this case, thereby becoming a political power that changes the course of history. Thus, we also follow Inoue and his band when they emerge if not quite onto the world stage then at least onto a Japan stage where they actually changed, with tragic consequences, the course of modern Japanese history. Once again, the changes they effected are viewed, at least initially, from Inoue and his terrorist band's perspective.

As noted above, I certainly recognize the danger that the "bad guys" may present a distorted image of themselves. As with anyone's self-description, one danger lies in its parochial and self-justifying, if not self-aggrandizing, viewpoint. To some readers, these self-descriptions may even come over as an apologia, bordering on hagiography, or as attempts to justify terrorist acts. A justification of terrorism, however, is far from the purpose of this book. On the contrary, its true purpose is exactly the opposite, for it seeks to illuminate a dark era in modern Japanese history. Once again, this is done in the hope that it will be possible to more effectively reach out to future, would-be terrorists *before* they engage in their heinous acts. However, this can only be done on the basis of first understanding what motivates them to act, especially when, as in this instance, there is a religious dimension to their conduct.

NO ILLUSIONS

Needless to say, I am under no illusion that the life and thought of one terrorist, or in this instance a band of terrorists, can be considered representative of all religiously motivated terrorists. However, it should be noted that there were two additional major terrorist incidents in 1930s Japan that had a strong connection to the Zen school, both Sōtō and Rinzai sects. Thus, as far as the Zen school is concerned, Inoue Nisshō and his band's terrorist acts were definitely not one-off aberrations. In fact, taken as a whole, these terrorist acts enjoyed the support of a sizeable number of Zen leaders at the time. See appendices 1 and 2 for an introduction to these additional terrorist incidents.

I am able to present the words of both Inoue and his accomplices in the first person, just as they spoke or wrote them, because Inoue left behind two major, as well as multiple minor, sources of his thinking, including a detailed biography as well as full transcripts of his extensive courtroom testimony. Inoue's 419-page biography, published in 1953, was titled *Ichinin, Issatsu* (One Person Kills One [Person]). Inoue's own courtroom testimony covers 375 pages, while that of his thirteen band members collectively accounts for an additional 2,370 pages. If the volume of this testimony is surprising, it is because the second chief judge in the trial, in a most unusual move for a Japanese courtroom, allowed each of the defendants to testify at length about their personal life histories as well as the "patriotic motives" leading to their terrorist attacks.

Thus, unlike typical terrorists, about whom little is known other than the heinous crimes they commit, Inoue and his band left behind what might almost be described as an "embarrassment of riches." On the one hand, this freed me from the onerous task of piecing together bits and pieces of the protagonists' lives and thinking into a coherent whole. On the other hand, the abundance of material forced me to limit what is included in this book while, at the same time, ensuring sufficient detail remains to make Inoue and his band's thoughts and actions comprehensible.

This does not mean, however, that having studied Inoue and his band over many years I have abandoned my responsibility to critically examine their actions and motivations, especially those relating to the terrorist acts they committed. This examination will be found in chapters 13 and 14, in which I look first at the historical and then at the religious significance of their acts. However, by the time readers reach these chapters, they will be in possession of sufficient information to come to their own conclusions and are encouraged to do so. In fact, it is my hope that both the historical and religious dimensions of this study will become the catalyst for further research, especially regarding the as yet unproven hypotheses I present at the end of the book.

I recognize that in relying so heavily on Inoue and his bands' depiction of events, the danger exists that the material presented may be not only self-serving but based on faulty recollections of events. When this is the case I draw readers' attention to contending or alternative narratives. The primary focus of chapters 3 to 12 is on Inoue's life from childhood to death, including his interactions with band members, his two Zen masters, and significant others. While readers may be surprised by the somewhat sympathetic figure that emerges, it is hardly surprising that Inoue, like any of us, attempted to depict himself in the most favorable light possible.

At the same time, readers may be equally surprised by the way Inoue honestly recounts the decadent lifestyle of his youth as well as his deep spiritual yearnings. There is, of course, no way to independently verify many of the events Inoue describes, especially those in his later life where Inoue claims to have gotten the better of his adversaries. For example, Inoue provides a detailed record of his interactions with various interrogators and prosecutors associated with the postwar Tokyo War Crimes Tribunal. At the time, he was under suspicion of having been a war criminal.[6] According to Inoue's recounting of his questioning, he was able to best his interrogators at every turn. Was this true?

Curious, I went to the repository for the tribunal's records held in the National Diet Library in Tokyo. There I learned that only the interrogation records of those twenty-eight Japanese military and political leaders who were eventually charged had been saved. It was, further, only after hours of reading microfiches that I could find a single reference to British Naval Lt. Parsons, whom Inoue identified as having been his chief interrogator. But even then there was no record of Lt. Parsons's first name, and Inoue himself did not record it.

In addition, I attempted to verify Inoue's version of events by consulting the diaries and other writings of the men with whom he claimed to have interacted, but beyond sometimes finding his name, there were few records of the substance of their conversations. I soon got used to this, for I realized that not many "normal people" would wish to see their interactions with a notorious terrorist become public knowledge. Thus, for better or worse, we are all too often left with Inoue and his band members' uncollaborated version of events.

I can, however, state that after an extensive review of secondary sources concerning Inoue and his associates, I have discovered no evidence indicating that either Inoue or his band members fabricated a particular incident or were blatantly dishonest in their recounting of events. At most, Inoue and his followers can be charged with having omitted important, and sometimes embarrassing, details, typically about their personal lives. In Inoue's case, this was especially true regarding references to his role as husband and father.

Thus, as a supplement to the "firsthand" accounts contained in this book, interested readers may wish to review the many academic books and articles describing this period and the role Inoue and his terrorist band played in it. Unfortunately, most of the works that mention Inoue and his band do so in a perfunctory manner, as just one more example of the instability of the period and the "deranged" nature of Japan's ultranationalists. Further, the degree of objectivity or simple accuracy of these references, especially regarding Inoue, is questionable since nearly all of them base their narratives on the mistaken assertion that Inoue was affiliated with the Nichiren sect of Buddhism, typically describing him, as previously noted, as a Nichiren priest. While this distinction may seem little more than a sectarian squabble, it will become clear that in seeking to understand Inoue and his band's terrorist acts, the Zen connection is of crucial importance.

THE ULTIMATE GOAL

The ultimate goal of this book is to take readers inside the mind, inside the very
"skin," of one terrorist leader, a leader who, together with his followers, felt he had
found in his Zen training the basis and justification for acts of terrorism. At the same
time, I hope to give readers an insider's view of the Zeitgeist of prewar Japan, especially as it relates to those figures typically identified as "ultranationalists" or simply
right-wing thugs and fanatics. In the process, readers will find themselves engulfed
in an Alice in Wonderland subterranean world of "religious idealism" gone mad, a
religious idealism that played a major role in propelling Japan toward a totalitarian
society at home in conjunction with its imperialist aggression abroad. Inoue's descriptions of events are so vivid that you can almost picture them in your mind, as if
you were reading a Japanese *manga* (an adult comic book).

However, readers should be aware that what they are about to read is not an
objective history of prewar Japan and later. In the first instance, this is because, as
mentioned above, it has been impossible for me to independently verify many of
the claims Inoue and those around him made. I can report, however, that on those
relatively few occasions when I have been able to collaborate Inoue's descriptions of
events, they have been congruent with one another. For example, Inoue's postwar
interactions with Mark Gayn (1902–1981), an American journalist covering the War
Crimes Tribunal, were collaborated in the latter's 1948 book *Japan Diary*. The only
contention between the two men in their descriptions of each other was who had
won the arguments between them.

In any event, even though uncollaborated for the most part, the claims made by
Inoue and his band members have the merit of being those of "insiders" who were
themselves participants in the events they describe. In that sense, what follows may
be considered one of the "raw materials" from which a well-documented, objective
history of the period is constructed. However, as the book's author, I do recognize
the responsibility to aid readers in placing the material included in context, including
possible interpretations of events and indicating promising leads for future historians. If this book is a history of any kind, it is the *spiritual* history of a group of men,
beginning with Inoue, who collectively had a significant, and devastating, impact on
prewar Japanese history.

TOTALITARIANISM

Note that the term *totalitarian* is not used here lightly, for I am well aware that, in
contrast to the term *fascism* describing wartime Germany and Italy, a definitive term
describing wartime Japan has yet to be universally accepted. For many years, "Japanese militarism" filled that role, but in recent years, thanks to books like Herbert
Bix's *Hirohito and the Making of Modern Japan*, it is now clear that as important
as the military's wartime role was, there was an even more powerful entity in the

background, that is, the emperor and his advisors. This is evidenced by the fact that General Tōjō Hideki, the wartime prime minister, was summarily dismissed from his post in July 1944, a full year before Japan's surrender. Emperor Hirohito removed Tōjō for having failed to successfully prosecute the war. By contrast, there was no political entity in either Germany or Italy sufficiently powerful to dismiss Hitler or Mussolini even as they led their nations to catastrophic defeat.

I am also aware that in recent years, the term *totalitarian* has fallen out of favor in English-language scholarship and now seems rather dated. Nevertheless, it is far more accurate than the descriptive term "Japanese militarism," suggesting, as it does, that the military was solely responsible for Japanese aggression. There is, however, an alternate word that was actually employed within wartime Japan with a sense of pride, *zentai-shugi*, which literally translated means "total-ism." Unfortunately, *totalism* is not yet a widely accepted political term in English, but it refers to an authoritarian ideology advocating the massive centralization of power in the state with a concurrent focus on military power, and the willingness to spread its ideology by force.

In wartime Japan, totalism was fused with an almost mystical or spiritual belief in the *kokutai*, literally, "nation-body," typically translated as "national polity." This resulted in an ideology in which all Japanese, military and civilians, men, women, and children alike, were required to fuse or merge with the nation-body headed by its divine emperor. In this way, the entire nation was to become "one heart, one body." Each and every Japanese would be assimilated into the body of the emperor, just as each and every Japanese would fuse with one another. As the body's "head," the emperor, and he alone at least in theory, did the "thinking" for the body and made all major decisions, most especially those relating to war and peace. It was the responsibility of the subordinate elements of the nation-body, within a strict hierarchical framework, to carry out the emperor's orders without question, and without concern for the consequences of their acts to themselves or others.

Inasmuch as totalism is not yet widely accepted in scholarly literature, I have settled for the closely related term, totalitarianism, though within a clearly Japanese wartime embodiment of that term. How closely the two terms are related can be seen from the fact that, like totalism, totalitarianism is destructive of individual freedom and autonomy in that it subordinates citizens to the absolute authority of the state and regards them as no more than a means to achieve the state's ends, the emperor's ends in this case. In addition, totalitarianism has no faith in the natural equality of humanity and promotes both hero worship and the social superiority of its citizens, fostering extreme ethnic chauvinism. Ethnic chauvinism, together with emperor worship, was something that richly characterized the Japanese people during the wartime era.

Needless to say, totalitarian states are the sworn enemies of pluralism and constitutionalism. They inevitably destroy democracy and establish the monopoly of a single political party or personage, abolishing free and open competition for political power. In this way, they pave the way for the monopoly of political power and the strict hierarchical, and brutal, regimentation of society. Totalitarianism glorifies force

and violence, and it uses them to bring about complete conformity and unquestioning obedience. Whether called "totalism" or "totalitarianism," this is an accurate
description of wartime Japanese society.[7] And, in terms of this book, the individual
acts of terrorism it describes ultimately morphed into "state-sponsored terrorism,"
the Asia-Pacific War of 1937–1945, the ultimate result of which is only too well
known—massive death and destruction.

CONCLUSION

In concluding this chapter, I cannot help but note that while the events described
in this book belong to the "past," the terrorism to which they are connected is,
tragically, very much a part of our collective "present," and no doubt our collective
future as well. Thus, the nature of the terrorism described in this book, especially its
religious dimension, must also be examined for the enduring lessons it may offer. In
the course of writing this book, I came to realize the events it describes offer more
than a few insights into the nature of contemporary terrorism, especially religious
terrorism. These insights, I believe, can aid in understanding, and confronting, the
terrorism we face today.

To give but one example, it will become clear that Inoue and his terrorist band
were neither lone nor independent actors. Inoue, especially, enjoyed close connections to some of Japan's most important political and military leaders. Moreover,
these leaders aided him in substantive ways even though the details remain murky,
perhaps deliberatively so. Almost unbelievably, one of these leaders, Japan's then
prime minister Konoe Fumimaro (1891–1945), appears to have rewarded Inoue in
the aftermath of his deadly terrorist acts. This suggests, even if it does not prove, that
large, organized groups of terrorists, requiring financial and logistical support as they
do, may well be recipients of aid from hidden or unknown actors. These actors provide their aid in order to manipulate terrorists into accomplishing the actors' goals,
typically the enhancement of their own (or their nation's) interests.

No less a luminary than then secretary of state Hillary Clinton provided the following testimony to the House Appropriations Committee on April 23, 2009: "Let's
remember here, the people we are fighting today, we funded twenty years ago, and
we did it because we were locked in this struggle with the Soviet Union. . . . There's a
very strong argument, which is—it wasn't a bad investment to end the Soviet Union,
but let's be careful what we sow because we will harvest."[8] Building on this testimony,
Max Blumenthal wrote in his recent book *The Management of Savagery*, "If the CIA
had not spent over a billion dollars arming Islamist militants in Afghanistan against
the Soviet Union during the height of the Cold War, empowering jihadist godfathers
like Ayman al-Zawahiri and Osama bin Laden in the process, the 9/11 attacks would
have almost certainly not taken place."[9]

No doubt some readers will agree with former secretary of state Clinton that U.S.
support for terrorists in Afghanistan "wasn't a bad investment to end the Soviet

Union." But if Blumenthal is correct, it shouldn't be forgotten that this "investment" cost the lives of nearly 3,000 innocent American civilians in the 9/11 attacks. Although the reference is uncertain, on June 6, 2017, President Donald Trump stated, "We underscore that states that sponsor terrorism risk falling victim to the evil they promote."[10] Further discussion of this and other "lessons to be learned" will be found in the epilogue to this book.

I now invite readers to join me as we descend the proverbial rabbit hole into the subterranean world of Japanese ultranationalism as it has rarely, if ever, been seen or described in English. Moreover, the description is provided, primarily, by one of the chief inhabitants of that world, Inoue Nisshō. Fascinating though the journey be, following Inoue's tempestuous life can be something of a bumpy ride, so readers are asked to metaphorically "buckle up" before diving in. At the end of the journey, in chapters 13 and 14, we will resurface to try to "make sense" of it all. First, however, chapter 2, "Setting the Stage," will introduce readers to what was going on in prewar Japan "aboveground."

2

Setting the Stage

Japan from the 1860s through the 1930s

This chapter introduces readers to both the accomplishments and most especially the shortcomings of a momentous period of change in modern Japanese history. This period began with the Meiji era of 1868 and was followed by the Taishō era (1912–1926) and then the Shōwa era (1926–1989). Readers who are already familiar with this period can proceed directly to chapter 3.

While the positive accomplishments of this period are well known, this chapter will focus on the lesser-known social costs associated with Japan's rapid modernization and industrialization, particularly the plight of villagers engaged in agriculture and fledgling industrial workers, both classes on whose backbreaking labor the government's policies of economic growth and enhanced military power rested. In addition, the human costs associated with the Sino-Japanese and Russo-Japanese Wars are introduced within the context of the establishment of a military based on universal conscription.

As subsequent chapters further describe, the social deprivation and suffering that were an integral part of the Meiji period and its aftermath had a direct effect on the subsequent birth of both the political left and the political right in modern Japan. This period also saw the growth of the modern use of assassination, something that had begun as early as 1860 with the murder of Chief Councilor Ii Naosuke (1815–1860), predating the beginning of the Meiji period. In subsequent years, assassination became a tool regularly used, primarily but not exclusively by right-wing elements, to eliminate their foes and, as noted in the preface, to terrorize other political and economic leaders into acceptance of the terrorists' demands for a major social revolution.

Chapter 2

THE SITUATION IN THE COUNTRYSIDE

Following the Meiji Restoration of 1868, which overthrew the samurai-dominated feudal system that had governed the country for eight centuries, Japan's leaders embarked on a path of Westernization and industrialization that privileged the urban sector over the still undeveloped agrarian economy. The new modernizing state was heavily dependent on taxes disproportionately extracted from the rural sector, and many farmers were hard pressed to make ends meet. As time passed, the plight of many of them became worse rather than better.

Whereas World War I stimulated a war boom in Japan's industrial sector, it simultaneously damaged much of the rural economy. Land rents as well as the costs of tools and fertilizer accelerated the descent of many small landholders into foreclosure and tenancy. Higher rents exacted in kind by an emerging cadre of new landlords forced the swelling class of tenant farmers into the position of having to buy rice to feed their families.

Hunger closely followed mounting poverty and was among the major reasons behind the rural unrest that culminated in the nationwide rice riots of 1918. Although the government interceded by cutting the price of rice in half, price controls evaporated when economic recession hit Japan in the early 1920s. The recession exacerbated rural hardship, and one conspicuous result of this was a mounting exodus of poor farmers who migrated to the cities to seek factory work. With the onset of the Great Depression in 1929, rural Japanese suffered a further blow from the collapse of the export market for silk, which farm families relied on for supplemental income.

Many political activists devoted themselves to organizing grassroots associations of poor farmers, and more than a few advocated the necessity of forging strong labor–farmer alliances. Beginning in 1921 and continuing into the early 1940s, the number of tenancy disputes numbered over 1,500 annually—reaching an annual peak of around 6,000 in the mid-1930s. Regardless of how one analyzed these numbers, they were certainly sufficient to alarm the ruling elites—especially when paired with parallel incidents of protest by urban workers.

Beginning in the 1920s, activists and organizers spanning a broad ideological spectrum devoted attention to rural problems and the desirability of building bridges between poor farmers and blue-collar workers. However, by the early 1930s, their factionalism mirrored the fratricidal rifts that plagued the urban labor movement and precipitated the splintering of the movement into eleven "proletarian" parties, several of which included *farmer* in their names. Centrist and right-wing socialists vied with hard-line communists; parties changed their names with bewildering speed; and by the mid-1930s, as in many countries, many erstwhile socialists found it expedient to change their colors, as in Nazi Germany, to "*national* socialist" and join forces with the militarists and their expansionist agenda. However, the longer-term legacy of rural unrest remained substantial.

THE SITUATION AMONG URBAN WORKERS

The 1920s and 1930s were host to a surprising number of diverse political parties. Passage of the General Election Law establishing universal manhood suffrage in 1925 seemed to harken the emergence of a representative democracy for men of all classes.

The turbulent campaign for manhood suffrage—led by coalitions of intellectuals, social reformers, labor unions, tenant-farmer movements, and political parties—compelled the national Diet (parliament) to take notice of the widespread desire for an expanded franchise. Enactment of the 1925 law invested millions of men with the ability to affect social change through electoral politics. On the one hand, this resulted in revitalization of the conservative mainstream parties, the Seiyūkai (Association of Political Friends) and Minseitō (People's Government Party). At the same time, it also paved the way for formation of many progressive and leftist parties—ranging from the moderate Shakai Minshūtō (Social Democratic Party) to the centrist Nihon Rōnōtō (Japan Labor-Farmer Party) to the rurally based Nihon Nōmintō (Japan Farmers' Party) to the decidedly communist-oriented Rōdō Nōmintō (Labor-Farmer Party).

Although women's organizations also participated vigorously in the grassroots demands for universal suffrage, women would not acquire the right to vote until after Japan's defeat in World War II. Their exclusion from the formal political process led to their being painted out of the left-wing political posters and handbills of the interwar period, but this was misleading. Women continued to remain significant actors in social movements that supported political parties on both the political left and right.

Despite the 1925 election law, and despite the support they received from labor and farmer organizations, the position of the leftist parties was always precarious and sometimes dangerous. Various factors figured into this. Even as suffrage was expanded, the Diet was losing power to the constitutionally independent state bureaucracy. More significant still, the 1925 law was enacted in tandem with the Peace Preservation Law, which placed various legal constraints on public political activity. The latter law was specifically intended to mute the effect of extending the vote to working-class men.

The leftist parties and their affiliated organizations were also plagued by internal schisms. The minutia of internal ideological differences often led to bitter fratricidal division. Solidarity was also undermined by mounting economic disparities between rural and urban areas—to the point that the urban-centric parties and labor unions often seemed blind to the plight of rural farmers plagued by low crop prices, high rents, disproportionate tax burdens, and desperate poverty.

Such factional strife, coupled with government repression, caused the dissolution of many radical parties even before the first general election to be held under universal male suffrage took place in 1928. Still, several restructured parties on the left—notably, the Labor-Farmer Party, the Japan Labor-Farmer Party, the Socialist Party, and the Social Democratic Party—survived to take part in that widely heralded election.

In 1926 rural labor activist Asanuma Inejirō attempted to create a basis for a leftist intervention in rural Japan by founding the Nihon Rōnōtō (Japan Labor-Farmer Party), which he envisioned as a means to bridge the growing economic and cultural chasm between rural farmers and urban workers. His effort to create a formal alliance between the labor movement and leftist political parties backfired when the Nihon Rōdō Sōdōmei (Japan Federation of Labor) ordered the Japan Labor-Farmer Party leadership to resign their membership in the federation and respect the federation's status as a nonpolitical organization. This further inflamed the splits in the leftist press that characterized the lead-up to the 1928 general elections.

Despite a fresh field of new political parties in the nationwide 1928 election, the established parties lost little ground in the popular vote. Only eight of the 88 non-mainstream candidates fielded—from seven different parties (the four main leftist parties and three local independents)—won a seat in the House of Representatives, where the total number of seats was 466. Although leftist candidates did slightly better than they had done in the 1927 prefectural assembly elections (winning 5 percent as compared to 1927's 3.9 percent of total votes cast), they lacked the name recognition and established local constituencies of the mainstream parties.

Unsurprisingly, the radical positions of the left-wing parties also cut them off from the largest source of campaign funding: the corporate conglomerates known as *zaibatsu*. The established conservative parties—the Seiyūkai backed by the Mitsui *zaibatsu* and the Minseitō backed by the Mitsubishi *zaibatsu*—held a monopoly on campaign finance. These handicaps were compounded by repressive state interventions in the form of disruption of meetings and arbitrary arrests. Although the proletarian parties attempted to regroup in the wake of their overwhelming defeat in 1928, the government banned the communist-oriented Labor-Farmer Party before the end of the year, and the remaining leftist parties remained divided over ideological issues.

Another factor contributing to the poor showing of the political left in 1928 was the inability, or unwillingness, of the leftist parties to cooperate, which meant they were often unable to strategically place candidates in a national field. Many districts saw leftist candidates run against each other, which usually enabled an established candidate to win. Additionally, it is doubtful the voters themselves were fully aware of the differences between the various parties, a problem the Minseitō in particular exploited by presenting itself as the only viable party to improve the lot of the common people.

Political weakness helped to precipitate even worse electoral results in the 1930 general election. The worldwide depression of the early 1930s prompted the labor federation Sōdōmei to withdraw official support for political parties and adopt a policy of "nonpolitical unionism." Although Sōdōmei retained informal ties with a few leftist parties, it also worked with Minseitō. This meant that leftist parties were not even assured of dependable backing from labor unions.

The late 1920s and early 1930s thus saw the emergence of leftist parties with bewilderingly similar names. Some newly named parties represented short-lived mergers, and almost none survived past 1932. Their campaign posters featured agendas and images ranging from stridently radical to moderate, although usually with a consistent critique of capitalism and explicit appeal to workers and tenant farmers. The only nominally leftist party that the government allowed to continue operating through the 1930s was the Shakai Taishūtō (Social Masses Party), which emerged out of a 1932 merger and promoted an essentially centrist agenda calling for agrarian reform alongside close ties with the urban middle class, especially small shopkeepers who felt squeezed out by the economic dominance of the *zaibatsu* conglomerates. Although this party initially called for cuts in military spending to help pay for agrarian reform, it nevertheless cultivated ties with a conservative faction within the army, known as the Control Faction (Tōseiha), that supported Japan's expansion into Manchuria and eventually all of China. This collusion helps explain its survival when more radical parties on the left disappeared from the scene.

LABOR ACTIVISM

On September 5, 1905, a major citywide riot erupted in Tokyo's Hibiya Park to protest the terms of the Treaty of Portsmouth, which ended the Russo-Japanese War of 1904–1905. The spontaneity and decentered nature of this explosive riot, which spread to other cities, demonstrated the political diversity of public protest in modern Japan, as well as the impact such protest had on policy makers and the popular media. While the state used the Hibiya riot as an excuse to further crack down on political activists, the founding of the Yūaikai (Friendly Society) by Christian convert Suzuki Bunji in 1912 helped to precipitate a period of union activism. Ostensibly apolitical, Suzuki's organization was well timed: lower-class neighborhoods in Osaka and Tokyo were beginning to take on the characteristics of an industrial working class, and when World War I (1914–1918) opened new markets for Japanese industries, the booming economy combined with a more liberal political moment to allow for an interlude of sustained union activism in the heavy industrial sectors.

Wealth from the war boom, however, did not spread evenly. Nationwide rice riots followed the end of the boom in 1918 and drew attention to the material concerns of the urban working class. This helped precipitate vigorous reform movements aimed at quelling what corporate managers and government officials increasingly feared to be a working class ripe to give birth to leftist movements.

Yūaikai organizers benefited from the development of new patterns of traditional forms of lower-class collective action (nonunion disputes), as well as from company initiatives to replace traditional labor bosses with systems of direct managerial control. The success of the Yūaikai between 1912 and 1918 was also due in part to the emergence of what historian Andrew Gordon has called an "ideology of imperial democracy," which enabled male and female workers to conceive of themselves as possessing full political rights within a political system that still excluded them.

The Yūaikai also established the first union-affiliated women's organization, which sought to encourage more women to support the labor movement by creating an organization dedicated to their interests. Although the 1916 Factory Law had established minimum employment standards protecting women and children, the law had limited provisions for enforcement. Managers seeking greater control over their workforce continued to enjoy success in asserting authority over their female employees.

Female activists affiliated with the Yūaikai sought to help wage-earning women by advising on policy decisions, developing organizing literature, and participating in key strikes and walkouts throughout the 1920s. While the Yūaikai women's department established important precedents for women's union activism, they succeeded in persuading no more than a few thousand wage-earning women to join unions.

By the mid-1920s, the Yūaikai—renamed the Japan Federation of Labor (Nihon Rōdō Sōdōmei, or Sōdōmei for short) in 1921—had grown to represent nearly a half million industrial workers in the Osaka and Tokyo metropolitan areas. Organized strike actions spiked in 1921 when organizers coordinated a successful strike by 30,000 dockworkers at the Kawasaki-Mitsubishi shipyards in Kobe. In the mid- and late 1920s, labor leaders staged a number of strikes in the heavy industrial and transportation sectors that drew national attention and led to a series of unprecedented coordinated campaigns for political change.

Despite conservative opposition to the emerging alliance between left-wing parties and organized labor, unions were a significant force behind the successful campaign for universal manhood suffrage that culminated in 1925 and extended the vote to every male over the age of twenty. Whereas the Yūaikai advocated cooperation between labor and management and promoted a moderate policy of mutual assistance and worker education, Sōdōmei soon adopted a more radical and militant agenda emphasizing class struggle. This radicalization reflected the dramatic industrial expansion that took place in Japan in the early 20th century, especially during and after the war boom stimulated by World War I. The factory labor force of male workers in heavy industry grew rapidly. Militant workers challenged the Yūaikai's policy of conciliation. And the influence of Marxism, Leninism, and communism following the 1917 Bolshevik Revolution in Russia contributed significantly to the enhanced attraction of left-wing ideologies (and imagery).

By the mid-1920s, the nationwide labor movement claimed nearly a half million members. In addition to organizing strikes and other protest activities, unions joined other leftists in promoting outreach activities such as youth organizations and cooperative schools. Partly in response to this agitation—and partly spurred by changing production technologies and new theories of labor-management practices—the state and private sector intensified their imposition of hierarchical systems of control. Combined with outright repression, especially after adoption of the Peace Preservation Law in 1925, this turned the late 1920s and early 1930s into a period of intense but increasingly futile labor protest.

This confrontation was compounded by the inexorable march to all-out war that followed Japan's invasion of Manchuria in 1931. Sōdōmei carried on until 1940, making it the longest surviving of Japan's prewar unions. Its durability, however, was facilitated by the increasing takeover of leadership by right-wing elements. Beginning in the mid-1920s, the federation experienced splits and the hiving off of leftist and then moderate member unions. In the 1930s, it was again advocating collaboration with the state and managerial class, which now presided over an economy that was increasingly directed to production for war. In 1940, Sōdōmei and other still existing unions were dissolved and replaced by the ultranationalistic Industrial Association for Serving the Nation (Sangyō Hōkokukai, popularly known as Sampō), which stressed the importance of harmony in labor–capital relations, with particular emphasis on the "family" nature of every enterprise.

Even during the years of intensified government repression that took place after the passage of "peace preservation" legislation in the mid-1920s—and even after the Japanese invasion of Manchuria in 1931—workers' movements continued and constituted such a potential threat that they, especially their leaders, were under constant threat, including both imprisonment and torture. Nevertheless, labor organizations and agitation remained until they were finally snuffed out in the later half of the 1930s.

THE ROLE OF THE EMPEROR

Hirohito's accession to the throne in December 1926 helped move Japan in a more nationalistic direction.[1] It was based on the theocratic myth of an imperial house whose destiny was defined by the emperor—a human in form but actually a deity ruling the country in an uninterrupted line of succession. No matter what project the emperor undertook, his "subjects" were presumed and required to be absolutely loyal in "assisting" him from below. In newspapers and on the radio, the message echoed throughout the land that Japan had broken with its immediate past; it now had a monarch cast in the mold of his illustrious grandfather, Emperor Meiji, who (in the words of Hirohito's first imperial edict) had "enhanced the grandeur of our empire" and never allowed himself to be treated as a puppet.

For Hirohito, like most Western heads of state, empire, national defense, and national greatness were primary. Given his strongly opportunistic nature, he sought to extend Japan's control over China when given the chance. In other words, as a traditional imperialist and nationalist, he was firmly committed to protecting Japan's established rights and interests abroad, even in the face of the rising world tide of anticolonial nationalism. But he was also highly sensitive to the internal balance of political forces and even more totally dedicated to preserving the monarchy.

Hirohito differed from other contemporary rulers in the type of Machiavellianism that he practiced in order to maintain the monarchy and extend the reach of the Japanese state. Like successful Western imperialists, Hirohito was able to effectively deploy the rhetoric of ethics, virtue, and morality as a means to mobilize his nation for war. He and the elites who protected him treated international law as a fetter on their freedom of action, and they were not averse to using scheming and trickery for purposes of national defense. Hirohito alone, however, could display leadership by using the technique of the substantive question that carried the force of a command. He was also unique in his view of Japan's colonial and semicolonial rights as his genealogical inheritance from his dead ancestors. Since childhood, he had been taught that his ancestors, not his living "subjects," were the source of his authority and the object of his responsibility—the sole entities to whom he was morally accountable. Hirohito's denial of responsibility for errors of policy and judgment pervaded the entire structure of Japanese collective decision making.

The young Hirohito was neither bellicose nor intellectually shallow. He was serious, methodical, energetic, and intelligent; he was also physically slight and quite inarticulate. He had been carefully groomed to exercise imperial oversight through building and maintaining consensus so as to achieve unity in policy making. Above all, he had been trained to make rational judgments as both head of state and supreme commander. Yet from the start, occasions arose when passion and ideology intruded; on these occasions, Hirohito, the unifier, blundered badly.

The Meiji constitution gave him great power and authority that could not be restricted by the political parties in the Diet. It positioned him at the intersection of politics and military affairs—allowing him on occasion to move the entire government. Eager to assert the prerogatives of imperial power that his own sickly father had been unable to exercise, Hirohito, with the strong encouragement of his entourage, soon fired his first prime minister. The main grievance against Prime Minister and General Tanaka Giichi was that Tanaka wanted to punish the two young officers who in June 1928 had assassinated the Chinese warlord Chang Tso-lin (Japan's chief collaborator in China's Manchuria) rather than hush up their crime as Tanaka's cabinet ministers wanted.

Hirohito persisted in influencing from behind the scenes the policies and conduct of the two prime ministers that followed. In 1930 his determination to achieve arms control in concert with the United States and Britain led him and his close advisers to give inadequate attention to consensus-building among the elites. They forced through Japan's acceptance of the London Naval Treaty of 1930 over the objections of the navy's minority faction, who believed that Japan had to be able to brandish naval power on a par with the Anglo-Americans if it was to achieve its national goals. The backlash from the minority factions in both services, and from politicians in the Diet who agreed with them, came swiftly.

By making the Imperial Court a new, institutionally independent player in an era of party cabinets, Hirohito and his advisors undermined the tenuous system of party cabinet government that had begun to develop around the time of Meiji's death. Meanwhile, out of public view, Hirohito was slowly forming his own political space within a complex system of institutions and processes designed to protect him, so that he could exercise positive leadership at will, and not merely serve as a passive monarch, sanctioning policies presented to him by the cabinet. Over time, Hirohito improved his modus operandi, becoming more adept at practicing self-restraint and avoiding actions and comments that could incur criticism.

After elements of the Japanese Army staged the Manchurian Incident in September 1931,[2] in the face of the global Great Depression, Japan's domestic political situation became increasingly unstable. Hirohito and the men surrounding him made a series of decisions with disastrous consequences for both China and Japan. Instead of demanding the punishment of insubordinate officers who had staged that incident, Hirohito accepted the army's fait accompli, joined in covering up the facts, and failed to back the efforts of the incumbent party cabinet to bring the Kwantung Army to heel. However, since Hirohito was not yet in actual control of the army, he cannot be deemed criminally liable for the actions committed by senior- and intermediate-level officers in both Tokyo and Manchuria. Nevertheless, after learning the true facts, Hirohito not only failed to punish the wrongdoers but actively joined in aiding and abetting the army's seizure of Manchuria. In these ways, Hirohito allowed the military in general, and army field commanders in particular, to effectively take over Japan's China policy and turn it openly aggressive.

As this book will detail, following the assassination of Prime Minister Inukai Tsuyoshi by young naval officers in May 1932, Hirohito and his advisors abandoned their support for constitutional government conducted by party cabinets, thereby quickening the militaristic drift in Japanese politics. Cabinets of national unity headed by admirals moved to the fore. Japan was a signatory to the Nine-Power Treaty of 1922, which stipulated respect for China's sovereignty and territorial integrity, and the Kellogg–Briand Pact of 1928, which obligated it to refrain from using force against other states. However, when Japan formally recognized its puppet state of Manchukuo in the fall of 1932, it violated both treaties. For his part, Hirohito was pleased that the army had expanded the empire and partially redressed Japan's strategic weakness in natural resources such as coal and iron, but also agricultural land and its produce. So rather than abandon this huge territorial gain in the face of vehement United States and Chinese criticism, Hirohito sanctioned Japan's withdrawal from the League of Nations in March 1933 and issued an imperial edict announcing the move.

The rhetoric of "national emergency" and endangered "lifeline," generated during the Manchurian crisis, continued to affect thinking about Japan's domestic situation. Lethal conflicts involving military officers were shaking the country, and Hirohito was uncertain how to proceed in the face of multiple pressures. Radical rightist politicians in the Diet called for the dissolution of political parties. The army and navy, dissatisfied with their respective budgetary allocations, wanted a complete break with the Washington treaty system and an end to the court's pro-Anglo-American line in diplomacy. Hirohito, keenly aware of Japan's economic dependence on the West for resources, technology, and markets, initially hoped to cooperate with Britain and the United States, while simultaneously seeking to isolate China diplomatically.

Over the next four years, Hirohito groped for ways to restore discipline among alienated military officers impatient for domestic political and social reform, a major component of which was accelerated rearmament. Although concerned about the army's overreach on the continent, Hirohito worried even more about domestic disorder, which could undermine the monarchy. It was at this point that military and civilian ultranationalists acted to eliminate all constitutional restraints preventing the emperor from ruling "directly" without relying on popularly elected political parties. Their nationwide campaign included an attack on law professor Minobe Tatsukichi's organ theory of the constitution, about which more details will be provided in chapter 13. Suffice it here to state that, up to that time, the organ theory had been used to legitimize party government and lodge the monarchy more firmly within the constitutional order, that is, subordinate to the state. For Hirohito and his advisors, the organ theory represented one more impediment to their efforts to take complete control of the government. It had to be swept aside.

It was against these turbulent times, whether in the countryside or in the cities, that Inoue Nisshō was born. He would grow up to lead his own "revolution," something he and other ultranationalists called a Shōwa Restoration, firmly restoring all political power to the emperor. Inoue's personal role was to prepare for, and direct, Zen-related acts of terrorism leading to this goal.

3

A Troubled Youth

Inoue Nisshō was born in Kawaba village in Gumma prefecture, northwest of Tokyo, in the nineteenth year of the reign of Emperor Meiji, 1886. He was the fourth of five sons of the village doctor, an early supporter of Japan's colonial expansion onto the Asian continent. Inoue remained close to his father throughout his life but went through a process of estrangement from his mother beginning at the age of three. By then Inoue's younger brother had been born, and as his mother was nursing him, she refused to allow Inoue to touch her breasts.

Inoue's decisive break with his mother came when he was six. It was then that his mother, angry with him about something he had done, told him that he wasn't really her child. "I found you abandoned on the side of the road," she said, "left in front of a statue of the Buddha. I felt sorry for you, but if you don't behave, I'll put you back there!"[1] It was also around this time that Inoue found a bottle of whisky in the kitchen of his house and secretly had his first taste of alcohol. This began a habit that only increased in frequency and amount the older he got. He also started smoking soon after entering primary school.

Expressed in today's language, Inoue was a mixture of a "rascal," a "troubled youth," and a "juvenile delinquent" even in his preteen years. However, behind his delinquency lay a burning question, a question that became more pressing as he grew. The age-old dilemma was, "What are the standards for determining what is right and what is wrong?" For him, the standards adults followed seemed completely arbitrary and were consequently unacceptable.

This led Inoue to get in trouble in his village from an early age. One of his favorite pranks was to fill a paper bag full of dog poop and place it at the entrance to someone's home. He would light the bag on fire and knock on the door. When the occupants came to door, they saw the bag on fire and tried to stamp it out—with predictable results.

If this weren't bad enough, Inoue also took pleasure in setting fires in the open from the fall through the winter months. One time he would set a recently harvested rice paddy on fire, the next time an open field. "Once I set a field on fire that ended up spreading to an adjoining public forest where it burned down the entire mountain," he proudly claimed.[2]

When Inoue reached the age of nine, his father arranged for him to start *kendō* (bamboo swordsmanship) lessons. Instead of teaching him self-discipline, however, the lessons spurred Inoue's interest in what he could do with a real sword. Thus, early one New Year's morning, Inoue snuck out of his house with his father's short authentic samurai sword in hand and proceeded to cut in half every pine and bamboo decoration placed in front of village homes. This time, however, Inoue's pranks had gone too far, and a group of young villagers decided to teach him a lesson. They threw him headfirst into a large snow bank. Had it not been for the timely intercession of a passerby, he likely would have suffocated to death. However, this experience only caused Inoue to become even more incorrigible as a way to demonstrate he couldn't be intimidated.

As might be expected, Inoue's father tried various methods of punishing his son for his misdeeds. These included spanking him with an oak stick and even, on one occasion, turning him over to angry villagers for punishment. However, nothing helped until one day Inoue thought of a plan to show both his father and the villagers just how far he was willing to go. He set his family's storage shed on fire. As was the village custom, everyone came rushing to extinguish the blaze, thereby preventing it from spreading to the main house. From then on, both his father and the villagers realized that Inoue was not to be trifled with. Instead of scolding him, they all tried to stop his misdeeds by getting on his good side with kind words and gifts of his favorite foods.

As for his education, Inoue's attitude was no better. On the one hand, he did go to the village primary school on time but only because at the outdoor morning assembly he was able to stand by a girl he fancied. However, since boys and girls had to sit separately in the classroom, the rest of the school day was of no interest to him. Thus, he succeeded in getting a seat next to the window and the first chance he had jumped out the window to wander through the fields and woods, all the while planning his next prank.

SETTLING DOWN

Inoue finally began to settle down around the time he entered middle school. As he did so, a more reflective side of his personality came to the fore, and everything he saw and heard, from the color of flowers to the sounds of insects, became a source of doubt in his mind.

It was for this reason that once in middle school, "morals class" was the one and only class he never missed. It was taught by the school principal, who, Inoue admitted, took the subject very seriously. For his part, Inoue hoped that his deep-seated doubts would be answered in this class, but he was ultimately disappointed. For example, Inoue once asked the principal, "Over the past hundreds, even thousands of years, there have been tens, even hundreds of people who have done great things. Yet I don't think I can do any of these things. Are you able to?" Irritated by his question, the principal replied, "Well, I can't do such deeds either, but I can try my best." Inoue continued, "So if the best you can do is to try, isn't the whole thing a waste of time?" The principal fell silent.[3]

On another occasion, Inoue asked his father, "Where do we come from and where do we go after death?" "Go ask your teacher" was the reply. When Inoue did so, the principal confidently responded, "We come from our mother's stomach." "Well, then, where do we go when we die?" "We go to the grave." Not one to give up, Inoue continued, "Alright, but where do we go from there?" "Well . . . ," said the exasperated principal, once again at a loss for words.[4] As a result, Inoue's painful doubts about the meaning and purpose of life only grew stronger. These doubts eventually led him to take an interest in religion.

HIGH SCHOOL

With his village being too small for its own high school, Inoue had to travel some twelve kilometers (seven and a half miles) away to continue his schooling. This required him to board there as well. Still consumed by his doubts, it was there, in the provincial city of Numata, that Inoue first encountered Christianity. At age seventeen, Inoue went to the home of the local pastor and explained his doubts to him. In response, the pastor said, "The standards for right and wrong are all contained in this Bible. I'll give you a copy; please read it carefully, for there is no other way than to believe in God."

Thereafter, Inoue read the Bible earnestly and attended church on a regular basis, listening carefully to the sermons. However, as Inoue explained, "I realized that in Christianity God was the foundation and standard for all things. Yet I was unable to either experience Him directly or become aware of His presence in my life. Instead, I became more and more of a 'lost sheep.'"[5]

Equally important, it was at this time that Inoue consciously rejected his father's standards of right and wrong, summed up in the patriotic phrase, "Chūkun aikoku" (Loyalty to the emperor [and] love of country). Inoue asked himself why one should be willing to sacrifice his life for the emperor or what was so good about loving one's country? "It seemed to me to be just so much foolishness, but, feeling sorry for my father, I couldn't tell him."[6] Nevertheless, unable to rid himself of his deep-seated doubts, Inoue did eventually come to what he considered at the time to be a "big discovery." Namely, "People say something is good if it's convenient for them, and call it bad when it isn't."[7] Yet Inoue realized there was a problem with this way of thinking, namely, to base standards of right and wrong on what is simply convenient for this or that person is in fact to give up on the idea of any standards at all, for there are an untold number of people, each with different needs. Based on this, Inoue came to believe that the whole reason ethics and morality had originally been created and enforced was because in their absence there would only be endless conflict and divisions in society. In other words, people had to learn to compromise with each other in the course of fulfilling their own needs.

Out of this realization, Inoue came to the conclusion that from then on "good" would consist of whatever was convenient for him and nothing more. He wouldn't indulge himself in any form of self-deceit by thinking otherwise. After all, no matter what he did, death was the final and inevitable outcome. Yet he also recognized that in following this rebellious way of thinking he was bound to come into conflict with society, leading him to either kill others or take his own life, in short, leading to death. "I plunged into the depths of a deep, dark despair."[8]

A RAY OF SUNSHINE

At this point, a ray of sunshine entered Inoue's life, though it certainly didn't appear that way at the time. That is to say, Inoue's family went bankrupt when he was in the fourth year of high school. His parents lost the family home and moved away. Fortunately, Inoue was taken in by one of his mother's relatives, who also agreed to continue to pay for his education. He addressed the mother of the family as *oneesan* (elder sister) and, due to her concern for his well-being, experienced something like a mother's love for her child or love between brothers and sisters. "For someone like me who had never known human affection before, it was a warm and joyous experience that I can't begin to describe in words."[9]

As for his real mother, Inoue had realized she was truly his biological mother by the time he entered high school. She hadn't, in fact, found him lying abandoned in front of a statue of the Buddha. Thus, when he returned home during school vacations, he always intended to reconcile with his mother but never succeeded in doing so. On the one hand, the old pain from his childhood came back when he saw her; on the other hand, his mother always seemed to turn away from him. "Given that I had been an incorrigible child, widely disliked by everyone and then from a bankrupt family, the fact that I was able to graduate high school without either going crazy or committing suicide was entirely due to the indescribably warm love that I experienced from *oneesan*."[10]

Inoue's high school days were also memorable for several other reasons. First, it was then he encountered socialism for the first time. This came in the form of a popular schoolmate who was particularly close to his mother. Upon graduation, the schoolmate went to Kyoto to study at Dōshisha University. Not long afterward, he dropped out of university and returned home, but not before having become a dedicated socialist.

Shortly after his return, Inoue chanced to meet him and received a basic introduction to socialist thought. Inoue agreed with much of what his friend said but nevertheless felt a lack of human warmth in socialist theory. This led him to ask his friend, "You say everything can be explained on the basis of the theory of materialism, but how does this explain your close relationship with your mother?" When his friend was unable to respond, Inoue continued, "There's no other explanation for it other than the tender affection existing between a mother and her child."[11]

A second memorable event from Inoue's high school days was his first experience in a traditional Japanese-style restaurant attended by *geisha*. He was still only fifteen at the time. This was one of two awards he received for having won three matches at a *kendō* competition in which his opponents were all experienced teachers of swordsmanship. Because of his youth, Inoue made a big hit with the *geisha*, especially the younger ones who were still in training. This marked the beginning of Inoue's frequent visits to Japan's "gay quarters," or at least as frequently as he found the money to do so. Inoue's second award was an authentic, short *samurai* sword, presented to him by a member of Japan's nobility.

Inoue also fell seriously in love during his high school years. He was seventeen at the time and in his last year of school. It was a mutual attraction, the girl being a distant relative whom he fully intended to marry. One day, however, he invited her to go for a walk only to be told that she had decided to marry someone else. This came as a severe shock to Inoue, and he asked, "What's going to happen to me?" "I don't know anything about that," she coldly replied.[12] Inoue subsequently fell into a depression and concluded that he could no longer believe in anyone. In the future, a marriage based on love was out of the question for him.

The academic side of his life wasn't going any better. This time, however, it wasn't because Inoue was uninterested in such things as math, biology, or history, but rather because in some sense he was "too interested" in these topics. In other words, he was unwilling to simply memorize facts and charts but always wanted to understand what made $1 + 1 = 2$ or why two hydrogen atoms bonded to a single oxygen atom produced water. Unsurprisingly, nearly all of Inoue's teachers were angered by repeated questions of this type. Since his textbooks didn't address these fundamental questions either, Inoue lost faith in both people and books.

Inoue finally came to this conclusion: "Even if I continue to live, there's no purpose to it. If I die, I won't be able to do good things, but at least I won't be able to do anything bad. There is at least some meaning in that, so I chose to die."[13] Additionally, Inoue still had no idea what the basis of good and evil was anyway. This led Inoue to the point where he was ready to commit suicide except for one problem. He couldn't decide how to do it since he wanted to use a method he felt good about. Hanging himself or taking poison were out of the question.

SERVICE IN THE RUSSO-JAPANESE WAR

Given his decision to die, Inoue was fortunate in that his graduation from high school came in early 1905, just as Japan was in the midst of the Russo-Japanese War.

Though he was still too young to become a soldier, Inoue was old enough to serve in a civilian capacity as an apprentice steward on the *Kobe-maru*, a military hospital ship. He was convinced, even hoping, that he would be killed in the process of aiding wounded soldiers.

By August of that year, however, Inoue was frustrated since he had yet to see combat. Thus, as the ship sailed through Japan's Inland Sea one bright moonlit night, Inoue determined to finally end it all by jumping overboard. However, just as he began to climb the deck railing, he was roughly pulled down by an older crew member who shouted, "Don't you have any parents!"[14] Shaken by these words, Inoue was left in limbo, unable to kill himself yet having no desire to live further.

Rumor had it that the Russian fleet would soon launch a surprise attack. Everyone on the ship was very worried about this possibility except Inoue. Finally, he thought, he would get his chance to die. But it didn't happen. On the contrary, Inoue ended up being decorated for his "heroic action" in having single-handedly carried eighteen seriously wounded sailors from the navy's flagship *Mikasa* to his medical ship for treatment. In fact, Admiral Tōgō Heihachirō, Combined Japanese Fleet Commander and war hero, personally commended him.

Inoue recalled his feelings at the time: "I took no pleasure in receiving a military decoration that as far as I was concerned was nothing more than a plaything. That's because my life was devoid of all hope; hence fame was entirely worthless."[15] Yet Inoue admitted one thing did attract his interest. "The only thing I wanted was money. This had nothing to do with getting a lot of it but simply having enough money so that I could buy women and *sake*. Otherwise, money was of no more value to me than used postcards."[16]

A SHORT-LIVED CAREER AS A "LEFTIST"

Following the end of the war, Inoue began a brief career as a temporary worker in the Mitsubishi shipyards located in Nagasaki. It was hard, dirty work with considerable overtime, but Inoue was fortunate to find an experienced fellow worker from his hometown who offered Inoue a place to stay and whose family looked after him. Inoue needed the job because he would soon be turning twenty-one, meaning he would have to return home to undergo a preinduction military medical exam.

Inoue's work was physically demanding and included frequent overtime. However, his fellow workers treated him well, and for the first time in his life he felt really happy. The happiness only increased after he met Otama, the only daughter of one of the veteran workers in the shipyard. Inoue was also amused to learn that a number of the female workers thought he must be Chinese because of his long hair.

As the weather turned colder, Inoue noticed a marked increase in the workers' dissatisfaction with their nighttime working conditions. The supervisors stayed indoors huddled around warm stoves while the workers were left to keep warm as best they could, including drinking industrial alcohol mixed into a little tea. As the complaining increased, Inoue told them, "Instead of just grumbling all the time, why don't you take your complaints directly to the company? If the company won't listen to you, you can always go on strike, right? The company is really busy now, so if you went on strike the company would be in trouble. You're sure to win!"[17]

To Inoue's surprise, not only did his fellow workers agree with him, they asked him to help organize the strike. Inoue agreed and from then on spent nearly every night meeting to make plans and increase the number of strikers. But as the agreed-upon day approached, it became clear to Inoue that a company spy was in their midst. First, his landlady reported that the police were coming around to ask questions about him. Then, one night as he walked home around 11 p.m., he realized he was being followed. Inoue knew then he was a marked man, left with only one choice—get out of town fast.

Inoue successfully eluded the police and boarded a ship heading north from Nagasaki. He later got word that the strike had started as planned, but, leaderless, it quickly collapsed in the face of police repression. Inoue took away an important lesson from this experience: "It doesn't matter what the issue is, if someone isn't firmly in charge it's bound to fail."[18] This realization would have a strong impact on Inoue's future actions. Further, this event marked both the beginning and end of what Inoue himself regarded as his "left-wing" activism.

A TASTE OF MILITARY LIFE

Following his return home, Inoue underwent, and in May 1906 passed, the mandatory preinduction physical for twenty-one-year-olds. However, since he didn't have to report for basic training until spring of the following year, he first worked for a few months as a substitute teacher in the village primary school. While doing this, Inoue fell ill, so seriously that he thought he would be excused from military training. But the military doctor who examined him dismissed his illness as nothing to worry about. Thus, Inoue began his three months of basic training in a military engineering unit in Tokyo on April 1, 1907.

Inoue initially felt that his military training was "ridiculous," but he then decided that as long as he had no choice in the matter he might as well do his best.[19] The first thing that surprised him was that in the course of his training his illness completely disappeared. Secondly, upon finishing training three months later, Inoue was the only recruit in his unit to be issued a certificate recognizing him as a "superior soldier."

LIFE AS A UNIVERSITY STUDENT

Upon returning home, Inoue still had no direction or purpose in life. Although his father had recovered somewhat from his earlier bankruptcy, he was unable, on his own, to fund Inoue's further education. At that point, a family discussion ensued during which one of Inoue's older brothers, a navy lieutenant junior grade, volunteered to help out. Thanks to the combined financial support of his father and older brother, Inoue was able to enter Waseda University, a prestigious private school in Tokyo. Inoue enrolled in the English Literature Department, entertaining the idea, albeit not too seriously, that he might one day become a novelist.

Not long after starting his studies, Inoue formed a drinking club with four of his fellow students and began drinking more heavily than ever. With money from two members of his family, Inoue could afford his drinking habit, at least initially. But his fellow drinkers could not, and Inoue ended up paying for everyone's drinking, placing him in ever-deepening debt. In order to deal with this, Inoue began thinking up ever more unlikely excuses to get his father to send him extra money. Finally, on a visit home, his father exploded in anger: "Do you intend to deceive your father? You've come to me seeking additional money numerous times in the past, but I knew your excuses were lies all along. However, I sent you the money because I didn't want you to bother those around you. I'm not a fool who can be deceived by the likes of you!"

Yet even this scolding didn't stop Inoue. Instead, he only became more cunning in the way he got his drinking money. During school vacations, he went so far as to sneak a look at his father's financial records in order to identify those patients who had outstanding debts. Inoue then went around to these patients' homes, claiming to be collecting the monies owed his father. When even this wasn't enough, Inoue went so far as to pawn his quilted bedding so he and his schoolmates could continue drinking.

Unsurprisingly, Inoue's increasingly dissolute life included not just alcohol but frequent trips to Tokyo's famous "gay quarters" in Yoshiwara. By waiting until the other customers had left the next morning, Inoue was able to get a special discount for his favorite partner's favors. Additionally, Inoue found that he could put his waiting time to good use by doing his class homework. He was, however, unprepared for what happened on the evening he decided to try a new establishment.

After Inoue was shown to a room on the second floor, several women came by but they didn't interest him. Finally, in a fit of pique, he crawled into the bedding spread out on the floor and refused to even look at the next woman to come in. To his surprise, however, she called him by name! Yet when he peeked out from his bedding, he didn't recognize her face. How did she know who he was?

It turned out the young woman had seen him numerous times back in Numata, where she had delivered box lunches for the teachers at Inoue's high school. Her mother had run an inn in the same town that later went bankrupt. In order to settle outstanding debts, the mother was forced to sell her daughter into prostitution, a not uncommon occurrence in prewar Japan. But this prostitute had a surprising message for Inoue:

> Let me tell you something for your own good. Make tonight the last time you come to Yoshiwara. . . . If you don't listen to me and continue your dissolute life, you'll eventu-

ally find yourself thrown out of your lodgings and living on the street. Not only that, by then you will have likely caught syphilis and end up losing your nose, ashamed to show yourself in front of ordinary people. That's what's in store for you![20]

Inoue listened to her in stunned silence, realizing that she was saying these things because she cared about him. In particular, he was worried about the possibility of losing his nose! As a consequence, Inoue's near nightly visits to Yoshiwara come to an abrupt end. Although not directly connected, it was also about this time that he decided becoming a novelist didn't really interest him. Inoue came to this decision after realizing he wouldn't be able to write about himself.

A NEW SCHOOL

The final result was that Inoue quit Waseda and continued his education at the Tōyō Kyōkai (Oriental Society), a vocational school designed to train Japanese local and colonial administrators as well as overseas merchants. What made this school particularly attractive was that entering students signed a contract stating that upon graduation they would be guaranteed a permanent job in one of Japan's colonies, either in Taiwan, Korea, or Manchuria. Inoue wrote, "Whether looking to the left or to the right, I felt enveloped in anxiety. Maybe if I went to a new world, things would be different."[21]

Even though Inoue gave up his visits to Yoshiwara, his drinking habits did not change. Short of drinking money as always, Inoue next pawned the mosquito netting that his new school lent him. Further, having drunk away the money sent to him for winter clothing, Inoue was always cold at school. He did, however, come up with a solution to this problem—consume still more alcohol to keep warm. This, however, resulted in frequently dozing off in the classroom, especially during afternoon classes.

Unfortunately for Inoue, he had a very strict Chinese-language instructor. One afternoon, as Inoue dozed off, the instructor called out his name in Chinese and ordered Inoue to begin reading the Chinese text. Needless to say, Inoue hesitated because he had no idea where to begin reading. Seeing this, the instructor yelled at him in Chinese, "Fool!" To which Inoue immediately responded, also in Chinese, "Before I came to this school I wasn't so foolish. It's because I came here and was taught by a foolish teacher like you that I ended up being such a fool!"

To Inoue's surprise, the instructor burst out laughing and said, "You're pretty funny! But we instructors aren't little fools like you, Inoue; we're big fools who can reach the heavens!" and laughed even harder.[22] After that, Inoue got along well with the instructor, who always gave him 90 percent or better on classroom tests. Inoue, for his part, became a dedicated student of Chinese. Furthermore, thanks to their mutual interest in drinking, Inoue became close with yet a second Chinese-language instructor who frequently invited him over to indulge. This was a big help to Inoue, for on those occasions he didn't have to pay.

However, just when things seemed to be going well, perhaps for the first time in his life, Inoue faced a calamity. A full year had elapsed since Inoue began his studies. It was just then that a serious disturbance took place at school, a disturbance for which Inoue was blamed. The student who created the disturbance was Inoue's close friend, but Inoue himself was not involved. Yet, while some of the school's administrators supported Inoue, he nevertheless ended up being suspended from school for several months.

Inoue was eventually found innocent of involvement in the disturbance and had his suspension lifted. However, by this time the final exams in his courses had taken place, and the hard work Inoue had put into his classes meant nothing. There were suggestions he sue the school, but Inoue refused to do so. As he explained, "I had been a skeptical child who found no hope in life. Now, faced with this further unpleasantness, I got genuinely sick of this world."[23] But what would he do next?

Inoue once again came to the conclusion that it was time to die, preferably in a roadside ditch somewhere. The problem was, if he did this in Japan, he would be viewed as having been insane, thereby bringing shame on his family. Thus, if he were going to die, there was only one place his corpse was unlikely to be discovered—Manchuria. With only the clothes he was wearing, and a traditional bamboo tobacco pipe hanging from his waist, he boarded a ship to carry him to his death.

4

An Adventurer in China

SPYING IN MANCHURIA

In 1909 Inoue arrived by ship in Dairen (Ch., Dalian) with only one silver fifty-sen coin, half of one yen, in his pocket. While Inoue had changed his mind about dying by the time he reached Manchuria, he had no idea how he would support himself and spent his first month searching for work. In effect, he had become what was popularly known as a *Manshū-rōnin*, or a Manchurian "masterless *samurai*." In other words, Inoue was now a soldier of fortune.

Inoue got his first break when he was hired by the South Manchuria Railway Company and placed in their employee training facility. The South Manchuria Railway had originally been built by Russia as part of the Chinese Eastern Railway in 1898–1903. However, following the Japanese victory over Russia in the Russo-Japanese War of 1904–1905, the southernmost section of the southern branch of the railway was ceded to Japanese control. The railway ran from Lüshun Port (aka Port Arthur) at the southern tip of the Liaodong Peninsula to Harbin, where it connected to the Chinese Eastern Railway. It also included an adjacent railway zone in which it enjoyed absolute and exclusive administrative rights, including extraterritoriality.

The South Manchuria Railway Company, held semiprivately, was created to operate the railroad with an initial capitalization of 200 million yen. However, it was further tasked with developing settlements for Japanese settlers and pro-Japanese industries along its route. The army's role in the railroad was clear from its inception, for General Kodama Gentarō (1852–1906), hero of the Russo-Japanese War, was chosen to head the organizing committee. Following Kodama's death in 1906, General Terauchi Masatake (1852–1919) was his replacement.

Count Gotō Shimpei (1857–1929), former governor of the colony of Taiwan, was appointed the company's first president, with company headquarters in Dairen.

The company grew rapidly and by the end of 1907 employed some 9,000 Japanese and 4,000 Chinese. By 1910, these numbers had increased to 35,000 and 25,000, respectively. Inoue arrived in Manchuria at an opportune time.

Inoue completed his initial employee training in August 1910. Ostensibly, Inoue was to work as a railroad shipping clerk. However, undoubtedly helped by his Chinese language ability and former military training, Inoue was soon recruited to begin his first true adventure. "In reality, I was to work as a spy for the Japanese army," he wrote.[1] Thanks to army funding, Inoue was able to turn over his entire company salary to a fellow employee who, Inoue notes, was deeply grateful.

In this time of great political instability in China, it is not surprising that the Japanese army needed spies. Uprisings against the collapsing Qing Dynasty were occurring with increasing frequency throughout the country. For Japan, these uprisings presented both an opportunity as well as a threat. On the one hand, properly understood, and perhaps even assisted, the uprisings might serve to enhance Japan's rapidly expanding position in the country. On the other hand, there was an undercurrent of increasing xenophobic nationalism, especially among Chinese youth, that left unchecked might threaten Japan's growing economic interests, especially in Manchuria.

Inoue's first assignment was to infiltrate a Chinese group planning an uprising in the city of Liaoyang, 190 miles to the northeast of Dairen. The initial goal of the uprising was to occupy Liaoyang's castle, employing a band of over one hundred men, sixty of whom were security guards for a local wealthy merchant. The remainder of this group were drawn from an additional band of *bazoku*, or "bandits," the merchant had hired. Inoue was the only Japanese member of the band. The attack on the castle was to take place in two stages starting in the early morning hours of December 1, 1911.

Inoue was ordered to wait in the railroad's employee dormitory until he received a signal to join the attack. The signal, however, never came. Instead, he heard the sound of gunshots. Inoue raced to the scene, and the first thing he saw was a trail of blood on the freshly fallen snow. Following the trail, he encountered the merchant's dead body lying facedown in the snow. Nearby he discovered the bodies of some forty-five additional members of the group, many with their heads cut off. Out of respect for his fallen comrades, Inoue initially tried to place the heads back on the bodies but stopped when he realized it was useless, not to mention how surprisingly heavy their heads were.

It was at this point that a detachment of Qing soldiers arrived. Inoue immediately pointed to his railway uniform and hat, expecting this would protect him. Nevertheless, the mounted detachment commander shouted at him in Chinese, demanding to know who he was. Inoue pretended he didn't understand Chinese and simply pointed to his railroad hat. The detachment head then ordered Inoue to leave the area.

By late morning, the abortive uprising was the talk of the town. The worst, however, was yet to come, for the Qing soldiers had managed to identify and arrest the remaining sixty-odd members of the group. Judgment was not long in coming, for on the afternoon of the following day the prisoners, condemned to death, were marched two abreast, hands tied behind their backs, to a wide area just outside the western gate to the city. Remaining to witness the proceedings, Inoue was surprised that many of his condemned comrades acknowledged and smiled at him as they walked past.

Divided into five groups, the prisoners were made to kneel in front of previously dug trenches. Once in place, the executioner began his work. Armed with a large, curved Chinese sword, it took only one swing of the sword to cut off each prisoner's head, which fell into the trench. An additional kick sent the decapitated body into the same trench. Inoue was appalled: "It took about two hours for all of the prisoners to be executed. I was filled with indescribable feelings of rage, sympathy, and sorrow, so much so I felt as if I were going mad. I then made a pledge to myself, 'I'll definitely get revenge on these enemies!'"[2]

Despite his thirst for revenge, the "old Inoue" was never far away. Namely, whenever he had the time and money, Inoue returned to drinking and associated pursuits. Only this time Inoue had an excuse for his indulgent lifestyle—he claimed to be overwhelmed by feelings of desperation. Yet, at the same time, Inoue accepted a request to become an instructor at the Liaoyang branch of the Manchurian Railway's *kendō* (fencing) practice hall. He nevertheless almost never went there. Instead, he devoted his free time to facilitating weapon sales to local rebel groups, using his share of the profits to support his drinking and carousing.

In the spring of the following year, 1912, the railroad transferred Inoue to the city of Gongzhuling, 175 miles to the northeast of Liaoyang. It didn't take long for him to discover and join yet another revolutionary group. The goal this time was to overthrow the regional warlord, Zhang Zuolin (1875–1928), and create an independent state in Mongolia. Inoue welcomed this opportunity, for he saw it as a chance to get revenge for the deaths of his former comrades.

A SECOND ENCOUNTER WITH CHRISTIANITY

In the midst of planning this uprising, Inoue had a second, albeit brief, encounter with Christianity. At the beginning of April 1912, the South Manchuria Railway Company invited the Japanese delegate to the London conference of the International Christian Youth Association to speak at several locations on his way to Europe. Inoue attended the lecture in Gongzhuling and took up the delegate's invitation to his audience to ask whatever questions they might have. Inoue began his response by briefly reviewing his earlier contact and doubts relating to Christianity. This in turn led to the following heated exchange:

Lecturer: Are you a believer [in Christianity]?

Inoue: I was in the past, but I am no longer able to acknowledge [the existence of] God, who is of such vital importance.

Lecturer: People like you are known over there [in the West] as "believers who have graduated" [the faith]. People like you have an extremely base personality and are unable to be saved.

Inoue: Hey, you! Didn't you say in your lecture that due to Christ's love there was no one who couldn't be saved? Further, didn't you invite members of the audience to ask questions? Not only have you failed to answer my concerns, now you're insulting me in front of everyone gathered here. Just what do you think you're doing!

Inoue's angry response caused quite a stir among members of the audience, some of whom, especially the women, attempted to intervene to calm things down. At that point, Inoue decided to leave the lecture hall but not before he shouted at the lecturer on his way out, "Fool! Liar!"[3] This was Inoue's last contact with any form of Christianity.

A FIRST ENCOUNTER WITH ZEN

In October 1912, two railway employees Inoue's age told him about a Sōtō Zen priest named Azuma Soshin (1883–1966) who had recently arrived in town.[4] They invited Inoue to join them in going to meet the priest. Inoue dismissed their invitation without a second thought. However, a few days later, the employees returned and repeatedly urged him to go with them. Inoue finally agreed but thought to himself, "In the past I was deceived by Christians, and now a [Buddhist] bonze will try to hoodwink me. I'll go along with them just to show what a fake he is, too!"[5]

When Inoue arrived at the small house serving as a temporary temple, thirty people were already present, facing a small Buddhist altar at the far end of the second main room. Azuma Soshin was a slightly built man around thirty years of age wearing a short Japanese-style padded coat. Just as soon as he had been introduced, Inoue confronted him, saying, "To tell the truth, I'm someone who's been suffering from a number of doubts for many years now."

Having said this, Inoue spent the next hour expounding his many doubts. His doubts included such topics as the essence of things, standards of right and wrong, the need to be loyal and filial, the question of life and death, and the true nature of reality. When, at length, Inoue finished, Azuma raised his head, looked him in the face, and asked, "Well, is that all you have?"

"No," Inoue replied, "I have many more questions, but I'll stop here for the time being to respectfully ask for your response." However, before Inoue could even finish his sentence, Azuma shouted, "Fool!"

Short-tempered as ever, Inoue couldn't bear to be made fun of in front of such a large group. Clenching his fists, he jumped up, menacingly approached the priest, and said, "What do you mean, a fool?" To Inoue's surprise, Azuma first smiled and then broke out laughing. Perplexed by his behavior, Inoue once again shouted, "Just what do you mean, a fool?"

"Ha, ha, ha, I'm the fool! A fool is someone who doesn't understand what's going on. I foolishly listened to you saying you don't understand this and don't understand that. Moreover, I remained silent when you told me you were unable to understand anything at all. That's why I called myself a fool for letting you get away with it!"

Inoue was dumbfounded by Azuma's unexpected answer, delivered so nonchalantly. Yet, having challenged the priest, he couldn't stop there and continued to press for an answer: "Well then, do *you* understand?"

"Of course, I do!" Azuma replied.

"Well, in that case," Inoue continued, "instead of taking time to call someone a fool, wouldn't it be better to just answer their questions?"

"What a lazy man you are! You expect someone who has risked his life to understand something to give you answers without having to make any effort on your part. That's not the way it works!"

"Is that so? Well, in that case, how about telling me the way you went about discovering these answers for yourself?"

By this time, Inoue had calmed down considerably, and Azuma responded, "Well, I don't know if it'll work for others, but since I'm a Zen priest, I practiced *zazen* [meditation]."

"So if I practice *zazen* I'll understand, will I?"

"Who can say? That's entirely up to you. I can't say one way or the other. The only thing I can tell you is that I practiced *zazen*."

"Alright," Inoue replied, "then I'll practice *zazen*, too." Placing both hands on the floor and bowing deeply, Inoue said to Azuma, "Please tell me how to go about doing it."[6]

This exchange marked Inoue's initial introduction to Zen and Zen practice. Although Sōtō Zen priests, unlike their Rinzai Zen counterparts, don't usually assign *kōan* (Zen dialogues) to their students as objects of meditation, Azuma assigned one to Inoue that very evening. Thereafter, no matter what the weather, Inoue meditated for two forty-minute periods every day, once in the morning and once at night. His meditation was so intense that it took him only a week to successfully present a response to his first *kōan*. At first there were five or six others meditating with him, but one by one they stopped coming. By the time Inoue passed his fourth or fifth *kōan*, he and one other practitioner were the only ones left.

In recognition of his dedication, Azuma gave Inoue the lay Buddhist name of Yuishin (唯心, mind only). For the next twelve months, Inoue continued to meditate, "almost forgetting to sleep or eat."[7] As a result, he was able to pass additional *kōans*, although by then his fellow practitioner had also dropped out. Only Inoue and Azuma, now his master, were left. For the first time in his life, Inoue found something and someone he could truly believe in. As such, this encounter became a major turning point in his life.

Although the two men could not have imagined the circumstances, they would meet once again in either 1933 or 1934 when Inoue was imprisoned in Tokyo's Ichigaya Prison in the aftermath of the Blood Oath Corps Incident of 1932. At the time Azuma had come back to Japan for a brief visit and, upon learning of Inoue's arrest, paid a "sympathy call" (*imon*) to show his concern. Inoue was deeply moved by Azuma's visit, writing, "How very fortunate I am to have met the master of my spirit while I'm still alive, providing me with the opportunity to express even a single word of gratitude."[8] By this time Azuma was the abbot of Busshinji (Buddha Mind Temple), a temple he had established in Gongzhuling. However, like all temples built by Japanese Buddhists in Manchuria and throughout China, Azuma's temple was destined to last only until Japan's defeat in 1945.

ATTEMPTING TO OVERTHROW ZHANG ZUOLIN

Inoue's Zen practice was, however, no impediment to his continued dedication to fomenting revolution in northern China, focused as before on the establishment of an independent Mongolia. Toward that end, Inoue used his position with the railroad company as a cover for smuggling weapons into the area, starting with some fifty infantry rifles. However, his actions soon came to the attention of Zhang Zuolin, the increasingly powerful regional warlord. Zhang demanded that the railway company turn Inoue over to him for punishment, which would have undoubtedly led to his execution.

The upper echelons of his railroad company did what they could to defend Inoue, initially claiming that no such person as "Inoue Shirō" worked for them. Zhang's lieutenants, however, knew better and rejected their claim. Unable to protect their employee any longer, Inoue's superiors finally told him he would have to leave. In itself this didn't bother Inoue, but it did mean he would have to part with his master. Inoue describes the bitter tears both he and Azuma shed at their parting. Azuma's last words were, "Had we had a little more time, I would have liked to introduce you to the *Lotus Sūtra*." At the time, these words didn't mean much to Inoue, but "in later years, they were to have a profound impact on my spiritual life."[9]

Dressed in Japanese clothing, Inoue departed for Beijing early on the morning of January 11, 1914. A single knapsack slung over his shoulder contained all of his worldly goods, starting with a bottle of whisky.

SPYING IN BEIJING AND BEYOND

Inoue arrived in Beijing with the name of only one contact, Japanese Army Colonel Banzai Rihachirō (1871–1950). Banzai was then a military advisor to Yuan Shikai (1859–1916), a former high-ranking Qing Dynasty military figure who had maneuvered himself into the presidency of the newly formed Chinese Republic, ousting Sun Yat-sen (1866–1925) in the process. Banzai, however, had a second and secret role, sending regular reports on Yuan's actions to the army's chief of staff in Tokyo.

Inoue had never met Banzai and didn't even know where he lived. Thus, he spent his first night in Beijing at the city's only Japanese inn, in a room that cost four yuan. The cost was important because Inoue arrived with only seven yuan to his name, leaving him with only three silver yuan coins. Living on the edge as always, Inoue presented these coins to the room maid as "nose paper money" (*hanakami-dai*). "Nose paper," or tissue paper, in this instance represented payment for sex. The maid accepted his offer, and once again Inoue was broke.

The next morning Inoue departed for Banzai's residence, not knowing if the colonel would even meet him, let alone employ him. About this Inoue wrote: "If I was unable to gain entrance to his home I wouldn't have been able to pass the night on Beijing's bitterly cold streets, for I would have frozen to death. It would have been the end."[10]

In fact, it very nearly was the end, for Inoue was not allowed to speak directly with Banzai when he telephoned the next morning. He got no further than Banzai's military orderly, Nakagawa, who only agreed to his visit after a thorough quizzing. When Inoue finally met Banzai in person, he introduced himself and immediately launched into the following conversation:

Inoue: It appears you have a lot of Japanese and Chinese around here. So I imagine there must be some food left over.

Banzai: Yes, there are lots of people around, so I think there must be leftover food. But why do you ask?

Inoue: I'd like you to let me eat that leftover food.

Banzai (appearing puzzled): What?!

Inoue: In return I'll be your servant or just do menial work for you. I'll do whatever you need done so long as it's within my ability to do so.

Banzai: I see. Well, we can't very well talk about these things standing up, so please take a seat and tell me about yourself.

To Inoue's surprise and delight, it turned out that Banzai had already heard about him and his activities in Manchuria. Thus, he readily agreed to employ Inoue, providing a two-man room for him in the rear of his mansion. Yet, after informing Inoue of this, Banzai was in for another surprise—this wasn't enough for Inoue.

Inoue: I do have one condition regarding my employment.

Banzai (laughing): You're telling me that you, whom I have just agreed to hire, have a condition regarding your employment? Well, let's hear it.

Inoue: Well, now that I've safely made my way to Beijing, I want to be able to study Chinese in my free time.

Banzai (smiling): Oh, that's no problem. Two teachers of Chinese come here every day, so you can join one of their classes.[11]

Banzai's orderly then showed Inoue to his room, and Inoue requested his rucksack be sent over from the Japanese inn. Inoue had left it there as a guarantee for the money he had borrowed from the innkeeper for the taxi fare to Banzai's mansion. The next morning Inoue began to work; his first assignment was cutting out articles of interest from Chinese newspapers.

There was one "house rule" that Inoue found hard, very hard, to keep: the rule prohibiting the consumption of alcohol on the premises. Unsurprisingly, Inoue broke this rule almost immediately by drinking the bottle of whisky he had in his rucksack. Banzai's orderly discovered the empty bottle in his rucksack during a room inspection and admonished Inoue severely.

At the same time, Inoue's drinking didn't stop him from his Buddhist practice. Instead of meditation, however, he now devoted himself to a full hour of sutra recitation from four to five in the morning daily. He chose to recite the *Kannon Sūtra*, a scripture much beloved in both the Zen sect and other Japanese sects. Yet Inoue admitted this devotional exercise was, in fact, but one part of his strategy to endure the cold in a room that was not only unheated but also lacked bedding. He had no money to buy so much as a single blanket. It was not until Banzai's "second wife," his Korean mistress, accidently discovered Inoue's plight that bedding was provided. Banzai's "first wife" remained in Japan.

Inoue had been employed for nearly five months when he was ordered to accompany Banzai's second wife as far as Mukden (today's Shenyang) in Manchuria, from where she would travel by herself to her parents' home in Korea. The reason for the trip was the imminent arrival in Beijing of Banzai's Japanese wife. Inoue expected the round trip to take him approximately a month since he had also been ordered to investigate the activities of Japanese intelligence agents in the area as well as report on the overall situation in Manchuria and beyond.

On departure, Inoue was given the not-insignificant sum of 250 yuan to cover his expenses, together with the promise of additional funds to be telegraphed to him as needed. However, early in his assignment, Inoue heard a rumor about a second revolutionary uprising being planned somewhere in the vicinity of the Yangtze (today's Chang Jiang) River. In response, Inoue was prepared to put everything aside for, as he writes, "I was no less interested in revolutionary movements than I had been earlier in Manchuria. If the participants were really serious, I was prepared to join them."[12] To his disappointment, Inoue was unable to get any further information about the rumored uprising and reluctantly decided to carry on with his original mission.

In the course of his travels, Inoue made one stop not on his itinerary—the German colony of Tsingtao (today's Qingdao). Tsingtao, located on the southern coast of Shandong Peninsula in northern China, had been a German colony since 1898 and was home to a strategically important naval base. Inoue decided he would survey the gun emplacements in the city, for he suspected that such information might one day be of value to Japan, a premonition that turned out to be highly accurate. Once in Tsingtao, Inoue took advantage of a moonlit night for his secretive survey and breathed a sigh of relief when the German garrison failed to notice his movements. Inoue noted, "The success of my survey of the gun emplacements would later prove advantageous to the Japanese military's attack [on the colony] following the outbreak of hostilities between Japan and Germany [during World War I]."[13]

After leaving Tsingtao, Inoue continued south until he finally arrived in Shanghai, where he encountered an all too familiar problem—he was penniless again. As so often in the past, his drinking and other "pleasures" along the way had consumed his funds. Walking the streets of Shanghai pondering how to pay for his lodging, Inoue was overjoyed to see someone he knew—another Japanese spy! Although Inoue didn't know him well, part of Inoue's duties had been to forward this spy's monthly allowance, using a foreign bank as an intermediary. Thus, from the spy's viewpoint, Inoue was an important superior.

Inoue took full advantage of his status by, first of all, ordering the spy, who went by the name of Sugiura, to pay off all his bills at his lodgings. He then directed Sugiura to purchase him a ticket on the next ship leaving for Nagasaki. On the spur of the moment, Inoue had decided to return to Japan for a short visit. Needless to say, Sugiura was mystified by all of this, yet not daring to oppose his superior, he was in no position to object. Ticket secured, the two men set out to engage in Inoue's favorite pastime—a night on the town.

Inoue returned to Japan at the beginning of July 1914. From Nagasaki, he traveled to Kumamoto, the birthplace of both of his parents. Although Inoue had never been to Kumamoto before, many of his relatives still lived there. He was given a warm welcome, especially as his visit coincided with the major celebration of *Obon*, an annual Buddhist event dedicated to ancestor veneration.

For his part, Inoue was particularly interested in the stories told by one of his now-elderly female cousins. Her father, Inoue's uncle, had died fighting in the failed 1876 Shinpuren Rebellion, one of a number of ex-samurai uprisings that took place in the early Meiji period against Japan's new central government. The 200 participants in the rebellion were members of the former samurai class unhappy with having lost their former privileged social status and income under the Tokugawa Shogunate (1600–1868).

By the end of July, it was time for Inoue to return to China. Inasmuch as he had traveled to Japan without permission, Inoue fully expected Col. Banzai to fire him when he got back to Beijing. On his return, Banzai initially told Inoue to take a day off to rest before they had their first meeting. The next day, Inoue told Banzai what he had learned during his travels before adding, "I returned fully prepared to be dismissed given everything I've done, especially as I didn't let you know where I was, not to mention the fact that I'm now opposed to Yuan Shikai, whom I know you support."[14]

To his surprise, Banzai, promoted to major general in Inoue's absence, responded in the same amiable way as always: "Inoue, it's true that if you had provided me with this same information a month ago it would have had a major impact. Nevertheless, because you invested the amount of time and money you did, you were able to acquire additional important information, so I'm not bothered at all. If you have a mind to, you can remain here just as before."[15]

Inoue was deeply touched by Banzai's generosity and thought, "I must be prepared to sacrifice my life for this man."[16] Shortly after their meeting, Inoue was surprised and delighted to learn that Banzai had ordered his spending money be increased by five yuan per month. "Apart from my father, I'd never encountered such a generous person," he remarked.[17] Banzai's generosity also impressed Inoue because it was common for senior intelligence officers to pocket most of the money the General Staff Office gave them for their operatives. Banzai, however, was the exact opposite, going so far as using his personal funds to take care of subordinates. "I respect him even now, for such a selfless person is rare," Inoue wrote.[18]

At the time, Inoue was unaware that with the outbreak of hostilities in Europe he would soon be earning every yuan of his salary.

5

Fighting in World War I

Japanese aggression during World War II has all but erased from memory Japan's very different role in World War I (1914–1918). Japan, then allied with the United Kingdom, Russia, France, and eventually the United States, played a significant role, first and foremost by securing the sea lanes in the West Pacific and Indian Oceans against the German navy. Additionally, the Japanese navy carried out antisubmarine operations and escort duties for troop transports both in the Mediterranean and from as far away as New Zealand and Australia. In February 1915, marines from Japanese navy ships based in Singapore even helped suppress a mutiny by Indian troops against the British government.

Japan formally declared war on Germany on August 23, 1914, following an official request from the British government, its ally since 1902. Britain asked Japan to destroy raiders from the German navy in and around Chinese waters. Taking advantage of the opportunity, the Japanese navy initially seized several of Germany's island colonies in the Pacific, including the Mariana, Caroline, and Marshall Islands.

On the Asian continent, Japanese forces landed in China's Shandong province on September 2, 1914, quickly surrounding the German colony at Qingdao (formerly spelled Tsingtao). The siege of Qingdao concluded with the surrender of German colonial forces on November 7, 1914. It was in the battle for Qingdao that Inoue's actions as a spy for the Japanese army would play an important role.

And for those readers who suspect today's Tsingtao beer from China is connected to this area's earlier role as a German colony, your suspicions are correct.

SPYING ON GERMANY

Although his memory was faulty, Inoue wrote, "As I recall, Japan began its participation in World War I on August 3, 1914. On Banzai's orders, I spent my days in the military attaché's office in the [Japanese] consulate drawing maps of the battlefield situation."[1] One day, however, an army captain, stationed at the Japanese garrison in Tianjin (Tientsin), visited Banzai's residence.[2] Banzai introduced Inoue to the captain and left the two of them to talk in the parlor.

The captain quickly came to the point, requesting that, for the sake of the nation, Inoue accept a position as a spy for the Tianjin garrison. Inoue blurted out, "No, thank you. Under these circumstances, when it is necessary for someone to sacrifice himself for the nation, dangerous work of this kind is better left to professional soldiers like yourself."[3] The captain said no more.

Matters, however, did not end here. A few days later, Banzai approached Inoue to ask if he were willing to accept a dangerous assignment that he couldn't ask anyone else to do. This led to the following conversation between the two:

> "Boss, as you know, I'm unable to do even ordinary work satisfactorily, yet now you're asking me to do something so difficult that others can't do it. There's no doubt I'll fail, so please ask someone else."
>
> "You're right, there's no one else who can do this. That's why I'm asking you. And don't worry, it's alright if you fail."
>
> "Well, in that case, I'll try."
>
> "You agree to do it then! It's dangerous work, so please take care. And just in case something happens, are there any words you'd like to leave behind?"
>
> "I have none," Inoue concluded.[4]

By accepting Banzai's request, Inoue hoped to repay his superior's kindness. As for the danger involved, Inoue had, as at so many times in the past, already made up his mind to die. Nevertheless, in light of the captain's recent request, Inoue found it something of a bitter pill to swallow when Banzai later informed him that he was to report to the very same captain at the Tianjin garrison for assignment.

The captain was very happy to see Inoue on his arrival in Tianjin. He informed him that his assignment was to secretly enter the German colony of Qingdao within three days in order to report on both its armaments and the overall situation. How he accomplished this mission was up to him. He could pick up money to cover his expenses from either local Japanese post offices or consulates. The Tianjin garrison would let the relevant offices know to expect him.

Inoue was initially unsure how he would get into the tightly guarded colony, especially since Japan, then a British ally, had already declared war on Germany. On reflection, Inoue thought he might succeed disguised as a Chinese "coolie" (lit., bitter labor). Like other coolies, Inoue arrived at the colony's main train station on board a third-class coach. While German undercover agents were checking arriving passengers, their attention was focused on passengers in the first- and second-class coaches, not those in third class. "I did it!" Inoue thought to himself, careful not to show any outward emotion.[5]

As soon as it got dark, Inoue went to the one Japanese inn still operating in the colony. There he encountered an unexpected problem when the inn attendant wouldn't allow him on the premises, thinking he was nothing more than a dirty Chinese coolie. "Call the manager!" Inoue demanded in a low voice. When the manager appeared, Inoue said, "The Tianjin garrison sent me."[6] With that, Inoue was quickly hidden in a room in the inn's basement.

Inoue initiated his spying activities by using his contacts in the colony to hire local rebels to snoop on his behalf. He paid them for each bit of news they brought him about the enemy. During the daytime, he stayed in his basement room writing notes, while at night he went out to personally gather still more information. In addition, Inoue had a more unusual source—the Japanese mistress of the German head of a major factory in the colony. Unhappy with being in a war zone, she wanted to return to Japan and befriended Inoue in the hope that he could arrange this for her.

While Inoue initially refused to help the woman, he discovered something that changed his attitude; not only was the German factory located in a heavily fortified and secret section of the colony, but her German lover had a detailed map of the area stored in his safe. Knowing this, Inoue promised that if she could secure a copy of this map, he would help her return to Japan. And to Inoue's delight, she did just that. For his part, Inoue arranged for the mistress to leave on board the last repatriation boat departing the colony.

But Inoue still had one big assignment to fulfill before his mission was complete, namely, determining, as precisely as possible, the layout of a new minefield being constructed just offshore from the colony. In the likely event Japan were to invade the colony from the sea, advance knowledge of this minefield would be critically important. But how could Inoue find a relatively high place in the colony to observe the minefield's construction?

In another fortuitous turn, Inoue met a Japanese Buddhist priest staying at the inn who was affiliated with the True Pure Land (Shin) sect. At first, Inoue kept his true identity a secret from the priest, but with time running out, Inoue decided to risk everything. Taking the priest aside, he disclosed his identity as an army spy and laid out his plan for entering a restricted area with a view of the minefield. The priest's assistance was necessary because the only place with a view of the minefield below was the colony's Japanese cemetery. While reconnoitering the minefield, Inoue would pretend to participate in ancestor memorial rituals conducted by the priest.

The priest was so surprised by Inoue's proposal that he began trembling, unable to speak. Anticipating his reaction, Inoue took out a pistol from the folds of his kimono, pointed the barrel at the priest, and said, "Master, please give your answer to *this*!"

Inoue recognized that he was asking a lot of the priest, no matter how much the priest might have, as a devout Buddhist, "transcended life and death." Additionally, he realized that if the priest refused his request, he would have no choice but to shoot him on the spot to ensure the secrecy of his mission. Thus, Inoue felt a genuine sense of relief when the priest finally responded, stating that he would be happy to participate in Inoue's plan. The priest went on to explain that he himself was in Qingdao as a spy for the navy!

Inoue was overjoyed to hear this and reached out to take the priest's hands in his own, saying, "If we make the slightest mistake, it could cost us our lives. Thank you for agreeing to do this. Please let the two of us die for our country!"[7] Inoue then shed two or three drops of "men's tears" on the table between them.

Inoue was further moved when the priest explained that his initial hesitation resulted from the fact that he had already accomplished his mission for the navy and was anticipating returning safely to Japan on the last repatriation boat departing the following day. However, although his plans were now in jeopardy, he was prepared for whatever might happen. He asked Inoue to explain just what he had in mind.

Inoue told the priest that the two of them would travel to the cemetery in separate cars, the priest taking a sign on which was written the words "Japanese Community Cemetery." Inoue, dressed in a business suit, would arrive in a second car carrying a flag inscribed with "Honpa Honganji branch of the True Pure Land sect." Then, while the priest was erecting his sign, Inoue would go behind the cemetery's crematorium to draw a map of the minefield under construction off the coast. In the event they were apprehended, they would say they had come to pay their final respects to the departed before they left on the last repatriation boat the following day.

Sure enough, not too long after their arrival at the cemetery a car pulled up at the lower entrance. The priest coughed loudly to warn Inoue, who then rushed to a nearby grave marker where he pretended to be paying his respects. The "blue-eyes," walking toward him in the company of the priest, shouted in Chinese, "What are you doing?" Feigning ignorance, Inoue replied, "As you see, sir." "Well, get out of here quick!" "Yes, yes, of course." As they followed the blue-eyes out of the cemetery, Inoue looked over at the priest and gave him the knowing smile of success. Inoue wrote, "I later learned that we had been questioned by a man named Walter, head of the colony's secret police. It was a miracle we got away with it."[8]

A few days later, Inoue was able to sneak out of Qingdao and return to Tianjin, where he presented an interim report to the staff officer who had dispatched him. His report was added to others, and what satisfied Inoue the most, even more than the verbal praise he received, was the captain stamping "trustworthy" (J., *kakujitsu*) on his report. Inoue still regarded himself as very much the "black sheep" of his family, and therefore to have something he had done deemed "trustworthy" was a source of great pride to him. In fact, it led him to volunteer for a second reconnaissance mission to Qingdao. Once this was accomplished, it was time for Inoue to revert to his favorite pastime—drinking and carousing.

INTERPRETING FOR THE ARMY

In the midst of his carousing, Inoue received another request for his services, this time as an assistant interpreter for an army equine hospital. Although not as exciting or glamorous as his spy missions, this assignment was important work since horses were still widely used in China for transporting both soldiers and military supplies. However, in what would turn out to be a fortuitous development, the hospital closed not long after his arrival, allowing Inoue to become a full-fledged interpreter, this time in a unit transporting Japanese war wounded. Inoue's job was to accompany wounded soldiers from either of two frontline hospitals to field hospitals in the rear. His services were needed to direct the more than one thousand Chinese coolies who actually transported the wounded Japanese soldiers.

There were, however, lulls in the fighting when Inoue's duties consisted of playing cards with a traditional Japanese floral deck during the day and drinking with army doctors at night. Eventually, Inoue was transferred to a military first aid station staffed by only one doctor, two nurses, and assorted support staff. The station was so close to Qingdao that the colony's buildings were visible to the naked eye. On November 3, 1914, while out on a walk with other staff, a Japanese cavalry soldier rode past shouting, "Qingdao has fallen!" Excited, they all looked in the direction of the city and saw a white flag hanging from the flagpole of the German governor-general's official residence.

Tragically, however, the fighting did not end with the raising of the white flag. When the Japanese troops stood up to celebrate their victory, the German troops directed their machine gun fire at them, killing many. Inoue was of the opinion that this was not a deliberate act of treachery on the German side but simply that the German soldiers, with their backs to the flag, were unaware of the surrender. In any event, Inoue and his companions rushed back to their first aid station to take care of the many wounded soldiers heading their way.

Despite the casualties on the final day of fighting, Inoue was impressed with the relatively few Japanese casualties overall during the siege of Qingdao. Inoue attributed this to the fact that the Japanese were well informed about the location of the colony's military facilities. Thus, the Japanese side was able to thoroughly destroy the enemy's artillery pieces before its infantry advanced. In claiming this, however, Inoue made no mention of the role he and the Shin Buddhist priest had played in identifying German defenses.

The German colony fell after only a little more than two months of fighting on both land and sea, primarily at the hands of the Japanese army and navy but also with minor assistance from the British. Compared with the massive and still ongoing carnage in Europe, the cost to Japan had been minimal—a total of 2,300 casualties, of whom 715 had died. By comparison, the British suffered only 83 casualties with 16 deaths. The defeated Germans suffered 493 casualties with 199 dead, plus 3,600 who became Japanese prisoners. As during the earlier Russo-Japanese War of

1904–1905, the Japanese side distinguished itself by its humane care of war prisoners. Needless to say, this would change in a massive way during World War II.

IN THE WAR'S AFTERMATH

In one sense, the best part of the war effort, at least for Inoue, followed the fall of Qingdao, for the military had the task of getting rid of its supplies as quickly as possible, including *sake*. Inoue and field hospital personnel drank barrel after barrel every night. This, however, led to the problem of showing up fit for work the next day. Inoue's method of sobering up was to drink a ladle full of milk at the hospital when he first reported for duty. He also napped whenever he could during the day, but on waking up he frequently experienced diarrhea. "I finally got sick, deservedly so," he wrote.[9]

It was just at this point that Inoue received a new assignment. He was dispatched to serve as an interpreter for a railway unit of the army now stationed at a railway factory in Qingdao. It was the same factory previously run by the German lover of the Japanese woman whom Inoue assisted in returning to Japan in exchange for a stolen map of the colony. On arrival, Inoue, his legs now swollen, consulted with a military doctor about his condition.

After finishing his examination, the doctor shook his head and said, "Your stomach is in bad condition. Can you think of anything that might have caused it?" Inoue frankly revealed his recent excessive drinking, only to have the doctor angrily respond, "You have gastric ptosis.[10] If you don't take very good care of yourself, you won't recover!"

REVERTING TO A "SOLDIER OF FORTUNE"

Following the fall of Qingdao, Inoue left the pay of the army and reverted to pursuing the goal that had brought him, and many others like him, to Manchuria in the first place, that is, to secure his fortune. Now his timing was excellent—excellent, that is, in the event the Republic of China accepted the Twenty-One Demands made by the Empire of Japan on January 8, 1915, under Prime Minister Ōkuma Shigenobu (1838–1922). These would greatly extend Japanese control over not only Manchuria but also the entire Chinese economy.

It was exactly for that reason that many of Japan's requirements were strongly opposed by Britain and the United States, who were seeking to protect their own political and economic privileges in China. Their combined opposition allowed the Chinese government to reject the most far-reaching of the Japanese demands though it eventually was forced, under threat of war, to accept thirteen. In the end, Japan gained little additional economic advantage but lost a great deal of prestige and trust in both Britain and the United States, later having far-reaching effects.

Additionally, Japan's demands added to growing anti-Japanese sentiment among the Chinese people, especially students and intellectuals.

As for Inoue, he was determined to seek his fortune by renewing his collaboration with a group of Chinese bandits headed by Wang Guolong. When Inoue approached Wang, the latter was surprised to hear that this time Inoue was focused on making as much money out of their relationship as possible. In the past, Inoue had never appeared interested in money matters. Wang, of course, remained unaware that Inoue had earlier been a spy in the employ of the Japanese military.

For his part, Inoue was surprised to learn that Wang also had his own hopes for their future relationship, namely, help in relocating to Japan once they had sufficient money. Inoue agreed to do what he could, and they were ready to work together on their first moneymaking project.

Inoue hoped to take advantage of the possibility that war might break out at any time between Japan and China if the latter refused to accede to the Japanese government's demands. Acquainted with a lieutenant commander stationed on a Japanese naval destroyer in the harbor, Inoue went to him with an offer to supply two thousand coolies to work for the Japanese military in the event that hostilities broke out, as expected, between the two nations. These were the same coolies who had earlier worked for the Japanese military in carrying wounded soldiers during the battle for Qingdao.

The typical daily wages for a coolie were the Japanese equivalent of 49 sen (49/100 of one yen). Inoue, however, was able to convince the lieutenant commander that the coolies he controlled were already skilled in transporting wounded soldiers, a hard job, and therefore should be paid between one to one and a half yen per day. Needless to say, Inoue and his compatriots planned to pocket the difference. Now all they had to do was sit back, partying at night and waiting for the war to start.

To their great disappointment, a telegram arrived not long thereafter that overturned their well-laid plans—the Japanese and Chinese governments had reached an agreement, there would be no war! In the first instance, this meant the two thousand assembled coolies had to be dismissed. Given Wang's reputation for personally killing anyone who failed to follow his orders, the dispersal of the coolies went smoothly. Yet, once again, as so often in the past, Inoue found himself broke, having spent nearly all of his savings indulging himself at night in anticipation of the profits he expected to make from the coming war.

Under these circumstances, it didn't take long for Inoue and his compatriots to make their next plans. Given that World War I was still raging in Europe, there were still profits to be made, even in China, related to the war. This time Inoue and Wang set their sights on commodities trading, specifically the purchase of copper coins in China that could be sent to Japan, where copper was in high demand, so much so that Chinese copper coins were worth 36 times more in Osaka than in China.

Getting started in the coin-buying business wasn't easy as Inoue had almost no capital to make his initial purchases. But thanks to Wang's contacts and reputation, plus Inoue's language skills, he was able to set himself up as a middleman between coin buyers who had come from Japan and local sellers. Eventually things started to go like clockwork. Inoue sent out coin buyers to villages in the morning, collecting and selling their purchases in the evening. One of Inoue's big advantages was that he didn't have to worry about any of his purchases being stolen by bandits since it was bandits bringing the coins in the first place.

As Inoue's business grew, he had to send his agents out to ever more distant areas to locate copper coins, while at the same time putting together ever larger packages of coins to sell. One of the reasons things went smoothly after Inoue had sufficient capital to cover his purchases was because the particular copper coins he purchased, those with holes in the middle, were no longer in use as currency. Thus, they had little monetary value. On the other hand, Chinese law forbade the export of copper from the country, the penalty for which was death for all involved.

This penalty, however, did not deter Inoue. Instead, he took advantage of a long-standing Chinese practice—bribing the necessary officials, in this case the governors of the three districts in which Inoue and his associates worked. These bribes meant that Inoue's goods not only remained unmolested but actually received police protection as they were being transported by horse-drawn cart. Even the village where Inoue established his business became prosperous, especially the Chinese restaurant across the street from the entrance to his premises. Outward appearances, at any rate, gave the impression that Inoue had become a successful businessman.

REVOLUTIONARY ACTIVITIES REKINDLED

As much as Inoue valued getting rich, there was something he valued even more—revolutionary activity. Thus, when Inoue got word that an uprising had broken out in southern China against the central government located in Beijing, he once again put everything aside to join it. Although Wang was a bandit leader, he shared Inoue's enthusiasm for revolution, the two of them having previously agreed that if an uprising occurred they would drop everything to take part. Inoue's first act was to take ten thousand won with him to Qingdao to buy weapons on behalf of the rebels.

Initially, Inoue didn't have an easy time of it, though he eventually succeeded in purchasing one hundred sticks of dynamite and twenty revolvers. The date was March 1916. The year is important because it marked the beginning of what became known as the "warlord era" in China, lasting until 1928.

Although Yuan Shikai (1859–1916) was then the legitimate president of the Republic of China, he wanted still more power and thus attempted to revive the monarchy, hoping to install himself as the new emperor of China. His ambitions, however, were opposed by military factions in the southern provinces, beginning with Yunnan, but quickly spreading to other areas. By March 1916, Yuan had been pressured into abandoning his attempt to revive the monarchy, but the military struggle against his rule did not end until his death in June 1916.

Thanks to Japan's earlier Twenty-One (later reduced to Thirteen) Demands, Qingdao was still firmly under Japanese control and would remain so until 1922. While in the city, Inoue once again made contact with Japanese military government officials, now eagerly engaged in supporting the southern revolutionaries, whom they believed would better advance Japanese interests in China. Inoue met with Lt. Col. Taga, an official in the military government, hoping he would introduce him to local representatives of the revolutionaries. Taga not only agreed to do so but personally took Inoue by car to the nearby revolutionary headquarters.

From then on, Inoue visited the revolutionary headquarters on a daily basis until one day he was approached by two representatives of Japanese Prime Minister Ōkuma Shigenobu. As noted above, Ōkuma's administration had previously drafted the Twenty-One Demands under threat of war. This time, however, his representatives, plus a technician from Japan, brought something new to the table—poison gas. According to them, they had acquired "the best poison gas in the world."[11] Nevertheless, the two representatives had a problem. The Chinese revolutionaries the Japanese were backing were so afraid of poison gas the two were unable to find anyone to either make the gas or place it in exploding canisters for use on the battlefield. Would Inoue, they asked, take on this task?

Inoue immediately agreed to do so but on one condition—that he be placed in sole charge of a detachment of thirty Japanese men of his choosing. The two representatives gladly agreed, and Inoue immediately sent telegrams to ten of his most trusted friends resident in Manchuria. The remaining twenty, all Japanese, were hurriedly recruited in Qingdao based on nothing more than their willingness to serve. When assembled, they set up shop adjacent to the local revolutionary headquarters and began their dangerous work, mixing the main ingredient of arsenic together with other highly poisonous substances before pouring the mixture into canisters equipped with explosive detonators.

By May it was already hot in Qingdao, especially as unit members were required to wear gas masks and special protective clothing. Highly uncomfortable, Inoue began casting aside his protective clothing and was happy to see he suffered no ill effects. When the others in his unit saw this, they were more than happy to follow his lead. The technician from Japan was the only one who clung to his protective gear. Although Inoue didn't voice his suspicions, he secretly began to wonder if the gas they were making was really poisonous.

Not long after, the representatives from Japan decided it was time to test the effectiveness of the poison gas being made. They found an empty field near the ocean where they placed a flock of sheep. When a gas canister was exploded nearby, it quickly covered the sheep in a yellow dust cloud. From inside the cloud, the sound of sneezing sheep could be heard, and as the dust dissipated the assembled onlookers expected to see a flock of dead sheep. Contrary to expectations, however, the sheep were still standing and soon resumed eating the grass in the field as if nothing had happened.

Although Inoue's suspicions were proven correct, he was, like the others, stunned by the failure they had witnessed. It was decided they would try again at a later date, but inwardly Inoue had given up on what was claimed to be the world's best poison gas. Fortunately, blame for the failed test fell on the Japanese technician, leaving

Inoue free to publicize far and wide just what a fearsome weapon the revolutionaries possessed. He even wrote a leaflet advising potential enemies that it would be better for them to surrender than suffer enormous casualties.

At the same time, Inoue prayed that actual warfare would begin as soon as possible, hoping he would be relieved of responsibility for the poison gas unit. However, when war did come, the first thing to happen was a major split over tactics. The Japanese military advisor, Capt. Sakurai, recommended the Chinese revolutionaries capture the enemy's two major military strongholds in Shandong, the province in which Qingdao was located. But by this time the Shandong provincial government had already joined the revolutionary side.

Inoue, and one of the other Japanese present, opposed this plan. Inoue argued that the central government's two main strongholds in the province, both located inside walled towns, were too well fortified to be taken by the still relatively weak revolutionary forces. Instead, he proposed first attacking the enemy's weakest outposts scattered throughout the province, thereby allowing the revolutionary forces to gather money, weapons, and additional soldiers. Furthermore, it would allow time for the arrival of the weaponry recently purchased from Japan. Capt. Sakurai, however, abruptly dismissed Inoue's proposal by saying, "That's the thinking of amateurs!"[12]

The next morning, as the revolutionary troops prepared to depart, Inoue requested his unit's members be armed. His request, however, was turned down on the basis that the poison gas his unit carried was already the strongest weapon available. Inoue, however, was undeterred, pointing out there was always an element of uncertainty in any battle. It was even possible that one or two of his unit members might face a situation where they were in danger of being taken prisoner. As Japanese this would be an unbearable humiliation, so they needed to be armed with at least a pistol in order to take their own lives. This explanation proved convincing, and Inoue's unit received a total of thirty revolvers, twenty Colts and ten Mausers.

The revolutionary troops arrived outside of the walls of the enemy's first fortified town on the evening of the first day. Inoue and his unit were housed for the night together with the other members of the headquarters staff. This told Inoue that his unit was also tasked with protecting headquarters staff.

The next morning Inoue's unit attacked an enemy barracks, located just outside the town walls. The soldiers it housed were responsible for guarding the nearby rail line and station. Inoue's unit would be supported by a total of 250 additional troops, 150 of whom were professional soldiers and the remainder bandits turned soldiers. This was not an unusual arrangement, for during the warlord era it was quite common for bandits to be hired as soldiers. In this case, however, the commanders of all of the units were Japanese.

Inoue and his unit approached the enemy barracks before dawn the next day. In addition to a pistol, each unit member carried four poison gas canisters. As they got close to the barracks, they formed a skirmish line with Inoue walking slightly behind in case anything unexpected happened. It was then that Inoue encountered an unexpected truth—while his ten trusted friends were advancing step by step in a straight line, the other twenty men hung back, clearly afraid of dying. It was at this point a voice rang out of the darkness from the enemy side: "Who's there?"

With this, shots rang out from both sides. This angered Inoue, for he had instructed his unit that when fighting in the dark unit members should not begin firing until they actually bumped into the enemy. However, due to their inexperience, Inoue realized, they had failed to appreciate what he was saying. In any event, Inoue immediately shouted out, "Stop! Don't fire! Throw your canisters!"[13]

With this, the air was filled with the sounds of exploding poison gas canisters. In response, firing from the enemy side abruptly ended as it became clear the sentry on duty had fled his post in the face of the poison gas attack. In fact, as unit members approached the enemy barracks, it appeared that all of its inhabitants had fled when they awoke to find themselves under poison gas attack. Inoue took four unit members with him to make sure no one was left inside but decided not to use his flashlight since it might give away their positions in the event enemy soldiers were still lurking in the area.

With only thirty members under his command, and not knowing what the enemy's next move might be, Inoue gave the order to his unit to quietly retreat to a nearby trench where they would await the arrival of the 250 supporting troops. Following the arrival of these troops, they would jointly occupy and secure the enemy barracks. However, to Inoue's consternation, the supporting troops didn't show up, not even after Inoue sent two unit members, one after the other, to find out where they were. Moreover, even the two unit members Inoue sent to find the supporting soldiers failed to return.

Just as Inoue was pondering what to do next, the first supporting unit, numbering some one hundred soldiers, finally arrived. Their Japanese commander admitted they were late because they had stopped to plunder along the way, a soldierly pursuit typical of the warlord era. Inoue guessed this was also the reason the remaining 150 soldiers had yet to show up.

As Inoue was discussing what to do next with the Japanese commander, some of the newly arrived troops began firing in the direction of the enemy's now deserted barracks. This, too, was typical of the actions of freshly recruited Chinese soldiers when they got hold of rifles for the first time. Inoue immediately demanded the Japanese commander order his men to stop firing, but by then some twenty rounds had been discharged, enough, Inoue thought, for the enemy to know the approximate strength of their combined forces.

For a while, the area fell silent, and Inoue decided to wait for the arrival of the remaining 150 troops before taking further action. By this time, the troops in the trenches, Inoue included, had grown tired of waiting and began to doze off. Not long afterward, however, Inoue heard a bullet whiz by, a bullet that had been fired from the rear. Inoue instantly realized what this meant and yelled out, "We're surrounded! Retreat!"

The dozing troops woke up instantly and scattered in all directions like a nest of baby spiders. Frightened and confused, the troops ran willy-nilly, coming under enemy fire in the process. As for Inoue, he and three of his closest friends initially walked to a nearby wheat field where they could observe the enemy's movements. They would have run, but Inoue had injured his knee and was forced to walk. His comrades, aware of his injury, refused to abandon him, for they were determined to either survive or die together.

The relatively slow pace of Inoue and his companions turned out to be a blessing in disguise since the enemy was firing at the other fleeing soldiers, who were by then far in front of them. Nevertheless, they soon encountered yet another serious problem. As they neared the field headquarters of the revolutionary forces, they were mistaken for the enemy, and their own side began firing at them. They took cover, and fortunately the revolutionary forces soon recognized their error and stopped firing. They were then finally able to return safely to their headquarters.

Inoue's unit was relatively fortunate, for only one man had sustained a minor leg wound while another suffered a nervous breakdown. One man, however, was missing. After breakfast the next morning, Inoue sent out a detail to search for the missing man, and it wasn't long before he was found, still hiding under a freight car in the rail yards near the train station. On returning to the unit, the man, a heavy drinker and braggart, who previously boasted how tough he was, immediately came to Inoue with a fervent plea. He would do anything he said, such as cooking for unit members, so long as Inoue didn't send him into battle again. Inoue agreed since the man had originally been a cook in Japan. Although other unit members made fun of him due to his cowardice, they all liked his cooking.

Inoue's unit of revolutionaries was not the only one to attack the enemy's stronghold that day. It was also not the only one to fail, for two additional attacks on the enemy's strongholds failed, just as Inoue predicted they would. Yet there was a silver lining of a sort, achieved at the expense of the life of one of the accompanying Japanese troops, who had been killed by a stray bullet. The Japanese side made his death into a cause célèbre, threatening to use his death as the pretext for a declaration of war by Japan, something the Chinese side was unprepared for. Filled with bitterness, the Chinese defenders of the two walled towns had no choice but to open their town gates to the revolutionary troops even though they had defeated them on the battlefield.[14]

Inoue continued fighting with the revolutionary forces until early July 1916 though he increasingly fought on his own. It was in July that an agreement was reached between the southern-based revolutionary forces and the northern Beiyang Army of the central government, thus bringing an end to the war known as the National Protection War of 1915–1916. While the actual fighting came to an end, the struggle for power between the contending military cliques throughout China would continue until 1928. In the meantime, Inoue once again found himself jobless.

In fact, Inoue's situation was worse than that. He claimed to have been caught in a fraudulent trap (J., *sagiteki bōryaku*) set up by the head of the notorious Japanese military police, or Kempeitai, and their Japanese collaborators in Qingdao. Inoue was suspected of having purchased the original one hundred sticks of dynamite and twenty pistols for his bandit friends, not for the revolutionary forces. As a result, Inoue was ordered to disband his unit, and Inoue himself had to flee Qingdao in disguise, taking refuge in Tianjin, located a little more than three hundred miles north of Qingdao.

In Tianjin, Inoue learned that Japan was considering sending troops to fight in support of the Tsarist troops fighting a rearguard action against the Bolsheviks in Siberia. Inoue and one of his close friends thought there might be an opportunity for them in this struggle and decided to travel to Siberia to find out. But first, Inoue had to find the necessary travel money.

Before Inoue could do so, however, an event of far-reaching significance took place. His wife, Ofusa, who was with him in Tianjin, became ill. Although Inoue provides no further details about her or their marriage, he abandoned his travel plans so that she could receive medical treatment in Japan. At the same time, Inoue realized that their return to Japan would give him the opportunity to hide out for a while in his wife's family home. Accompanied by his sick wife, Inoue left China at the end of July 1916, though it wouldn't be for long.

FISHING IN JAPAN

In Japan, Inoue first went to live with his wife's family in the fishing village of Matsunaga near Fukuyama city in Hiroshima prefecture. His wife's father was a broadminded man who had experienced both success and failure in his own life and consequently readily accepted Inoue into the family. Inasmuch as the family operated its own fishery business, Inoue's job was to catch young sea bream, with his wife bringing him a box lunch and *sake* at lunchtime.

In August 1916, Inoue received a letter from his father in Kawaba village requesting that both Inoue and his wife pay a visit. Inoue rejoiced at this invitation since he hadn't been home in eight years. On arrival, Inoue's father greeted both him and his wife warmly while his mother was, somewhat to his surprise, accepting of his wife. In addition, Inoue was pleased by the fact that his father didn't question him about his life in China nor ask him about his future plans. Instead, Inoue quickly returned to a daily schedule of fishing, with his wife once again bringing box lunches as before.

The most important change to occur in his absence concerned Inoue himself. His father had changed his son's name from *Shirō*, meaning "fourth son" to *Akira*, meaning "to shine." This change was done after Inoue's family consulted a traditional seer, analogous to a fortune-teller but more respected, who specialized in recommending changes to a person's name in order to realize desired ends. In this case, Inoue's family had had no contact with him after he went to China, and they were worried he might not return. The seer advised the family that in order to ensure Shirō's safe return, they should change his legal name to Akira. Not only did they do this, but they also used a family connection to register Inoue as a disciple of the abbot of Chōjūin, a Tendai sect–affiliated Buddhist temple in nearby Numata city. At least in name, but without his knowledge or consent, Inoue had become a Buddhist priest, albeit only a neophyte.

Inoue didn't object to his new name and henceforth identified himself as Inoue Akira. He doesn't indicate what, if anything, he did regarding his status as a novice Buddhist priest. He did, however, mention how impressed he was by his older brother, Fumio. While yet a student in middle school, Fumio had studied the Buddhist precepts under the guidance of the distinguished Shingon sect priest Shaka Unshō Risshi (1827–1909). After joining the navy, Fumio switched to the Zen sect when he began his practice of swordsmanship. Although Inoue admired his elder brother's stern self-disciple, he seemed so aloof that it was difficult for Inoue to get close to him.

RETURN TO CHINA

With his wife recovered from her illness, Inoue returned to China in November 1916 and first settled in Shanghai, where he spent an uneventful three months. From there he returned to Tianjin, where he quickly realized that the little money he had with him wouldn't last long. Thus he proposed to four of his acquaintances that they start a business in Tianjin's French concession. They chose the French concession because business regulations there were more lenient than in the Japanese concession.

The concessions dated from the aftermath of the Boxer Rebellion of 1899–1901. The major Western powers, plus Japan, forced the Chinese government to allow them to garrison Tianjin in order to ensure open access to Beijing. In addition to the Japanese, the British, Italians, French, Germans, Russians, and Austro-Hungarians all stationed troops in their respective concessions. However, when Inoue was there during World War I, the German and Austro-Hungarian garrisons were captured and held as prisoners of war by Allied forces.

Despite its location in the loosely regulated French concession, things quickly went wrong with Inoue's new business venture. Among other things, his four business partners turned out to be dishonest. On the one hand, they stole money from the business, and on the other hand they borrowed money from Chinese sources in the company's name and then absconded with the loans. Given this, it didn't take long for the company to fail, and Inoue found himself broke once more.

It was under these circumstances that Inoue fled Tianjin and made his way back to Beijing with a single 100-won note in his pocket. The date was February 1918. Thanks to his former spy master, now Maj. Gen. Banzai Rihachirō, Inoue was able to arrange the financing to get a new business going. He began by selling rice and wheat, expanded into operating a horseracing track, and then established a bank in addition to other business ventures. "I didn't make as much money as I had hoped," Inoue wrote, "but I did make a fair amount."[15]

Inoue was at pains to explain that he wasn't making money in order to become a capitalist or lead a life of luxury. Instead, what he hoped to do was make as much money as possible in order to financially support a large number of scholars who would devote themselves to finding answers to those questions still bedeviling Inoue, that is, standards for right and wrong, the meaning of life, and so on. Despite his earlier Zen training, Inoue was convinced that only outside experts could provide him with the answers to his deep-seated doubts.

It was these deep-seated doubts that had led Inoue to undertake the dangerous military actions he had been part of, for his goal was to use physical pain as a method of overcoming his mental agony. This is what led him first to become a spy and then to join the revolutionary army. Furthermore, by disposition Inoue was inclined to favor the weak. The revolutionary army was definitely weaker than the government forces and, moreover, had been repressed by the government. Angered by this, Inoue threw himself into the fight on the revolutionary side.

On the one hand, it is true that a number of Japanese had supported the revolutionary forces. Yet in Inoue's view very few of them had been willing to risk their lives in the process. Inoue, however, thought nothing of dying for their cause, consumed as he was by his own mental anguish. At the time, Inoue was reputed to have had such a fierce countenance that people were afraid to look him in the eyes. For Inoue, however, this was only the outward manifestation of the fierce internal struggle he was undergoing.

All of this led Inoue to look for an answer to his suffering outside of himself. He had consulted Buddhist priests but found them lacking because they used their religion as a means of supporting themselves, showing no interest in further investigating the nature of things. The same was true of Shinto priests. By comparison, scholars were relatively pure and could therefore be trusted, or at least so it seemed to him at the time. Even then, however, Inoue wasn't sure how things would turn out. In retrospect, as foolish as he may appear to have been, at the time he couldn't think of any other solution.

INOUE MEETS THE VENERABLE TŌYAMA MITSURU

One day, while Inoue was still in Beijing, he was approached by a man who identified himself as the younger brother of the wife of Japan's most important ultranationalist political leader, Tōyama Mitsuru (1855–1944). Tōyama was one of the founders of the Genyōsha (Dark Ocean Society), a secret society and terrorist organization whose agenda was to agitate for Japanese military expansion and conquest of the Asian continent. The society, founded in 1881, was initially composed of disaffected ex-samurai and organized crime figures (i.e., *yakuza*) who assisted in its campaigns of violence and assassination against liberal politicians, foreigners, and anyone else who stood in its way. Tōyama later helped create the even more notorious Kokuryūkai (Black Dragon Society) in 1901.

Tōyama's brother-in-law stayed with Inoue for some time before indicating his intention to return to Japan. Inoue also had some business to attend to in Japan, and the two made the return trip together. While in Tokyo, the brother-in-law arranged for Inoue to meet Tōyama at the latter's home in the Akasaka district. Tōyama, already more than sixty years old, presented a striking figure, a flowing white beard masking his traditional dress of kimono, white *hakama* skirt, and cotton *haori* jacket bearing his family crest. On entering the room, Inoue noticed that Tōyama put down a magazine, titled *Zen,* he had been reading.

The interview lasted for approximately an hour. Tōyama's brother-in-law did most of the talking, describing what he regarded as the high-handed actions of both England and the United States in China. During this time, Tōyama's only response was "I see." Finally, when at last the brother-in-law finished, Inoue was anxious to hear how Tōyama would respond. Tōyama's comment was simple: "The powerful are always vanquished."[16] Inoue had previously heard what a great man Tōyama was, but now he knew he was even greater than rumor made out. Tōyama's words made a deep impression on Inoue, and from then on Tōyama was a man Inoue kept close to his heart.

Inoue returned to Beijing as planned. By now World War I, millions of casualties later, had at last come to an end. So, too, had the opportunities both in China and Japan for war profiteering. Eventually Inoue underwent a change in his thinking. He came to realize that the only way he would ever find release from his mental anguish was to rely on himself and no one else. This led to a decision to return to Japan permanently in order to undergo religious training for as long as necessary.

6

The Winding Road to Enlightenment

When Inoue returned to Japan in February 1921, the Taishō era (1912–1926) was in full swing. On the positive side were such things as the emergence of a parliament, known in English as the Diet, that had an increasing say in determining state policy and exercising, via the power of the purse, a degree of control over the military. In addition, among ordinary citizens, especially in urban areas, there was growing demand for fundamental democratic rights, including freedom of the press and assembly, male universal suffrage, collective bargaining, and social welfare programs.

Internationally, the creation of the League of Nations following World War I, together with Japan's participation in the Washington Naval Arms Limitation Treaty of 1922, held the promise of long-term peace and stability. Domestically, however, both issues led to growing tension between military leaders and civilian politicians, resulting in growing Japanese criticism of both the league and the treaty.

On the one hand, World War I had initiated strong economic growth, for Japan enjoyed the benefit of serving as a supplier to the Allied powers, which were, due to the war, unable to produce needed war materials in sufficient quantity. This, however, led to inflation and a period of growing concentration of capital in the hands of the *zaibatsu*, the powerful financial combines that exerted a strong influence on Japan's political leaders. At the same time, the left grew in strength among workers, intellectuals, and educated youth. This led the state to mobilize against "radical thought," and in addition to the police and courts, it looked for "extralegal" assistance from ultranationalist organizations. These shadowy groups, often at odds with one another, were typically composed of toughs and their leaders, funded by the rich and powerful for the purpose of strikebreaking, voter intimidation, and union busting. When called upon by their patrons, these groups, claiming to be "patriots," intervened directly in the political process, including the assassination of designated opponents. Tōyama Mitsuru was the preeminent example of one such patriotic boss.

As for Inoue, once back in Japan, he was determined to settle, once and for all, his doubts concerning the standards for right and wrong. However, shortly after arriving in Yokohama, he was approached by an old friend with a job offer. His friend first expressed his deep concern about the recent growth of left-leaning labor unions in Japan. Then he asked, "Won't you spearhead the movement for a *patriotic* labor movement?" Inoue replied, "Please wait for three years while I address the deep distress I'm experiencing. Once that's done, I'll start a patriotic labor movement on my own. However, if after three years I still haven't resolved my distress, then I'll do as you request."[1]

Thereafter, Inoue returned to considering where he might find a refuge in the mountains of Japan that would allow him to address his longstanding doubts. At the same time he admitted, "I had no intention whatsoever of engaging in any kind of labor movement that might benefit society. I only harbored a small hope that I would be able to address my mental anguish within the year and then die. People who are contemplating death don't see the value of thinking about anything else."[2]

It was at this point that Inoue received a second request, this one contained in a letter from his mother. Inoue's mother asked for his help during her upcoming visit to Tokyo to see a major exposition being held in Ueno Park. This time Inoue couldn't refuse despite the fact that he had almost no money left. But he couldn't let his mother know his financial situation.

His mother's request wasn't surprising since his parents imagined their son was now a financial success. While Inoue was still resident in Beijing with a good income, he had paid for his parents to visit him for some three months, even purchasing a villa for them in the Italian concession of the city. His parents were unaware that Inoue had subsequently lost his wealth. What was he to do?

Ever resourceful, Inoue first traveled to Tokyo, residing at the Japanese-style inn his father stayed in when visiting the city and paying for it with his last one hundred yen. Next, he invited all of the *geisha* he knew in Yokohama to come visit him in Tokyo on their way to see the exposition in Ueno Park. He requested the assembled *geisha* to empty their purses in a single pile on the straw *tatami* mats. They did as he requested although complaining it would no longer be possible to know whose money it was. Inoue explained, "No need to worry about that. I'm going to take all of it. I'll give each of you enough money to get back to Yokohama."[3] With that, Inoue gathered sufficient money to look after his mother during her weeklong sojourn in Tokyo. As a consequence, Inoue's *geisha* friends from Yokohama stopped coming to visit him.

For all of his talk about dedicating himself to religious training, one might imagine that, at last, Inoue would have been off to one or another retreat in the mountains. This didn't happen. For another three months, Inoue, now accompanied by an old friend, remained in Tokyo eating, drinking, and carousing as in the past, even though he was broke. "Something will come up," he thought, and once again it did.[4]

The "something" was in the form of a visit from the male secretary of Count Tanaka Mitsuaki (1843–1939), former imperial household minister to Emperor Meiji (1852–1912). The secretary explained that Tōyama Mitsuru had suggested

Inoue as someone who might be of assistance. Although Count Tanaka would later play a decisive role in Inoue's future, at this stage his request, as conveyed by his secretary, concerned a relatively minor matter.

The problem involved a conflict between two business partners in a roofing company, one of whom was trying to oust the other in order to take sole control. The dispute had already been in court, only to have the judge direct the parties to settle the matter on their own. Still unable to reach an agreement, Tanaka's secretary asked Inoue to mediate the dispute, and Inoue agreed, though only after the secretary agreed to pay for Inoue's lodgings in Tokyo. "If you wait long enough, things always work out," Inoue chuckled to himself.[5]

The roofing company was located in the city of Mito, some seventy-two miles northwest of Tokyo. Inoue took a room at an inn near the train station but then proceeded to do nothing, other than spend his days drinking as always. Inoue explained, "If I had mediated the dispute quickly, they wouldn't need me anymore."[6] For the same reason, when each of the contending parties called on him to explain their position and seek his support, Inoue simply replied, "Oh, is that so."[7] Things went on like this for quite some time.

Finally, one of the partners invited Inoue to join him at a banquet attended by *geisha*. Inoue accepted the invitation but, at the same time, secretly invited the other business partner to attend the same banquet. Although the two partners were shocked to see each other at the banquet, before they had time to react or resume their quarrel, Inoue clapped his hands and called in ten *geisha* waiting in the adjoining room. The *geisha* quickly poured *sake* in everyone's cups, Inoue then lifted his own cup and said triumphantly, "Congratulations!" The *geisha* and other assembled guests joined in with another round of "Congratulations!" and bowed. The two quarreling business partners were flummoxed. Nevertheless, overwhelmed by the gaiety of the moment, they joined in the celebrations. The next day, Inoue phoned the judge to let him know the matter had been settled.[8]

Inoue was rewarded for his mediating efforts with an invitation to move to a nearby seaside villa owned by the company. Inoue arranged for his wife to join him, and they stayed there for a month. At that point, one of the business partners presented Inoue with a parting gift of one hundred yen, a portion of which Inoue and his wife used to return to Kawaba village. Once there, Inoue resumed his life of fishing as well as occasional bird hunting, not forgetting to send his best catches to Tōyama Mitsuru in Tokyo, albeit anonymously.

Inoue continued this lifestyle from the fall of 1921 to the spring of 1922. At that point, Inoue's wife, Ofusa, announced she no longer felt comfortable living off the money Inoue's father gave them every month and had decided to return home to help with the family business. As a result, and unlike his many turbulent years in China, Inoue found himself living a quiet life. Yet it was exactly due to his peaceful surroundings that Inoue's longtime mental torment returned stronger than ever. If he were to free himself, he thought, it had to be now or never. Unable to procrastinate further, Inoue decided to immerse himself in religious practice.

RELIGIOUS PRACTICE AT SANTOKU HERMITAGE

With nothing more than some Japanese-style bedding, Inoue moved into a small derelict hermitage named Santoku-an (Hermitage of Three Virtues).[9] Once a nun's residence, enshrining a statue of Kannon, the Buddhist personification of compassion, the hermitage had long been abandoned. It now served merely as a storage shed for funeral-related paraphernalia used in conjunction with the village graveyard located next to it.

Inoue began his religious training by once again engaging in the practice of *zazen* as he had under the guidance of Azuma Soshin, his former Sōtō Zen master in Manchuria. This time, however, Inoue trained by himself, and it was not long before he became frustrated:

> After having practiced [*zazen*] for some time, I noted that when seated my mind became clear. However, when I had to stand up to do things like relieving myself, there was no change in my state of mind, and I continued to be afflicted by the same doubts as before. Not knowing any other method of training, I continued to practice *zazen* day and night, but my mental anguish only increased.[10]

It was at this point that Inoue recalled a vivid dream he had while in China. This was despite the fact that he normally didn't have dreams or, if he did, had forgotten the details by the next morning. This time, however, the dream had been so vivid, so real, that he remembered it even though years had passed. The dream started with Inoue involved in a debate with two or three others. When Inoue won, those on the losing side started to physically attack him. Inoue struck back, and a big fight broke out with ever more men joining in against him. They started beating Inoue with a chair, and he was in mortal danger. In response, Inoue pulled out a dagger from an inside pocket, stabbed one of his attackers to death, and fled as quickly as possible with the others in hot pursuit.

One after another, his attackers caught up with him, and each time Inoue stabbed and killed one of them. Yet even though he killed three or four, the number of attackers kept increasing. All Inoue could think of doing was run as fast as he could, heading for some nearby mountains. Inoue climbed to the peak of a rugged mountain with his attackers still in pursuit. From his youth, Inoue had excelled at mountain climbing, but nonetheless, as he climbed down the other side of the mountain, he lost his footing and fell hundreds of feet, losing consciousness in the process. When he regained consciousness, he found himself lying at the bottom of the mountain with his bloody dagger nearby.

Inoue thought to himself, "I have killed a number of people. Even if I manage to escape, my crimes won't go away. There's nothing to be done but commit suicide."[11] With that, Inoue looked up only to see a nearby mound with steps leading to a stone pagoda inscribed with seven Chinese characters, a mantra pronounced in Japanese as *Namu-myōhō-renge-kyō* (I take refuge in the Wondrous Law of the *Lotus Sūtra*). Fine, Inoue thought, I'll climb up to the stone pagoda to commit suicide. With this, Inoue picked up his bloody dagger, climbed the mound, sat cross-legged at the base of the pagoda, and proceeded to commit suicide by cutting his stomach open in traditional *seppuku* style (popularly known as *hara-kiri*). Having done this, he lost consciousness.

Still dreaming, Inoue regained consciousness to find himself alive. However, when he looked at his knees, seated cross-legged, he found them covered with his intestines (as required in traditional Japanese suicide). Moreover, standing at the bottom of the mound was an old man with a white beard, smiling at him. Inoue addressed him, "Old man, you're standing there like a spectator when I'm finding it difficult to die despite having cut my stomach open. Don't you know some way to help me accomplish my goal?"[12]

In response, the old man replied that, thanks to having killed himself, Inoue's misdeeds had been forgiven. Proof of that could be seen in the way his wounds would heal if he put his intestines back in his stomach. Inoue doubted the old man, but having nothing to lose, he did as instructed. To his great surprise, once he replaced his intestines his injuries healed in short order. Maybe he had been forgiven, Inoue thought, and made a deep bow of gratitude to the old man. In return, the old man told him how to return to the city, finishing with, "When you get back, think of yourself as someone who has died and work for the benefit of the world and its people." "I'll do as you say," Inoue replied.[13]

On his way back, Inoue first passed by some farmers and then some laborers. Each time he met someone, he was filled with apprehension because he feared one of them would identify him as a murderer and seek to restrain him. Yet none did. Instead they simply exchanged normal greetings, even when he passed by a policeman. This led Inoue to believe that he had really been forgiven. With this thought in mind, he caught sight of a fine-looking city in the distance. "I'll go there to be of service," he thought, and hurried on his way.[14] It was at that point he awoke from his dream.

ON THE PATH TO INSANITY

Reflecting on his dream, Inoue decided, "I was saved by having died, so from now on I will repeat the mantra *Namu-myōhō-renge-kyō* as my form of religious practice as if my life depended on it."[15] With this, Inoue ended his practice of *zazen*, no longer sitting with his eyes half open and legs crossed in the lotus posture. Instead, he recited his new mantra over and over with his eyes shut, kneeling on folded legs in the formal Japanese *seiza* sitting posture. He filled a bottle with water and repeated the mantra, drinking from time to time and then returning to repeating the mantra. When he got hungry, he left the hermitage to eat wild plants growing around rice paddies or in fields, as well as pine needles, wisteria flowers, or anything else available.

After some time, his kimono became torn and soiled and his hair unkempt to the point that neighborhood children taunted him as if he were crazy. Inoue, however, didn't care what the children or anyone else in the village thought of his religious practice; he simply kept reciting the mantra over and over again. However, as time passed, he, too, began to feel there was something wrong with him and wondered, "I've been reciting the mantra, determined to die if necessary. . . . Is it possible I'm really going crazy?"[16] In addition, Inoue worried how his parents and siblings would react if he lost his mind without having repaid the debt of gratitude he owed them for having raised him. This all led Inoue to stop practicing for two or three days.

The extreme mental confusion Inoue had experienced disappeared, and he felt he had returned to normal. Yet, at the same time, his deeper mental anguish and accompanying doubts returned. He was, in effect, back to where he started: "As ever, I felt like a lost child with questions about the nature of life enveloping me like a dense, black cloud."[17] Not knowing what else to do, Inoue returned to reciting the mantra, and once again he began to feel as if he were going crazy. This led to a series of fretful stops and starts, but nothing seemed to help.

Time passed and the year was now 1923. Inoue was engrossed in a period of acute introspection:

> None of this is helping, maybe I should just die and get it over with. After all, as Confucius said, "If I can hear the Way in the morning, in the evening I can die content."[18] If in the course of searching for the truth one goes crazy, it can't be helped. That's one's destiny, and there is nothing to be ashamed of. Just think of the joy I'll feel should I succeed in my quest. No matter what, I'm determined to continue my practice even should it lead to an untimely death and bring grief to my family.[19]

Once Inoue had reached this decision, he was gratified to see that his doubts about his practice had disappeared. He recalled that when he had earlier considered committing suicide on board the *Kobe-maru* hospital ship, his life had been enveloped in darkness. Everything seemed meaningless, for he hadn't yet realized there was a bright side to Truth. In other words, he had turned his back on Truth and discarded life.

At the same time, Inoue realized it was thanks to Zen master Azuma Soshin's guidance that he now recognized the possibility of a bright side to Truth. He had never forgotten Azuma's parting words to him on the importance of the *Lotus Sūtra*. Azuma had already given Inoue a copy of the *Lotus Sūtra* that included both its Chinese- and Japanese-language versions. It had been a constant source of reading for Inoue, and he imagined that it was due to Azuma's psychological influence that he had his dream about the sutra while in China.

Inoue once again reverted to his incessant repetition of the mantra. This time, however, he was able to successfully overcome his doubts about the effectiveness of this practice, for his mantra repetition served as a method to enter *samādhi*, a heightened state of mental concentration/awareness not to be confused with a trance. It was then that Inoue had another unexpected experience—he began seeing and hearing things. One night, for example, he was sleeping when he happened to open his eyes and, even though the hermitage was pitch black, saw an image on the paper door in front of him. Sitting up, he looked closely and saw the image depicted a spring scene in which the trees and flowers were in full bloom. It was then that a voice called out of nowhere, "You can die now!"[20]

Initially, Inoue didn't think too much of what had happened since he realized that it was only natural that anything that was born would die at some point. But as he lay back down, he realized just how strange the occurrence had been, for he had seen the image in an otherwise pitch-black setting. How was this possible? Mulling over this question, Inoue sat up once again, but by this time the image had disappeared. This was, however, only the first of many similar occurrences.

Another incident occurred when Inoue saw a large Japanese rat snake sunbathing on a cemetery marker near the hermitage. Inoue noted that the snake was missing part of its tail, a deformity Inoue attributed to the mischief of neighborhood children. Inoue was surprised that the snake didn't try to escape when he approached. Instead, it simply repeatedly stuck out its tongue in an upward motion. Inoue addressed the snake, saying, "I'll give you the opportunity to hear the precious *Lotus Sūtra*." With this, the snake stopped sticking its tongue out. And when Inoue repeatedly chanted the associated mantra, the snake lowered its head, prompting Inoue to say, "It seems you've understood. That's enough for today, so go home and come again tomorrow. I'll give you a chance to hear more. Now go."[21]

With this, the snake slithered away and down a nearby hole. The next day Inoue returned to the spot at the same time, wondering if the rat snake would return. And there it was! Once again Inoue repeated the mantra, and once again the rat snake lowered its head as if it understood. Inoue thought this might all be a coincidence, but the same thing happened the next day. At that point Inoue told the snake, "You've heard this precious mantra recited for three days now, so that's enough. Don't come back here anymore since the neighborhood children might harm you."[22] Inoue went back the fourth day to make sure the rat snake had understood him, and the snake wasn't there. He never saw it again.

This episode convinced Inoue that he could now freely communicate with anything from trees to flowering plants, even rocks. At first this felt strange, but after a while it all seemed natural. Further, one night as Inoue was about to go to sleep, he heard the footsteps of two men walking by the hermitage. One of the men coughed, and Inoue instantly realized that he was not well. Inoue rushed after the two and asked which of them had coughed. After the man identified himself, Inoue said, "You're going to get sick, so please take good care of yourself." The man responded angrily, "Talking like that brings bad luck, you know!"

Inoue had already forgotten about the incident when four or five days later the son of the same man dropped by to inform him that his father had suddenly taken ill with a fever. He requested Inoue come to his home to pray for his father's recovery. Inoue did so, and the sick man recovered almost immediately. As the word got out, an increasing number of ill visitors came to his hermitage hoping to be cured. When they did so, Inoue would chant the mantra repeatedly until he felt a cure had been effected. "You've recovered," Inoue would say, but even he was mystified to find that their ailments disappeared on the spot.[23]

The strange happenings did not stop here, for next Inoue had what might be described as "out of body" experiences. It started one morning after Inoue finished washing his face. Suddenly his legs started moving and took him outside the hermitage. This was not something he had consciously willed, and Inoue's mind could only observe what was going on. After walking some distance, he found himself back in his family home for the first time since he had moved to the hermitage. After greeting his parents, he asked his father for some writing paper, which he used to write his father's name with a traditional brush. He then showed his gratitude to his parents by prostrating himself before them nine times. Only then did he return to his hermitage, his mind continuing to wonder what was going on. Inoue's father, he later learned, treasured the sheet of paper with his name on it until his death.

Yet, this wasn't the strangest thing that happened. Having awoken in the middle of the night, Inoue found himself getting dressed and going outside. This time he walked to a farmhouse more than two miles away and knocked on the door. A young man opened the door, and upon seeing Inoue expressed his surprise, "Why, you're the religious teacher from Santoku-an, aren't you? I was just coming to fetch you since my father suddenly became ill." With this, Inoue knelt beside the father and placed his hand on his head, once again repeating the mantra. "How's that. It feels good, doesn't it? You'll soon be better."[24] And, as always, the sick man quickly recovered.

Inoue emphasized that in all of these actions he was, as it were, a bemused bystander since none of this was of his own doing. Instead it was the result of some higher power making it happen as if by command. At one point, Inoue made a conscious decision to turn back, only to feel a powerful force make him continue walking in the original direction. Inoue recognized he had no choice but to follow the "supreme command."[25] At the time, however, Inoue didn't understand what all this meant.

ENLIGHTENMENT APPROACHES

Extending over a three-day period at the beginning of 1924, a series of new apparitions appeared to Inoue. On the first day, in the midst of mantra chanting, Inoue saw a beautiful purple cloud appear in front of him. He noted a male figure looking like Emperor Jimmu (r. ca. 660–585 BCE), Japan's legendary first ruler, standing on top of the cloud with a female deity standing beside him. In addition, Inoue saw a vision of himself prostrated before the two of them. Inoue emphasized that this vision occurred while he remained seated, though it soon disappeared.

At the same time on the second day, a similar vision of the two figures atop a purple cloud appeared. However, this time the male figure was holding an infant, who suddenly pointed in Inoue's direction. For some reason, Inoue felt disconcerted by this and once again prostrated himself before them.

Finally, on the third day, again at the same time, the vision returned, with the infant stretching out its golden-colored hand and inviting Inoue to come forward.

Just at that moment, Inoue turned into the infant, and the Inoue who had been prostrating himself before the figures was no longer there. It was at this point that Inoue felt a sense of oneness that he was unable to explain.

HEAVEN AND EARTH ARE ONE

It was now the spring of 1924. As he did every morning, Inoue stood in the hermitage's garden chanting the mantra as the sun rose over the mountains in the east. Just as the sun broke free from the brow of the last mountain, he suddenly called out the word *nisshō*. Inoue had no idea why he had done so or what the word meant. Perhaps *ni* meant "sun" and *shō* "to ascend," but Inoue couldn't be sure without seeing the word written in Chinese characters. By this time, however, Inoue was used to having strange things happen, so he didn't think too much about it.

After Inoue finished chanting, he felt himself in good spirits. Next, when he went back inside the hermitage and resumed chanting, a faintly purple, bright light suddenly filled the hermitage from the east as if splitting heaven and earth apart! At that point, Inoue felt he should stand up, and when he did he saw everything in heaven and earth was in a state of great joy.

> I experienced a oneness in which the whole of nature and the universe was my [true] Self. I was overwhelmed with the feeling that "heaven and earth [and I] are of one substance," and "the ten thousand things [and I] are of the same root." This was something I had never felt before, a truly strange and mysterious state of mind. I thought to myself, "This is really strange!" And then I thought, let me examine my past doubts in light of the enlightened realm I had just entered. As I quietly reflected on these doubts, I was astounded to realize that my doubts of thirty years standing had disappeared without a trace.[26]

It goes without saying that Inoue's description of his enlightenment experience is a seminal passage in his writings. Although he doesn't explain their origin, the two phrases Inoue quoted above are contained in the fortieth case of the *Blue Cliff Record* (J., *Hekiganroku*; Ch., *Biyan Lu*), the famous twelfth-century collection of one hundred *kōan* that has been described as containing "the essence of Zen."[27] In the case in question, the conversation partner of the famous Zen master Huairang (677–744) cites a passage from an earlier essay written by Sengzhao (384–414) describing the oneness of heaven, earth, and humanity.[28] Significantly, Sengzhao is known for the deep influence Daoist thought and terminology exerted on his understanding of Mahāyāna philosophy, especially the Mādhyamaka school's teaching of "emptiness" (Skt., *sunyata*; J., *kū*). A further investigation of Inoue's enlightenment experience in terms of his Zen background will be found in chapter 14.

Inoue also used this occasion to examine his long-held doubts concerning the standards for determining good and evil, right and wrong. Up until that point, Inoue had thought that good and evil were two opposing entities. Now, however, Inoue realized,

It is truly a case in which, from the very beginning, "good and evil do not differ [from each another]." Rather, when our thoughts and actions are in accord with the truth of a nondualistic universe, this is good. When they are not, this is evil. For example, in the case of a relationship between two people, if you think and act on the basis that "self" and "other" are one, that is good. On the other hand, if you do no more than think (without action), that is evil. Yet concrete manifestations of good and evil do differ from one another according to the time, place, and those involved. Thus, there is no need to be attached to a particular concept [of good and evil] or think about what is right or wrong.[29]

In light of his subsequent career as the leader of a band of ultranationalist terrorists, it is significant that Inoue's enlightenment experience freed him from having to "think about what is right or wrong."

Inoue was also concerned about the difference between "differentiation" and "equality." Inoue claimed the basic reason it is possible to share one's thoughts with frogs and snakes, plants and trees, is because all share an essence that makes oneness possible. While seeming quite different, they nevertheless originate from a single element in the universe. It is because they equally share this element that they can manifest their essence and, consequently, communicate among themselves.

Inoue explained that the reason everything in the universe appeared to rejoice was because he himself rejoiced, filled with the joy of the Dharma in the aftermath of his enlightenment and the deliverance accompanying it. This rejoicing was reflected in the many objects he encountered. Because he was at one with these objects, his eyes reflected their rejoicing.

Nevertheless, Inoue wondered if he might finally have gone mad. At least, that is what the neighborhood children yelled when they saw him wildly waving his arms about and jumping up and down in the hermitage garden. So great was his ecstasy! When at length Inoue calmed down, he methodically went through all of the doubts that had tormented him for thirty years. He found himself able to answer every one of them to his satisfaction. His reasoning was clear, and there was nothing to suggest he had lost his mind. On the contrary, he became more convinced than ever he had finally realized enlightenment.

As a further test, Inoue picked up his copy of the *Lotus Sūtra*. As he did so, Inoue was reminded just how important Zen master Azuma Soshin's parting words about the *Lotus Sūtra* had been. In the past, Inoue had been unable to understand the sutra's opening chapters, and he regarded them as nonsensical. Now, however, Inoue was surprised to find these chapters embodied Buddhism's deepest philosophical principles, expressing Shakyamuni Buddha's deep compassion, in which he sought to aid the unenlightened in their quest to understand the truth of the universe. It was, he now realized, a veritable vehicle of great deliverance.

The *Lotus Sūtra*'s most critical message was "differentiation is equality" and "equality is differentiation." This message corroborated the realization he had at his enlightenment, namely, "the ten-thousand things are of the same root." Although Inoue didn't know who had compiled this sutra, he was convinced that it contained

Shakyamuni Buddha's greatest truths. Further, as Inoue read the *Sūtra*'s twenty-eight fascicles, he realized that each one of them accurately reflected a portion of his life up to that point. Reading through the *Sūtra*, he found himself repeatedly nodding his head in agreement.

IN ENLIGHTENMENT'S AFTERMATH

Interestingly, Inoue realized that his enlightenment experience differed from the typical Zen experience. He claimed the reason not many strange phenomena appeared during training was because of the use of *kōan* (Zen dialogues) during the practice of *zazen*. *Kōan* facilitate a spiritual unity that promotes the rapid acquisition of Wisdom. The strange phenomena that Inoue encountered were one step this side of Wisdom. Religious training undertaken on one's own is truly dangerous, for the practitioner can easily end up going mad or becoming a mountain spirit (*tengu*).

Although Inoue didn't use the term, he was clearly referring to what is known in the Zen school as *makyō*, literally the realm of devils. This is a realm of self-delusion typically consisting of visual and auditory hallucinations that sometimes arise during the course of meditation. These hallucinations often stem from repressed traumatic experiences, especially those from one's childhood. Practitioners can be disturbed, deeply disturbed, by their encounters with *makyō* or, alternatively, falsely convince themselves they have realized enlightenment. In Inoue's case, because he meditated by himself, there was no one present to explain the cause or nature of his hallucinations. Despite this, he appears to have ultimately recognized their hallucinatory nature without "going mad." When Zen training is conducted under a Zen master's guidance, if there is the slightest hint of something strange going on, the practitioner can be counseled in private meetings with the master (*dokusan*) or, during meditation, brought back to reality, typically by being struck with a long, thin waking stick known as a *keisaku* (aka *kyōsaku*). In this way the practitioner is prevented from being sidetracked.

Inoue continued:

> In my case I devoted myself totally to the practice of mantra recitation in order to escape my pain, not from any desire to acquire Wisdom. This is what led to the appearance of strange phenomena. Thus, only later was I able to acquire Wisdom. Because I practiced on my own without anyone's guidance, I suffered a great deal. However, it was exactly because I suffered so much that I was able to thoroughly penetrate my spirit. Compared with Zen practitioners today, we find that while they acquire Wisdom with their minds, there is a tendency for only a few to acquire it with the totality of themselves.[30]

Despite what may be interpreted as Inoue's critique of the state of Zen training in his day, Inoue recognized that his own enlightenment experience was as yet insufficient. Something more was necessary—the longstanding Zen practice of *post*-enlightenment (*gogo*) training. Inoue explained its importance:

The Buddha Dharma contains two kinds of practice—practice prior to enlightenment and practice after it. Post-enlightenment practice is important because the dregs of one's past habits and preconceptions gradually disappear. No matter where you go, you will never be separate from the truth "the universe is one." Additionally, there is no "graduation" from practice since the more you practice the broader your vision becomes and the more luminous the light you possess. Five candles become ten and ten candles become one hundred as your Wisdom shines ever brighter.

Based on the fundamental Truth of enlightenment, it is possible to thoroughly examine the occasional problems you encounter and to have an increasing ability to resolve them. This in turn gives you the Wisdom to immediately respond to whatever may occur, for enlightenment provides the basis of all criticism. Therefore, you will never go astray no matter what happens.

At this moment I possess a very confident outlook for both Japan and the world. However, this is not just my exclusive possession but is a realm shared by anyone who has experienced enlightenment.[31]

POST-ENLIGHTENMENT LIFE AT SANTOKU-AN

Although Inoue recognized the importance of formal post-enlightenment training, he did not immediately undertake it. First, he still had his life at Santoku-an to address, a life composed of an increasing number of followers centered on those whose illnesses he had cured. On the one hand, Inoue continued to treat all those seeking his assistance, for enlightenment had diminished neither his healing powers nor his willingness to use them on behalf of those in need. On the other hand, Inoue did not seek to profit from his abilities. Instead, he gave the money he received in gratitude from his recovered patients to those in need around him.

One morning not long after his enlightenment, Inoue told his assembled followers, "My work is complete. Now I can die."[32] Both surprised and upset, his followers entreated him not to die. However, this did not mean that Inoue intended to commit suicide, but rather he simply felt the time had come for him to die naturally. In response to his followers' repeated entreaties, Inoue said, "My life was given to me by my mother and father. Therefore, if you will call them here, it is possible that my life might be spared through their power."[33] While one of his followers ran to get Inoue's parents, Inoue, still sitting upright, gradually slipped into a deathlike state. Inoue invoked his last remaining willpower to remain alive until his parents arrived.

Inoue's mother arrived in a fluster and immediately grabbed her son's left hand. As she did so, Inoue felt a jolt go through him and his physical strength returned. However, his spirit felt as if it were still somewhere far removed. This feeling continued until, at length, his father was located and also came running to the hermitage. When his father grabbed his right hand, Inoue once again felt a jolt run through him. This time it was his spirit that returned, and as a consequence, Inoue felt reborn in both body and mind.

At this point, it was as if a spirit had once again taken possession of him. Standing up, Inoue took his father and mother by the hands and led them into the next room, where he had his father sit directly in front of him. By this time, scores of people in the village, hearing about the strange happenings at the hermitage, had gathered together to find out what was going on. Inoue began delivering a sermon that would continue for more than three hours. It was phrased in such a way that both young and old could understand and contained, at least in Inoue's view, an exposition of the deepest truths he had understood. Inoue was astonished by the words that came out of his mouth since they expressed knowledge that he had never read or heard before.

Inoue asked himself how it was possible that he could give such a great sermon whose content surpassed his knowledge and ability. His answer was that he had succeeded in combining the power of the entire universe into one. It was this unified power that had borrowed his mouth to express itself. "When I became one with the universe, the universe became me."[34]

Inoue recognized that from a psychological viewpoint he would be regarded as suffering from some kind of personality disorder. It is impossible, he knew, for someone to be able to communicate with a snake. But such things are not really a question of sharing the same words with this or that animal but of communicating intuitively. It is a question of the *spirit* of language. With words it is impossible for even Japanese and Americans to communicate with one another, but all things share the spirit of words, making communication possible.

Based on this realization, Inoue asked himself if his spirit possession was really a sign of madness but came to the conclusion that it was not. In light of his insight, it is not surprising, Inoue thought, that psychology had created a category known as the "psychology of religion." Inoue had been given a new life thanks to the psychologically mysterious experiences he had undergone. And although he didn't know what it was at the time, he realized he had also been entrusted with a new mission.

7

The Voice of Heaven

One of the most important factors leading Inoue to his new mission in life was what he referred to as the "voice of heaven" (*ten no koe*). The first time he heard it was not long after his enlightenment at Santoku-an. One day Inoue was sitting at the base of a pine tree basking in the sun. Suddenly, a voice said, "Get up!" Inoue looked around but could see no one. Once again, the voice spoke, "You are the savior of the world. For the sake of all sentient beings, get up!"[1]

Inoue found the whole thing strange and replied testily: "What are you talking about? I'm sitting here enjoying the sunshine after having found answers to questions that had long tormented me. That was my only goal. How is it possible that a person like me, who breaks all the Buddhist precepts and lacks compassion, could be the savior of the world?"[2] Although the exchange ended at that point, a few days later Inoue heard the same voice, saying, "You know nothing about repaying the debt of gratitude you owe others. You found relief from the pain you suffered for so many years thanks to the mercies of Heaven and earth. How is it possible that you would not try to save all sentient beings from their suffering?"[3] Inoue continued to ignore these words, convinced he lacked the qualifications or character for such a role, especially as the purpose of his recent training had nothing to do with saving others. A few days later, however, the voice came back and said, "You're a coward. Can't you hear the suffering voices of the masses? Get up!"[4]

Inoue continued his resistance to the voice and began to think that he was being subjected to a test of some kind. Perhaps this is what the Christians meant by the temptations of the devil. This possibility only served to strengthen Inoue's resolve to ignore the voice. Not long afterward Inoue ceased to hear anything further.

This incident did serve to remind Inoue of the biographies he had read of the founders of Buddhist sects, many of whom began teaching others only after hearing the voice of heaven. It was only natural, Inoue thought, that they would have done so in the wake of the Dharmic joy they experienced following their enlightenment, a state of extreme clarity for both body and mind. But this didn't apply to Inoue because of the deep sense of guilt he felt regarding his past conduct.

It was at this time that Inoue began to dislike being around other people. Instead, he preferred the peace and quiet of the mountains. Even Santoku-an was no longer of interest as he spent more and more time in the mountains, eating wild plants available there in abundance. One of his greatest pleasures was conversing with birds. One day a dove came to warn him of an impending earthquake, and soon the ground was shaking. Birds even came to warn Inoue when other human beings were approaching, giving Inoue ample time to find another area to wander in.

In the midst of his solitary life, Inoue came to a new realization, namely, that his current life of conversing with birds and insects, enjoyable though it be, was completely meaningless. It was simply wrong of him to disregard the suffering of all sentient beings. Although he lacked the qualifications for becoming a leader, he determined to serve them to the best of his abilities. With this, Inoue returned to Santoku-an and sought to resume a normal life even though he vomited on eating his first raw egg and didn't feel normal until he had drunk two bottles of sweet potato wine. He then became the talk of the village when he fell off a bicycle. "Look," the villagers said, "the wizard hurt himself!"[5]

There was a price to be paid for Inoue's return to normal life, as he gradually lost his prophetic powers. However, before they had disappeared completely, Inoue astounded villagers with his prediction of the Great Kantō Earthquake of September 1, 1923, a magnitude 7.9 earthquake killing well over 100,000 residents of Tokyo and environs. Closer to home, he also predicted a fire in one of the villagers' homes six months before it happened. Nonetheless, Inoue found it difficult to believe his own prophecies.

Of all Inoue's predictions, the most surprising concerned the outbreak of war between the United States and Japan, a prediction made in May 1924. It occurred one day when, by chance, Inoue observed a struggle taking place between two colonies of ants. Just then, Inoue once again heard the voice of heaven, only this time it whispered into his ear:

> A war between Japan and the United States will begin in year 16. At first Japan will be victorious, but after a while the United States will start winning, leading to Japan's sound defeat. Despite this, the Japanese flag will eventually flutter throughout the world. Look, the colony of small black ants is the Japanese military. The colony of big, red ants is the United States military.[6]

As Inoue observed the struggle between the black and red ants, he saw that initially the black ants were successful in pushing the red ants back. However, after a while, the tide was reversed and the red ants emerged victorious. Nevertheless, Inoue found himself unable to believe the prophecy since the sixteenth year of Emperor Taishō's reign, according to traditional Japanese chronology, was less than three years away, and there was no sign of war breaking out between the two countries.

Inoue wasn't worried about this inconsistency since he freely admitted that not all of his prophecies came to pass. On the one hand, there are those who believe that prophecies are the result of having been taken over by a godlike deity. Since such a deity is all-powerful and all-knowing, it is impossible for the deity to be mistaken. On the other hand, Inoue believed no such thing. "There are no deities!" he emphatically said.[7] "The reason prophecies occur is because of the prophet's ability to unify his spirit, thereby clearing his mind to receive the truth just like a radio antenna. That's all there is to it."[8]

Inoue realized that not all prophecies come to pass. This is because humans also have conceptual knowledge, and conceptual knowledge can sometimes interfere with the accurate reception of the truth. Originally, human beings were very open to intuitive understanding, but over time, with the acquisition of conceptual knowledge, intuitive understanding became ever less necessary. Inoue claimed this is the situation human beings find themselves in at the moment. It is not until the realization of enlightenment that it becomes possible to unify one's spirit, leading to a momentary stoppage of conceptual knowledge and recovery of intuition.

When it becomes a question of how it is possible to know the future, words like *past, present,* and *future* are, according to Inoue, only artificial divisions of uninterrupted time. Therefore, it is only natural that if you truly understand today's events you will understand tomorrow's events as well. Events occur because of the necessity for their occurrence. If you understand the nature of that necessity, you will understand the reason behind events that have yet to occur. There is really nothing strange about any of this.

As for his earlier prophecy about war with the United States, it was only later that Inoue learned he had been correct after all. This is because war between Japan and the United States did in fact break out in year 16. However, it was in the sixteenth year of Emperor Hirohito's reign, 1941, not the sixteenth year of Emperor Taishō's reign, as Inoue had originally believed.

ORDERED TO THE SOUTHEAST

In July 1924 Inoue once again heard the voice of heaven. This time it simply told him, "Travel to the southeast on September 5." Inoue responded, "But where am I supposed to go in the southeast? How can I go anywhere when I don't have any money?"[9] Although Inoue had continued to treat those who came to him with various illnesses, for which he was paid either in money or in kind, he still gave it all away to those in need, leaving him without funds. Inoue once again forgot about the voice until, on the evening of September 4, one of his followers gifted him five yen. Recalling the voice's earlier instructions, Inoue interpreted the gift as a sign that this time he should do as instructed. "Alright," he thought, "Tokyo lies in a southeasterly direction from here. I'll use this money to go there."[10]

In Tokyo, Inoue went to live at the home of his wife's younger brother. While he didn't have any particular goal in mind, he did continue his daily recitation of the mantra, *Namu-myōhō-renge-kyō* (I take refuge in the Wondrous Law of the *Lotus Sūtra*). Hearing this, his wife's friend asked if he were a follower of the uniquely Japanese Nichiren Buddhist sect, inasmuch as the sect's main religious practice was the recitation of the same mantra. At the same time, she offered him a book about Nichiren (1222–1282) titled *Nichiren Shōnin no Kyōgi* (The Doctrines of St. Nichiren). The book's author was Tanaka Chigaku (1861–1939), a layman who had become famous for his highly nationalistic interpretation of the sect's founder.

With nothing else to do, Inoue read the book and was both surprised and deeply moved by what he read: "I discovered the book containing St. Nichiren's teachings described circumstances just like my own. Furthermore, this was the first time I realized how great Nichiren was and was filled with admiration for him. My religious practice consisted of paying homage to the *Lotus Sūtra*, but this was done without any knowledge of Nichiren."[11] From then on, whenever Inoue had any money, he used it to buy books on Nichiren. Inoue learned that in 1274, at age fifty-three, Nichiren had gone to Mount Minobu in Yamanashi prefecture, where he established Kuonji Temple. As a result, Mount Minobu became the spiritual center of the Nichiren sect, and Inoue decided he would go there for further training.

Before he departed for Mount Minobu, however, Inoue visited journalist and right-wing commentator Asahina Chisen (1862–1939) to discuss his plans. Asahina encouraged Inoue to undertake this training, noting that the single Chinese character for his name, Akira, consisted of two parts, the first part on the left meaning "sun" and the second part on the right "to invite." Divided in this way, Inoue's personal name would be pronounced in Japanese as *Nisshō*. Inoue immediately realized that Nisshō was the name he had mysteriously heard when undergoing training at Santoku-an, only at that time he had no idea what it meant. Asahina told Inoue that his new name meant he had been "invited by the sun" to undertake whatever mission awaited him. Additionally, Inoue now shared the first of two Chinese characters, those for "sun," that composed Nichiren's name. Delighted, Inoue henceforth referred to himself as "Inoue Nisshō."

Upon his arrival at Mount Minobu, Inoue initially joined the Nichiren monks in their early morning sutra recitation service but found the service "unsatisfactory" (*i ni mitanakatta*).[12] As a result, he moved to a small temple next to Nichiren's gravesite on the mountain. There he passed his time reading Nichiren's writings as well as undertaking periods of fasting, returning to Tokyo at the end of December of that year.

Upon learning that Tanaka Chikaku, whose writings had first attracted Inoue to Nichiren, was giving a weeklong series of lectures in Shizuoka city from January 1, 1925, Inoue decided to participate. However, Inoue found Tanaka's lectures full of nothing but theory and therefore, once again, "unsatisfactory."[13] This marked the end of any direct connection between Inoue and the traditional Nichiren sect or Tanaka's highly nationalistic interpretation of Nichiren's teachings known as Nichirenism (*Nichiren-shugi*).

In light of this, the reader may be surprised to learn that Inoue has nevertheless been universally, though mistakenly, regarded by both Japanese and foreign scholars alike as either a "Nichiren priest" or at least a lay adherent of Nichirenism. The significance of this mistaken identification will be explained in chapter 14, which will also detail the nature of *Nichiren-shugi*, together with the significant influence it exerted on prewar Japanese nationalism and right-wing extremism.

A NEW ROLE TO PLAY

In the summer of 1925, Inoue went back to his hometown of Kawaba village to visit his family. While there, Inoue received a message from his wife, Toshiko, who was still in Tokyo. Inoue noted that his first wife, Ofusa, was taken ill in Osaka and died but provided no further details.[14] Inoue had married Toshiko, a native of Kawaba village and a nurse, in September 1924. Toshiko's message stated that she had just given birth to a baby girl, Ryōko!

As broke as ever, Inoue asked his father for the money to return to Tokyo, where he found both mother and child sick in bed. His wife had experienced chills after giving birth and then developed a fever. In turn, his newborn child had developed diarrhea from nursing at the breast of her sick mother and was now receiving medical treatment. Fortunately, Toshiko's fever soon dissipated, but only pus came out of her left breast, leaving too little milk for the baby. With only a little money between them, they were reduced to eating the bony parts of fish with a little rice.

Even though they took care to pay the doctor, he eventually stopped calling. Inoue believed it was either because the doctor thought the baby was beyond saving or he didn't want to get too involved with the impoverished family. Every morning, Inoue bought one small bottle of milk for the baby, but it was never enough. The baby's hunger quickly returned, leading to crying from morning to night. Inoue realized this was having a detrimental effect on his wife's recovery and, in desperation, decided to offer the baby his own nipples, knowing full well they offered no nourishment. What Inoue hadn't expected, however, was just how strong the baby would suck his nipples, and it wasn't long before they swelled in pain, making it impossible for Inoue to continue.

Things came to a head one day when Inoue returned home to find his wife sitting on the floor despondently. On questioning, she explained that she and the baby had just eaten rice porridge made from the last grains of rice the family had left. Inoue replied, "Don't worry, maybe the three of us will die tonight. But should we still be alive tomorrow morning we can worry about what to do then, so let's just go to bed."[15] Sure enough, the next morning one of Inoue's friends came by to give his wife five yen, noting, "Mrs. Inoue, your husband has always been that kind of man."[16]

A few days later, Inoue scheduled a meeting with Navy Admiral Kobayashi Seizaburō (1883–1956), a leading military ultranationalist. Inoue was quite late for the meeting, and when asked what happened Inoue explained he had no choice but to walk all the way since he didn't have money for the train fare. Surprised to hear this, the admiral began a monthly stipend to Inoue of between ten and twenty yen. The admiral was only one of the many right-wing leaders Inoue met at the time through introductions by Asahina Chisen and others. What these right-wing leaders shared was a nationalist, though somewhat vague, ideology known as *Nihon-shugi* (lit., "Japanism," aka Japanese Principles).

In general, Inoue was disappointed by the caliber of the people he met. However, he was impressed by Ōkawa Shūmei (1886–1957), even though the two had serious disagreements. Ōkawa was an ultranationalist, pan-Asianist, and scholar who maintained that money was the most important factor in a successful movement dedicated to state renewal. For his part, Inoue maintained the most important factor was the right people, for people used money, not the reverse. Ōkawa further asserted it was necessary to liberate Asia by driving white people out. Inoue, however, asserted the equality of all beings, based on his enlightenment experience that all things stem from the same root. Yet, despite their differences, Inoue admired Ōkawa's dedication to the movement.

At this time there were a variety of proposals concerning the way to bring about state renewal. One proposal called for an initial massacre of some six thousand leaders of Japanese society. Inoue was invited to participate in this plan but declined, for at the time Inoue thought it was still possible to accomplish the renewal by legal means. Only later would he come to realize how "naïve" he still was, explaining,

> Renewal means the destruction of tradition or at least the destruction of the current system. Further, the current system is firmly protected by today's laws. Thus, it stands to reason that without violating today's laws it will be impossible to effect a change in the current system. Reality is more important than theory. Has there ever been an example anywhere in the world, either past or present, when state renewal has been accomplished without breaking the law? At the time, however, I was still bound by my previous sense of morality and regarded illegal activities as something in the nature of a crime.[17]

In the end, Inoue decided to join a "movement to found the country" (*kenkoku undō*), first proposed in 1925 by Akao Satoshi (better known as Akao Bin, 1899–1990). Originally an anarchist, Akao had subsequently moved to the radical right, where he became a vocal opponent of both the Soviet Union and communism. In order to counter the left wing's May Day celebrations, Akao proposed the creation of a National Foundation Festival (*Kenkoku-sai*), the first one of which was held on February 11, 1926. By April of that year, he had garnered sufficient support to establish the National Foundation Society (*Kenkoku-kai*), destined to become one of the major ultranationalist organizations of the 1920s. Installing himself as the society's first managing director, Akao enlisted such right-wing luminaries as Tōyama Mitsuru and Nagata Hidejirō (1876–1943), former head of the Home Ministry's Public Security Bureau, as cofounders. Inoue was also invited to become a member.

The stated purpose of the society was the creation of a people's state based on unanimity between the people and the emperor. Founded only six years after Hitler created the National Socialist German Workers' Party (G., Nationalsozialistische Deutsche Arbeiterpartei—commonly known in English as the Nazi Party), the society also called for state socialism, including the demand for the state to control the life of the people so that there would not be a single disadvantaged individual among the Japanese people. The society also embraced pan-Asianism and, still further, declared it was Japan's mission to stand at the forefront of all colored people, bringing a new civilization to the world. Behind the scenes, however, society members organized gangs of strikebreakers, working closely with the police in defeating strikes by miners, factory workers, streetcar workers, and tenant farmers. Further, in 1928 the society bombed the Soviet embassy in Tokyo. At its height, the society had more than ten thousand members throughout Japan.

Inoue's assignment was the recruitment of new members for the society in Gumma prefecture, the area of his birth, as well as increasing readership of the society's virulently anticommunist newspaper, *Kenkoku Shimbun*. The newspaper typically featured such headlines as "Death to Communism, to Russian Bolshevism and to the Left Parties and Workers' Unions!" Inoue successfully recruited more than four hundred members for the society, all of whom were dedicated to smashing the left, eradicating what they viewed as the current, corrupt political system and effecting the renewal of Japan.

As time passed, however, Inoue began noticing something strange—the society's newspaper was gradually losing interest in social renewal. Frustrated, Inoue felt he owed an explanation to those whom he had recruited and returned to Tokyo to find out what was going on. There he found the society's leaders more interested in improving the yearly National Foundation Festival than expanding the society. This resulted in a lack of funds, so that even the continued publication of the newspaper was in doubt.

Shortly after Inoue's arrival, the society's leaders held an emergency meeting. Inoue also participated but quickly became dismayed by the barrage of angry accusations and left the meeting. Unsure what to do next, Inoue later went to the home of the society's president, Uesugi Shinkichi (1878–1929). Annoyed by Inoue's critical questioning, Uesugi became agitated and said:

"Don't you realize I have a Ph.D.?"

"Does having a Ph.D. mean that you know a lot about things?"

"That's right!"

"In that case, who knows more, you or the sum of knowledge contained in the library at Tokyo's Ueno Park?"

"Um . . . ," Uesugi's voice trailed off.

On departing Uesugi's home, Inoue said, "Being a Ph.D. is really quite tiresome, isn't it!"[18] Thereafter, Inoue returned to the society's headquarters and submitted his resignation.

ZEN TRAINING ONCE AGAIN

Inoue's participation in the National Foundation Society marked his first overtly political activity since his return to Japan from China, not to mention his enlightenment. While Inoue was one of the first members of the society to resign, he certainly wasn't the last. In 1927 Uesugi dropped out, followed by others who were opposed to the "direct actions" (*chokusetsu kōdō*), often illegal and sometimes violent, undertaken by Akao Bin and those close to him. Eventually, the society ended up with only a handful of members and became Akao's private preserve.

In the meantime, Inoue was set adrift. He thought about returning home but couldn't bring himself to face all those whom he had convinced to join the society on the basis that they were building a new Japan. It was at this point he remembered some unfinished business, namely, the need for post-enlightenment training. As noted in the previous chapter, Inoue was following a classic Zen paradigm, especially in the Rinzai Zen sect, that had long recognized the need, if not the requirement, for such ongoing training.

Inoue first went to the famous Rinzai Zen monastery of Kenchōji, located in Japan's former military capital of Kamakura, south of Tokyo. Kenchōji was the home of a priest whom Inoue had long admired. Inoue explained the purpose of his visit:

> I was involved with some people but I failed, for they were undependable. I thought I could put into practice the way I had discovered on my own. When I look around Japan today, I see a country full of lies. The first thing that needs to be done is to change Japan from a land of lies to a land of truth. Then it will be possible to go on to save the world. However, I lack the virtue and ability to do this. I believe if I am to stand before the masses of the people and expound the way, then I need to accumulate sufficient virtue to be trusted by the people. I would like to ask your assistance in accumulating such virtue.[19]

The Kenchōji priest responded, "If that's your goal, Kamakura is the wrong place for you. Various people come to Kamakura to undergo religious practice, but they all do it for show. It's not a place for a serious practitioner like you. There is, however, one place in Japan that would be appropriate for someone like you—Ryūtakuji Temple in Mishima."[20]

Inoue quickly put his few belongings in a cloth pouch, bought a train ticket, and headed for Ryūtakuji in Shizuoka prefecture. After eating near Mishima train station, he arrived at the temple with only ten sen in his pocket. Ryūtakuji was one of Japan's most famous Zen temples, closely associated with Hakuin (1685–1768), the great seventeenth-century reformer of Rinzai Zen.

On arrival, Inoue shouted in a loud voice the customary greeting of someone who hoped to train in a Zen temple: "Tanomō!" (I beseech [to be allowed to enter]). Inoue explained why he had come to the novice monk who came out to greet him. The novice informed him that all of the senior monks were out and wouldn't return until evening. He then showed Inoue to a room where he could practice *zazen* while awaiting their return. Toward evening, in accord with Zen custom, a senior monk came to tell him to leave because the severe training regimen wouldn't be to his liking. As expected of an aspiring entrant, Inoue was undeterred and repeated his request. In response, the monk indicated he couldn't make the decision on his own and would have to wait for his superior's return. Thereafter, Inoue was invited to have dinner with five or six of the training monks.

Following the meal, yet another senior monk came into Inoue's room to inform him to leave, saying, "I've heard what you have to say, but even professional priests find this practice difficult, so it would be better if you went to a school or someplace where you could read books about it. Give up religious practice!"[21] Undeterred, Inoue replied as earnestly as he could, "I've staked my life on the decision to come here. I won't be surprised by something like hardships, so please allow me to stay."[22]

Despite Inoue's entreaties, the senior monk continued to dissuade him from undertaking practice at Ryūtakuji. For his part, Inoue fervently repeated his desire to do so. After a while, Inoue's earnestness appeared to impress the senior monk, who then explained this was not a decision he could make on his own. Instead, the final decision was up to the temple abbot, Zen master Yamamoto Gempō. Zen master Gempō, however, was also the abbot of a second temple, Shōinji, in the nearby town of Hara. This was where Gempō was residing at the time, and Inoue would have to go to Shōinji the next day to request the abbot's permission. Inoue did as he was instructed but took the precaution of purposely leaving his cloth pouch behind just in case Gempō refused his request. Inoue hoped this might lead to a second chance to show how serious he was about practicing at Ryūtakuji.

Inoue arrived at Shōinji the next day around noon and was shown into Gempō's quarters. It was their first meeting but not, at least initially, a happy one. Just as he had done previously, Inoue detailed why he wished to train at Ryūtakuji but received the same response. "In any event, I can't allow you to stay here," Gempō replied. Once again, Inoue wouldn't take no for an answer and repeated his request. Gempō then said:

"I can't accept you because we don't have any food at this temple."

"In that case, I'll beg for food," Inoue replied.

"And we don't have any extra bedding."

"Then I'll sleep on the floor without bedding. Please allow me to stay."[23]

Even after this exchange, Gempō, following Zen tradition, still wouldn't allow Inoue to stay. Yet Inoue wouldn't give up, and after every refusal earnestly repeated his request. Gempō finally became convinced of Inoue's determination, saying, "In that case, I'll permit you to remain." Feeling as if he had just been granted permission to enter heaven, Inoue replied, "Thank you so very much. I'll immediately return to Ryūtakuji." "Wait," Gempō said, "I meant that you can stay here." "That's even better," replied Inoue, overjoyed at the prospect. He then went back to Ryūtakuji, but only to fetch his cloth pouch with his few belongings.[24]

TRAINING AT SHŌINJI

In addition to Inoue, there were two other laymen training at Shōinji. One was a lay student whose education Gempō had supported from junior high school through university. He was then working in the temple kitchen while preparing himself to take the Higher Civil Service Examination. The other was a former artillery lieutenant who had lost his sight when a shell burst during training. Finally, there was one priest at the temple in charge of the temple's finances. He had formerly worked at a bank but lost his position due to an undisclosed error and was now Gempō's disciple.

Inoue's assigned duties consisted of cleaning the entire temple complex as well as making the fire to heat the bath water. Before breakfast, he cleaned the temple's living quarters, the main worship hall, and the Hakuin Memorial Hall. After breakfast, he cleaned the temple garden, the path leading to the temple, and the graveyard. At three in the afternoon it was time to heat the bath water, and at eight, time to go to bed. However, instead of retiring, Inoue went to practice *zazen* in the Hakuin Memorial Hall until at least eleven and sometimes until one in the morning.

Sometime later, the lay student preparing for the civil service exam moved to Ryūtakuji because it was more conducive to his studies. This meant that Inoue had to take over his kitchen duties, leaving Inoue without a moment's rest. Inoue got up at four, poured water over his head, cleaned the living quarters and other areas, and prepared breakfast by seven. He then went outside to clean the garden and adjacent areas before coming in to make the noon meal. When he finished heating the bath water at three, it was time to prepare the evening meal. Then at eight he would begin his practice of *zazen*, leaving no time to enjoy a cigarette let alone a cup of tea. This left him with less than five hours of sleep a night.

As Inoue got used to this routine, he found he no longer needed a watch since the amount of time required for each task never varied by more than three minutes. Actually, he had already gotten used to this kind of tight schedule from his previous experience as a spy in China.

ACCEPTING ALMS IN THE FORM OF GIANT JAPANESE WHITE RADISHES

Shōinji had a tradition that took place every year in November. It involved pulling a cart to surrounding farmhouses, which would donate large, white radishes (*daikon*) for pickling to the temple, while accompanying monks recited sutras for the spiritual benefit of the donors. On the specified day, all of the trainees at Ryūtakuji came to support Inoue as he pulled the cart, and by the end of the day the cart was overflowing with donated radishes. After saying goodbye to the Ryūtakuji contingent, it was up to Inoue to get the cart back to Shōinji on his own.

By then the cart was quite heavy and difficult to pull. At first Inoue was able to move it, but then one of wheels slipped into a deep rut in the road. No matter how hard Inoue tried, he couldn't pull the cart out of the rut. His first thought was to go to the main and well-traveled road to get some help, but then he realized that the responsibility for getting the radishes back to the temple was his and his alone. Even if he died in the attempt, no one would blame him for having tried to fulfill his responsibility.

Inoue found a long pole nearby and used it, after much effort, to lift the cartwheel out of the rut. This, he thought, was the power of religious faith. The next thing he knew, he and the cart were on the main road, where he immediately fainted, pole in hand. This caused quite a stir among passing farmwomen, who stopped to minister to Inoue. He quickly recovered and sincerely thanked the women who had aided him. After that Inoue successfully pulled the cart back to Shōinji.

THE ABBOT'S INVITATION

One day in the fall, Gempō telephoned to tell Inoue to quickly finish his duties at Shōinji in order to view a special exhibit concerning Zen master Hakuin being held at Ryūtakuji. He also mentioned that Ryūtakuji's autumn foliage was at its peak. This sparked Inoue's interest, and he decided to bring a cart full of pickles he had made along with him. Since the distance between the two temples was approximately ten miles, it was evening by the time Inoue arrived at Ryūtakuji. As luck would have it, the trainees there had just run out of pickles and were delighted with Inoue's gift, so much so that they presented him with his favorite beverage—*sake*.

Inoue soon became drunk and fell asleep. He awoke at one in the morning and immediately realized the predicament he was in. Namely, he had to be back at Shōinji by early morning to make breakfast. Fortunately, the cart was now empty, and Inoue reached Shōinji at daybreak, in time to prepare the meal for the 7 a.m. service.

BEING TREATED WITH AFFECTION

A short time later, Inoue was outside cleaning the temple grounds as always. When he got to Hakuin's gravesite, he was filled with the urge to stop a moment and practice *zazen* seated on the large, flat rock in front of the grave. Shortly thereafter he heard some footsteps, and upon standing saw Zen master Gempō coming out of the temple. Seeing Inoue, Gempō said, "Inoue, you had some good Zen practice recently." Inoue was deeply moved by his words, for he realized that in a comparable situation the man in charge would normally praise his subordinate by telling him what a good job he had done. But Gempō didn't praise Inoue. Instead, he told him what good Zen practice he had experienced. Inoue took this as a sign of just how much affection Gempō had for him.

"SWINGING BALLS"

On another occasion, Inoue participated in a program of intensive weeklong *zazen* practice at Ryūtakuji, known as a *sesshin*, literally meaning to "touch the heart/mind." During the short break after lunch, one of the training monks, known as something of an incorrigible, informed Inoue that he had been given the nickname "Swinging Balls" (*Kinpura*). Surprised to hear this, Inoue asked more about it. The monk explained that when Inoue first arrived at Shōinji he was wearing a thin summer kimono, lacking even underpants. Thus, when he bent over to clean the floor, the lower part of his body was exposed. When Gempō described this scene to the trainees at Ryūtakuji, they started referring to Inoue as "Swinging Balls." After finishing his explanation, the monk laughed, and Inoue also broke out in a broad smile. He now understood why Gempō had bought him a knit undershirt and underpants soon after his arrival. Not only that, Gempō also gave him one of his own lined kimonos together with a Japanese half coat known as a *haori*. He later provided him with a skullcap for wintertime as well.

Inoue was, however, disturbed by the attitude of Gempō's disciples at Ryūtakuji. Whenever Gempō gave him something, they would all say, "I wish I had one, I wish I had one." Inoue regretted that the disciples who weren't favored as he was were so consumed with envy that the only way they could think to conceal their disappointment was to ridicule him with the nickname "Swinging Balls."

8

The Blood Oath Corps Incident

PART ONE: PREPARATION

The road to the Blood Oath Corps Incident (*Ketsumeidan Jiken*) of early 1932 can be traced back five years to April 1927. It was then that one of Inoue's old friends came to Shōinji with an invitation to meet Count Tanaka Mitsuaki. Realizing the importance of this invitation, Inoue immediately bid farewell to Shōinji and returned to Tokyo. Inoue had met Tanaka some time before when he sought the latter's aid in building a religious center to train thirty youth per year to undertake activities leading to the reform of Japan.

Inoue's original plan involved dividing the thirty youth into two groups of fifteen each. On any particular day, one group would engage in religious practice while the second group either grew food or collected alms in nearby villages. They would continue this schedule for a full year, after which they would be sent countrywide to attract additional recruits to the renewal movement. At the same time, thirty new trainees would begin their year at the center, repeating this until the renewal movement had members scattered throughout Japan.

When Inoue approached Tanaka requesting support for his plan, Tanaka asked the purpose of his proposed training center. "I want to launch a rebellion," Inoue replied. "A rebellion!" Tanaka responded. "What's your plan?" Inoue explained his goal was, first of all, to exterminate communist ideology. Additionally, he sought to eradicate the corruption that existed within political parties and among *zaibatsu* financial leaders. Tanaka replied, "I will be eighty-three this year, but I still have the physical and mental strength to cut down three to five men. Do your best!"[1] Inoue was deeply grateful for Tanaka's support but eventually abandoned the idea for unexplained reasons. Nevertheless, Tanaka retained his interest in Inoue's plan and was now in a position to assist in bringing it to fruition.

When Inoue and his friend arrived at his home, Tanaka first shared how great a man Emperor Meiji (1852–1912) had been and the close relationship between the two men during Tanaka's many years of military and government service, including as minister of the Imperial Household Agency. One example involved Tanaka's proposal for the liberation of a traditional outcast class known as *burakumin* (lit., "hamlet people"). Tanaka recalled the emperor had immediately given his consent to this measure. Tanaka added, "If I ever realized I had failed to fulfill the wishes of the emperor, I was prepared to immediately commit *seppuku* [ritual suicide]."[2] Tanaka's reminiscences concerning Emperor Meiji, coupled with his dedication to the late emperor, made a deep impression on Inoue.

Tanaka, however, was not happy with the way Japan had developed in the years following Emperor Meiji's death in 1912. In particular, he was disturbed by what he considered the corruption in the Imperial Household Agency. Tanaka therefore commissioned a bronze statue of Emperor Meiji and had it placed in the entrance to the agency's offices in such a way that employees would have to bow to it as they passed by every morning. The irritated employees eventually succeeded in having the statue removed and placed in storage.

Tanaka reacted by having a replica made. The new statue was to become the centerpiece of a museum dedicated exclusively to the emperor and including Tanaka's extensive collection of emperor-related artifacts. Tanaka's goal was to inspire the spirit of the Japanese people and assist in the renewal of Japan by opening the museum to the general public. Named the Meiji Kinenkan (Meiji Memorial Pavilion), the facility was to be built with the financial support of Takeuchi Yūnosuke, head of Ibaraki Kōtsū Transportation Company. It was in Takeuchi's self-interest to build the museum since it would be located in Ōarai, a seacoast village sixty miles northeast of Tokyo serviced exclusively by his company's rail line. The increase in passenger traffic, he believed, would repay his investment.

The plan also called for the construction of a small temple near the museum that would enshrine a statue of Nichiren. Nichiren was the medieval Buddhist priest widely admired, including by Inoue, for his love of country, as evidenced by his efforts to protect Japan from two Mongol invasions in the late thirteenth century.[3] The new temple's patriotic orientation would also be reflected in its name, Risshō Gokokudō, or Temple to Protect the Nation [by] Establishing the True [Dharma].[4] The intent was to utilize Buddhism as a means to promote patriotism among worshippers. This was the reason Tanaka had requested Inoue's visit, for he knew Inoue had wanted to establish just such a patriotic Buddhist training center. As the temple would be unaffiliated with any sect, Inoue could serve as its head despite his lack of clerical qualifications.

Despite the widespread belief in the postwar period that Inoue was connected to the Nichiren sect, or even was a Nichiren priest, it should be noted that Inoue was no more than an interested bystander in the construction of this nonsectarian temple. Somewhat surprisingly, the presence of a statue of Nichiren as the main object of devotion on the altar indicates the nonorthodox nature of the temple. In traditional Nichiren Buddhism, the primary object of devotion is not a statue of Nichiren but, instead, a scroll containing Chinese and Sanskrit characters written in the form of a *mandala* on either paper or silk. Known as the *Gohonzon* (object of devotion), the original *mandala* was created by Nichiren to transmit what he regarded as the essence of the *Lotus Sūtra*.[5]

The planning and fundraising for the temple's construction were in the hands of former imperial household minister Count Tanaka and Takeuchi Yūnosuke. As temple records indicate, contributions for its construction came from scores of Japan's top political and military leaders, including Prime Minister Konoe Fumimarō (1891– 1945). From its outset, the temple was promoted as the "foundation for reform of the state" through its training of Japanese youth.[6] Its location immediately adjacent to a memorial hall to Emperor Meiji only served to reinforce its patriotic nature.

On the one hand, Inoue was asked to head the temple because of his undoubted religious fervor coupled with his connections to leading right-wing patriotic figures like Tōyama Mitsuru. These connections were the domestic manifestation of those he had previously developed with influential army and right-wing figures in Manchuria and northern China. On the other hand, Inoue initially hesitated to accept the invitation to head the temple for the simple reason that the temple, lacking traditional parishioners, had no guaranteed source of income. "Even I need food to eat," Inoue said, "A temple that can't provide that is impossible." Nevertheless, after being repeatedly asked to head the temple, he finally agreed.

Life in a "Patriotic Training Temple"

Once persuaded to direct the temple's activities, Inoue played the role of a Buddhist priest and temple abbot even though this was an act entirely of his own making, unsanctioned by any Buddhist organization or sect. It was this "imitation" of a Buddhist priest, coupled with the presence of Nichiren's statue on the temple altar, that further contributed to both Japanese and non-Japanese scholars alike mistakenly identifying Inoue as a Nichiren sect adherent.[7] Inoue, however, never identified himself as a member of this sect.

Having agreed to head the temple, Inoue threw himself into his real work: training a group of youth dedicated to the reformation of Japan and endowed with a "do-or-die" spirit. Toward this end, he employed a variety of training methods that included practicing Zen meditation (*zazen*) in the morning and evening, assigning Zen dialogues (*kōan*) as objects of meditation, conducting private interviews with disciples (*dokusan*), reciting the *daimoku* mantra, and fasting.[8] Except for the last two, all of Inoue's training methods were based on traditional Zen practice. Initially, there had been no meditation hall (*zazendō*) at the temple, but Inoue prevailed upon Takeuchi to donate an empty railroad car to be used for meditation practice. Inoue had it placed immediately behind the temple with a simple shed erected over it and straw *tatami* mats on the floor.

Inoue successfully attracted approximately twenty youth to his movement, mostly residents of Ibaragi prefecture. This was actually no small accomplishment given the high hurdle Inoue set for entry. Namely, each young man who hoped to participate had to first complete a seven-day fast. This was an unusual requirement in the Zen tradition, for typically, a testing period, lasting up to a week, was the norm. During this period, the trainee was expected to continuously practice *zazen* during waking hours, albeit three meals a day were provided. Inoue justified his fasting requirement as follows: "Prior to the training of their spirits, youth must first go through a toughening-up experience. Without this, they just start spouting off, talking nothing but theory and unable to undertake true religious training. The reason why so many training centers fail is because they forget this key element."[9]

Most youth, Inoue noted, started fasting with confidence. However, by day three the bravado disappeared, only to be replaced by the temperament of a sheep, coupled with calls of "Please let me stop now." The youth were unaware that days three and four were the hardest, for thereafter the hunger pangs gradually disappeared. Failing to understand this, they were overcome with fear, thinking it possible they were going to die. For those who stuck it out, this experience served as their ticket of admission or qualification to become a member of Inoue's group.

Switching to Illegal Activities

Inoue initially intended that the training center's activities would be entirely legal. A cadre of methodically trained youth would, in turn, train others until a critical mass of reformists had been formed throughout the country. His plans changed, however, after a chance meeting with Navy Lieutenant Junior Grade Fujii Hitoshi (1904–1932) at an informal meeting of reformists held at the home of an employee of the Ibaragi prefectural government. While everyone in attendance was interested in government reform, Inoue was disappointed, even angered, by what he regarded as a lack of seriousness coupled with the fanciful nature of their discussion. This led Inoue to disrupt the discussion with scathing words of criticism. In response, Fujii angrily replied:

"Well, reverend sir, do you have a concrete plan for the reformation of Japan?"
"I do indeed!"
"Well, then, let's hear it!"
"Fine, come with me to the Temple to Protect the Nation!"
"I certainly will!"[10]

This angry exchange marked what would become a close and long-term relationship between Inoue and Fujii as well as other like-minded young aviators stationed at the Naval Air Training Base on the shores of Lake Kasumigaura, south of Ōarai. On the evening of the same day as their heated discussion, Fujii brought Lieutenant Junior Grade Suzuki Shirō with him to the temple, and the three of them talked through the night. From then onward, Inoue considered both Fujii and Suzuki to be members of his group.

Little by little, Fujii succeeded in convincing Inoue that the situation prevailing in Japan in 1930 was so dire that purely legal activities would no longer work. The reason was the state of the two major political parties of the era, Rikken Seiyūkai (Friends of Constitutional Government) and Rikken Minseitō (Constitutional Democratic Party). According to Inoue, both parties had become representatives of Japan's competing financial elites, the interlocking corporate conglomerates known as *zaibatsu*. Thus, Seiyūkai was closely associated with the interests of the Mitsui *zaibatsu* while Minseitō represented the Mitsubishi *zaibatsu*. True, elections were being held on the basis of recently enacted universal male suffrage,[11] but economic policies favored these financial elites, no matter which party came to power. At the same time, the masses continued to suffer from the effects of the Great Depression of 1929 with high levels of unemployment and poverty and increased taxation.

Inoue noted that the economic power of the *zaibatsu* had steadily increased in the years following the Meiji Restoration of 1868 because they succeeded in acquiring a combination of both financial and industrial power. They used this as a means of exploiting the labor of the masses, allowing them to produce products cheaply and sell them at a high price. Profit was their only motive, slowly driving small and medium-sized businesses bankrupt. The loss in purchasing power of factory workers had a further negative effect on the nation's farmers, who lost customers for their crops. It was especially hard on tenant farmers in the northeast of Japan, who also suffered from a series of natural disasters, leaving them in a pitiable situation.

The end result was not only an increase in labor disputes and strikes, but a rise in support for socialist and communist ideology. In particular, the nascent Communist Party's propaganda was so effective that there even appeared elements advocating a change in the nation's fundamental political structure. Among other things, this meant the possible end of the imperial system centered on the emperor. At the same time, those citizens who had lost hope in the future sought outlets for their frustrations in debauchery of various kinds, endangering the continuation of Japanese culture developed over what was claimed to be a history of three thousand years.

In the face of all this, the two major political parties showed no concern for the plight of ordinary citizens, only the continued success of their own political party. The *zaibatsu* were likewise indifferent to the suffering of the people, while the country's senior statesmen, forgetting their duty to the country, allied themselves with the *zaibatsu* in pursuit of benefits for themselves. The result was that the close relationship between the emperor and his subjects was impaired, leaving the people with nowhere to turn to seek relief from their abject circumstances. And as if this were not enough, the country's scholars, religious leaders, thinkers, and journalists not only failed to point out the inhumanity of the actions of the rich and powerful but allied themselves with these figures, becoming their pawns and speaking in their defense.

Inoue's analysis of Japanese society, coupled with his involvement in "patriotic movements," might lead one to think that Inoue would use the corruption of Japan's financial and political leaders as the justification for his right-wing activities. Surprisingly, however, Inoue was as dismissive of right-wing "fascism" as left-wing "Bolshevism."

The various injustices committed by the ruling class have filled both the left and right wings with the desire to overthrow the existing order. However, from my viewpoint, the thinking on both sides is no different than that of the ruling class, for they all base themselves on discriminative antagonisms that are unqualified to become the guiding principles for saving the people and reforming the state. Therefore, I cannot promote either fascism or Bolshevism.[12]

If, in the face of Japan's many ills, the right wing was as unacceptable to Inoue as the left wing, what was his position? "No matter what others may think, I stand on the truth of the universe acquired through my experience of enlightenment. I have my own unique faith."[13]

Interestingly, it was not only the ruling class, together with both the left and right wings, that were consumed by "discriminative antagonisms." Additionally, both the army and navy blatantly displayed the same fundamental flaw. According to the then popular slogan, the Japanese military was to serve as the "emperor's arms and legs," united in its dedication to defend the nation. Yet the reality was that the right arm was exchanging blows with the left arm, the right leg with the left leg. The blame lay with the major political parties that suppressed the military, making it impossible for them to fulfill their duties. The military was so enfeebled that it had given up hope.

In short, Japanese society as a whole was lost in strife, confusion, and corruption at the hands of the rich. It was impossible to find even a trace of Japan's past glory in which emperor and subjects were united in a body politic based on coexistence and coprosperity. Inasmuch as the true nature of Japan had become a complete lie, the situation called for uncommon determination coupled with concrete action. What was necessary could no longer be described as simple social reform. *Revolution* was the only word capable of fully expressing the extent of the drastic changes necessary.

Inoue became convinced that an emergency situation required emergency measures. Giving life to the nation was his uppermost concern; discussions on what and how should only come later, much later. In seeking to overthrow the ruling class, it was utterly foolish to argue about whether one's actions were legal or illegal, inasmuch as the ruling class used the legal system to protect itself. Inoue admitted he had initially believed social reform could be done legally, but he gradually realized such an easygoing attitude was unacceptable in the face of the dire situation facing the nation. He was, furthermore, prepared to accept the consequences of his lawbreaking.

Faith Healing

As Inoue gradually embraced this way of thinking, it became increasingly difficult for him to remain living at a temple in the countryside. In addition, there was external pressure that made it difficult for him to stay. This pressure came as a result of a widely circulated leaflet touting his efficacy as a faith healer. Although distributed without his permission, it was not long before hundreds of sick people appeared at the temple on a daily basis seeking to be cured. For the first month or two, Inoue willingly responded to their requests, with the temple becoming so popular that outdoor food stalls were set up on its grounds. And, of course, many of the sick came by train, so ridership increased significantly.

Inoue's popularity as a faith healer also came to the attention of the local police. Concerned that he might be a fraud, a police detective came one day to conduct an investigation. Inoue explained the nature of his spiritual treatments to the officer, but the latter refused to believe him. This prompted the following exchange: "It's quite understandable that you don't believe me, so let me demonstrate what a spiritual treatment can do. (Pause.) Alright, now I want you to try to stand up, but you will be unable to do so."

The detective tried to stand up but couldn't. Inoue explained that it was the detective's own spirit that made it impossible for him to stand, a phenomenon Inoue described as "spiritual sympathy" (*seishin kannō*). The detective was flustered by this turn of events, at which point Inoue said, "Don't worry, just close your eyes, and I'll make it possible for you to stand up." Inoue then recited an incantation and said, "Go ahead, now you can stand up." Upon standing, the detective said, "I see. It's not superstition after all!" and quickly left.[14]

Reflecting on this event, Inoue pointed out that one is apt to deny something one doesn't understand. However, if someone has a strong mind, they will be able to overcome a person with a negative mind. When someone comes for the first time, they arrive with a conflicted mind—half believing and half doubting. However, they are already half hypnotized, for if they didn't believe at all they wouldn't have come in the first place.

Although no longer under police suspicion, Inoue's practice of faith healing remained a mixed blessing. On the one hand, it brought income to the temple, but at the same time, it increasingly interfered with what he considered to be his true purpose—the training of a cadre of youth dedicated to social change. Frustrated, Inoue began to cut back on his healing activities, much to the consternation of all who had previously benefited financially. As far as they were concerned, Inoue's usefulness had come to an end. In later court testimony, Inoue also referenced his departure to the fact that, for legal purposes, the temple had to be registered with a traditional Buddhist sect, the Nichiren sect in this instance. Once the registration was complete, Inoue, neither a Nichiren adherent let alone a cleric, would no longer be qualified to serve as the temple's abbot.[15] It was a combination of these circumstances that finally led Inoue to bid farewell to the temple in October 1930.

The Plotting Begins

If one intended to reform Japan, there was only one place it could be done—Tokyo, the heart of Japan's political and economic life. Fujii Hitoshi had long urged Inoue to move to Tokyo. It was he and his fellow officer Suzuki Shirō who arranged a place for Inoue to stay upon his arrival—Kinkei Gakuen (Golden Pheasant Academy). Located in the house of Count (and House of Peers member)

Sakai Tadamasa (1893–1971), Kinkei Gakuen was established in 1927 by Yasuoka Masahiro (1898–1983) as a private school. Yasuoka was an influential right-wing backroom power broker whose lectures emphasized Confucian-inspired filial piety and loyalty to the emperor. Yasuoka attracted young government officials and army officers to the school, hoping to encourage them to join the movement for the reformation of Japan.

Despite the fact that Inoue and Yasuoka had similar goals, their relationship was not a happy one. This was because, according to Inoue, Yasuoka aroused his students with stories of daring feats by past rebels in Japanese history but never went beyond talking about the past. Thus, even as the number of youth coming to hear Yasuoka's lectures increased, so did their unhappiness with Yasuoka's lack of a concrete plan for Japan's reform.

It was this unhappiness that led more and more of the students to visit Inoue in his room at the school to discuss concrete measures that could be undertaken. Among his visitors was Yotsumoto Yoshitaka (1908–2004), a student at Japan's elite Tokyo University who went on to become one of Inoue's chief lieutenants.[16] Inoue became so popular that students no longer attended Yasuoka's lectures but came to talk with Inoue instead. Disturbed by this, Yasuoka pressured Inoue to leave the school though not without finding him a new place to live.

A New Home

Inoue's new home was the Tokyo headquarters of the Dai Nihon Seigidan (Greater Japan Justice Organization), headed by Sakai Eizo (1872–1939). Like many right-wing "patriotic organizations" of the day, this group claimed to have lofty ideals, in this case supporting morality and social improvement. In reality, Inoue notes that it was essentially a gangster organization with Sakai acting as the muscleman for the Ōkura-gumi, one of Japan's smaller *zaibatsu*. The organization's overall mission was to fight left-wing groups, especially in the event of strikes and labor disputes.[17]

In December 1930, not long after his arrival at his new home, Inoue attended a secret meeting of his fellow activists. The meeting was held at the Kashii hot springs resort in the city of Fukuoka on the southernmost island of Kyūshū. Attended by some fifteen "comrades" (*dōshi*), the meeting was primarily composed of both young army and naval officers, including Fujii Hitoshi. As Ben-Ami Shillony notes, the meeting was of seminal importance in that it "fostered the links between the Army and Navy components of the nascent Young Officers' Movement as well as between them and civilian radical rightists."[18] The Young Officers' Movement referred to would eventually lead to the largest military insurrection in Japan's modern history—the February 26, 1936, Incident. This incident will be described in detail in chapter 10.

Of immediate significance was that this secret meeting demonstrated Inoue's plans were not those of a "lone wolf," nor a fringe quixotic enterprise. Instead, Inoue, as a "guest of honor" at the meeting, was at the center of a much broader, and lethal, movement to launch a violent coup d'état against what was then a democratic government, however imperfect it may have been. The importance of this meeting was further enhanced by the fact that, albeit secret, the meeting had the blessing of Lieutenant General Araki Sadao (1877–1966), then commander of the Sixth Army Division in Kyūshū and one of Japan's principal right-wing political theorists. Not only was Araki an up-and-coming general in the army, but he was also a close friend of General Mazaki Jinzaburō (1876–1956), then vice chief of the Japanese Army General Staff. Both generals sought to strengthen patriotism and nationalist values in the military and were also sympathetic to the need for drastic social reform.

Following the conclusion of the meeting, Inoue went to meet Araki at his headquarters in Kumamoto. Inoue had previously met Araki in Tokyo when the latter had been attached to the military police (Kempeitai). Araki had interviewed Inoue about his espionage work in China, and as a result of the trust they had developed, Inoue openly discussed the combined plans of the young military officers and civilians for a major uprising to reform Japan. Araki not only indicated his support for their plan but added that once he heard the uprising had occurred he would lead the Sixth Division to Tokyo to ensure its success. "I was greatly encouraged by his words and returned to Tokyo in high spirits," Inoue reported.[19]

Shunned Again

Not long after returning to Tokyo, Inoue found himself forced to move yet again. Sakai Eizo, head of the Dai Nihon Seigidan, gave a variety of excuses as to why it was "inconvenient" (*fuben*) for Inoue to remain at the organization's headquarters. Nevertheless, like Yasuoka before him, Sakai found a new home for Inoue, this time with Imaizumi Sadasukei (1863–1944), a Shinto scholar who also served as an instructor at Seigidan's headquarters. Inasmuch as Imaizumi provided Inoue with room and board at no cost, Inoue made sure to keep him happy by sharing a bottle of *sake* on occasion. In doing so, he learned that both Sakai and Imaizumi had developed their own plans for social reform, using Seigidan members to execute their plans.

Inoue's discussions with Imaizumi also provided him with an opportunity to learn more about Shinto, at least the increasingly nationalistic version then in vogue. This is not to say that Inoue had been ignorant of Shinto up to that point, for he already counted himself an adherent based on his reading of the *Kojiki* (Records of Ancient Matters), an early eigth-century collection of myths concerning the origin of Japan and its indigenous deities (*kami*). Inoue's understanding of this Shinto classic, however, was rooted in his previous enlightenment experience at Santoku-an. Thus, given that Shinto scholars in 1930s Japan were typically highly antagonistic toward Buddhism, Inoue's discussions with Imaizumi often turned into debates. Imaizumi's intolerant and self-righteous attitude, not to mention his farfetched arguments, were a cause of deep disappointment to Inoue.

Fortunately, Imaizumi was willing to listen to Inoue's point of view and changed a number of his views as a result. Inoue admitted that he, too, had benefited from his exchanges with Imaizumi, claiming that he now comprehended the "true meaning" (*shingi*) of Shinto.[20] Imaizumi also introduced Inoue to the still nebulous, but increasingly important, concept of the "Imperial Way" (*Kōdō*), linking emperor, subjects, land, and morality together as one, with the emperor as undisputed head. At the same time, Inoue was filled with nostalgia as he recalled his experience at Santoku-an. None of this interfered with Inoue's frequent meetings with his comrades, including Fujii, Suzuki, and Yotsumoto, among others. Truthfully or not, Inoue would later testify at his trial that Imaizumi didn't know anything about these meetings, thus saving the latter from being implicated in Inoue and his band's terrorist acts.

The Manchurian Incident

In June 1931 Inoue first heard a rumor that an army clique stationed in Manchuria was preparing to undertake some kind of action. A month later, Nishida Mitsugi (aka Zei, 1901–1937), on the recommendation of Kita Ikki (1883–1937), approached Inoue, providing him with concrete information on the plan and seeking his assistance. Nishida was a former army first lieutenant who had organized a secret group of young officers from the Military Academy to discuss political affairs as early as 1922. Due to illness, he was released from active duty in 1925, but he created a more formal secret military society in 1927, the Tenkentō (Party of Heaven's Sword). Army officials, however, quickly learned of the party's existence and ordered Nishida to disband it. He did as ordered, but without first informing the other youthful military members, who as a result felt Nishida had betrayed them. In the aftermath, Nishida drew close to Kita Ikki, the leading civilian theorist and philosopher of the ultranationalist movement in 1930s Japan.

Born on the small island of Sado, Kita spent his youth in Tokyo developing his own brand of socialism. In 1906 he wrote his first book, *Treatise on the National Polity and Pure Socialism* (*Kokutai-ron oyobi Junsei Shakai-shugi*). Kita advocated ending the oligarchic rule of Japan by the *zaibatsu* financial combines and their bureaucratic supporters. This would enable a true union of the people with their sovereign, the emperor, whom Kita embraced as a national symbol acting in the name of Japan. At the same time, Kita advocated universal male suffrage, the enactment of which would lead to genuine representatives of the people comprising the membership of the Diet. Together with the emperor, the two groups would make up the highest organ of the state and enact major social reforms.

In October 1911 Kita had gone to China in support of the Chinese revolution. This support led to a second book in 1915, *An Unofficial History of the Chinese Revolution* (*Shina Kakumei Gaishi*), including criticism of Japanese policy makers for their failure to understand the true nature of Chinese revolutionary ferment. In 1919 Kita was one of the founders of the Yūzonsha, a political group attempting to realize his vision of pan-Asian nationalism as set forth in a third book, *Outline of a Plan to Reorganize Japan* (*Nihon Kaizo Hōan Taikō*). This book exerted a major influence on the thinking of the radical young officers, including those close to Inoue, not least of all because it advocated a coup d'état to be carried out by a civilian elite aided by the military.

Like Inoue, Kita was a devout follower of the *Lotus Sūtra*. As noted by George Wilson, Kita used a phrase from the *Lotus Sūtra* to define the nature of revolution. "Revolution," Kita wrote, "means entry into the Buddhist truth of the unity of loyalty and treason" (*jungyaku funi no hōmon*). By this he meant that in a revolutionary vortex, what is loyal from one standpoint may be equally traitorous from another. Kita further borrowed insights from the Zen tradition to claim that revolutionary theory "cannot be set down in writing" (*furyū monji*; lit., "does not rely on words and letters"). Revolutionary theory could, he insisted, only be understood intuitively.[21]

Given the similarity of their thinking, it is not surprising that Kita and Inoue, who had known each other for some time, held each other in high esteem. Kita always referred to Inoue as "Master" (J., *oshō*). For his part, Inoue placed a high value on Kita's skills.[22] Although Nishida had initially sought Kita's aid in connection with the military's upcoming action in Manchuria, Kita recommended Nishida contact Inoue instead, for he claimed to be deeply immersed in his study of the *Lotus Sūtra*. This was the background to Nishida's approach.

Nishida informed Inoue that on an as yet undetermined date, Japan's Guandong (aka Kwantung) Army would stage an incident. The Guandong Army had been stationed in Manchuria since 1906 in order to defend the Guandong Leased Territory and areas adjacent to the South Manchurian Railway, that is, the "fruits of battle" (*senka*) Japan had secured following its victory over Tsarist Russia in the Russo-Japanese War of 1904–1905. Simultaneous with the incident in Manchuria, elements of the army would carry out a coup d'état in Japan proper. Nishida requested Inoue to take an active role in the domestic coup.

The military leader of the domestic coup was to be Army Colonel Hashimoto Kingorō (1890–1957). Hashimoto had first become politically active in 1927 while serving as a military attaché at a Japanese consulate in Turkey. It was there he encountered the revolutionary thought of Turkish army officer and founder of the Republic of Turkey Mustafa Kemal Atatürk (1881–1938). Concretely, Hashimoto was to lead a group composed of both military and civilians in taking over the Imperial Palace. Following this, a military government would be installed, leading to a series of major social reforms. The brains behind the coup was identified as Ōkawa Shūmei (1886–1957), one of the most influential and long lasting of Japan's ultranationalist writers, who would later play a critical role in Inoue's own plans.

Inoue's first reaction to the coup proposal was one of doubt—that such a major plot could be carried out without being discovered by the military authorities. Nishida, however, informed him that two leading officers in the General Staff Office, Generals Tatekawa Yoshitsugu (1880–1945) and Koiso Kuniaki (1880–1950), secretly backed the plot. Hearing this, Inoue reluctantly agreed to participate as a representative of the civilian side. Reluctantly, because although unspoken, Inoue still harbored reservations about the plan.

In Inoue's mind, the military intended to use illegitimate means in both Manchuria and at home to come to power. In other words, he felt their plan was one of pure militarism. In attempting to usurp power from the nation's leaders, whether they be rich *zaibatsu* or political parties, the coup plotters were enveloped in the same divisive worldview based on discriminatory thought as their opponents. Inoue, however, continued to embrace his enlightenment experience characterized by "pacifism based on a unitary view of the world" (*ittaikan ni tatsu heiwa-shugi*).[23] Inoue's goal was to change Japan from "a country of falsehood to a country of truth," while the plotters sought to change Japan from "a country of falsehood to a country of even greater falsehood."[24]

Inoue recognized, however, that he lacked both the funds and the manpower necessary to realize his own plan. Thus, he felt he had no choice but to go along with the coup. However, as Inoue learned still further details, it became clear to him that he could not support it. This was because the plotters intended to completely ignore the "august mind" (*ōmi-kokoro*) of the emperor. In fact, Ōkawa had already written a draft of the imperial edict the plotters expected the emperor to sign even if they had to force him to do so. When Inoue learned of this, he was incensed and secretly decided on a new course of action. He would wait until the coup succeeded, and then, at the first cabinet meeting of the military government held in the imperial presence, he and his band members would kill Generals Tatekawa and Koiso and the remaining military members. He informed Yotsumoto and others close to him of his intention while continuing to lay ever more detailed plans for the coup.

In August, Inoue was informed that the incident in Manchuria would take place on September 18, 1931, and it was agreed the domestic coup would take place on the same day. All that was left to do was await the designated day. To Inoue's surprise, however, even with the designated day fast approaching, he failed to receive word from Col. Hashimoto. Even more surprising, on September 18 the incident planned for Manchuria occurred, but nothing happened in Japan itself. When Inoue tried to find out what was going on, he was told the coup leaders were hesitant to act. In Inoue's mind there was yet a second reason for the failure to act—the tension that developed during the coup planning between Ōkawa and Nishida Mitsugi. Col. Hashimoto had been unsuccessful in his attempt to reconcile the two men, with the result that unity among the coup plotters was lost and communication strained.

When both the military and civilian members of the intended coup finally got together, they decided on two lines of action. First, the coup would be rescheduled for exactly one month later, October 18, 1931. Second, in order to placate the anger and disappointment of the younger officers involved in the plot, it was decided to send a threatening letter, signed by anonymous "Young Army Officers," to leading government officials, including the prime minister and the ministers of the army and navy. The letter stated, "If you do not carry out domestic reform in the immediate future, we concerned young army officers will rise up, questioning the role you are playing and enacting reform with our own hands."[25]

Inoue strongly supported the young officers' decision, telling them, "Do it, do it!"[26] The letter was sent in the latter part of September, and as expected, the prime minister and others were very surprised. In the meantime, what became known as the Manchurian Incident (*Manshū-jihen*) was making rapid progress. On September 18, 1931, Lieutenant Kawamoto Suemori, acting on the orders of Guandong Army Colonel Itagaki Seishirō (1885–1948) and Lieutenant Colonel Ishiwara Kanji (1889–1949), detonated a small quantity of dynamite close to a railway line owned by Japan's South Manchuria Railway near Mukden (now Shenyang). The explosion was so weak that it did little damage, with a train safely passing over the rail line minutes later. The Japanese army, however, accused Chinese soldiers of sabotage and quickly mounted a full-scale invasion, leading to the occupation of all of Manchuria. Less than six months later, on February 18, 1932, the Japanese puppet state of Manchukuo was proclaimed under the nominal rule of the last emperor of China, Puyi, who was himself Manchurian.

As for the planned coup in Japan, it once again ended in failure. The letter the young officer plotters had sent had an effect, though not the intended one. Instead, the letter served to alert Japan's political and senior military leaders that something was afoot. Additionally, leaked details concerning the plot reached the ears of War Minister General Minami Jirō (1874–1955) who requested Gen. Araki Sadao pacify the young officers. Araki attempted to reason with Hashimoto and other leaders, but to no avail. Since they refused to abandon their scheme, Araki had them all arrested by the military police on October 17, 1931. Nevertheless, the punishments for this abortive coup were quite mild, as Gen. Minami publicly excused the plotters on the basis of the patriotic zeal that had motivated them. Hashimoto, for example, was punished with only twenty days of house arrest.

Despite their light sentences, the question remained of who had leaked the coup plans to Gen. Minami. The young officers first suspected Nishida Mitsugi. Nishida, however, charged Ōkawa was responsible due to his habit of boasting about everything. This exchange only angered the young officers more, and they pledged to find the guilty party. Shortly thereafter, when the officers got together at a private officers' club known as Kaikōsha, they decided to first bring Nishida in for questioning. Going to his house, representatives of the young officers told Nishida to accompany them to Kaikōsha. Nishida, however, refused. Angered, one of the officers said, "We have the responsibility to accomplish our duty. Come with us to be judged!"

As chance would have it, Inoue happened to be visiting Nishida when the officers arrived. In light of the emotional split between the officers and Nishida, Inoue intervened in the conversation and said,

> What are you talking about? It's not a question of passing judgement or not. If all of us share the same concern for our country, there will be a chance to make a second or even a third plan. Doing something like passing judgement is foolish talk. Inasmuch as Nishida says he doesn't want to go, it's stupid to talk about it. If you still insist on taking someone, take me instead![27]

On hearing this, one of the officers said it would be meaningless for Inoue to accompany them. In addition, the officer agreed that what Inoue said was correct and indicated his intention to return to Kaikōsha and tell the others. With this, the officers departed Nishida's home, while Nishida, for his part, expressed his deep appreciation to Inoue for his timely intervention.

PART TWO: TIME TO ACT

Although Inoue had not been arrested in connection with the attempted coup, there were indications he was under police surveillance. As a result, Inoue visited Tōyama Mitsuru at his home in Tokyo, explained the situation to him, and sought his protection. Tōyama agreed to help and allowed Inoue to stay with him for a week. Inoue later learned that the morning after he left his previous lodgings at Imaizumi's home, the police had come searching for him. He was definitely under suspicion.

In November 1931 Inoue moved into a row house managed by Gondō Nariaki (aka Gondō Seikyō, 1868–1937). Gondō was an ardent supporter of Japanese expansionism and publisher of the journal *Tōa Geppō* (East Asia Monthly News). In 1920, he founded the Jichi Gakkai (Self-government Society) in Tokyo to promote his ideas, including the proposal that Japan adopt a policy of self-sufficient village communities, without bureaucratic or capitalist interference, under the direct authority of the emperor. This proposal, contained in his 1927 book *Jichi minpan* (Guide for the People's Self-Government), was especially popular among young army officers, many of whom were themselves from rural families.

It was the young officers who had first introduced Gondō to Inoue, who quickly became impressed by the latter's encyclopedic knowledge. He identified him as being "just like a case full of books," as capable of talking about politics and economics as he was about culture.[28] Inoue recalled their first meeting, when Gondō sought to find out what kind of man Inoue was. Gondō asked, "I hear you wish to make a revolution, but do you really know what a revolution means?" Inoue replied,

> It's because scholars ask those kinds of questions that I dislike them so much. We have no intention of becoming scholars, so we have no need to go on and on about the meaning of revolution. We simply intend to carry one out. It will be fine if, once you see the flames of revolution lit, you observe the happenings from your window, thinking, that fellow Inoue did it after all.[29]

Following this exchange, Gondō treated Inoue respectfully, addressing him as "Master, Master."[30] It also led Gondō to request that Inoue gather a group of youth together in order to create a private school where his proposals for social reform could be taught. This was a perfect opportunity for Inoue, for it meant, in addition to the new school, there would be room to have his own followers, like Yotsumoto Yoshitaka, live with him in the row house. Additionally, it provided a convenient meeting place for other members in the Tokyo area.

Inoue was also interested in learning more about Gondō's proposals and, to that end, began reading the latter's writings. Inoue soon discovered, however, that Gondō's proposals were too difficult for him to understand. Yet this didn't bother Inoue in the least, for as he explained,

> We had accepted the role of destruction, prepared to destroy ourselves in the process. We had no intention of studying proposals for constructing a new society. Further, it was not a question of having to first read Gondō's books and listen to his lectures before deciding to rise up in revolt. We had already made up our minds before doing any of that.[31]

In one area Inoue was strongly opposed to Gondō's thinking—Chinese poetry. Gondō claimed that culture and ideology were two separate spheres. Thus, even a communist could compose a Chinese poem with a patriotic theme. Inoue was taken aback when he heard Gondō claim this. To Inoue, this was an absurd idea, for it meant that a person's actions and character were separate entities. "I thought," Inoue wrote, "Gondō was really an irresponsible person. Ordinary people admired him because they got caught up in his aura, failing to understand his true character."[32]

Another Failed Attempt

At the beginning of December 1931, Inoue got wind of yet another terrorist plot being organized by Ōkawa and Hashimoto. Inoue had two young officers close to him, including Fujii Hitoshi, approach the two organizers without letting them know of Inoue's involvement. The plot called for the assassination of Prime Minister Inukai Tsuyoshi (1855–1932). While Inukai was to be given an initial opportunity to resign, if he refused he was to be shot, precipitating a declaration of martial law and the creation of a military government.

The two young officers' approach was so successful they succeeded in convincing Ōkawa and Hashimoto they should be the ones to organize it. Ōkawa also gave the officers what was then the large sum of two thousand yen for planning expenses. He also promised that just before the uprising he would provide twenty revolvers as well as hand grenades. The grenades, however, were to be of a type that did no more than make a loud explosive sound. Before the coup could be organized, fate intervened once again, this time in the form of what became known as the First Shanghai Incident, starting on January 28, 1932, and lasting for a little over a month. Building on its success in Manchuria, the Japanese military had launched another plot to increase Japanese influence in China, this time in Shanghai, where Japan, along with various Western powers, had extraterritorial concessions.[33]

In this instance, the Japanese military's Shanghai Incident dealt a direct blow to right-wing military and civilian plotters at home. This was because many of the young officers who were to have been involved in assassinating Inukai were, instead, dispatched to fight in Shanghai. In particular, the plot suffered a major blow when Fujii, then a naval aviator stationed on the aircraft carrier *Kaga*, was shot down and killed on February 5 flying over Shanghai. Would everything come to naught once again?

An Alternative Plan

When the Shanghai Incident began, Inoue was not in Tokyo but taking a rest back in Ibaragi prefecture because he hadn't been feeling well. Intuitively, he claimed, he realized something strange was going on at his lodgings in Tokyo. Returning immediately, he discovered that Yotsumoto and Navy Lieutenant Junior Grade Koga Kiyoshi (1908–1997) were acting strangely. Koga was a close friend of Fujii and, like him, a naval aviator stationed at the same Naval Air Training Base near Inoue's former temple in Ōarai. Unlike Fujii, Koga had not been ordered to Shanghai and remained determined to take some kind of action.

Inoue called Yotsumoto and Koga to his room to find out what was going on. The two explained they had purposely hatched a plot in his absence in order to protect Inoue from being implicated in it. Inoue asked whether their plan reflected only their thinking or that of all their comrades. They assured Inoue they had secured agreement from everyone involved. The new plot called for the assassinations of twenty political and economic leaders, to be carried out on February 11, 1932, a national holiday known as Kigensetsu (Empire Day). Kigensetsu had been created in 1872 to focus the people's attention on the emperor by celebrating the alleged foundation of Japan and the accession of its first emperor, Jimmu, on February 11, 660 BCE. The coup plotters considered this to be the perfect day to carry out their "patriotic act."

While not opposed to their plan, Inoue was nonetheless taken aback by it. This was because he had not given serious thought to concrete plans for another coup in the aftermath of the previous failed attempt in October 1931. However, the only concern he voiced was whether the necessary planning could be accomplished in such a short time. Ultimately, he agreed to leave the timing up to the plotters themselves. Yotsumoto left Tokyo the next day for the Kansai area to gather together the band members living in that area.

As Inoue had anticipated, things did not go smoothly. In the first instance, Inoue lost contact with Yotsumoto at the end of January. Then Ōkawa proved unreliable and didn't deliver the pistols on the date promised. Inoue realized there was no way the plot could take place on February 11. Forced to reschedule, Inoue gathered his band members together and told them the plot would have to be postponed until the thirty-day period preceding the general election of February 20, 1932. The political leaders would be out campaigning for reelection and thus easier to target.

The strategy to be used was "one person kills one person" (*ichinin issatsu*). However, inasmuch as only ten band members were deemed fit to participate, each one would have to kill two persons. Each was to determine their first and second preferences and thereafter cease all contact. Inoue would distribute the pistols and necessary funding directly to each of them, for by this time the military members of Inoue's band had supplied the necessary pistols and ammunition.[34]

The band members collectively selected a total of twenty targets, including both political and business leaders. These were men who could not evade their responsibility for having caused the crisis facing Japan—men who gave false advice to the emperor, men who threw the government into disarray, and men who preyed on the people's welfare. First and foremost among these was Prince Saionji Kinmochi (1849–1940), one of the most liberal of Emperor Hirohito's advisors, who, believing in parliamentary government, sought to diminish the political influence of the army and opposed the emperor's direct participation in politics.

Other major targets included Count Makino Nobuaki (1861–1949), Dan Takuma (1858–1932), and Inoue Junnosuke (1869–1932). Makino shared Saionji's belief that the emperor should not be directly involved in political affairs. After a long career as both a diplomat and a politician, Makino had relinquished his formal positions but still exercised significant power and influence behind the scenes as an advisor to Emperor Hirohito. Dan was director-general of Mitsui, one of the leading *zaibatsu*, and favored closer relations between Japan and the Western powers. Inoue was a Japanese businessman, central banker, and politician who served two terms as both governor of the Bank of Japan and minister of finance. Inoue was one of the political figures who would be out campaigning for reelection preceding the February general election.

Inoue and his band members, military and civilian, had long believed there were leaders of various military cliques who also deserved to be assassinated. For the time being, however, they were not to be targeted, for it was decided to leave their assassination to the military members of Inoue's band, many of whom were still in Shanghai. Once the military members returned, the plan called for the young officers to launch a second wave of attacks, at which time they would determine the military leaders to be targeted. Additionally, Inoue felt a degree of sympathy for the Japanese military, whom he viewed as being oppressed by the ruling classes. True, the military had been involved in some "mischief" (*itazura*) in Manchuria, but that was about it. "Never in my wildest dreams," Inoue wrote, "did I imagine these military cliques would grow to the point that they would subsequently start the major war they did."[35]

Inoue made it clear that his band consisted of more than the ten members he had selected to participate in the uprising. Some members, Inoue thought, still lacked the necessary willpower to participate, while others were simply too physically weak. Another had dedicated himself to developing a set of principles for undertaking revolutionary acts, and Inoue felt his theoretical work was too important to be interrupted. Each of them, Inoue believed, had their own path to follow, as did he.

There was one final source of concern for Inoue: how would his father react to what was about to happen, for the clearly illegal incident was sure to create quite a social stir? Inoue therefore went to meet his father in order to sound out his reaction. He began by patiently explaining to his father what he believed to be the decay and corruption present in every corner, including high-ranking officials in the Imperial Household Agency, the political parties, the *zaibatsu*, and other members of the ruling class. In response, his father, who had long been immersed in loyalty to the emperor and love of country, was visibly angered and said, "Is there no one who will cut down traitors to the country like them? What are the young people of today thinking about?" With that, Inoue's concern vanished as he thought to himself, "Great, everything will be fine if father feels this way."[36]

Awaiting News

At this point Inoue relaxed and awaited the "good news" (*kippō*). On the morning of February 10, he received word that twenty-two-year-old Onuma Shō (aka Onuma Tadashi, 1911–1978), a onetime baker's assistant and carpenter's apprentice, had shot and mortally wounded Inoue Junnosuke, general-secretary of the Minseitō and former minister of finance. Junnosuke had been shot the previous evening as he entered Komamoto Elementary School in Tokyo to deliver an election speech. Onuma had decided to shoot Inoue as he entered the school instead of as he exited in order to lessen the danger that members of the public seeing off the former finance minister might be injured in the process.

Shortly after receiving this news, Yotsumoto arrived to request Inoue find somewhere else to stay. Yotsumoto was concerned that if Inoue were arrested at Gondō Nariaki's house, the latter would be implicated in the incident. For this reason, Inoue left Gondō's house around eight in the morning and once again sought refuge at the home of Tōyama Mitsuru. At their meeting, Inoue asked Tōyama if he had seen the morning's newspaper, and when Tōyama indicated he had, Inoue explained the whole situation to him, including the need for him to find a hiding place, at least until all twenty of the intended victims had been killed. Tōyama immediately ordered Inoue to be hidden in a second-floor room above his son's nearby martial arts hall, home of the Tenkōkai (Heavenly Action Society).

An Informer

For the first few days after Inoue Junnosuke's death, Inoue was pleased to see that, according to the newspapers, police suspected his death was the result of a political feud. Because Inoue was a member of the Rikken Minseitō, suspicion initially fell on the party's major political rival, the Rikken Seiyūkai. Although the assassin, Onuma Shō, had been captured alive, he wasn't talking. Police suspicions appeared to be confirmed when, on March 5, Dan Takuma was shot and killed by Hishinuma Gorō (1912–1990) just as his car pulled up to the side entrance of the Mitsui Bank Building. Mitsui was regarded as being close to the Seiyūkai, and thus Dan's death was suspected of having been retribution on the part of Minseitō.

Inoue welcomed the police suspicions, for it meant that his band members had just that much more time to carry out their plan. Inoue was not surprised by the police failure to suspect that the assassinations might have been the work of right-wing extremists. This was because, as he noted, "Up to that point, the right wing had served as bodyguards for the *zaibatsu* in their struggle against the left wing."[37] It would only be after this incident that the police recognized right-wing organizations could also be opposed to the *zaibatsu* and existing political parties.

Inoue was quite content in his new home, for it gave him ample time to practice *zazen* as well as read.[38] However, just when everything appeared to be going well, Inoue happened to look outside his second-floor window and saw a policeman mounted on horseback passing by below. At first, Inoue was not too concerned, but in the days that followed suspicious visitors began showing up one after another until one day a policeman suddenly pushed open a window and surveyed a first-floor room where Inoue was engaged in a game of *shōgi* (Japanese chess). The next day Inoue saw what appeared to be plainclothes policemen standing in a nearby open space, twenty-four hours a day. Inoue was clearly under surveillance, but why had the police become suspicious of him?

It would not be until after his arrest that a police official would inform Inoue what had happened, that an informant had come forward in order to protect himself. The informer's name was Yasuoka Masahiro, head of Kinkei Gakuen (Golden Pheasant Academy), where Inoue had first stayed on his arrival in Tokyo. At least two members of Inoue's group, including Yotsumoto, had initially been Yasuoka's students, and he therefore feared that he, too, might be implicated in the plot. Yasuoka told the police that if they would simply arrest Inoue as the ringleader, the incident would come to an end. Yasuoka received a reward of fifty thousand yen for his information.

Although Inoue wasn't aware of Yasuoka's role at the time, both he and Tōyama realized that it was only a matter of time before his arrest. However, even though Tōyama was coming under increasing pressure from his subordinates to make Inoue leave, he said nothing to Inoue. While Inoue was grateful for Tōyama's attitude, he realized his situation was untenable. What should he do?

Inoue's first thought was to reveal himself to the police and then cut down as many of them as he could. Convinced of this, he drank five bottles of cold sake he had on hand and took a nap. However, by the time one of Tōyama's subordinates, Honma Kenichirō (1889–1959), came to wake him, Inoue had decided to kill himself instead. "Once I commit ritual suicide by cutting my stomach open," he said to Honma, "I want you to cut off my head and place it in a wrapping cloth. Then take it to the Metropolitan Police Department and tell them you brought Inoue with you before throwing my head at them."[39]

In response, Honma asked Inoue to think the matter over a little more. He left the room and shortly came back with Amano Tatsuo (1893–1972) one of Tōyama's senior lieutenants. Amano addressed Inoue, saying,

> I've been told about your situation. If you were to die now it would be a worthless dog's death. You should wait a while to see how the situation develops. There's no doubt reform will happen, and at that point I would sincerely like you to be a part of it. Fortunately, the chief of the Metropolitan Police Department is a friend of mine. He told me he would treat you as a patriot and will ensure that police detectives don't lay a hand on you. I recommend the three of us go by car to the police, where you can turn yourself in.[40]

Reflecting on Amano's words, Inoue thought it would indeed be heartless of him to kill innocent detectives and police. Additionally, he had recently instructed Koga that even if something were to happen to him, there would be a further uprising by the returning officers of the army and navy in May, at which time Koga should take part. Even in jail, Inoue realized, he would be able to see how things turned out. With this, Inoue agreed to Amano's suggestion and prepared to turn himself in. When Tōyama was informed of Inoue's decision, he simply said, "Well, if that's Inoue's decision, fine."[41]

By the time Inoue was ready to leave the martial arts hall on the morning of March 11, all arrangements had been made. Thanks to the aid of Lt. Gen. Araki Sadao, no repercussions would befall Tōyama for having hidden Inoue. Additionally, Araki arranged for Inoue to be accompanied by military police on his way to police headquarters. This was to ensure Inoue would not be subject to the humiliation of arrest as a criminal on his way to surrender himself.

Before departing, Inoue went to Tōyama's residence to express his gratitude and bid farewell. Before leaving, Tōyama's wife poured some *sake* for him. When he returned to the martial arts hall, he was surprised to see that all of the detectives and police had been withdrawn.

Just as Inoue was preparing to leave his room, the maid came to inform him that Tōyama was waiting for him in a downstairs room. Inoue entered the room and bowed to Tōyama, at which point the maid prepared to break five quail eggs in a rice bowl. Before she could do so, however, Tōyama quietly told her, "Give them to me." He then broke the eggs himself and, adding chopsticks but without saying a word, gave the rice bowl to Inoue to consume. Inoue noticed that both the rice bowl and the chopsticks were those that Tōyama used on a daily basis and was overcome by emotion. For him, it was the act of a compassionate father to a beloved son. Inoue drank the mixture in one go and then silently bowed again.

At that point, Tōyama said in his uniquely quiet yet sonorous voice, "Take good care of yourself," and left the room.[42] Inoue accompanied him as far as the entrance to the martial arts hall; however, as much as he tried, Inoue could no longer see Tōyama, for his eyes were filled with tears. At the same time, Inoue couldn't help recalling the dream he once had in China of an old man with white hair. Tōyama appeared to be the very incarnation of that man. Inoue then climbed into the waiting car and, accompanied by Amano and a second Tōyama subordinate, left to turn himself in.

For sensationalist purposes, newspapers labelled the entire event as the Blood Oath Corps Incident (*Ketsumeidan Jiken*). The name originated with one of the public prosecutors, Kiuchi Tsunenori (1896–1976). This is despite the fact that the band members never undertook a "blood oath" or even gave their group a name.[43] Only two of the twenty intended targets had been killed. Moreover, the incident failed to precipitate a declaration of martial law, the establishment of a military government, or the immediate restoration of absolute political power to the emperor, let alone major social reform. For these reasons, this incident may be regarded as yet another failed uprising. However, the two men who were assassinated were major political and economic leaders in their respective fields. Henceforth, both communities were alerted to the threat posed by right-wing terrorism, a threat that would once again prove deadly only two months later. By that time, however, Inoue would view it from behind bars.

9

Patriots on Trial

QUESTIONING AND INCARCERATION

On arrival at the metropolitan police headquarters, Inoue was treated with the respect promised. In fact, he was personally greeted by the smiling superintendent-general of the Metropolitan Police. Following introductions, the superintendent announced he had to leave to supervise the police protection provided for Empress Nagako during her visit. After his departure, Inoue, still accompanied by one of Tōyama's subordinates, reported to the office of the chief public prosecutor. At that point, Inoue regarded himself as a witness to an incident who, having come of his own free will for questioning, was able to come and go as he liked.

Following introductions, the prosecutor suddenly said, "Among St. Nichiren's writings is the statement, 'The law of the sovereign is also the law [of the Buddha].'" Surprised by his words, Inoue quickly realized the prosecutor believed him to be a Nichiren adherent and hoped to use Nichiren's words to ensnare him. The words "law of the sovereign" referred to the law of the state, and in effect the prosecutor was saying that the law of the state is identical with the law of the Buddha. Therefore, inasmuch as Inoue had broken the law of the state, he had also broken the law of the Buddha, something no Buddhist should do.

However, based on his Zen-derived enlightenment experience, Inoue rejected this dualistic way of thinking, believing the law of the sovereign was *both* the law of the Buddha and *not* the law of the Buddha. Inoue explained his position by creating a traditional Zen *mondō* (question between a Zen master and disciple):

Question: Is the law of the sovereign the law of the Buddha or is it not?

Answer: "Is" and "is not" are One.[1]

Inoue meant by this that his actions were based on the non-dualistic "law of the universe" (*tenchi no hō*).[2] Therefore, whether or not his actions impinged on the law of the state was of little import. Given this, it stood to reason he could not have broken the law of the Buddha. On the contrary, he claimed, "I was the one who dealt a blow to the transgressors of the Buddha's law."[3] Nevertheless, Inoue realized that whether or not the law of the sovereign was identical with the law of the Buddha, he had clearly violated the law of the state. Just as it was his job to judge his actions based on the law of the universe, so it was the prosecutor's job to judge his actions based on the law of the state. Inoue had no objection to the latter doing so and made no attempt to rebut the prosecutor or dissuade him from his belief that Inoue was a Nichiren adherent. Inoue's silence made it possible for the prosecutor to claim in his memoirs that his arguments had been responsible for persuading Inoue to cooperate.

After a further short discussion, the chief prosecutor handed Inoue over to his assistant, who then took Inoue to another building for additional questioning. There he was provided with a tasty lunch of eel and rice before undergoing a second, but short, round of questioning. Inoue was then ushered into the detectives' lounge, where a barrel of *sake* was opened for all to consume. Inoue downed five bottles before he was given bedding and shown to a room where he slept alone. The next morning Inoue was formally placed under arrest though only after he had agreed to skip the legal formalities. From then on, questioning began on a daily basis immediately after breakfast, continuing all the way through to the evening meal.

At first, Inoue was determined not to collaborate with this ongoing and lengthy questioning. He maintained his innocence while drawing out the process by talking in general terms about the abject state of the country and the need for true patriots to take action. At the same time, despite his disdain for the police, he could not help admiring the honesty of the elderly, and decorated, detective interrogating him. As the detective explained, his job was not to judge Inoue's guilt or innocence but only to compile as much relevant evidence as possible before turning the matter over to the prosecutor. Upon hearing this, Inoue agreed to collaborate with the detective, telling him everything he wanted to know.

Although Inoue only learned of it later, sometime after he turned himself in, Tōyama, accompanied by his secretary, went to Kawaba village to express his sympathies to Inoue's father. Unfortunately, Inoue's father was ill with pneumonia and unable to meet Tōyama at the time but was deeply touched by his unannounced visit nonetheless. Upon recovery, Inoue's father came to Tokyo to express his gratitude in person, marking the beginning of an enduring friendship between the two men. While in Tokyo, Inoue's father also visited his son in Sugamo Prison, where he was awaiting trial. Filled with emotion, his father tearfully told him, "Mr. Tōyama kindly told me that while your collective actions were insufficient, they were fine nonetheless."[4]

Around April 20, 1932, the police completed their questioning of Inoue and thirteen other members of his band who were now in police custody. At that point, they were all moved to Toyotama Prison in Tokyo, used in large part to house "thought criminals" (*shisō-han*). This period was the calm before the storm.

The May 15 Incident

Although history books record the May 15 Incident of 1932 as a separate coup attempt, in reality it was the second stage of Inoue's plan, this time chiefly carried out by the military members of his band. Naval Lt. Koga Kiyoshi, Inoue's trusted subordinate, was in charge of a group of eleven young naval officers, supported by army cadets and right-wing civilians, including Ōkawa Shūmei and Tōyama Hidezō (1907–1952), the younger of Tōyama Mitsuru's two sons. Integral to his ultranationalism, Hidezō was devoted to enhancing the "Japanese spirit" (*Yamato-damashii*) through promotion of the martial arts at the Tenkōkai *dōjō* (practice hall) he headed.

Inoue explained the reasoning behind having a two-stage plan. First, his band had only ten pistols between them, and second, only ten civilian band members were deemed ready to participate. Inoue continued:

> If we were successful in toppling around five of the twenty targets, it might cause the leaders of the ruling class to come together to take the first steps toward social reform. However, if we were only able to take down one or two, we would end up being wiped out without having had any effect on genuine social reform. Inasmuch as we [in the first wave] were prepared for inevitable defeat, the best plan was to hold our naval members in reserve, waiting for the right time for them to form a joint force composed of both army and navy comrades who would then launch a second wave.[5]

The chief target of the second wave was Inukai Tsuyoshi, prime minister and head of the Rikken Seiyūkai party. He was shot by a group of nine naval officers who forced their way into the prime minister's residence. Inukai's final words were, "If you would let me speak, you'll understand" (*hanaseba wakaru*), to which his killers replied, "Questions and answers are of no use" (*mondō muyō*). At least in format, the verbal exchange between the naval officers and Inukai was similar to that between a Zen master and his disciple, a Zen *mondō* (dialogue).

Surprisingly, the original plan had also called for the assassination of English film star Charlie Chaplin, who had just arrived by ship on a goodwill visit to Japan on May 14, 1932. The assassins planned to attack the prime minister's residence during a reception hosted by the prime minister in Chaplin's honor. At his trial, Lt. Koga explained their motive as follows: "Chaplin is a popular figure in the United States and the darling of the capitalist class. We believed that killing him would cause a war with America, and thus we could kill two birds with one stone."[6] Fortunately, Chaplin wasn't at the prime minister's residence at the time of the attack, having been invited by Inukai Takeru (1896–1960), the prime minister's third son, to go to a sumo wrestling match. Their absence probably saved both their lives.

The plotters were organized into four groups, each with their respective targets. The primary target of the first group was the prime minister. A second group of five, led by Koga, attacked the residence of Count Makino Nobuaki, Lord Keeper of the Privy Seal and head of the Rikken Seiyūkai party. As readers will recall, he had also been one of the main targets of the first stage attack but managed to escape injury for a second time. A third group of four took a cab to the headquarters of the Rikken Seiyūkai party, where they threw hand grenades, damaging the entrance. A fourth group also used hand grenades and damaged the outer walls of Mitsubishi Bank. Finally, seven rural civilian participants attempted to throw Tokyo into panic by causing a blackout, attacking, but not seriously damaging, six electrical transformer substations. Apart from the death of the prime minister, their collective actions resulted in only minimal damage though there was one serious injury—Nishida Mitsugi. One of Inoue's four original band members still at large shot Nishida, who they had become convinced was a traitor. Although he suffered a massive loss of blood, Nishida survived.

At 6:10 p.m. on May 15, the eighteen military participants of the first three groups went to the Tokyo headquarters of the Kempeitai (military police) and surrendered themselves. The other participants were arrested in the days that followed. Although already incarcerated, Inoue once again underwent lengthy questioning, this time by the minister for navy affairs. However, he wasn't charged for being involved.

As with the first stage, the second stage of the plot must also be considered a failure in light of their goal to provoke martial law, establish a military government, and enact massive social reform in the emperor's name. Nevertheless, as Herbert Bix noted, the combination of both incidents "precipitated the start of a fundamental transformation in Japanese politics."[7] Specifically, the emperor and his advisors decided to suspend appointment of cabinet-based governments in Japan. Among other things, this suspension led to the effective end of civilian control of the military, especially in budgetary matters. "Taishō Democracy," for all its imperfections, was dealt a severe blow from which it would never recover. From that point on, the emperor and his advisors would appoint and remove prime ministers and their governments as they saw fit.

The emperor's personal involvement, if any, in these events remains a matter of debate.[8] What is clear, however, is that the combination of these two stages of the attempted coup ensured the Japanese people, particularly Japanese men (aged twenty-five and over), who had only gained universal suffrage in 1925, would henceforth have little or no influence on government decisions. No longer would the political party that garnered the greatest electoral support from the Japanese people be allowed to form a government and attempt to implement its election promises.

Given this, and despite their repeated failures, it is fair to say that Inoue and his military and civilian band's dedication to "destruction" was well on its way to becoming a reality even though not in the way they had envisioned. Their demand for social reform, however, remained alive, not only among young military officers but also at the higher echelons as well. General Araki Sadao, then army minister in the Inukai cabinet, commented:

> We cannot restrain our tears when we consider the mentality expressed in these pure and naïve young men. Theirs are not actions for fame, or personal gain, nor are they traitorous. They were performed in the sincere belief that they were for the benefit of Imperial Japan. Therefore, in dealing with this incident, it will not do to dispose of it in a routine manner according to short-sighted conceptions.[9]

Araki's comments suggest he expected the perpetrators to escape severe sentences. He was not disappointed, for the punishment handed down by the court was extremely light by Japanese standards. While the two military officer leaders were sentenced to fifteen years in prison, the majority received four years or less. The Japanese press, reflecting favorable public opinion, accurately forecast that the prime minister's murderers would be released in a couple of years at the most. In light of this, it was only a matter of time before further terrorist acts occurred. The deep social unrest that lay at the root of these incidents had by no means disappeared.

Life in Prison

Once the repercussions of the second incident died down, Inoue faced the question of how to pass his time in jail while awaiting trial. He first thought of attempting to solve some further *kōan* (Zen dialogues), but that seemed pointless. Pointless, because the public prosecutor had told Inoue during questioning, "You're going to be sentenced to death!"[10] Inoue wasn't disturbed by this statement, however, since he had long resigned himself to that fate. But until that time arrived, what should he do?

Inoue finally decided to revisit one of the interests he enjoyed as a child but had abandoned when he was thirteen or fourteen—composing seventeen-syllable haiku poetry. He received special permission to enroll in a twelve-month haiku correspondence course but realized along the way he lacked the talent for writing poetry and quit the course.

In March 1933 Inoue and members of his band were moved once again, this time to Tokyo's Ichigaya Prison. There he spent his days writing down his thoughts with the pen and paper the prosecutor provided him and reading books provided by the education office. One of these books was a famous Buddhist text entitled *Tannishō* (Passages Deploring Deviations of Faith). It consists primarily of a collection of sayings attributed to St. Shinran (1173–1263), founder of the True Pure Land (Shin) sect of Buddhism in Japan. Although it wasn't a Zen writing, Inoue read it with an open mind and was particularly attracted to the second chapter, in which Shinran addresses his disciples:

> I [Shinran] believe that the reason you have come here, crossing over more than ten provinces at the risk of your lives, is solely to ascertain the path that leads to birth in the Pure Land.[11] But if you suspect that I know ways other than the *nembutsu*[12] to attain birth, or that I am versed in the scriptures connected with them, you are greatly mistaken. If that be the case, there are many eminent scholars in the monasteries of Nara and on Mt. Hiei, so you should go to see them and ask in detail about the way to attain birth in the Pure Land.
>
> As for myself, Shinran, I simply take to heart the words of my dear teacher, Hōnen, "Just say the *nembutsu* and be saved by Amida [Buddha]." Thereafter, I entrust myself to the Primal Vow [of Amida].[13] Beyond this, there is nothing more.
>
> I really do not know whether the *nembutsu* may be the cause for my birth in the Pure Land, or the act that shall condemn me to hell. But I have nothing to regret,

even if I should have been deceived by my teacher, and, saying the *nembutsu*, fall into hell. The reason is that if I were capable of realizing Buddhahood by other religious practices and yet fell into hell for saying the *nembutsu* I might have dire regrets for having been deceived. But since I am absolutely incapable of any religious practice, hell is my only home.

If Amida's Primal Vow is true, Shakyamuni's teaching cannot be false. If the Buddha's teaching is true, Shantao's commentaries[14] cannot be false. If Shantao's commentaries are true, how can Hōnen's words[15] be empty of meaning? If Hōnen's words are true, what I, Shinran, say cannot be meaningless. In brief, such is the true entrusting of this foolish one. Now, whether you accept the *nembutsu*, entrusting yourself to it, or reject it, that is your own decision.[16]

Inoue was deeply moved by these expressions of Shinran's religious modesty. He felt forced to ask himself how he compared with such modesty. Inoue acknowledged that while he believed he had transcended all things, he was still overcome, at the deepest level, with the desire to penetrate what the Zen sect calls the "no-self"(*muga*).[17] "I realized," Inoue wrote, "just what an arrogant person I was!"[18]

Overcome by feelings of shame and remorse, Inoue lost control of his emotions and began to weep incessantly. He tried to control his tears by using the traditional method of placing strength in his abdomen but to no avail. Finally, desperately trying to muffle his plaintive cries, he plunged his head into his bedding that lay folded on the straw *tatami* mats of his cell. He then continued to cry and cry until he could cry no more. Exhausted by his crying, he fell asleep.

When Inoue awoke, he went to the window of his cell and saw a truly wondrous sight. The cherry trees in the garden outside were in full bloom, their blossoms radiant. Each tree seemed to be rejoicing in *nembutsu-zammai* (the concentrated state of mind achieved through *nembutsu* recitation).[19] Seeing this, Inoue experienced the same exceptional frame of mind he had first encountered during his training at Santoku-an. Inoue later described his experience in the following poem he sent to Yamamoto Gempō, the Rinzai Zen master under whom he had previously trained at Shōinji:

> Looking out
> from inside Ichigaya Prison,
> Understanding nothing,
> large or small

Recognizing the depth of spiritual attainment Inoue expressed in his poem, Yamamoto bestowed on him the Buddhist name Gentetsu (lit., Mystery Piercer).[20] Like D. T. Suzuki's lay Buddhist name Daisetsu, granted by Suzuki's Rinzai Zen master Shaku Sōen, it was a distinct honor to receive a lay Buddhist name from a famous master liked Yamamoto. It was also a sign of the continued close master–disciple relationship that existed between the two men. This is not surprising given that even after leaving Shōinji, Inoue had continued to train under Yamamoto's guidance.

This ongoing training was possible because, as Yotsumoto Yoshitaka noted, Inoue and members of his band frequently practiced *zazen* at the Rinzai temple of Ryū-un-in in Tokyo's Bunkyō ward.[21] It was here that Yamamoto conducted *zazen* practice sessions lasting for a week on his monthly visits to the Tokyo area. Yamamoto, however, does not appear to have been directly involved with Inoue and his band's plans for "revolution."

THE TRIAL BEGINS

Inoue and his band's trial began on June 28, 1933. According to one description, the courtroom atmosphere was "as melodramatic as a revival meeting." This was thanks not only to the religiously impassioned court testimony of Inoue and his "right-minded" young followers, but to the similarly emotional pleadings of the defendants' lawyers as well.[22] The trial so captured the nationalist-oriented imagination of the nation that when, six weeks later, the three presiding judges attempted to limit testimony to events directly related to the assassinations, the defendants demanded the judges step down from the case due to their alleged "inattention."[23]

In an almost unheard of move in Japanese jurisprudence, the judges were replaced, ostensibly due to illness on the part of the presiding judge. Thus, when the trial finally resumed on March 27, 1934, the new chief judge granted the fourteen defendants, Inoue among them, the right not only to wear formal kimono, complete with family crests, in court, but to expound at length on the "patriotic" motivation for their acts. For his part, Inoue made it abundantly clear that his Buddhist faith lay at the heart of his actions: "I was primarily guided by Buddhist thought in what I did. That is to say, I believe the teachings of Mahāyāna Buddhism as they presently exist in Japan are wonderful. That's what I believe. . . . No matter how many sects Mahāyāna Buddhism may be divided into [in Japan], they all aim for the essence, the true form of the universe."[24] If Inoue took a rather ecumenical stance in his testimony, it is also true that he went on to express his indebtedness to both the Pure Land and Nichiren sects for having contributed to his "salvation." With regard to Zen, however, he said, "I reached where I am today thanks to Zen. Zen dislikes talking theory so I can't put it into words, but it is true nonetheless."[25]

Inoue made another reference to the Zen-like manner of thinking when he was asked about the particular political ideology that had informed his actions. He replied, "It is more correct to say that I have no systematized ideas. I transcend reason and act completely on intuition."[26] As D. T. Suzuki would write in 1938, acting according to "intuition" has long been regarded as one of Zen's distinguishing characteristics:

Zen has no special doctrine or philosophy, no set of concepts or intellectual formulas, except that it tries to release one from the bondage of birth and death, by means of certain intuitive modes of understanding peculiar to itself. It is, therefore, extremely flexible in adapting itself to almost any philosophy and moral doctrine as long as its intuitive

teaching is not interfered with. It may be found wedded to anarchism or fascism, communism or democracy, atheism or idealism, or any political or economic dogmatism.
It is, however, generally animated with a certain revolutionary spirit, and when things
come to a deadlock—as they do when we are overloaded with conventionalism, formalism, and other cognate isms—Zen asserts itself and proves to be a destructive force.[27]

Although Suzuki wrote these words only four years after Inoue's trial, there is no
evidence to suggest Suzuki either knew or supported Inoue and his band's terrorist
acts. Nevertheless, Suzuki's identification of intuition, as well as destruction, as Zen
characteristics suggests a similar understanding.

Inoue also testified about the contribution Buddhism made to his band's acts.
He first noted that Buddhism was a religion that taught the existence of "Buddha
nature" (*bushō*). Although Buddha nature is universally present, Inoue argued, it is
concealed by passions, producing ignorance, attachment, and degradation. Japan is
likewise a country that possesses a truly magnificent national polity, a polity that is
in fact identical with the "absolute nature of the universe itself." However, human
desires for such things as money, power, and the like worked to conceal this incom-
parable national polity and resulted in dualistic ways of thinking, leading to the
failure to comprehend the fundamental truth that matter and mind are one. Thus,
even though Japan's national essence is excellent, degradation had occurred.

At this point the judge interrupted to ask, "In the final analysis, what you are
saying then is that the national polity of Japan, as an expression of universal truth
[*shin'yo*; Skt., *tathatā*], has been clouded over?" Inoue replied, "That's right. It is due
to various passions that our national polity has been clouded over. It is we [band
members] who have taken it on ourselves to disperse these clouds."[28]

Yet why had Inoue and his band chosen assassination as their method of revolution? Were there no other more humane ways of bringing about the fundamental
reform of Japanese society? Inoue stated,

> In explaining why "assassination" was the most appropriate method to employ, I would
> first point out that the upper classes have status, fame, wealth, and power and want for
> nothing. Although they believe no one is in a position to challenge them, they are nev-
> ertheless confronted by one thing—death. Death is the only thing they have no control
> over; therefore, it is the only way to bring them to their knees. Apart from this method,
> we thought there was no other way to save either them or the nation.
>
> We believed it was necessary to assassinate two or three members from each of the
> privileged classes, that is, representatives of the *zaibatsu*, politicians, and military cliques,
> for a total of some twenty in all. Thereafter, we anticipated that out of their own self-
> interest the remaining members of these groups would come together to form an alliance
> to placate those seeking change, listening to the voices of the whole nation. Of course, if
> this method were to be successful, it would, at first, be necessary for it to take the form
> of a union between the Imperial Court and the military. Then in a second and third
> stage it would be possible for the reformist forces, gradually accruing political power, to
> use legal means to complete the transformation of society.

Secondly, this method was the most appropriate because it required, whether successful or not, the least number of victims. That said, there is no question the twenty or so band members dedicated to the reformation of society would die in the process, either at the hands of the police when they killed their victims or later after they were arrested. That is to say, on the surface it would appear they had failed, but at the same time they would have a major impact.

Additionally, this small number of comrades would serve, by virtue of having climbed the hangman's scaffold, as a beacon for the army of reformation, the comrades' lifeblood stimulating the self-sacrificing conscience of each branch of the right wing. In time, the branches of the right wing would unite together, hastening the unity of both the civilian and military members of the reformation army and spurring them to act. . . . The critical issue is that there was no better method than implementing what I felt sure was best for the country, untainted by the least self-interest.[29]

Inoue maintained it was this point that distinguished the revolution he led from those that had taken place in Western countries. In the French and Russian Revolutions, Inoue claimed, the revolutionaries had worked to ensure their own survival in order that they might secure a leadership role for themselves in the post-revolutionary era. As a consequence, they were quite willing to kill any and all persons who stood in their way. The result was a massive loss of life.

Inoue and his band, however, were prepared from the outset to perish in the process of the revolution. The "selflessness" of their Buddhist faith enabled them to willingly sacrifice themselves, firm in the belief that others, particularly their comrades in the military, would follow in their footsteps and bring about the ideal society they sought. By being prepared to sacrifice themselves, they could ensure that as few persons as possible became victims of revolutionary violence. In short, they described themselves as so many "revolutionary *sute-ishi*" (lit., cast-off stones).[30] Similar to pawns in chess, the sacrifice of *sute-ishi* at opportune times in the Japanese game of *go* may lead to final victory.[31]

In addition, Inoue noted that during his Dharma talks at his former temple, he had often spoken on the thirteenth-century Zen collection of *kōan* known as the *Mumonkan*. In case number fourteen of that collection, Inoue taught that it was Buddhist compassion that had motivated Nansen (Ch., Nanquan, 748–834) to kill the monastery cat. Building on this, Inoue claimed,

> Revolution employs compassion on behalf of the society of [our] nation. Therefore, those who wish to participate in revolution must have a mind of great compassion toward the society of [our] nation. In light of this there must be no thought of reward for participating in revolution. A revolution that does not encompass a mind of great compassion is not Buddhist. That is to say, revolution is itself the mind of great compassion.[32]

The judge was curious as to how Inoue was able to link "a mind of great compassion" with not just "revolution" but, specifically, to the act of killing. Inoue began his response with a reference to Nichiren's use of a traditional method of propagating

Buddhism known as *shakubuku* (lit., break and subdue).[33] Inoue explained that the harder the intended recipient resisted conversion, the more rigorous the application of *shakubuku* had to be. Yet, at the same time, when this method was employed, it had to be accompanied by a second component—compassion. Inoue explained,

> Mahāyāna Buddhism requires the exercise of compassion. However, this is not a question of always patting someone on the head or acting in a lukewarm manner. For example, there are times when the Buddha takes the form of Kannon [Skt., Avalokiteśvara, the embodiment of compassion] and embraces [those in need] with affection. On the other hand, there are figures like Fudō Myō-ō [Skt., Acala Vidyārāja, the Immovable One] who force an enemy to surrender [with his sword and lasso]. This is clearly written in the *Nirvāṇa Sūtra*. This is Mahāyāna compassion.
>
> Although I don't know much about the Nichiren sect, it is said that St. Nichiren taught a small good deed can turn into something heinous. I was greatly surprised when I encountered this teaching, but the reason a small good deed can turn into the opposite is because of great compassion. For example, [my Zen teachers] Azuma Soshin and Gempō-rōshi are truly men of precious and indescribable compassion. However, their compassion doesn't consist of just smiling and patting you on the head. When I was at Gempō-rōshi's temple, I was frightened out of my wits [by his sternness], but it is due to his great compassion that I became the man I am today. That's what *shakubuku* means. Pointing our pistols at the ruling classes and shooting them is like the figure of demon-conquering Fudō Myō-ō brandishing his sword. We don't deal with relative, conceptual ideas about compassion. But I think the kind of *shakubuku* I have just described is true, complete Mahāyāna compassion.[34]

In light of this, the judge wanted to know how Inoue viewed himself. Inoue answered,

> I live in revolution. I'm a revolutionary *unsui*. However, I'm not talking about whether or not the revolution is successful, for no matter what, I'm a revolutionary *unsui*. This is my entire life, my everything. That's the feeling I had. From the beginning I lived in Zen; therefore, I felt I was disciplining myself for the sake of the reform movement. That's all.[35]

In describing himself as an *unsui* (lit., cloud [and] water), Inoue once again revealed the impact Zen had on his life, for the term *unsui* is unique to the Zen school and refers to a novice priest in training who is regarded as the embodiment of impermanence, floating like clouds and flowing like water. It therefore represents the Buddhist ideal of nonattachment. At a deeper level, an *unsui* represents an enlightened priest who has actuated nonattachment in his life, the goal to which all Zen priests should strive. In Inoue's case, however, he was still clearly attached to one phenomenon—revolution.

In concluding his testimony, Inoue recited the following short poem:

> Dew taken up in the palm of the hand
> fades away in the summer morning.[36]

When the judge asked if he had anything left to say, Inoue began his reply with the most famous word in the Zen lexicon: *Mu*, a word that can be translated as "nothing" or "naught" but far transcends these meanings within the Zen school.[37]

Hishinuma Gorō's Testimony

It was Hishinuma Gorō who had shot and killed Dan Takuma as he arrived by car at the entrance to Mitsui Bank in Nihonbashi, Tokyo. Hishinuma explained the rationale behind his act as follows:

> It is the innate duty of Japanese citizens to always put the country first and self, second. If it is impossible to find a way out of the present situation facing the country using legal means to make those [in power] reflect on their conduct, then as a last resort it is necessary to employ [the strategy of] "killing one that many may live." It is necessary to slay the culprits with the demon-destroying sword that benefits others in order to reveal the truth and refute evil. I believed the only way to save the country was to cleanse it with the culprits' blood and therefore decided to participate in this incident sometime around October 1930.[38]

When the judge asked Hishinuma to explain what he hoped to accomplish by assassinating Dan, he replied, "In the first place, I wanted to wake up the sleeping citizens of this country. Secondly, I wanted to strike terror in the hearts of people like Dan. And finally, I hoped to encourage those comrades not yet involved to take action."[39] "Did you think about how you wished to reform the country?" the judge asked. "I didn't think about construction at all," Hishinuma replied, "only destruction."[40]

Upon being asked if he had anything additional to say, Hishinuma replied that he would like to share two spiritual incidents that had influenced his actions. The first occurred in October 1929 when he went to a nearby Shinto shrine to have his fortune told by an elderly female fortune-teller. The shrine was dedicated to Inari, the deity of plentiful rice harvests. At the time, Hishinuma was debating whether he should run away from home in order to continue his education in Tokyo. The fortune-teller first asked his age, and Hishinuma replied he was eighteen. The fortune-teller nodded, and then began to repeatedly chant the mantra *Namu-myōhō-renge-kyō* (I take refuge in the Wondrous Law of the *Lotus Sūtra*) some twenty to thirty times. She then let out a cry and said, "Listen well, eighteen-year old, you are definitely going to make a name for yourself. But you have to wait for the right time. If you go to Tokyo now, you won't succeed. Further, once you've made a name for himself, you must come back to this shrine and thank Inari for his aid. If you fail to do so, you'll be punished."[41]

Hishinuma didn't immediately take the fortune-teller's words seriously because he suspected she was trying to get him to return to the shrine in order to make more money. Therefore, he didn't put too much stock in what she had said. Later, however, reflecting on her words, he thought if what she was saying were true, that is to say, if he did make a name for himself by participating in a revolution and returned to the shrine to thank Inari, this would mean the (Shinto) deities endorsed his actions. Thinking this, he decided to do everything in his power to make a revolution.

The second incident Hishinuma spoke of is even more esoteric and magical. Once, when Onuma Shō and other band members were leaving his house after holding a religious service in March 1930, Hishinuma saw a "ball of fire" (*hi no tama*) fall from the heavens. He thought this was strange and wondered whether it was a good or evil omen. On reflection, he decided it was a good omen, for he knew of someone who had the same experience who said that deities manifested themselves as balls of fire in order to show their joy. The *Lotus Sūtra* and Inari were said to be like brother and sister. Given that the band members had just finished reciting the *daimoku* at his home, plus the fact that Inoue had brought along a related piece of calligraphy to give to him, Hishinuma was convinced that the deities had taken the form of a ball of fire to express their joy to the assembled youth. From this, Hishinuma concluded that the revolution they were planning represented the will of the gods, further encouraging him to participate.

Readers may well be surprised by these incidents: for example, the story of a fortune-teller at a Shinto shrine repeatedly reciting a Buddhist mantra, popularly known as the *daimoku* (title), in order to tell Hishinuma's fortune. In the first instance, it should be understood that itinerant fortune-tellers like the elderly woman are not Shinto clerics nor sponsored by the shrine. Instead, they merely rent space on the shrine grounds for their booths. Second, there is a very close relationship at the folk level between Shinto and Buddhism, so much so that in the minds of many lay believers the two religions are nearly one faith though with separate, albeit often overlapping, areas of efficacy. When it comes to esoteric rituals, including those related to fortune-telling, Buddhism is widely regarded as the more powerful of the two. At the same time, strange natural phenomena, such as "balls of fire," are the purview of Shinto deities, who are believed to not only control natural events but also to use them to send messages or omens to believers. And, of course, at least in prewar Japan, the emperor was revered as a direct descendant of the chief Shinto deity, the Sun goddess (Amaterasu-ōmikami), thus making him divine.

Hishinuma also testified to having been introduced to the teaching of St. Nichiren, and the practice of *zazen*, after joining the band. In response, the judge asked Hishinuma whether Nichiren's thinking had influenced his actions. Hishinuma replied, "I did not make a very deep study of Nichiren's teachings. Therefore, I was not influenced to take part in the revolution on the basis of his teachings."[42]

Finally, in one more sign of Shinto's influence on Hishinuma's actions, he recounted an episode that had occurred just days before he carried out the assassination. Then resident in Tokyo, and in anticipation of what he was about to do, Hishinuma went to pray at the city's best known Shinto shrine, Meiji Jingu. As its name suggests, it enshrines Emperor Meiji, reverently regarded as the father of modern Japan. Hishinuma explained his motivation for visiting this shrine as follows:

I don't really want to talk about this, but it is the truth so I will. At the time my conviction was still weak. First, I explained in my prayer that we pure-minded youth intended
to undertake our actions out of our utmost concern for the welfare of the country. If
our actions have your protection, I pray that you will grant us success. However, if His
Excellency [the emperor] thinks that our movement is truly bad for the country, I pray
that you will make not just me but all comrades fail.[43]

Even though nearly all of his comrades failed, Hishinuma was successful.

Yotsumoto Yoshitaka's Testimony

Like Inoue, Yotsumoto Yoshitaka killed no one though he nevertheless played
a major role in the incident. Additionally, of all Inoue's band members, including
Inoue himself, Yotsumoto would have the greatest impact on Japan's postwar political leaders. Yotsumoto's postwar role was that of a close advisor and backroom ma-
nipulator to at least nine prime ministers. This is not as surprising as it might seem
because as a student at Japan's prestigious Tokyo University, Yotsumoto was the best
educated member of the band.

Yotsumoto began his career as a right-wing activist soon after entering Tokyo
University in April 1928. It was there he joined the Shichisei-sha (lit., Seven Lives
Association), a name derived from a famous historical incident in which a samurai
general named Kusunoki Masashige (1294–1336) vowed, facing defeat, to be reborn
seven times in order to destroy the enemies of the emperor. Appropriately, the association's motto was "Repay the debt of gratitude owed the state, with loyalty and
utmost sincerity" (*shisei-ikkan-hōkoku-jinchū*). The association's real purpose was to
counter the growth of left-wing student activism on campus.

Yotsumoto began attending lectures at Kinkei Gakuen in the spring of 1930, and
in November of that year met Inoue for the first time. Although not initially, Yotsumoto soon became convinced Inoue was a pure and straightforward person, deeply
committed to the revolutionary reform of Japan. What he admired most about Inoue
was that he was a man of action who, unlike his other teachers, didn't speak about
revolution at the level of theory but was prepared to carry it out.

Yotsumoto was also attracted to the following two aspects of Inoue's teaching
about revolution:

> The first thing Inoue taught us was to come and follow him, doing as he did. Inoue said
> various things about revolution, but the first was that it entails destruction. We shouldn't
> say we can't do this because it's bad, or let's wait and see what'll happen. We are now
> in a situation where things have come to an impasse, so this is no time to talk about
> theory, only destruction. Even if you don't know what will come after, if something is
> bad, destroy it. Destroying something in the attempt to make it better can never result
> in making something bad.
>
> One more thing has to do with how we revolutionaries determine what is good or
> bad, right or wrong. We should make this determination using the masses as a mirror for

our actions. That is to say, if our actions are in accord with the happiness of the masses, then they are just. Further, and this is an important point, a revolution is not a question of engaging in some kind of work. Outside observers view revolution as simply work, regarding it as something apart from themselves, treating it as a plaything. But this is wrong, for you must live the revolution.

Those who treat revolution as a plaything are not revolutionary comrades. True revolutionary comrades are those who live the revolution and unite together as one. This is why Master [Inoue] never talked to us about things like revolutionary theory or logic. The first thing was for the Master and me to become one, truly one. It was only then that the two of us could, for the first time, engage in actual revolutionary work.[44]

Yotsumoto also testified about his first taste of Zen, something that had occurred even before meeting Inoue:

My family consisted of a long line of Shinto priests, and therefore I had no interest in Buddhism. However, around the time I graduated high school I started to feel I would like to try Zen and began reading various books about it. In university, I went to Seikenji Temple [in Shizuoka] every summer, where I did *zazen* and listened to the priests. The first summer I returned to Kagoshima after visiting the temple, but the second summer I stayed on to participate in their mental training program. Nothing special happened, but I found the Zen life suited me. I very much enjoyed eating with the monks training there as well cleaning the temple and grounds.

After going to Seikenji to practice Zen for the last time, I became convinced that I didn't need to train any further. At that point, I went to say goodbye to the temple priest. It was a very serious time for me in light of the various things that had happened the day before. When I met the priest, he started to criticize me severely. I had never imagined him attacking me so viciously and became really, really angry. However, as I got to know the priest better, I gradually came to understand what he was talking about. However, I imagine I didn't really understand what he was saying, but I acted as if I did.[45]

Upon his return to Kinkei Gakuen, Yotsumoto found a copy of the *Rinzai-roku* (Sayings of Master Rinzai) in the library. Zen master Rinzai Gigen (Ch., Línjì Yìxuán, d. 866 CE) was the founder of the Linji (J., Rinzai) school of Chan (J., Zen) Buddhism during the Tang Dynasty (618–907) in China. When Yotsumoto informed Inoue what he was reading, the latter recommended that upon waking in the morning he should immediately do *zazen* seated on his bedding for at least thirty minutes. Feeling that this book would make him wiser, Yotsumoto always kept it close by even though he admitted there were parts he didn't understand. "I think the *Rinzai-roku* influenced my thinking to some extent," Yotsumoto testified.[46] Unfortunately, the judge did not ask Yotsumoto to explain how the *Rinzai-roku* had influenced his thinking.

Yotsumoto did, however, testify on the important role *zazen* played in what he considered to be revolutionary action. Like Inoue, Yotsumoto also regarded himself as a "revolutionary *unsui*":

Although the amount of destruction we caused was small, it was nevertheless the first step in the revolution. Even though I consider it to have been just a little step toward revolution, I believe it was only natural for us to have followed this path. Therefore the *zazen* I practiced was revolutionary *zazen*. The books I read were read for the revolution. I was truly a revolutionary *unsui* [novice Zen monk].[47]

The judge also asked if he was acquainted with Kita Ikki. Yotsumoto replied,

Yes, I know Kita; he always talks about nothing but Buddhist sutras. There are those who say that a man of his ability and knowledge must be trying to hide something by feigning an interest in the sutras. However, from where I stand, that isn't true. Kita recites sutras in order to unify his spirit. . . . I know that when Kita recites sutras, it is different from the way Buddhist priests chant them as a means of getting donations. Kita uses a statue of Emperor Meiji as the object of worship in his altar at home. His statue is a small version of the statue of the emperor located in the Meiji Memorial Hall in Ōarai. Kita showed me this statue and said that revolution in Japan would come through revering this figure.[48]

It is noteworthy that in his discussion of Kita, Yotsumoto did not discuss, nor criticize, Kita's political leanings, for Kita was one of the main proponents of "national socialism" in Japan, albeit a clearly emperor-centric version of the ideology the Nazis had already embraced. This might be taken as a sign that, like many of the radical young officers in the right-wing revolutionary movement, Yotsumoto's goal was also the creation of a national socialist state. However, as the following testimony indicates, this was not the case:

There have been some young people of late who advocate the adoption of national socialism. However, when this ideology is examined, it is nothing but a left-wing fake, using left-wing terminology. These young people are attempting to get the masses to launch an insurrection. Further, they think things like Marxism or socialism will save society. Not only that, they attempt to attach the emperor or the national polity to this ideology, but I think this is a big mistake.[49]

As Yotsumoto's testimony shows, there were clearly significant differences of opinion among band members about what kind of state would emerge from their revolutionary activity. Yet these divergent opinions played no role in the actions of Inoue and those following him. As Yotsumoto's testimony, like that of Inoue, reveals, they all shared one conviction in common—destruction comes first. Yet the judge was curious why Yotsumoto imagined that assassinating just a few people would have much of an impact. Yotsumoto explained,

We felt we had no choice but to create something new by destroying Japan as it presently exists. Yet we never believed that with our small numbers we could successfully destroy the powerful, existing structure of the state with one blow. Nevertheless, we could throw a stone that would lead to a better nation. If Japan is eternal, then something new will be born. I believed we would be able to punch a hole in the large dike.[50]

Even so, the judge wanted to know, why had Yotsumoto failed to assassinate his intended victim? Yotsumoto explained,

My target was Makino Nobuaki [Lord Keeper of the Privy Seal and head of the Rikken Seiyūkai party]. . . . After having been forced to abandon my initial plan to assassinate him on February 11, I heard he sometimes went to Okitsu [in Shizuoka city]. I wondered if there might not be a chance to assassinate him when he went out walking, so I paid close attention to the newspapers. It was then I read Makino had been in Okitsu but returned to Tokyo on the day the newspaper was published. The newspaper was named something like the *Tokyo Taisei Shimbun*. At any rate, inasmuch as Makino was already back in Tokyo, I thought I'd missed a good opportunity.

"Didn't you have any other detailed plans?" the judge asked. "No, I had none," Yotsumoto answered.

Onuma Shō's Testimony

It will come as no surprise to read that Onuma Shō, assassin of former finance minister Inoue Junnosuke, began his testimony as follows:

> Our goal was not to harm others but to destroy ourselves. We had no thought of simply killing others while surviving ourselves. We intended to smash ourselves, thereby allowing others to cross over [to a new society] on top of our own bodies. I think this is what our master Inoue meant when he told us that our goal was not to sacrifice personal affections at the altar of justice but to destroy ourselves. In the process of destroying ourselves it couldn't be helped if there were [other] victims. This was the fundamental principle of our revolution. A mind of great compassion was the fundamental spirit of our revolution.[51]

Like both Inoue and Yotsumoto, Onuma stressed the importance of a "mind of great compassion." Employing Zen terminology, Onuma added, "We sought to extinguish Self itself."[52] Nevertheless, Onuma admitted to having been anxious when the time came to actually carry out his assignment. On the morning of the day of the assassination, he was so disturbed he wondered if he would actually be able to pull the trigger. It was at this point that he sought strength from his Buddhist training. Visiting the home of Inoue's wife in downtown Tokyo, Onuma asked for a room where he could conduct a Buddhist service. After setting up a makeshift altar, he first lit a stick of incense and then quietly recited four sections of the *Lotus Sūtra* to calm himself. Thereafter, he recited the *daimoku* four or five times before beginning to practice *zazen* in the full lotus posture. About this, Onuma said,

> After starting my practice of *zazen*, I entered a state of *samādhi* the likes of which I had never experienced before. I felt my spirit become unified, really unified, and when I opened my eyes from their half-closed meditative position I noticed the smoke from the incense curling up and touching the ceiling. At this point it suddenly came to me—I would be able to carry out [the assassination] that night.[53]

Onuma also testified about Yamamoto Gempō's role in the plot. While, as mentioned above, Yamamoto does not appear to have been directly involved, Onuma's court testimony makes it clear Yamamoto was aware, at least to some degree, of Inoue's plans. Onuma referred to Yamamoto's role as follows:

> Gempō-rōshi[54] said, "Inoue, the ideals you embrace will fail." Inoue, however, had never believed he would succeed; he knew he would fail. Although he knew he would fail, Inoue has devoted his life to revolution so there is neither success nor failure, only living. In living, there is neither success nor failure, for one simply lives unconsciously. It is only in comparing oneself with others that success or failure can be spoken of.
>
> Did Inoue vacillate because Yamamoto Gempō told him he would fail? No, he did not. It's because Inoue didn't vacillate that he was able to reach where he is today. Although he knew he would fail, he accomplished what he has because he knew that revolution is not a question of ideology, but living. Ordinarily, if someone is told they are going to fail, they would be shaken. Inoue, however, expressed his gratitude to Gempō-rōshi for his guidance, yet didn't drop his plans. He thought that it would be fine if he died, for his death would benefit the young people who came after him.[55]

As Onuma's testimony shows, Yamamoto was aware, at least in general terms, of Inoue's intentions. Although not necessarily opposed to Inoue's "ideals," Yamamoto nevertheless believed Inoue was bound to fail. In this, Yamamoto may be said to have been the more realistic of the two men. Yet it is clear that, as far as Inoue and his band members were concerned, success or failure meant nothing. Their only interest was in "living," even as they showed not the slightest concern for the deaths of their victims. As for Yamamoto, he still had an important role left to play.

Yamamoto Gempō's Defense

The September 15, 1934, morning edition of the *Asahi Shimbun* carried the following headline: "Zen Master Yamamoto Gempō, spiritual father of Inoue Nisshō, arrives in Tokyo to testify in court. Yamamoto claims, 'I'm the only one who understands his [Inoue's] state of mind.'"[56] Commencing his testimony at 11:10 a.m., Gempō stated,

> The first thing I would like to say is that Inoue has engaged in spiritual cultivation for many years. This led him to a direct realization of the most important element in religion—the true nature of the mind, something Buddhism calls perfect wisdom. Perfect wisdom is like a mirror that reflects humans, heaven, earth, and the universe. Inoue further realized that the true form of humans, heaven, earth, and the universe is no different than the true form of the Self. The manifestation of this truth of the universe is the Spirit of Japan, that is to say, the polity of Japan. It is in these things that Inoue's spirit is to be found.
>
> In light of the events that have befallen our nation of late, there is, apart from those who are selfish and evil, no fair and upright person who would criticize the accused for their actions in connection with the Blood Oath Corps and subsequent May 15 Incidents. Since agreeing to appear in court on behalf of the defendants, I have received several tens of letters. All of these letters, with but one exception, have expressed support for the defendants, identifying their actions as being at one with the national spirit.

Notwithstanding this, however, it is utterly impossible to express by the spoken or written word the true meaning and intent of either Inoue or those allied with him in these two incidents.

No doubt there are those who would ask why, in light of his devotion to religion, a believer in Buddhism like Inoue would act as he did? This is especially true given that Buddhism attaches primary importance to social harmony as well as repaying the four debts of gratitude owed others and practicing the ten virtues.[57]

It is true that if, motivated by an evil mind, someone should kill so much as a single ant, as many as one hundred and thirty-six hells await that person. This holds true not only in Japan but in all the countries of the world. Yet the Buddha, being absolute, has stated that when there are those who destroy social harmony and injure the polity of the state, then even if they are called good men, killing them is not a crime.

Although all Buddhist statuary manifests the spirit of Buddha, there are no Buddhist statues, other than those of Shakyamuni Buddha and Amida Buddha, who do not grasp the sword. Even the guardian Kṣitigarbha Bodhisattva holds, in his manifestation as a victor in war, a spear in his hand. Thus Buddhism, which has as its foundation the true perfection of humanity, has no choice but to cut down even good people in the event they seek to destroy social harmony.

Although Inoue came to visit me in the midst of his spiritual training, I most definitely did not give him my sanction [i.e., confirming him as being fully enlightened] nor say that his practice was complete.

Thus, on December 14 of last year [1933], I received a letter from Inoue stating that now more than ever he wished to become a Buddha, that is to say, to realize the fundamental unity of the universe and Self and become one with all things. Since then, I have visited him [in prison] and verified his intention. The [Buddha] Dharma is like a great ocean; the further one enters into it, the deeper it becomes. I believe that Inoue's true work is set to begin from this point onward. However, in the event he were to be sentenced to death, his wish would remain unfulfilled. This much I can vouch for.

Inoue's hope is not only for the victory of Imperial Japan, but he also recognizes that the well-being of all the colored races (i.e., their life, death, or possible enslavement) is dependent on the Spirit of Japan. There is, I am confident, no one who does not recognize this truth.

Although there is much more I would like to say, I have no doubt that both the lawyers for the defense who have thoroughly researched this case, as well as each one of the judges present who, possessed of a truly pure mind, graciously adjudicate it, are well aware of what I have to say.

At this point the defendants are not thinking of themselves, but state they have entrusted themselves to the judgment of the law. For my part, I am absolutely certain they have truly become one with the spirit of the gods and Buddhas.[58]

Given that Buddhism's first precept, binding for clerics and laity alike, is "not to kill," Yamamoto's claim that because the Buddha is "absolute . . . then even if they are called good men, killing them is not a crime" is one of the most chilling statements in Buddhist history. The Buddhist basis for Yamamoto's testimony will be explored further in chapter 14.

VERDICT AND AFTERMATH

As expected, Inoue and the members of his band were all found guilty and sentenced on November 22, 1934. Inoue and the two actual assassins were given life sentences, while the others received sentences ranging from fifteen down to as few as three years. While the sentences for the three chief defendants were severe, as Yamamoto had hoped, none of them were sentenced to death, as the state prosecutor had demanded. As the following paragraph in the verdict reveals, the judge clearly expressed some sympathy, or at least understanding, of the "nondualistic" Buddhist motivation for the defendants' actions:

> [The defendants maintain that] to overthrow the old system of organization is a destructive or negative act. To establish the new system of organization is a constructive or positive act. Without destruction, however, there can be no construction. Since ultimate denial is the same as genuine affirmation, destruction is itself construction, and the two are one and inseparable.[59]

In this formulation, the judge demonstrated his familiarity with the Madhyamaka school of Buddhist thought, including as it does an emphasis on the identity of opposites (J., *sokuhi*). In the Zen sect, a central theme of many *kōans* is this identity of opposites, pointing to an original nonduality. In turn, the recognition or realization of nonduality forms the core of Zen "enlightenment" (*kenshō*, aka *satori*). Given this, one is forced to confront the question of what doctrine or teaching exists in the Zen sect that would have prevented the identification of "destruction" with "construction," even when this consisted of terrorist acts directed against innocent civilians. Once again, this question will be revisited in chapter 14.

10

Imprisonment

The Zen of Pasting Envelopes

The sentences Inoue and members of his band received were, especially by Japanese standards, clearly on the lenient side. Nevertheless, they faced many years in prison—Inoue, Onuma, and Hishinuma for the rest of their lives. At the beginning of December 1934, Inoue, together with Onuma, Hishinuma, Yotsumoto, and one other, were transferred to Kosuge Prison in Tokyo, while the remaining nine convicted band members were sent to prisons near their homes. The immediate question all faced was how to spend their time in prison. For his part, Inoue decided to regard his prison cell as a Buddhist priest's hermitage, especially as he was placed in solitary confinement.

As for the required prison work, Inoue chose to paste envelopes since the repetitive nature of this work would provide him with the opportunity to focus his mind. "I felt like being in a Zen meditation hall," he wrote, "but now I pasted envelopes together just as I once practiced *zazen* using *kōan* to enter *samādhi*."[1] In early February 1935, however, Inoue fell victim to neuralgia that affected his entire body, especially his face. He was placed in the prison infirmary until he recovered sufficiently to be returned to his cell at the end of March.

Unskilled with his fingers, Inoue was only able to paste about one hundred and fifty envelopes per day when he started, but by June he could do a thousand a day and soon reached twenty-five hundred. He was so good that even his guards praised him. Inoue was greatly encouraged by their praise since he had never succeeded in using his hands like this before. "If one tries hard, it can definitely be done, so I'll do it!" Inoue said to himself and worked even harder.[2]

The prison guards couldn't help but notice how dedicated Inoue was to his work. They would say, "Inoue, you needn't work so hard. Take a break!" or "Today's a holiday, so relax like everyone else."[3] In response, Inoue would just smile and continue working. What the guards didn't realize is that by virtue of the repetitive nature of pasting envelopes, Inoue was able to enter *samādhi* with its attendant lucid mental state. At times, he was able to experience the same truth of a non-dualistic universe that he had intuitively encountered when training at Santoku-an. Thus, he spent his days contentedly, engrossed in the joy of the Dharma.

Yet it was Inoue's apparent self-satisfaction, or self-sufficiency, that raised another question in the guards' minds. Given Inoue's Buddhist background, why, they wondered, had he never asked for a visit from the prison's Buddhist chaplain. When the guards spoke about this with the head of the prison's education section, he called Inoue to his office and asked:

You've never once asked to see the [True Pure Land sect–affiliated] prison chaplain. Is it because you belong to a different sect of Buddhism?

Inoue: No, that's not it. I simply have no need of a chaplain.

Section head: That can't be true given your responsibility for such a big incident. You can't claim to have no earthly passions.

Inoue: Well, if you insist, let me ask you this: who is more precious, Amida Buddha or the emperor?

(Silence)

Inoue: According to the Shin (True Pure Land) sect, Amida Buddha's Pure Land is more than ten billion [Buddha]lands to the West. When you sermonize about this, you often say that is where the merciful and compassionate Amida Buddha is to be found. Have you ever been to the Pure Land? Have you ever met Amida Buddha?

(Silence accompanied by an angry look)

Inoue: Well then, you believe in something you've never seen and a place you've never been to! And let me add that I've visited the Pure Land and met Amida Buddha. Not only that, the Amida Buddha I met is not the vacuous one you talk about.

(Silence accompanied by a quizzical look)

Inoue: The Amida Buddha I'm talking about is the emperor!

(Looking astonished)

Inoue: In the first place, Amida Buddha is not someone out there, for no matter how hard you look for Amida in the sutras you won't find him. Amida Buddha was created simply to symbolize the human virtue of compassion. How fortunate we [Japanese] are to have been favored with an emperor who is richly endowed with the virtue of compassion. In other words, Amida Buddha is enshrined within the emperor.

Impressed, the section head said, "Inoue, you say some clever things!"

Deeply offended by his words, Inoue responded: "What do you mean by saying I speak cleverly? I'm not using flattery!" The section head looked stunned. Inoue continued, "If you think what I've said is nothing more than flattery, how about if I make the content of our conversation public and let the public decide. Is that what you want?" Frightened by what might be seen as a lack of respect for the emperor, the section head humbly apologized to Inoue and retracted his words.[4]

As in his past references, Inoue revealed his utmost reverence for the emperor, elevating him to the status of a Buddha, or at least possessing the compassion of a Buddha. This reverence for the emperor was, of course, one of the distinguishing characteristics of all right-wing activists at the time. No matter how much their agenda for social reform may, in certain aspects, have overlapped with the left wing, the near absolute reverence for the emperor was a major, if not insurmountable, barrier separating the two groups. Nevertheless, some ultrarightists, including those at the highest echelons of the military, were prepared to manipulate the emperor to achieve their goals of social reform. Inoue was definitely not one of them.

PRISON CORRUPTION

Inoue also made it clear that he had a very poor opinion of the section head, who the above conversation suggests may have doubled as the prison chaplain, though Inoue doesn't say this. Inoue does, however, explain exactly why he not only disliked but actually despised the section head—he was corrupt. Specifically, Inoue learned that the section head regularly accepted bribes in return for favors.

The Japanese penal system was such that it was possible to receive a temporary release from prison if a prisoner's good conduct was attested to by the prison's education section. While the final decision was made by the Ministry of Justice, the first and crucial step was to receive the support of the head of the education section. Inoue first learned of this arrangement in connection with one of the civilians convicted and incarcerated in the same prison for his role in the May 15 Incident. Typically, it was the family of the convicted prisoner who paid the necessary bribes, but in this case it was the medical company where the convicted civilian once worked that paid a bribe, not only to the head of the education section but to the prison warden and other section heads.

In short, all of the leading prison staff were taking bribes, but there was nothing Inoue could do about it other than be angry and write the facts down in a little "black book" he kept. This was the reason why Inoue had become so angry when the section chief referred to the "clever words" Inoue used during their conversation. In Inoue's eyes, it was the section head's "clever words" that had secured him, and other prison officials, bribes amounting to tens of thousands of yen. Inoue soon learned this was not the only example of prison corruption.

A second scam was related to the prison's haiku poetry club. Inoue had firmly refused to join such a club when initially imprisoned, believing that he lacked the necessary poetic talent. However, as time passed, Inoue changed his opinion. One day, engrossed in the *samādhi* of pasting envelopes, Inoue realized,

The mental state of haiku is the same as pasting envelopes! There are no haiku apart from me, for nature and I are one. The physical expression of this reality is what haiku are all about. Whether written skillfully or not is just a matter of technique, not the essence of haiku. As long as they're not connected to anyone else, it'll be fine for me to compose haiku about my own life.[5]

Following this insight, Inoue joined the prison haiku club and soon found his haiku earning praise and being reprinted in outside poetry journals. Yet here, too, Inoue found corruption, for the very person who had first encouraged Inoue to start writing poetry, the prison's medical doctor, was engaged in illegal practices. Specifically, the doctor and other medical personnel in the Justice Ministry were using the prison's printing facilities, operated by prisoners, to publish a medical journal on prison medicine, distributed nationally, with a paid subscriber base of more than two thousand medical professionals. Inasmuch as the journal was printed in the prison, using prison labor and paper, there were no production costs. The prison doctor and other medical personnel involved simply pocketed the subscription income. Thanks to a few honest, lower-level prison employees who were disgusted by the corruption going on around them, Inoue learned of more and more cases like these but still could do nothing about it.

THE FEBRUARY 26 INCIDENT

Just as Inoue was facing increasing turmoil in prison, a momentous event took place outside of it. Known by the date of its occurrence, February 26, 1936, the February 26 Incident was the largest military insurrection in Japan's modern history. Nearly fifteen hundred soldiers under the command of twenty-five young right-wing army officers attempted a coup d'état in hopes of purging the government and military of leaders whom they deemed responsible for a corrupt and unjust society. "To cut away the evil ministers and military factions near the emperor and destroy their heart: that is our duty and we will complete it," they wrote in their manifesto.[6]

The young officers and their subordinates initially succeeded in assassinating several leading officials, including Lord Keeper of the Privy Seal Saitō Makoto (1858–1936), Finance Minister Takahashi Korekiyo (1854–1936), and the relatively moderate Inspector General of Military Education General Watanabe Jōtarō (1874–1936). The rebels also seized the Army Ministry and the Metropolitan Police Headquarters in central Tokyo. Their actions, they believed, would bring about a Shōwa Restoration, restoring full political power to the emperor and eliminating fractious political parties, corrupt ministers, and *zaibatsu* manipulation.

Although by no means united in their ideological goals, the young officers believed that once political power had been restored to the emperor, the latter would, as a benevolent ruler, initiate massive social change at home in line with the emperor-centric, national socialist–oriented ideology of Kita Ikki as well as other reformers focused on the plight of the nation's rural poor. In addition, they expected the emperor to significantly increase military expenditures for the army.

While not involved in the rebellion, Inoue nevertheless stood to be one of its first beneficiaries, for prominent among the young officers' slogans was "Attack Kosuge Prison and free Inoue!"[7] Thus, had the rebellion been successful, Inoue stood to be released if not immediately then soon after the creation of a new government. However, the immediate effect of the rebellion was a frantic call by the head of the prison to the metropolitan police requesting reinforcements to fend off a possible attack.

Despite the large numbers of soldiers involved, the rebellion ultimately ended in failure, like so many in the past. In the first instance, the rebels were unsuccessful in their attempts to assassinate Prime Minister Keisuke Okada (1868–1952) and secure control of the most important prize of all, the Imperial Palace. While coup supporters in the higher echelons of the army, including Generals Araki Sadao and Mazaki Jinzaburō, tried to support the rebels behind the scenes, they were ultimately unsuccessful.

The fundamental reason for the rebellion's failure was the implacable opposition of the figure in whose name the rebellion had been waged—Emperor Hirohito (1901–1989). Far from endorsing their actions, Hirohito ordered loyal elements of the army and navy to move against the rebels, employing force if necessary. He had been deeply offended by the killing of his ministers and the movement of troops without his permission. Encircled by twenty thousand government troops and twenty-two tanks, the young officers had no choice but to surrender on the afternoon of February 29, ordering their troops to return to their barracks.

Unlike previous examples of right-wing political violence involving the military, this coup attempt had severe consequences. In the first instance, the rebel officers were immediately tried in closed military tribunals, without defense lawyers or the opportunity to garner public support for their actions. Nineteen of the uprising's leaders, including two civilians, Kita Ikki and Nishida Mitsugi, were found guilty of mutiny and sentenced to death, while forty more were imprisoned. The rebellion marked the last attempt by those in the army seeking domestic social reform to influence the government. In the face of the emperor's staunch opposition, their cause was doomed.

The young officers, together with higher-echelon supporters like Generals Araki Sadao and Mazaki Jinzaburō, composed the radical right wing of the army, known as the Imperial Way Faction (Kōdō-ha). The Imperial Way Faction envisioned a return to an idealized preindustrialized, pre-Westernized Japan, in which social reform was to be enacted through the elimination of corrupt bureaucrats, opportunistic politicians, and greedy *zaibatsu* capitalists. Following the declaration of a Shōwa Restoration, the state would be run directly by Emperor Hirohito (aka by his reign name, Shōwa) with the assistance, if not direction, of the military. War with the Soviet Union would be necessary in order to eliminate the threat posed by communism. They believed military spirit, as expressed in the *Bushidō* code, could overcome any deficiency in weaponry.

The effective demise of the Imperial Way Faction opened the way for the Control Faction (Tōsei-ha) to emerge as the main, if not exclusive, center of power within the military. The Control Faction recognized that future wars would be total wars, requiring the cooperation of the bureaucracy and *zaibatsu*-affiliated corporate leaders to maximize Japan's industrial and military capacity. The Control Faction, under the leadership of General Tōjō Hideki, sought to avoid war with the militarily powerful Soviet Union, instead striking south into the militarily weak countries of China and Southeast Asia, especially the oil- and mineral-rich Dutch East Indies (today's Indonesia).[8] If this brought Japan into conflict with the Western powers, including the United States, so be it.

It must be stressed that both factions shared the common belief that national defense should be strengthened through a reform of national politics. Both factions borrowed ideas from totalitarian, fascist, and national socialist political philosophies, sharing a strong skepticism of, if not outright opposition to, political party politics and representative democracy. Additionally, although Control Faction followers took control of the army, the Imperial Way Faction ideals of spiritual power and imperial mysticism remained embedded in the army and, albeit to a lesser extent, the navy. Following the conclusion of the Tripartite Pact on September 27, 1940, Control Faction leaders also believed they had an invincible military partner in the form of Nazi Germany.

As for Inoue, his memoirs are strangely silent regarding his view of the coup. This is despite his earlier association with Gen. Araki and the young navy officers who tended to support the Imperial Way Faction, especially its emphasis on spiritual power. On the one hand, Inoue makes it clear that he was aware of the rebels' demand for his release. At the same time, he wrote that the rebels' demand actually caused his incarceration to be extended. "Due to the uprising, I lost my opportunity to be released from prison," he wrote.[9] This is a surprising comment in light of the fact that in 1936 Inoue was only in the second year of a life sentence.

Inoue's comment is explained by the fact that he already knew he only faced three years in prison thanks to his father, who brought him this news during a prison visit. "Tell Inoue he only has to serve three years," Tōyama Mitsuru told his father.[10] Tōyama made this prediction because he was aware Count Tanaka Mitsuaki had appealed for leniency to then president of the House of Peers Konoe Fumimarō. In turn, Konoe appealed directly to Emperor Hirohito.[11] It is also noteworthy that despite the rebellion, Inoue was granted a one-day parole in order to attend the funeral of his father, who had died on Inoue's birthday, April 12, 1936. This was the first time in modern Japanese penal history such permission had been granted.[12]

Whether Inoue's pique at having to remain in prison for an extended period was the sole reason for Inoue's uncharacteristic silence regarding the February 26 Incident is unknown. Inasmuch as Inoue was clearly opposed to "military cliques" of any kind encroaching on the emperor's prerogatives, this may be part of the explanation. At the same time, Inoue may not have criticized the rebellion because, as he and his band frequently stated, they were only interested in "destruction."

It is also noteworthy that Inoue failed to mention the Zen training of many of the young officers in the February 26 Incident as well as the earlier Aizawa Incident. In the latter incident, Zen-trained and Imperial Way–affiliated Lieutenant Colonel Aizawa Saburō assassinated General Nagata Tetsuzan, a leader of the Control Faction, on August 12, 1935. Interested readers will find details concerning Zen's connection to both incidents in appendices 1 and 2.

CLEANING HOUSE

The February 26 Incident did not lessen Inoue's interest in seeking internal prison reform in the least. His chance finally came in September 1938 with the arrival of a new prison head. Although those prison officials fearing his revelations prevented a meeting with the new prison head for more than a month, Inoue eventually prevailed. The new prison head answered affirmatively when Inoue asked if he would be willing to eliminate corruption in the prison, leading to the following exchange:

Inoue: I trust you realize it won't be sufficient simply to have the willingness to address the corruption. If done poorly, it could cost your life. Are you still willing to do it?

Prison head: Like others, I value my life, but as a government official I have a duty to perform so, yes, I would certainly address any corruption.

Inoue: Since arriving here, I imagine that every section head has given you various reports and will continue to do so, but you mustn't believe any of them. At the same time, you mustn't immediately believe what I'm about to tell you either. It's your job to compare my words with theirs and decide for yourself who is correct. After you determine that what I'm telling you is the truth, then I want you to take action.

Prison head: I understand.[13]

After this exchange, Inoue revealed everything he knew. The prison head took a week to check on the facts and informed Inoue he had determined that everything Inoue told him was true. Thereafter, the reforms began, and Inoue drew close, so close to the prison head that not only was he appointed as an assistant to the head of the education section but he was released from solitary confinement and given freedom to go anywhere in the prison. One of the first things Inoue did was to start a haiku poetry club for interested prisoners, gathering them together on a regular basis.

RETRIBUTION

Unsurprisingly, when the prison head started putting his reforms in place, the corrupt officials quickly realized the source of his information. At first, they initiated low-level attacks against Inoue, for example by informing officials in the Justice Ministry about what they claimed was the falling work output of prisoners who participated in Inoue's haiku club meetings. This resulted in a formal investigation, but much to the chagrin of the corrupt officials, the results showed that participating prisoners' work output actually increased. Inoue was also surprised by this because other than when the guards walked by, he spent his time joking and telling stories to the members of the haiku group. However, this turned out to be exactly what the prisoner participants needed, for by relieving stress and making them feel better about themselves, their output increased.

But the corrupt officials didn't give up. In particular, the prison doctor, who lost a sizable, illicit income, was determined to have his revenge and, moreover, was in a position to do so. Inoue continued to suffer not only from neuralgia but from heart trouble as well. When Inoue consulted the doctor, he was simply told there was nothing to worry about and given a minimal prescription that had no effect. Fortunately, there was a second, young medical doctor on the prison staff who took a liking to Inoue and secretly gave him appropriate injections. However, when the corrupt doctor learned of this, he arranged with his medical cronies in the Ministry of Justice to have the young doctor moved to another prison.

Although Inoue's health recovered, his trials were not yet at an end. When Inoue subsequently came down with a serious case of dysentery, the prison doctor had another chance to strike. This time, the doctor gave Inoue a prescription that he would later learn had nothing to do with curing dysentery. Instead, it had the effect of further injuring his heart to the point that he couldn't sleep at night. The doctor planned to use Inoue's dysentery as a cover for causing heart failure. Fortunately, by this time the prison warden had grown suspicious and intervened, replacing the doctor just in time to save Inoue's life. On reflection, Inoue realized he was the one who first believed the warden's life would be endangered if he attempted to reform the prison. However, it turned out to be Inoue's own life that came close to ending.

TENKŌ (CONVERSION)

Inoue's newfound freedom of movement inside the prison came at a price. The warden asked Inoue to conduct personal interviews with those left-wing "thought criminals" (*shisō-han*) who were imprisoned for having violated the Public Order Preservation Act of April 1925. The thought criminals to be interviewed claimed to have discarded their left-wing beliefs as a result of undergoing *tenkō* (ideological conversion). *Tenkō* was a program that relied on social pressure and induced feelings of guilt, but also coercion, to turn leftists into loyal subjects of the emperor. Initially, this was done by making the prisoners recognize the shame their disloyal conduct and beliefs had brought on their families, a very effective tactic in a family-oriented, Confucian society. The coercion aspect came from the fact that it was only after having undergone *tenkō* that thought prisoners were eligible to be set free.

Inoue's work consisted of determining whether those claiming to have undergone *tenkō* had genuinely done so. There was always the lingering suspicion among both police and prosecutors that those who made this claim had only done so in order to hasten their release. One of the best known of these prisoners was Tanaka Seigen (1906–1993), onetime chairman of the Japanese Communist Party Central Committee. He had been arrested in July 1930 after leading the party in conducting armed terrorist attacks against the police. Although Tanaka issued a *tenkō* statement in 1933, he was still suspect. Inoue got all of the targeted thought prisoners together and held the following conversation based on the basic Buddhist doctrine of the impermanence of all things.

Inoue: All of you believe that materialism is the absolute truth, right?

Prisoners: Yes, we do.

Inoue: In that case, let me ask you, what are material objects?

Pointing to tables and chairs, the prisoners said, "These things."

Inoue: The things you pointed to are changing, moment by moment. In other words, nothing in all of existence possesses an unchanging essence. Isn't it clear that making such unstable things the basis of your theories precludes them from ever becoming absolute truth?

None of the prisoners was able to reply, so Inoue continued: "*Tenkō* means to change the direction your life had up to this point and head in a different direction. However, while you have discarded communist theories, you all have completely failed to find a new direction. You're not someone who has done *tenkō* but simply someone who is dead. Given this, it would be manlier to never claim to have done *tenkō* at all!"[14]

Following this exchange, Inoue interviewed the prisoners one by one, but his opinion remained unchanged—none of them had been through the complete change *tenkō* required. The only prisoners who even came close were those few who had participated in Inoue's haiku group. Inoue then reported his findings to the warden, including, of course, his negative assessment of Tanaka Seigen. Possibly due to his assessment, Tanaka remained in prison for eleven years, not gaining release until 1941. It was, in fact, not until Inoue's Zen master Yamamoto Gempō visited Tanaka in prison that he completely disavowed communism.[15] This is not surprising, for Inoue himself enjoyed regular prison visits from Yamamoto, under whose guidance he continued to practice *kōan*-centered meditation.

Likewise, it is not surprising that the prison authorities had requested Yamamoto to speak to Tanaka, for Buddhist priests were prized for their ability to promote *tenkō* among left-wing prisoners. In particular, Zen priests were prized for their ability to speak to prisoners in a down-to-earth, readily understood manner, emphasizing the Confucian virtue of not bringing disgrace on the family. As for Tanaka, in the postwar period, he became a well-known anticommunist activist, successful construction company president, and influential behind-the-scenes fixer for a number of prime ministers. In this, Tanaka played a role similar to Yotsumoto Yoshitaka in the postwar era.

GREAT TREASON INCIDENT (*TAIGYAKU JIKEN*)

There was one other prisoner who caught Inoue's attention, a Korean by the name of Park Yeol (Japanese pronunciation, Boku Retsu, 1902–1974). Park was a political activist who had embraced both political anarchism and nihilism. He and his common-law wife, Kaneko Fumiko (1903–1926), were arrested and placed in "protective confinement" (*hogo kensoku*) two days after the Great Kanto Earthquake of September 1, 1923. Following the earthquake, false rumors spread throughout Tokyo alleging that Korean residents in the area had begun a revolt, setting fires, poisoning wells, raping, looting, and organizing an army. These rumors led to a sudden wave of killings of Koreans in the disaster area, with more than six thousand Korean men, women, and children murdered at the hands of vigilante groups, police, and soldiers.[16]

On the one hand, the government eventually set up camps to protect remaining Koreans from vigilante attacks. In the case of Park and Kaneko, however, the motivation for their arrest was not to protect them but rather to show that the rampage had been justified because of the existence of Korean radicals. Under questioning, Park and Kaneko admitted they had once discussed the possibility of assassinating then Crown Prince Hirohito. Although their discussion never went beyond the talking stage, this was deemed sufficient to charge and convict them of high treason. Although initially sentenced to hang, their sentences were subsequently reduced to life imprisonment. Kaneko, however, died in prison on July 23, 1936, allegedly at her own hands. Prison officials stated she hung herself but allowed no independent investigation to verify the claim.

This was not the first time that charges of high treason had been used as the pretext for getting rid of left-wing activists. The precedent was set in 1910 when twenty-six anarcho-socialists were arrested for their alleged participation in a plot to kill one or more members of the imperial family. All of them were convicted and twenty-four sentenced to death, though later twelve had their sentences commuted to life imprisonment. Among the twenty-six were three Buddhist priests, two of whom were affiliated with the Zen school. One of these, Sōtō Zen priest Uchiyama Gudō (b. 1874), was hung together with eleven others on the morning of January 24, 1911. Uchiyama had dared to criticize the imperial system in an underground pamphlet he produced.[17]

Park, however, was still alive, giving Inoue an opportunity to listen to his story. Inoue did not question Park's guilt, but he was concerned about the treatment Park received in prison. From Inoue's viewpoint, Park was already imprisoned and serving his sentence. Therefore, there was no need to further mistreat him, yet that was exactly what was happening. Prior to being transferred to Kosuge Prison, Park had been incarcerated in a prison located outside of Tokyo in Chiba prefecture. While there, Park reported having been the object of cruel treatment by the prison guards. Even after his transfer to Kosuge, his harsh treatment continued. In the face of this, Inoue admired Park's earnestness and tried his best to comfort him. At the same time, he admonished the guards, saying, "You all lack compassion. If you truly understood the August Mind of the Emperor, you would not treat Park so cruelly."[18]

Park was eventually released from prison, but not until October 27, 1945. It was Japan's defeat that made this possible. Park took advantage of the opportunity to create a Korean residents' association for the tens of thousands of Koreans remaining in Japan. He eventually decided to return to Korea but ended up being taken prisoner by communist forces during the Korea War. In North Korea, Park wrote he had accepted communism, but according to Tanaka Seigen, Park was nevertheless suspected of being a South Korean spy and shot in 1974. As for Inoue, his release from prison was drawing near.

FREE AT LAST

Readers will recall Inoue had been incarcerated in Kosuge Prison since December 1934. Despite his life sentence, Inoue's father had relayed a message from Tōyama Mitsuru that he would only have to serve three years. However, a series of further right-wing incidents, culminating with the February 26 Incident of 1936, put a hold on Inoue's release. Nevertheless, on November 16, 1938, Inoue's sentence was reduced from life to twenty years. Two years later, on February 11, 1940, on the occasion of Japan's National Foundation Day (Kigensetsu), it was reduced further to fifteen years. This last reduction was especially important in that Inoue was now eligible for parole; incarcerated for slightly more than five years, he had served the legally required one-third of his sentence. Finally, on October 17, 1940, Inoue was released on parole in honor of the mythical 2,600th anniversary of the founding of the Japanese state.

Normally, as far as Inoue's imprisonment is concerned, this would have ended the matter, but it didn't. On April 29, 1941, on the occasion of the emperor's birthday, Inoue was granted an unprecedented special pardon (J., *tokusha*) in which Inoue's very conviction was rescinded. Inoue noted, "The action to declare my conviction null and void was the first of its kind in Japanese penal history."[19] This meant the slate was wiped clean; Inoue no longer had a criminal record of any kind. Those members of Inoue's band still in prison, including Onuma, Hishinuma and Yotsumoto, were also amnestied at the same time, in the name of promoting national unity.[20]

Although Inoue was free, without the stigma of a criminal record, he once again found himself unemployed and penniless. At that point, he had no idea he would soon be invited to accept a position unlike that offered few, if any, terrorists in history. One of the most important events in his life still lay in the future.

11

From Prison Cell to Prime Minister's Estate

This chapter focuses on the relationship between two men that can only be called amazing, if not nearly unbelievable. Reflecting the political milieu of the day, Inoue, convicted head of a band of terrorists, was invited by the prime minister of Japan, Prince Konoe Fumimarō (1891–1945), to become his live-in advisor and confidant. Borrowing words from Inoue's trial testimony, what happened reveals just how "clouded over" Japan's national polity had become.

The process began with fifty-four-year-old Inoue's release from prison a little after 1 p.m. on October 17, 1940. As one might expect, Inoue's wife and daughter were waiting for him with a change of clothing as was his lawyer. However, they were not alone, for Yotsumoto Yoshitaka and other members of Inoue's band who had already been paroled were there to welcome him as were scores of other ultranationalist supporters. There were so many that it took a fleet of nearly twenty cars to hold them all as they accompanied Inoue on a very important pilgrimage, a pilgrimage that began with a visit to the Shinto Daijingu shrine in central Tokyo.

The purpose of the visit to Daijingu shrine, enshrining the Sun goddess Amaterasu, progenitor of the imperial family, was to prepare Inoue for an even more important event—a visit to the outer grounds of the Imperial Palace. First, however, Inoue had to undergo a series of purification ceremonies, employing a combination of water and salt, to ritually cleanse him. The final purification ceremony consisted of drinking cold *sake* offered in the same bright red lacquered cup used in traditional wedding ceremonies. This point wasn't lost on Inoue, for after drinking the *sake* he said, "Well, now I am married to the gods (*kami*) of Japan and the national polity."[1]

Ritually cleansed, and wearing a traditional kimono emblazoned with his family crest, Inoue proceeded to the outer grounds of the Imperial Palace. After everyone accompanying him had lined up beside him, Inoue kneeled down on the rough gravel with his legs tucked beneath him in the formal Japanese sitting posture (*seiza*). Hands placed on the ground in front of him, Inoue made a deep vow of obeisance in the direction of the emperor, who remained, as ever, at the center of his life. Thereafter, Inoue worshipped at the major shrine dedicated to Emperor Meiji—that is, Meiji Shrine—before paying his respects to Tōyama Mitsuru. Only then was Inoue able to go to live with his wife and her family in Tokyo.

Inoue's wife had visited him regularly in prison, but, with a long history of illness, she was now sick again. However, following Inoue's release from prison her health improved. This was fortunate because a steady stream of visitors kept his wife busy. Inoue's visitors, many whom he knew but others not, all stopped by to congratulate him on his release. At the same time, following eight years of imprisonment, Inoue found it difficult to adjust to his newfound freedom, especially as so much had occurred in his absence.

Once things calmed down, Inoue again called on the man to whom he owed so much —Tōyama Mitsuru. Upon meeting, Inoue said, "From today onward, I am going to call you father. In my late father's will, he told me to regard you as my father and serve you as if I were serving him."[2] The two men then exchanged *sake* cups in a time-honored Japanese tradition made all the more significant because, according to Inoue, this was the only time Tōyama is known to have consumed alcohol.

Inoue asked Tōyama to introduce him to someone in need of a political advisor or consultant. In response, Tōyama contacted Ogawa Gōtarō (1876–1945), an economist, educator, politician, and most importantly, railways minister in the cabinet of Prime Minister Konoe Fumimarō. According to Inoue, Ogawa and Tōyama had been jointly responsible for making Konoe the powerful politician he was. Ogawa repeatedly urged Inoue to meet Konoe, but Inoue initially hesitated to do so.

Inoue's hesitation was not because he disliked Konoe, for although the two men had never met, Inoue was aware that as early as June 1937 (i.e., during his first term as prime minister) Konoe had sought, albeit unsuccessfully, to arrange a general amnesty for Inoue and the other imprisoned members of his band. Then, in March 1941, Inoue received an unexpected telephone call requesting a meeting. Inoue initially thought the call was from Konoe's secretary, but it turned out to be from Konoe himself. Taking this as proof of his sincerity, Inoue agreed to a meeting at the prime minister's residence. On the appointed day, Konoe was late for the meeting, explaining he had been delayed by a cabinet session that ran longer than expected.

Konoe said he had contacted Inoue directly because eight of his acquaintances strongly recommended he do so. In response, Inoue mentioned that numerous friends had also urged him to contact Konoe, but he hadn't done so because "I felt you and I were too far apart in every way, beginning with our thinking and personalities. However, since you called me directly, I immediately decided to meet you."[3] In light of his joblessness, let alone his past, one might have thought Inoue would flatter, or at least show deference to, the prime minister. On the contrary, during their first meeting, Inoue accused Konoe of having a "split personality" (*nijū-jinkaku*).[4] Konoe showed his displeasure at this accusation and wanted to know why Inoue said it. Inoue replied,

> When you were a student at Kyoto University, you had socialist ideology instilled in you by the likes of Kawakami Hajime [1879–1946] and other professors. Even today, at an intellectual level, you are still inclined to affirm socialism. At the same time, the intuitively antisocialist spirit of Japan pulsates through your blood just as it did that of your ancient [Shintō] ancestor, Ama-no-Koyane-no-mikoto.[5] Thus, you have a split between your intellect and your intuition that results in your indecisiveness in the face of problems you encounter. That's what I call a split personality.[6]

Hearing this, Konoe recovered his composure and said, "It's just like you say. That's why I'm so troubled."[7] Konoe's honest response impressed Inoue because he felt most people subject to criticism made excuses for their conduct. The fact Konoe didn't convinced Inoue he was dealing with an honest man. In ensuing years, Inoue's appreciation of Konoe's honesty only grew, including the latter's relationship with the emperor. Inoue claimed that before Konoe took over, Japanese politics consisted of "politics by report." This meant the political-party-based government of the day decided policy on its own and only then reported its decisions to the emperor as it saw fit. The result, Inoue claimed, was a lot of fabrication.

Once Konoe became prime minister, however, things changed. No matter what the issue, Konoe first sought the emperor's consent. It was only after the emperor gave his approval that a policy was implemented. Government administered directly by the emperor came about in this way. According to Inoue, both Konoe and the emperor were advocates of peace, so the relationship between sovereign and subject was very close. It was for this reason that during Konoe's tenure as prime minister Japan was able to avoid war with the United States. While there were those like Tōjō Hideki who lied to the emperor out of self-interest, Konoe never did so. Inoue believed this was probably the biggest reason the emperor trusted Konoe the way he did.

"Given the emperor's confidence in him, if only Konoe had a more resolute character," Inoue wrote, "things would have turned out a bit better for Japan."[8] Unfortunately, Konoe was not the kind of person to force his opinion on others. On the contrary, others continuously forced their opinions on him, especially in the case of the military. This belief lead Inoue to take Konoe to task once again.

Inoue: Prince, from childhood on, have you ever been involved in a fight?

Konoe: No, not even once.

Inoue: That's exactly what's wrong with you. Your ideas swing back and forth from left to right just like a clock's pendulum. It's when they finally stop balanced in the middle that you imagine Japan is saved.[9]

Konoe nodded in agreement.

PURGING THE MILITARY

The military was the next topic the two men discussed. This time Konoe began:

> Although I'm the prime minister, I can't find out how the war between Japan and China is progressing. As prime minister, it's a problem if I don't know what's going on. For example, I'll go to the General Staff Office and explain that, as prime minister, I'm responsible for the government of the country. I further explain that I can't do my job properly without this knowledge. The staff officers, however, just ignore me, saying they can't reveal anything because of military secrecy. I end up having to go to the emperor to find out anything about the war. Whether it's a question of politics or diplomacy, the military acts so willfully it's unbearable.

"I completely agree with you," Inoue replied, "As long as the militarists are in control of Japan, reform is impossible."[10] Inoue went on to express his strong antipathy to the actions of the military cliques in the aftermath of the October Incident of 1931. The October Incident was yet another unsuccessful coup attempt carried out by the Cherry Blossom Society (*Sakura-kai*), a secret group of officers within the army. Aided by civilian ultranationalist groups, the Cherry Blossom Society intended to bring about political reform by eliminating party-based government and establishing a new cabinet based on state socialism. Their avowed goal was a Shōwa Restoration, which they claimed would restore Emperor Hirohito to his rightful place, free the country of party politics, and eliminate evil bureaucrats. Yet in the event the emperor resisted their demands, they were prepared to threaten him with physical violence.

Inoue was utterly opposed to the threat of physical force against the person of the emperor. Konoe shared his opinion. Thus, the two men found themselves in total agreement, including the need to purge the army of its radical elements.

A UNITED FRONT

Finding themselves in agreement, the question was how the purging could be accomplished. Inoue was convinced that as prime minister Konoe had it within his power to carry it out.

> Inoue: Prince, as prime minister, I imagine you can tell the emperor anything you like.

> Konoe: Unfortunately, as far as being an adviser to the throne is concerned, all cabinet members have the same right as the prime minister. Each of them is authorized to report to the emperor concerning affairs relating to his ministry. Therefore, the minister of military affairs can report to the emperor about military matters without my knowledge.[11]

On hearing this, Inoue realized more than ever the importance of overthrowing the despotic obstruction of the military cliques. Yet it also became clear that Konoe and he did not necessarily share the same views regarding the nature of the reform required. In this connection, Konoe said, "I don't think I'm the appropriate person to take charge of reforming Japan. Furthermore, I don't think this is the right time to do so."[12] Inoue agreed with Konoe, for he realized the latter represented Japan's old traditions and could not be expected to eliminate them. Nevertheless, Inoue felt Konoe had an important role to perform:

> While you can't be expected to reform Japan, it'll be sufficient if you use your position and responsibilities to move Japan even one step closer to reform. No matter how much noise the people at the bottom of society make, nothing will change without an authoritative pronouncement from the emperor. Inasmuch as I represent the people, it will be enough if you frankly convey my opinion to His Excellency.[13]

Inoue anxiously waited for Konoe's response, for he was convinced that the emperor's sanction was the key to reform. No one would dare oppose the emperor's dictates, meaning that societal reform could be accomplished with the fewest number of victims possible. At length, Konoe replied, "I can do at least that much."[14] Satisfied by his pledge, Inoue engaged in a frank discussion with Konoe, leading to the conclusion of a pact between them. At the end of the meeting, Konoe asked Inoue's permission to address him henceforth as "Master" (*oshō*), a term of respect for a Buddhist priest. Inoue, however, declined, saying, "Prime Minister, you shouldn't do that, for you are in the service of the emperor and a representative of the people. A degenerate priest like me doesn't deserve that name." "Alright," Konoe said, "I'll call you, Inoue."[15]

KONOE'S SECRET CONFIDANT

At their second meeting, Konoe asked Inoue to make sure when telephoning that he requested to speak directly with him. On the occasion of their third meeting, Konoe added, "Inoue, it's bothersome to have to make arrangements by phone every time we get together. Isn't there some way we could meet more easily?"[16] Half jokingly, Inoue responded by noting that since Konoe lived in a large mansion he must have a room somewhere in which Inoue could stay.

> Konoe: Well, in that case, the second story of a cottage behind the house is empty. It's dirty, but if you wouldn't mind . . .
>
> Inoue: Don't worry, I won't be surprised no matter what shape it's in.

After moving in, Inoue was surprised to find that Konoe hadn't explained his presence to anyone in the household. In particular, Konoe's wife didn't know what to think about this development. The only thing she knew about Inoue was his background as the onetime leader of a band of terrorists. Out of concern for her husband's safety, she asked Inoue, "You're not going to kill Fumimaro, are you?" Angered by her insinuation, Inoue replied, "My association with the prince is for the sake of the nation. Therefore, should the need arise for the sake of the nation, I may kill the prince." Konoe's wife left without saying a word, but the next day a smiling Konoe said, "Inoue, I hear you're going to kill me."[17] With this, Inoue couldn't stop himself from bursting out laughing.

Over the course of the next days and weeks, Konoe's wife was not the only one close to the prime minister whom Inoue managed to offend in one way or another. This was primarily due to the pledge Konoe had made to Inoue at the beginning of their relationship—namely, they would always talk directly with one another without a third party present. In practice, this meant that when others were around they simply exchanged greetings but never engaged in extended conversations. Instead, the two men got together to talk late into the night. Konoe's associates couldn't help but notice this and wonder what was going on, especially given Inoue's terrorist background. The fact that Konoe never explained Inoue's role to them made them only more suspicious.

YAMAMOTO GEMPŌ ISSUES AN INVITATION

Despite his new position, Inoue's relationship with Zen master Yamamoto Gempō had by no means come to an end. Even before Inoue became Konoe's advisor, that is, at the beginning of 1941, Yamamoto approached him with a proposal.

> Yamamoto: I've got something to discuss with you. Are you willing to die with me?
>
> Inoue: Fine, what's it all about?
>
> Yamamoto: [Army General] Yamashita Tomoyuki [aka Yamashita Hōbun, 1885–1946] has agreed to provide an airplane, so will you accompany me to [China's wartime capital] Chongqing [aka Chungking]? If Jiang Jieshi [aka Chiang Kai-shek] is half the man I think he is, I'm confident that from a humanitarian point of view he will understand our peace proposal. You'll serve as my interpreter. However, should we be captured by the Chinese Communists on the way, it means the end for us. Nevertheless, if we succeed in meeting Jiang, I have no doubt we will succeed in finding a solution to the current conflict between Japan and China.[18]

While the reader may find Yamamoto's proposal bordering on the quixotic, Inoue did not, and he immediately agreed to accompany his master. Aside from the close relationship between the two men, this can be explained by the ample historical precedent for such a role. For hundreds of years, Zen Buddhist priests served as government envoys in charge of trade between Japan and China, especially during the Ming Dynasty (1368–1644). Equally important, General Yamashita was both an admirer of Yamamoto as well as an ardent Zen practitioner. As such, he would have been comfortable supporting this mission.[19] Unfortunately, not everyone was equally supportive. Thus, when the faction-ridden Japanese military and Ministry of Foreign Affairs heard of the proposal, they quickly moved to prevent it.

Inoue was deeply disappointed by the failure to carry out Yamamoto's plan and regarded his new position with Konoe as a golden opportunity to revive something similar. This time he proposed that Konoe gather together men interested in relations between Japan and China like Tōyama Mitsuru and have them undertake nongovernmental peacemaking efforts. Additionally, Konoe would approach the emperor to ask him to make an imperial grant of one hundred million yen in support of this effort. Konoe responded favorably to Inoue's proposal and agreed to approach the emperor.

After some time passed, Inoue asked Konoe what had happened. Reluctantly, Konoe replied, "Unfortunately, someone close to the emperor opposed your plan."[20] Although Konoe didn't share the name of the "someone," Inoue immediately knew who it was—Kido Kōichi (1889–1977), Lord Keeper of the Privy Seal from 1940 to 1945 and one of the emperor's closest advisors. Inoue's suspicions grew out of three meetings he had with Kido during 1941, either on his own or on Konoe's behalf.

While generally regarded as Konoe's friend, Inoue claimed that behind the scenes Kido took the lead in opposing Konoe's proposals. Although still in the future at that point, Inoue also held Kido responsible for recommending Gen. Tōjō Hideki to follow Konoe as prime minister on October 17, 1941. In any event, Inoue was so deeply disturbed by Kido's interference that he asked a mutual friend to inform the latter of his anger. The friend did so and later informed Inoue that Kido responded by placing his hands around his neck as if being strangled and asking, "Am I next?"[21] Inoue took some satisfaction in learning that Kido was afraid of him.

These repeated failures by no means brought Inoue's peacemaking efforts to an end. Through a mutual friend, he next approached Matsukata Otohiko to enlist his aid in what was to be a purely nongovernmental effort. Matsukata was the influential son of a mercantile and political family who had enjoyed a personal friendship with Franklin Roosevelt since their student days together at Harvard. However, inasmuch as this effort was unsanctioned by the Japanese government, funding was a problem. As a consequence, Inoue devised a plan to process and sell cotton yarn to raise the necessary funds. This meant he would need permission from the Ministry of Commerce and Industry, headed by Kishi Nobusuke (1896–1987). Through an intermediary, Inoue sought Kishi's permission, but due to what Inoue labelled as his "insincerity" (*fusei-i*) it was not forthcoming. This brought an end to Inoue's third and final effort at peacemaking.[22]

Kishi went on to become one of Gen. Tōjō Hideki's closest associates during the war years, best known for his brutal rule of the Japanese puppet state of Manchukuo in his role as its economic czar. In postwar years, despite three years of imprisonment as a suspected Class A war criminal, Kishi became prime minister of Japan from 1957 to 1960.

INOUE AND JAPAN'S MILITARY LEADERS

If Inoue's peace activities all ended in failure, he was nevertheless successful on one front: engendering the wrath of the army leadership that was seeking a military victory in China as well as, if necessary, going to war with the United States. This was not entirely Inoue's fault, for Konoe had been opposed to the military's ascendency long before Inoue became involved. On numerous occasions, Konoe had secretly dispatched emissaries to China with personal letters addressed to Jiang Jieshi containing peace proposals. The core of the proposals focused on conditions for the withdrawal of Japanese troops from China. However, either before embarking by ship in Kobe or disembarking in Shanghai, his emissaries had been arrested by the feared Kempeitai (military police) and his letters confiscated. When Konoe shared this history, Inoue tried to offer words of encouragement, saying, "Don't let that discourage you!"[23]

War-espousing military leaders were not the only players Konoe and Inoue had to worry about. Japan had signed the Tripartite Pact with Nazi Germany and Fascist Italy in September 1940, and Konoe's foreign minister, Matsuoka Yōsuke (1880–1946), was one of its fervent advocates. When Matsuoka returned from Europe in the summer of 1941, he continued to promote the pact in concert with those Inoue identified as "so-called patriots."[24] According to Inoue, it was as if Matsuoka and his supporters had gone "completely mad" (*shōki no sata*).[25]

Matsuoka's attitude came as a deep shock to Konoe, for prior to his trip to Europe Matsuoka often said, "I'm deeply indebted to Prince Konoe for having appointed me as foreign minister. Additionally, the Konoe family and my family have a special relationship, and therefore I have a duty to serve Prince Konoe to the end of my life."[26] Inoue, too, was disappointed with this change in Matsuoka, for he knew him personally and, up until then, had admired him.

When Matsuoka later referred to Konoe as "that jerk" (*ano yarō*) in Inoue's presence, his disappointment turned into an angry confrontation:

> Inoue: Have you forgotten that you previously said you were going to serve Konoe to the end your life?!
>
> Matsuoka: In the past I thought that way, but for the sake of the nation I have to disregard personal feelings!
>
> Inoue: A foreign minister's fundamental duty is to pursue foreign policy in a peaceful manner. Isn't it contradictory for a foreign minister to advocate war before anything else?

Matsuoka didn't reply, and Inoue realized Matsuoka couldn't, or wouldn't, understand what he was saying. This led to a permanent break in their formerly amiable relationship. But the matter didn't end here, for Matsuoka and his supporters sought to silence anyone opposed to the pact, including both Konoe and Inoue. Both men were attacked under the banner "Topple weak-kneed Konoe and get rid of Inoue!"[27] The attack escalated to the point they both received mounds of threatening letters on a daily basis. It even reached the point where the directors of both the Bureau of Military Affairs and the Bureau of Naval Affairs came to Konoe's estate by car after midnight and demanded the prime minister force Inoue to leave immediately. However, neither Konoe nor Inoue let any of this bother them.

The reason for their opposition to the Tripartite Pact was, first of all, because both men were convinced Japan mustn't continue the war with China, a country with which Japan had, by then, fought a largely stalemated war for four long years. In this situation, they believed, binding Japan to untrustworthy countries like Germany and Italy, thereby making new enemies in the process, was like placing a noose around one's neck. In other words, it was the height of stupidity.

On top of this was the telegram sent to Konoe by Japan's ambassador to Nazi Germany, Army General Ōshima Hiroshi (1886–1975), at the time of Germany's invasion of the Soviet Union at the end of June 1941. Ōshima wrote, "Germany's attack on the Soviet Union is more in the nature of a police action than a war. Inasmuch as the Soviet Union will be subjugated within three weeks, Japan should march south with all possible haste."[28]

When the normally gentle Konoe read this, he flew into a rage: "Ōshima isn't Japan's ambassador, he's Hitler's waiter!"[29] Inoue was in complete agreement. Two or three days later Konoe told Inoue, "Since I'm not knowledgeable about warfare, I asked the opinion of the military's General Staff Office. They said that while they couldn't be certain about three weeks, Germany should be able to defeat the Soviet Union within a month or, at the latest, three months."[30]

It was around this time that Konoe ordered a study done on the relative strength of Japan and the United States. The result was, simply put, there was no comparison. Therefore, the study concluded, Japan must definitely not go to war with the United States. Based on this, Konoe said, "Inoue, in light of the figures researched by these specialists, I just can't bring myself to fight a war with the United States."[31] Once again, Inoue found himself in complete agreement.

KONOE'S WEAKNESSES

Although Inoue genuinely admired Konoe, he also recognized his weaknesses. Chief among them was his lack of willpower—in particular, the courage to repulse evil. In the case of Tōjō Hideki, for example, had Konoe explained the situation to the emperor when Tōjō was still minister of war in his cabinet, it would have been possible to get rid of him. In fact, Inoue repeatedly urged Konoe to do exactly that, but Konoe, fearing the military, was unwilling to take effective action.

Konoe devised an alternate plan to control the military, a plan that sought to utilize military factionalism to control the military's violent actions. Concretely, Konoe's strategy consisted of using the higher-echelon remnants of the Imperial Way Faction (Kōdō-ha) to suppress the Control Faction (Tōsei-ha). Inoue strongly opposed this strategy, advocating, instead, that Konoe honestly explain the situation to the emperor with the expectation that the latter would find both factions at fault. This, Inoue believed, would make possible the creation of a new military leadership.

In this instance, Konoe rejected Inoue's advice, for he felt there were already too many things troubling the emperor. In contrast, Inoue believed everything should be presented to the emperor for his decision. Konoe, however, felt it was his duty to bear the heavy loads, no matter how personally painful, in order to avoid disturbing the emperor. As things turned out, while Konoe was on good terms with retired, but still influential, Imperial Way Faction generals Araki Sadao, Mazaki Jinzaburō, and Yanagawa Heisuke (1879–1945), he was never able to suppress the Control Faction headed by Tōjō Hideki. Although Konoe tried still other methods of control, they also failed. "In short," Inoue wrote, "Prince Konoe's fatal flaw was his lack of courage to resolutely repulse evil."[32]

THE ROAD TO WAR

The year 1941 was a momentous one for relations between Japan and the United States. Early in Konoe's third term as prime minister, beginning in July 1941, a proposal emerged for a direct meeting between Konoe and President Franklin Roosevelt to discuss ways of avoiding war between the two nations. When Konoe asked his opinion, Inoue enthusiastically endorsed the proposal, including a request, which Konoe granted, to secretly accompany him. After securing cabinet approval, Konoe formally proposed this meeting to the American side, and to everyone's surprise, the Americans responded positively, even suggesting a tentative location for the talks. However, when powerful elements within both the Japanese military and American government got wind of the proposal, they successfully blocked the meeting.

Nevertheless, diplomatic negotiations between the two governments continued. By the beginning of August, however, there was growing frustration on the Japanese side with the lack of progress, especially on the part of the allegedly patriotic elements who continued to strongly support the Tripartite Pact. It reached the point where a physical attack on Konoe was a distinct possibility.

To head off this danger, Inoue decided to hold a meeting between Konoe and Tōyama Mitsuru as well as right-wing Shinto scholar Imaizumi Sadasukei. Inoue hoped that if these two ultranationalists accurately understood Konoe's thinking, especially about war with the United States, they would take steps to ensure the prime minister's safety. The meeting took place over dinner at Konoe's mansion from 6 to 9 p.m. This setting allowed the participants to talk candidly and sincerely to one other. Inoue thought the exchange went well and was especially impressed by Konoe's final words: "Preparations will be finished by the end of October, and I will start the war [with the United States] at the beginning of November [1941]."[33]

In response, Tōyama quietly placed both hands on his knees, bowed deeply, and said, "I would like to thank you for your strenuous efforts on behalf of the nation."[34] This exchange made a deep impression on Inoue though he was quick to add this did not mean Konoe had abandoned his search for a peaceful resolution of Japan's disagreements with the United States. Instead, it reflected a decision that had already been made in a cabinet meeting held in the imperial presence. Namely, if a peaceful resolution proved impossible, Japan was prepared to go to war.

The following evening Inoue invited a second group of ultranationalist leaders to Konoe's mansion and repeated the process. It was in this way that Inoue ensured not only Konoe's safety but his cabinet ministers as well. For example, at the time of the formation of the Imperial Rule Assistance Association in October 1940,[35] Inoue was approached by an unnamed ultranationalist seeking Inoue's support for the assassination of Home Minister Hiranuma Kiichirō (1867–1952), deemed responsible for the association's creation. Inoue, however, refused his support, thereby saving the minister's life.[36] Even when it became clear that war was inevitable, Konoe, Tōyama, and Inoue hoped that things might develop differently than they did, but they all ended up engulfed by the frenzied determination to defeat the United States and Great Britain. Commenting on this development, Inoue wrote, "It can only be described as fate."[37]

WAR WITH THE UNITED STATES

On October 15, 1941, War Minister Tōjō, at a cabinet meeting, proposed the immediate cessation of diplomatic relations with the United States and the start of war. This led to the resignation of Konoe's entire cabinet, bringing an end to his third term as prime minister. In response, Lord Keeper of the Privy Seal Kido recommended Emperor Hirohito appoint Tōjō as the new prime minister. However, when Tōjō went to discuss the matter with the emperor, he recommended the appointment of Prince General Higashikuni Naruhiko (1887–1990) in his stead. Higashikuni was an uncle-in-law of Emperor Hirohito twice over. Hirohito, however, rejected Tōjō's recommendation. Hence, Tōjō ended up becoming Japan's fortieth prime minister on October 17, 1941, serving to July 22, 1944.

Inoue had hoped Higashikuni would succeed Konoe, for he believed domestic reform could be accomplished with the fewest number of victims under the leadership of an imperial prince. However, when he shared this opinion with Konoe, the latter informed him that, outside of an emergency, the emperor would never agree to have a cabinet headed by a member of the imperial family. In the event the war went badly, the imperial system as a whole might be placed in jeopardy. As a result, Inoue wrote, "As planned, Prime Minister Tōjō executed an attack on the United States [on December 8, 1941(Japan time)], beginning Japan's tragedy."[38] For his part, Tōjō was well aware of Inoue's presence and importance. So much so that soon after he became prime minister he sent an emissary seeking Inoue's assistance. Inoue, however, rebuffed him, as well as those Tōjō sent later.

THE *HIMOROGI* MOVEMENT

With the war underway, Inoue proposed to Konoe that they create what he called the *himorogi* movement. While *himorogi* refers to a sacred offering made to a Shinto deity, it was anything but a religious activity. Instead, its name was purposely chosen to obscure its real purpose—the development of a national network of social activists who would be ready to launch a legal, domestic reform movement just as soon as Japan lost the war. "From the outset," Inoue wrote, "there was no question that Japan would lose the war."[39]

According to Inoue, the reason the domestic reform movement hadn't succeeded in the past was because the military blocked it. However, following Japan's defeat, the military would lose power, making reform extremely easy. It was therefore critically important that, until the time came, close attention be paid to ensure the movement was not seen as an antiwar or peace movement. For this reason, it would engage in no conspicuous, public activities. Instead, it would establish private schools and martial arts halls throughout the country and recruit members on a voluntary basis.

Konoe's role was to provide the necessary funds for these activities, including the creation of a movement periodical titled *Himorogi*. It was imperative this periodical carry no writings related to current affairs that might arouse the suspicion of the military. Therefore, it would only contain various kinds of traditional poetry and related news, all designed to maintain contact with members nationwide. On occasion, the movement's headquarters would dispatch liaison personnel to the movement's regional centers to inform them of the state of affairs in the headquarters, while the regional centers would report developments to the headquarters on a monthly basis.

Although the majority of the membership would be unaware of the movement's true purpose, a cadre of leaders would be informed. The main leaders were composed of Inoue's freed former band members, starting with Yotsumoto Yoshitaka and Hishinuma Gorō. At the beginning, the movement was successful and gradually expanded its presence throughout the country. However, its very success raised suspicions, leading the military authorities to employ their own national network to clamp down on regional activities. Nothing could be done to stop this, with the result that contact with the district centers lessened to the point of ending altogether.

INOUE AND THE MILITARY POLICE

Although Inoue survived the collapse of the *himorogi* movement, his greatest wartime challenge was yet to come. It began simply enough when he went to hear a lecture on "Imperial Way Economy" (*Kōdō Keizai*). Inasmuch as Inoue was not the speaker, it should have been a simple event, but things didn't turn out that way. Inoue was unable to restrain himself from engaging in a lengthy criticism of the speaker's presentation. This is not surprising in that there were as many interpretations of the meaning of "Imperial Way Economy" as there were speakers. In general, the thrust of this economic program was a heavily state-directed economy that was neither capitalist nor communist.

Inoue didn't stop with a mere critique of the speaker's presentation but went on to present his own proposals for economic reform. Only later did Inoue learn from a fellow attendee that the head of Japan's dreaded military police, the Kempeitai, had been in the audience. Inoue was surprised to learn of his presence. Given the scathing nature of Inoue's criticism, there was a distinct possibility Inoue would be accused of throwing the national economy into disorder.

On reflection, Inoue realized if only he had known in advance of the presence of the Kempeitai's head, he would have spoken more moderately. But that was water under the bridge and couldn't be changed now. Hence, in light of his past strained relations with the military, the only thing Inoue could do was put his affairs in order and wait for the order to report to military police headquarters. To his surprise, however, though the days passed, the order never came.

In light of this, Inoue asked an acquaintance in the Kempeitai what had happened. His acquaintance replied, "To tell the truth, your speech did become a topic of discussion at headquarters. The question was, what should be done about it. Eventually, the conclusion was reached that what you said had been correct, so no action was taken."[40] While Inoue was relieved to hear the Kempeitai realized his arguments were correct, he also knew none of the proposals would be enacted. "That was where the cancer infecting the military existed," he concluded.[41]

PREPARING FOR DEFEAT

Although the *himorogi* movement failed, Inoue's "common front" with Konoe continued unabated, with the two men holding secret meetings on a regular basis. They discussed the end of the war and, especially, the steps to be taken following Japan's defeat. Early in the war, Inoue intuitively sensed the navy had just experienced a great defeat. When he shared this with Konoe, the latter replied, "I can tell you the navy has definitely not told me that!"[42] Only later did the truth emerge that the navy had covered up the major defeat it experienced at the Battle of Midway in June 1942.

As the war situation worsened, especially following Japan's defeat and withdrawal from the Solomon Islands in February 1943, Tōjō was increasingly desperate for outside assistance, realizing he was losing the support of even his own cabinet ministers. In fact, by this time Kishi Nobusuke (1896–1987), his munitions minister and close friend from their days together in Manchuria, was rumored to be plotting against him. This led Tōjō to reach out to Inoue once again. Colonel Akamatsu Sadao (1900–1982), Tōjō's private secretary, invited Inoue to dinner in Tokyo's Akasaka *geisha* district. In response to Akamatsu's request for assistance, Inoue stated,

Alright, I'll tell you how I feel. From the time Tōjō became prime minister, a number of people have asked me to assist him. However, I refused because it isn't my responsibility to do so, nor do I harbor any weakness compelling me to. It would be a lie if Tōjō decided to use me because you told him I'd changed my mind and was now ready to assist him. Tell that to Tōjō on your return. Also, tell him that if he decides to have the Kempeitai kill Kishi Nobusuke, I'll immediately assassinate him. That's all I have to say![43]

Assuming the accuracy of this conversation, the degree of Inoue's animosity toward Tōjō is not surprising given Inoue's long-held opposition to the Control Faction of the army, headed by Tōjō. More surprising is Inoue's willingness to directly confront the man who, next to the emperor, was still the most powerful man in wartime Japan. Inoue's position as Konoe's advisor must have afforded him substantial protection. At the same time, it is true that Kishi Nobusuke was behind a movement to remove Tōjō from the premiership, a goal finally achieved on July 22, 1944.

Returning to Inoue and Konoe, when the two men got together on March 9, 1945, Inoue informed Konoe that he had a premonition there would soon be a major air attack on Tokyo, leaving nothing but smoldering ruins. Only hours after they parted, on the night of March 9–10, that is exactly what happened. The Tokyo Metropolitan Police Department claimed 83,793 residents died, 40,918 were wounded, and 286,358 buildings and homes were destroyed.[44]

Inoue was deeply moved by the accuracy of his premonition and the following month reported to Konoe his conviction that the war would end in August. As he watched the war situation deteriorate, Inoue could not help but recall his experience of 1924 in the garden at Santoku-an. Readers will recall it was then Inoue observed a struggle taking place between two colonies of ants. Initially, the black ants (i.e., the Japanese military) were successful in pushing the red ants (i.e., the United States military) back, but after a while the tide turned and the red ants emerged victorious.

JAPAN'S DEFEAT

The war ended on August 15, 1945, with Japan's unconditional surrender. Only two days later, on August 17, General Prince Higashikuni Naruhiko became Japan's first postwar prime minister, a position he held until October 9, 1945. Konoe joined the cabinet as deputy prime minister. For Inoue, these were very welcome developments, for at long last the opportunity for major social reform had arrived. The military, *zaibatsu* financial conglomerates, and their bureaucratic supporters had lost power. In Inoue's eyes, the ensuing social chaos provided an unprecedented opportunity to eradicate past evils and renovate politics. Not only that, the government was finally headed by a member of the imperial family, facilitating rapid change with the least resistance.

With these thoughts in mind, Inoue went to confer with Konoe in the cabinet offices. In response, Konoe agreed to share Inoue's proposals with the new prime minister. In particular, Inoue believed it was time to establish a new major political party that would serve to light the fire of reform throughout the nation. Shortly thereafter, however, Inoue encountered a problem he had not foreseen. An economist acquaintance informed him that if things continued as they were, there was the danger of some twenty million people dying of starvation by March 1946.

Deeply concerned by this news, Inoue once again approached Konoe to ask if the government had a plan to address the situation. "The truth is, the government has no plan," Konoe confided. Hearing this, Inoue said,

In that case, I have a proposal. First, please ask the emperor to surrender the assets of the imperial household. Then I will stake my life on convincing every *zaibatsu*, whether they want to or not, to restore their assets to the emperor. After all, it's only a matter of time before the *zaibatsu* are broken up, so they might as well leave looking good. Using these funds, we will then purchase all of the excess rice in the country and distribute it equally among the people. While it might not meet everyone's needs, with some hunger still remaining, at least no one will die of starvation. If this is not sufficient to meet people's needs, we can think of other methods at that time. In any event, not having any plan is unacceptable, so how about this as a first step?[45]

As with his earlier justification of terrorism, Inoue remained convinced that an emergency situation required emergency measures. Although Konoe supported Inoue's proposal, both Prime Minister Higashikuni and his cabinet rejected it. Not only did his proposal come to nothing, Konoe was told to inform Inoue that he was no longer welcome in the cabinet offices. From there, matters escalated to the point that the prime minister even stopped holding direct discussions with Konoe himself, instead addressing communications through his chief secretary. In such a situation, reform measures were out of the question. Yet again, Inoue was forced to realize just how corrupt things were.

KONOE'S SUICIDE

With the Allied occupation taking hold, Konoe came under suspicion of having been a war criminal. Learning of this, Inoue feared that Konoe might commit suicide. Through an intermediary, Inoue sent word to Konoe that he had something important to tell him, and therefore he must definitely not commit suicide until they had a chance to talk. But Inoue's efforts came too late, for Konoe had already taken poison and died early on the morning of December 16, 1945.

For Inoue, Konoe's death represented the loss of a valuable witness who could have clarified events at the time of the Tokyo War Crimes Tribunal (aka International Military Tribunal for the Far East, convened on April 29, 1946). Had he lived, Konoe could still have served the state even though it might have been personally painful. But why had he committed suicide?

Inoue believed it was because Konoe could not accept the shame of arrest. In other words, as a member of the aristocracy, he was unable to bear having his pride injured. In Inoue's eyes, Konoe was a true aristocrat. In fact, the only aristocrat in Japan who acted like one. When Konoe contemplated giving testimony in the upcoming tribunal, he was, no doubt, unable to bear the thought of having to expose the crimes of his friends and colleagues. One of Konoe's distinguishing characteristics was that he never lied or spoke disparagingly of others.

When Inoue said something that made Konoe uncomfortable, you could tell by the latter's facial expression. Nevertheless, he never made excuses. Whenever Inoue made a proposal, Konoe clearly stated, "I can do that," or "I can't do that."[46] Even when rebuffed, Inoue felt good about the way he had been treated. When Inoue spoke disparagingly about men like Tōjō or Kido Kōichi, Konoe listened quietly but never joined in. Even when Inoue's criticism was excessive, Konoe simply replied, "He's not as bad as you make him out to be."[47] In Inoue's eyes, Konoe was truly a man of integrity.

"Konoe's suicide was a question of fate [*unmei*]," Inoue wrote. "The past never returns."[48]

12

An Ultranationalist in Postwar Japan

Four months had passed since the end of the war, and it was an early winter's morning in 1945. The streets of central Tokyo were now clear of rubble even though most of the surrounding buildings still lay in ruins. Streetcars were functioning again albeit overflowing with passengers. There was, however, one major building still intact, the Dai-Ichi Insurance Building. This building, facing the giant moat surrounding the unscarred grounds of the Imperial Palace, now served as the General Headquarters (GHQ) of the Supreme Commander for the Allied Powers (SCAP), Gen. Douglas MacArthur (1880–1964).

Inoue had received a letter from the occupation authorities ordering him to report for questioning at 9 a.m. Shortly before nine, Inoue, now fifty-nine years old, shabbily dressed, balding, and somewhat portly, walked up the stairs of the entrance to the Dai-Ichi. He first showed his letter to the uniformed United States military guard and then entered the building, where he again showed the letter to a receptionist at the entrance. The receptionist directed him to an office down the hall on the first floor. Inoue entered the office, once again showing his letter to the office receptionist, and was immediately taken to the office of British Naval Lieutenant Parsons.[1]

Parsons informed Inoue that, beginning tomorrow, he would be interrogated by an unnamed German American first lieutenant. Hearing this, it occurred to Inoue this might not be to his advantage. A German American interrogator, he felt, might feel under pressure due to his ethnic background to prove his loyalty by treating Japanese war criminal suspects harshly. Therefore, Inoue asked Parsons if he would be willing to interrogate him instead. Parsons thought about this for a moment and agreed.

The next morning Inoue arrived promptly at nine and was shown into Lt. Parsons's office. Parsons spoke with an interpreter at his side:

Parsons: You're Nisshō Inoue, correct?

Inoue: Yes, I am.

Parsons: Mr. Inoue, I didn't request your appearance today in order to find out what you did before and during the war. We already know what you did. We know you were not only an ultra-right-wing nationalist but the leader of a band of terrorists as well. In fact, it is a matter of common knowledge the world over that it was you who started World War II. There's no point denying it. It's therefore unnecessary for me to inquire about any of this.[2]

If in speaking to Inoue so harshly, Parsons hoped to frighten him, Parsons simply didn't know the character of the man he was dealing with.

Inoue: I'd like to ask a question. May I?

Parsons: Go ahead.

Inoue: Just now you said that I was a right-wing leader. Now, I may be a little bit clumsy, but I nevertheless regard myself as a human being. From where you sit, do I look like a bird?

Parsons: Mr. Inoue, why do you ask such a stupid question? No one here has called you a bird!

Inoue: Well, didn't you just call me a right-wing leader. Look, when I spread my arms, I don't have a right wing, much less a left![3]

Inoue spread his arms to show that he was "wingless." With this, Parsons turned pale and, sitting erect, apologized to Inoue. "Excuse me for having spoken rudely. I take back what I said." Hearing this, Inoue thought that Parsons was a true English gentleman and, at the same time, "Great, now I know I have little to worry about."[4]

Thereafter, Parsons's interrogation was extremely polite. While looking at a memo on his desk, he asked for the names of the leaders of various right-wing organizations and their ideological viewpoints. Inoue, however, explained that the right-wing organizations of interest to Parsons were those that had been active while he had been in prison, and therefore he had little knowledge of them. At that point, Inoue said, "One of my comrades, Maeda Torao, was free during that time, and I believe he is knowledgeable about the groups you are asking about. If you like, I can bring him along tomorrow and you could ask him." Parsons readily agreed to Inoue's proposal.

The next morning, Inoue brought his old friend Maeda (1892–1953) with him. Maeda, whom Inoue had known since their days working together in Manchuria, was an ultranationalist civilian activist who became a leader of the 1933 Divine Soldiers Incident (*Shimpeitai Jiken*). Composed of both civilian activists and right-wing military officers, the incident called for assassinating the prime minister and other important politicians, bombing the Diet building, and creating general chaos in the heart of Tokyo. This would lead to a declaration of martial law followed by the promulgation of the Shōwa Restoration. However, in the aftermath of the May 15 Incident of 1932, the police were keeping close watch on ultranationalist radicals and arrested the key conspirators on July 10, 1933, just one day before the attempted coup. As so often in the past, the defendants, Maeda included, received only short prison terms, accompanied by immediate remission of their sentences.

As for Parsons, he began asking Maeda the names of the leaders of one rightist group after another. Maeda wrote down their names but each time included his own as well. After doing this a number of times, Parsons asked if the name "Maeda" referred to the same person. Maeda replied it did, and Parsons asked Maeda if he was the same person. Maeda said he was.

> Parsons: Mr. Maeda, this is not a simple investigation, for your very destiny is at stake. It's only natural that, when asked, someone in your position tries to hide their involvement. Yet, in your case, you've written your name each time. What's this all about?

> Maeda: For me it's not a question of whether it's connected to my destiny or not. I'm simply responding to the questions you asked me; that's all. I'm not someone who can deceive based on whether or not it's to my advantage.

Letting out a short sigh, Parsons said, "That'll be enough for today. I appreciate your cooperation."[5]

The following morning, instead of questioning Inoue, Parsons said, "Mr. Inoue, you certainly have a fine friend. Even in my country it is rare to meet such an honest man." Hearing these words, Inoue thought to himself they reflected the pride if not the arrogance of the English. While Inoue couldn't be sure whether the English were honest or not, he felt words like "my country" reflected the English conviction that whether in terms of culture in general, constitutional politics, or parliamentary government, England was a world leader, with countries like Japan having done nothing more than imitating them.

Nonetheless, it was clear Parsons had been genuinely impressed with Maeda's courage and honesty. Inoue noticed that Parsons wrote in the margins of his interrogation notes, "Honest man." Thanks to those words, Inoue believed, Maeda avoided any further questions regarding his wartime actions. As for Inoue, Parsons informed him that his interrogation had come to an end. Any further summons would come directly from the International War Crimes Tribunal. As Inoue left his office, Parsons told his interpreter to help Inoue on with his overcoat and accompany him as far as the main entrance.

INTERROGATION AT THE INTERNATIONAL WAR CRIMES TRIBUNAL

It was not long before Inoue received a directive to report to the International Tribunal, housed in the Army Ministry's former headquarters in Tokyo's Ichigaya area. This began the first of twenty-seven interrogations. In the course of being subjected to the same questions by one prosecutor after another, Inoue grew irritated and decided to fight back with questions of his own. For their part, each prosecutor approached Inoue with the idea of besting him in an argument. Inoue was reminded of the classic manner in which the master of one martial arts hall went to another martial arts hall and first had to fight his way up through that hall's lower ranks until he finally earned the right to confront the head of the second martial arts hall. In similar fashion, Inoue eventually earned the right to challenge William Flood Webb (1887–1972), Australian head of the International Military Tribunal for the Far East.

The first prosecutor Inoue encountered immediately launched into an attack from the outset.

> Prosecutor: I wish to ask about the responsibility you feel for Japan's war of aggression?
>
> Inoue: In order to answer your question, some prior knowledge is necessary. May I ask you a question?
>
> Prosecutor: Fine. Ask what you like.
>
> Inoue: Alright, let me ask who made the earth. Was it England? Or the United States?

His face turning red in anger, the prosecutor replied, "What kind of stupid question is that! Nowhere in the world is there someone who made the earth. No matter whether in the United States or England, or anywhere else, everyone was born on this earth. By asking who made the earth, are you trying to be funny?"

> Inoue: No, I'm not. I'm deadly serious. I agree with you that the earth doesn't belong to anyone. Nor does it belong to any one country. It's simply a question of the world's most powerful nations, that is, England, the United States, Japan, and Germany, having gotten together to plunder the earth for themselves. In Japanese, we say it's a matter of behaving like "would-be robbers" [*dorobo-gokko*]. At the moment, the victorious big robbers are in the midst of giving the defeated small robbers a hard time. That's the true meaning of the International Tribunal. If Japan is guilty of having engaged in aggressive warfare, the same is true of England and the United States. In light of this, how can you ask me about my sense of responsibility for one side only? There's no point in taking this verbal tug-of-war seriously.[6]

In response, the prosecutor didn't simply get angry but hopping mad, gripping his desk with both arms. But then he appeared to have second thoughts and abruptly ended the interrogation. From then on, whenever the two met in the tribunal's hallways, the prosecutor smiled, approached Inoue with outstretched hand, and spoke to him pleasantly about one thing or another.

THE QUESTION OF THE IMPERIAL SYSTEM

The second prosecutor, an American, began his interrogation by not only expressing his personal opposition to Japan's imperial system but disparaging the emperor. This offended Inoue, who when asked his thoughts about the imperial system replied,

We Japanese don't cherish the emperor because we have an imperial system. Domestically, the term "imperial system" [*Tennō-sei*] was created due to the presence of communists. Externally, it began because of the arrival of people like yourselves. We Japanese have never even thought of this term, let alone employed it. The relationship between the emperor and the people of this country is the same as the relationship between a parent and his children.

If the emperor weren't our parent, why would he do his duty as a parent. It is for this reason we call him our "Great Parent." If we weren't the emperor's children, why would we do our duty as children. For this reason, we are called "His Majesty's children." Not only this, but as history reveals, the emperor and the people of this country have always been one, differing only in their respective missions and stations in life. No matter what the organization, it is always made up of a center and its branches. The emperor is naturally at the center ruling over his subjects. It is for this reason that following the introduction of writing from China the phrase "sovereign and subjects are one" has been used to express Japan's national body politic.

By comparison, your country [i.e., the United States] is made up of people who got together while looking for work in another country. For that reason, there is no one to take a parental role in your country since it is made up of equal individuals. However, even in such a society you need a center. Thus, you must use a competitive system to decide who the father figure will be. In Japan, we have no need for that since we've had a father figure from the very beginning. In other words, Japan is the world's one and only "extended family state" [*daikazoku-kokka*]. Inasmuch as the family is the basic unit of society, it is only natural that the state took on this form. The extended family is the true form of the nation's body politic. Western countries are based on a foundation of utilitarianism in which life consists of nothing but advantage and disadvantage. Therefore, they are not true, national body politics.

Inoue said the above in one go and was not surprised to see how extremely angry it made the prosecutor. Nevertheless, as with the previous prosecutor, the next time the two men met, Inoue was treated very courteously. Perhaps, he thought, the prosecutor realized "the truth can't be beat."[7]

THE NATURE OF MARRIAGE

Inoue was aware the Allies believed they needed to destroy the traditional family system if they were to accomplish a democratic revolution in Japan. Knowing this, Inoue was not surprised when a third prosecutor wanted to know what he thought about the relationship between husband and wife.

Prosecutor: The basis of society is the family.

Inoue, agreeing immediately: Yes, it is.

Prosecutor: However, the Japanese family system is beyond belief. It doesn't even amount to a family.

Inoue: Well, what are families like in your country?

Prosecutor: A family consists of one man and one woman, both with equal rights and responsibilities, sharing life together.

Inoue: What a stupid thing to say! Let's assume the kind of family you have just described. Suppose the monthly expenses for this family totaled one thousand yen. This would mean the man paid five hundred yen and the woman paid the same amount. Each of them would have their own bedrooms. While that arrangement would be a fine shared life, no children could be expected. Without children, the family ceases to exist, eventually bringing an end to both society and nation. For a family and society to prosper, the man and woman in a family unit must occasionally become one, resulting in the birth of children.

Due to their different roles, something that was originally one [life] sometimes gives birth to a man and sometimes to a woman. The harmonious working of this single entity makes human reproduction possible. Therefore, in Japan we don't talk about husband and wife sharing with one another, but "husband and wife as one" [*fūfu ittai*]. The meaning of a family is not something as shallow as what you call a shared life in which a man and woman have equal rights. Or tell me, is it possible in the United States for a man to give birth to a child all by himself? Or can a woman give birth to a child all by herself?[8]

Inoue was chuckling as he posed these final questions, but the prosecutor's face turned pale.

THE MEANING OF THE "IMPERIAL WAY"

A fourth prosecutor questioned Inoue about the Imperial Way (*Kōdō*). The prosecutor prefaced his question by indicating he believed the Imperial Way was the guiding principle behind Japan's aggression as expressed in the wartime slogan "The eight corners of the world under one roof" (*hakkō ichiu*).

Inoue: It's fair to say that I'm an adherent of the Imperial Way. However, the Imperial Way I speak of isn't the Imperial Way of the military cliques.

Prosecutor: Well then, tell me what your Imperial Way consists of.

Inoue: How do you expect me to tell you that! The military cliques didn't understand it so they spouted nonsense that had nothing to do with the Imperial Way. As someone who believes and practices the true Imperial Way, I can say that the more you comprehend it the more difficult it becomes to say or write anything about it.

At that point, the prosecutor became angry and said, "I can understand that it's impossible to talk about something you don't understand. However, to claim that you can't say anything about something you truly understand is nothing but a cheap trick. You won't get away with that here!"

Inoue: Is that so. Well then, I have something I'd like to ask you—have you ever eaten an apple?

Prosecutor: I have.

Inoue: Do you know what it tasted like?

Prosecutor, boiling with anger and shouting: Of course, I do! What's that got to do with it?

Inoue, shouting back: Well, you talk big, so tell me, if you know what an apple tastes like, explain it to me!

Hearing this, the prosecutor groaned as his face turned pale while lowering his head. Inoue immediately repeated his question: "Well, if you know, tell me!"

Prosecutor: [silence]

Inoue: Just as I thought; you can't say anything. When you understand the essence of something, the more you comprehend it the less able you are to either speak or write about it. Just because your country happened to win the war, you come over here all puffed up and humiliate us. How about if you settled down and reflected on your conduct?[9]

Following Inoue's criticism, the prosecutor appeared sorry for what he'd said.

GETTING USED TO THE PROCESS

As Inoue effectively got the better of prosecutor after prosecutor, he relaxed to the point he felt he was reporting to the tribunal just to make fun of the prosecutors. Inoue became so familiar to the American guards at the building's entrance they just waved him through. Even the Japanese language interpreters at the gate thought Inoue was there as a tribunal informant, not a war criminal suspect, and urged him to request payment for his services. Although, as a suspect, Inoue was never paid, he did receive the benefit of delicious lunches at a time of severe food shortages in Japan.

In the course of his interrogations, Inoue became concerned for the well-being of his interpreter during questioning. Unlike other suspects, Inoue always had the same interpreter no matter which prosecutor was interrogating him. On the one hand, the interpreter was never supposed to interject his personal feelings into his work. On the other hand, he was expected to honestly convey not just the words but the feelings of the subject being interrogated. Thus, when Inoue shouted at the prosecutor, the interpreter was expected to shout as well. On those occasions when Inoue shouted, the prosecutor ended up being shouted at twice in rapid succession. Inoue feared this might cause problems for the interpreter, but at the same time, he couldn't help being amused by the whole situation.

In the course of going from one prosecutor to the next, Inoue noticed the difference in the national character of American and English prosecutors. In the case of American prosecutors, this meant a lack of good manners. They would, for example, take off their officers' coats, roll up their sleeves, and when angry pound their fists on the table as they hollered. Occasionally, they even placed their legs on the table, leaned back in their chairs and treated the Japanese like they weren't even human beings. On the other hand, when they found themselves on the losing side of an argument, they immediately changed their attitude, became well mannered, and expressed their respect. For this reason, Inoue admired Americans' honesty.

English prosecutors were exactly the opposite. No matter how hot it got, they wouldn't leave so much as a single button undone on their uniforms. However, when it came to attempting to intimidate their Japanese interrogees, they were no different from the Americans. Prosecutors from both countries clearly looked down on the Japanese though, at the same time, English prosecutors revealed they also regarded themselves as superior to their American counterparts. Moreover, when English prosecutors found themselves losing an argument, they would never admit it. Instead, they would say, "Let's change the topic," or "We'll stop here for today." For that reason, Inoue just couldn't bring himself to like the English. Yet Inoue couldn't help but wonder how he would have been treated had his interrogators been Japanese officials. When Japanese officials were on the losing side of an argument, Inoue believed, "they would, without a doubt, have resorted to whatever underhanded method necessary to get revenge."[10]

"INDICT ME!"

Inoue claimed to have become so successful at rebutting the various prosecutors questioning him that he became known as a "genius of sophistry" (*kiben no tensai*). Amazed by this, one of the prosecutors said, "Mr. Inoue, when one of us asks a question, you begin your rebuttal even before we finish, and without thinking. You truly have a ready wit!"[11]

What the prosecutors wanted to know was how Inoue had acquired his wit. Seeking an answer, one of them said, "Mr. Inoue, according to our records, you either failed your classes or dropped out of school altogether. Thus, you don't appear to have much of an academic background, so what books did you read?" Inoue responded,

> Well, I did read some books hoping to find answers to my longstanding doubts. However, I was unable to find the answers I sought, either from books or anyone I spoke to. Thus, I continued to suffer from the time I was seven years old over the next thirty years. During that time, I had one personal experience after another until, finally, I intuitively understood the essence of things.[12]

With this the prosecutor fell silent, saying nothing more. However, overhearing this exchange, another prosecutor said, "It's hard to tell which of us is being interrogated."[13] This turned out to be a seminal insight, for thereafter Inoue often took the lead in his interrogation sessions. For example, when it became clear he was unlikely to be indicted, Inoue initiated the following exchange with the prosecutor interrogating him:

Inoue: I want you to indict me!

Prosecutor, puzzled: Why do you want to be indicted?

Inoue: If you indict me, I'll be able to tell the whole world, in a way anyone can understand, that this foolish tribunal is something the civilized world should be ashamed of.

Prosecutor, surprised: Wait just a minute. We could never allow that.

Inoue: Well then, how about letting me observe the court proceedings? No doubt, it's a bunch of nonsense anyway.

Prosecutor: If we did that, it would be illegal for us to indict you.

Inoue: Alright, then put me on the witness stand.

Prosecutor: If we put you on the stand, there's no telling what you'd say.

Inoue: Well, if I said something you didn't like, you could press the button to cut me off, couldn't you?

Prosecutor, surprised: How do you know about the button?[14]

Inoue indicated that another prosecutor had already told him how the tribunal courtroom functioned, including the button that could be pushed to light up a red lamp, indicating the witness's testimony had been cut off.

BRIBERY

Inoue learned one additional fact about the tribunal—the size of the bribe required to escape prosecution as a war criminal. According to his informants, when interrogations had just begun, the going rate for exoneration was between ten and twenty thousand yen. As time passed, however, the cost went up, primarily due to the Japanese side bidding up the amount. Tribunal officials happily accepted the increased bribes.

Although he expected the prosecutor to get angry, one day Inoue dared raise this issue, resulting in the following exchange:

Inoue: I imagine everyone has taken bribes.

The prosecutor surprised Inoue by replying: When we selected tribunal officials from all of the Allied countries, we tried to do so carefully, but the need was so great. Why do you know about this? Do you have proof of bribe taking?

Inoue: If I had proof, I'd be a criminal, wouldn't I?

Prosecutor: That's true, but for you to make this charge I imagine you must have some kind of proof.

Inoue: Yes, I have. One is actual fact, and the other is something I intuited based on this fact. The fact is that there were four men who ought to have been indicted but were not. At the same time, there were four men who weren't guilty of anything but were charged nevertheless. I imagine that behind a contradiction like this there must be bribery or something like it going on.

Prosecutor: What are the names of the four men who should've been indicted?

Inoue: That's up to you prosecutors to investigate. I can't tell you because, as a Japanese myself, I would like to see even one fewer Japanese convicted as a war criminal. However, I will give you the names of four men who aren't war criminals: [Army General] Mazaki Jinzaburō [forced into retirement in 1941], [Navy Admiral and Prime Minister] Yonai Mitsumasa [1880–1948], [Minister of Justice in the Konoe cabinet] Shiono Sue-hiko [1880–1949], and [industrialist and backroom political fixer] Kuhara Fusanosuke [1869–1965]. These four men were not especially opposed to the war but neither were they supporters. Albeit indirectly, they were all sympathetic to Konoe's peace efforts. I'm not asking you to believe this because I said it. Why not use the various channels at your disposal to check to see if what I've said is accurate?[15]

Inoue brought up Konoe's name because by then he had learned Konoe was highly respected by both the English and Americans. They viewed him as a representative of the peace faction in Japan. This was demonstrated by the fact that when discussing imperial princes, they dropped their titles. In speaking of Konoe, however, they always addressed him as "Prince Konoe."[16] Inoue was convinced that had Konoe lived, he would have been found innocent of war criminal charges. As for the four allegedly innocent men Inoue mentioned, he was pleased to see all four were found innocent and released within a week.

BANISHED FROM HOLDING PUBLIC OFFICE

Even as Inoue grew confident that he wouldn't be indicted, he remained determined to prove his innocence. This led Inoue to tell the prosecutor,

> I want you to investigate me thoroughly, just as many times as you like. Should you become convinced that my thoughts injure the happiness and development of human beings, then indict me and sentence me to death. Alternatively, I am willing to commit suicide. On the other hand, if you discover that my thoughts can make even a small contribution to human development, I would like a certificate stating this fact.[17]

By this time, Inoue was aware the standard practice was for prosecutors to give statements of innocence to war criminal suspects once charges were dropped against them. However, if Inoue thought he was about to be found innocent, he was mistaken. Ordered to appear before yet another American prosecutor, Inoue was told,

> Mr. Inoue, since coming to Japan, we have had the opportunity to question you directly. We now understand that you belong to neither the right wing nor left wing. However, the International Tribunal is not composed of the United States alone. Even though we realize you are a unique thinker, belonging neither to the right nor left, the other allies

all believe you head the right wing, the very person responsible for starting war in the Pacific. In light of this, the United States is powerless to intercede on your behalf. Were we to try, it would become a major problem. In the near future, we are going to enact a measure banishing lesser guilty figures from holding public office. Your name will be included, and I can only express the hope you'll put up with it.[18]

In response, Inoue asked whether the prosecutor's request was his own or that of the Supreme Allied Commander. The prosecutor replied it was his own, to which Inoue said, "Fine, if you are asking me as a friend, I agree, for I have no intention of becoming a public official. Even if banished, I'll still be the same old vagabond I've always been. It makes no difference to me."[19] It was only later Inoue came to realize the full import of banishment since it prevented him from engaging in a wide variety of activities, including unauthorized writing for the public.

ONE FINAL PROSECUTOR

For the unindicted, the final step in the interrogation process consisted of a senior prosecutor reviewing the entire testimonies of suspected war criminals before approving the recommendation of subordinate prosecutors to drop charges against them. In Inoue's case, the reviewing prosecutor was Hugh Barnett Helm (1914–1999), associate counsel of the United States International Prosecution Section General Headquarters. Inoue noted Helm was unknown to the Japanese public since his name never appeared in Japanese newspapers.

On reporting to his office, Inoue was surprised by two things—first the office's spacious size and, second, the size of Helm himself, whom Inoue guessed must have weighed at least two hundred pounds. Inoue also noticed the mountainous piles of documents on his large desk. Looking grave, Helm began the interrogation with a typically American style of bluster.

Helm: Mr. Inoue, the pile of records I have on my desk are all yours. Each of the prosecutors has written the same thing, namely, that you claim that this world of unlimited differences is, just as it is, a single entity. Is that correct?

Inoue: That's right.

Hoping to unnerve Inoue, Helm raised his fat fist and waved it around his desk before pointing out the window: "How can you claim that this world of infinite differences is a single entity? Where is this single entity to be found?"

Angered by his attitude, Inoue decided to give Helm a hard time, saying, "Alright, but in order to answer you, may I ask a question?"

Helm: Fine. Ask anything you want.

Inoue: First, Mr. Helm, how many universes are there?

Helm: What do you mean, how many universes are there? Why do you ask such a stupid question?

Inoue: I don't know whether it is stupid or not. However, you did say I could ask any question I wished, so I'm asking.

Helm: Well, what you're asking is so stupid it's not even a question. Of course, the universe is an absolutely infinite single entity.

Inoue: That's right. I agree. This leads me to my second question. Mr. Helm, do you exist within this universe or outside of it?

Helm shouting, with his face turning red: Stop talking nonsense. Your insincerity is unacceptable!

Inoue: Please look at me. Do I look insincere? I don't want to say something so carelessly that I end up hanging at the end of a rope. Why would I speak insincerely? I'm extremely sincere!

Helm: What a bunch of crap—asking if I exist in the universe or outside of it! How could there be anything outside of an infinite universe? No matter how small, if there was something that existed outside of the universe, then the universe would be finite and relative.

Inoue: That's right. I agree. There is nothing outside of the universe. That's fine.

Helm: What do you mean, that's fine?

Inoue: You've answered the question you asked me by yourself.

Helm, looking exhausted and shaking his head back and forth: I don't understand.

Inoue, laughing: Do you mean that an eminent American like yourself doesn't know when you have answered your own question?

Chagrined and with a scowl on his face, Helm said nothing.

Inoue: Well, I see I have no choice but to ask a third question—do American snakes have legs?

At this point the interpreter looked at Inoue continuously, hoping to restrain him. Inoue, however, was quite confident about what he was saying, forcing the interpreter to translate exactly what he said. The moment Helm heard this, however, he became even madder.

Helm: You're saying the same ridiculous thing again. You're, you're rude! Are you trying to insult me?

Inoue: Listen, you, I'm not deaf. I can understand you even when you're speaking quietly. You said you didn't understand, so out of kindness I'm trying to inform you. However, you claim that I'm putting on an act and being rude. Aren't you the one being rude?

Helm: You're talking about snakes with legs. Whether it's a question of American snakes or snakes in any country, how could any of them have legs?

Inoue: That's right. Snakes in Japan don't have legs either. However, in Japan, when some-one adds something to a matter that is already abundantly clear, we call that a "snake's legs." In order to help you understand, I'll have to add legs to a snake. Listen carefully.

Helm, looking doubtful: I still think I'm being made a fool of.

Inoue: No, I'm definitely not making a fool of you. On the contrary, I respect you greatly. My initial question was how many universes are there. You answered only one, and I agreed. I then asked whether it was possible for there to be something outside of the universe, and you answered that was impossible. Once again, I agreed and stated that you had just answered your original question to me. Since there is nothing outside of the universe, you were born in America looking as you do, and I was born in Japan looking as I do. However, both of us exist as part of the universe. Therefore, even while retaining our individual differences, as for the universe we are one. Do you agree?

Helm, placing both hands on his desk and sighing: You're an amazing genius! . . . I'm sorry to have troubled you. That'll be all for today.[20]

This was to be the first of three times the two would meet. By the time of their second meeting, Helm's attitude toward Inoue had changed completely. Helm said, "Your thoughts are astonishing. Whether in America or Japan, or anywhere else, there shouldn't be anyone who likes war. I hope you will do your best for the peace and development of humanity. I'm not going to indict you."[21] At their third meeting, Helm was even more polite, going as far as to praise Inoue. At the conclusion of their meeting, Helm said, "I'm busy today so I'll have to end our meeting, but Chief Justice Webb has indicated he would like to see you since he has studied Buddhism for many years. Would you be willing to meet him?"[22]

Inoue indicated his willingness to meet Webb or anyone else. With that, Helm picked up his telephone, and shortly thereafter a thin man entered. This was Chief Justice William Flood Webb (1887–1972), who invited Inoue to join him in his of-fice where they sat down facing each other.

Webb: Are you an adherent of the Nichiren sect?

Inoue: No, I'm not.

Webb: Well then, what sect do you belong to?

Inoue: I don't belong to any particular sect. My family was affiliated with the Rinzai Zen sect. I received guidance from priests belonging to both the Sōtō and Rinzai Zen sects. Additionally, I went to Mount Minobu to study Nichirenism. However, at present, my thoughts are almost entirely those of the Mahāyāna school of Buddhism.

Changing the subject, Inoue continued:

According to what I've been told, you've also studied Buddhism. From the viewpoint of Mahāyāna Buddhism, what do you think of the present International Tribunal? I've heard this trial will judge Japan in the name of civilization, but this doesn't make sense. I say this because no one has made this world, and therefore it doesn't belong to any country. Despite this, England, America, Japan, and Germany got together and started quarrelling. The result is that the victorious, big robbers are now mistreating the little robbers, calling this a war crimes tribunal. All of this is being done in the name of civilization.

This would be understandable were this trial being held in a neutral country like Switzerland where both parties could be judged. From ancient times, there's been a verdict in Japan in which both sides are found at fault. That verdict would fit the current situation perfectly. Instead, we have a situation in which the winning countries judge the losing countries unilaterally. That's not a trial, only revenge. I find it incomprehensible, for could anything be more uncivilized barbarity? I don't know anything about the law, but I simply can't believe this is legitimate.[23]

Saying this, Inoue watched to see how Webb reacted. Webb hastily put his hand in his breast pocket and, taking out a big gold watch, said, "I'd like for us to meet on occasion to continue talking about various things, but, as you know, I don't have a second to spare. Thus, in my place I'd like to introduce an English gentleman with whom I hope you will meet frequently and speak freely."[24] With this, Webb pushed a button and a thirty-something gentleman came in accompanied by a pretty blond woman. Inoue's meeting with Webb lasted only five minutes.

Inoue saw Webb a few times after that walking in the hallway, but each time Webb ducked into an office and avoided talking to him. As far as Inoue was concerned, this was only natural, for he was convinced that as a result of their encounter, Webb had come to realize the tribunal was invalid. As its chief justice, Webb's position was equally invalid, and, moreover, he had lost face. Up until the members of the International Court left Japan at the end of December 1946, Inoue never met Webb again.

INOUE AS "AN HONEST MAN"

Webb introduced Inoue to Lee M. Kenna (1918–1997), a United States Army investigator for the tribunal.[25] The pretty blond woman accompanying him was his interpreter, whom Inoue noted spoke excellent Japanese indistinguishable from a native speaker. During their meetings, Kenna and Inoue spoke on a range of topics beyond the tribunal itself, including the following exchange:

Kenna: I imagine you already realized that in the course of your frequent visits to the tribunal's offices you have gradually earned everyone's respect. Do you know why?

Inoue: I never thought I was that respected, but now that you mention it, I see what you mean. What's the reason?

Kenna: Well, in the first place, at the end of each of your interrogation sessions, the relevant prosecutor commented that you are an "honest man." This made for a good first impression, to which successive prosecutors added things like a "serious man," a "religious figure," a "poet," and a "person worthy of respect."[26]

Inoue noted that in the West there appeared to be a tendency for religious figures and poets to garner respect. This was in contrast to Japanese bureaucrats, who lacked such sensibilities.

ENTER MARK GAYN

Inoue's direct connection to the tribunal had now come to an end. However, in the summer of 1946, Mark Gayn (1902–1981), an American journalist covering the tribunal, came to visit him. Gayn later recounted his experiences, including his meeting with Inoue, in a 1948 book entitled *Japan Diary*. On the day they were to meet, Gayn was late, and Inoue waited for him to arrive wearing nothing more than a *yukata*, a lightweight, summer kimono. "It wasn't the type of dress to greet an honored guest," Inoue opined, "but I wanted to see how he would react."[27] Not only that, when Gayn finally did arrive, Inoue purposely sat with one leg upright, exposing his crotch. Gayn, for his part, was dressed informally in an open-necked shirt. While not personally disturbed by Inoue's dress, Gayn did appear concerned about the female reporter who accompanied him, frequently glancing sideways to see how she was doing.

The first question Gayn put to Inoue concerned the nature of the Imperial Way.

Inoue: It's difficult to explain.

Gayn: You don't know what it is?

Inoue: It's because I know what it is that I can't explain it.

Gayn: Stop talking nonsense. If you know what it is, you should be able to explain it!

Inoue: Well, then, let me ask you, do you know what an apple tastes like?

With this, the conversation proceeded as it had earlier in the prosecutor's office, and with the same result. Inoue noted Gayn eventually ended up purring like a kitten.

Gayn: To tell the truth, this is the first time in my life I have encountered thoughts as wonderful as yours. I imagine there is probably no academic anywhere in the United States who could match wits with you. When the situation permits, how about coming to the United States? I'll serve as your guide and arrange a series of debates. By having these debates broadcast on radio and television, you'll become famous throughout the country.

Hearing this, Inoue thought to himself, "Just like a newspaper reporter to say such things."

Gayn continued: "Don't you have a book in which you've written your thoughts and experiences? If you do, I'll take it to the United States and have it published. I'm sure it'll become a bestseller."

When Inoue replied that he hadn't written such a book, Gayn urged him to do so. Inoue took this advice seriously and later wrote a book containing much of the material forming the basis of this present volume. Gayn also shared his interest in learning more about the Mito School (Mitogaku), a school of Japanese historical and Shinto studies that arose in the Mito domain, modern-day Ibaraki prefecture. Aware that Inoue had previously headed a temple located in Ibaraki, Gayn asked Inoue to introduce him to someone knowledgeable about this school that had exerted such a major influence on modern Japanese history. Inoue provided Gayn with the names of two acquaintances in the area.

The roots of the Mito School can be traced back to 1657, when Tokugawa Mitsukuni (1628–1700), second head of the Mito domain, commissioned the compilation of the *History of Great Japan* (*Dai Nihonshi*). This work, based on Neo-Confucianism, emphasized the influence of moral laws on the process of historical development. The *History of Great Japan* revealed Japan to have originally been a country ruled by successive emperors (rather than the warrior class) and emphasized respect for both the Imperial Court and Shinto deities. By the end of the eighteenth century, however, the Mito School branched out to address contemporary social and political issues. It thus became a major influence on the *sonnō jōi* (revere the emperor, expel foreign barbarians) movement, contributing to the Meiji Restoration of 1868.

In *Japan Diary*, Gayn described his trip to the Ibaraki area that began on September 26, 1946:

> The trip was so exciting, and so much fresh material seemed to wait ahead, that we were loath to turn back. We had brought letters of introduction from Nissho ("Sun-chosen") Inouye (aka Inoue), one of the three great political terrorists of Japan, and as we penetrated the "nationalist belt" near the city of Mito, we put them to good use. Mito had been wiped out in the air raids, and to be close to the patriotic killers, we lived in a bordello in the neighboring town. The place was busy, and at night from our porch we watched Mito officials make merry in the banquet hall, and take the girls in relays to a back room. Sally [Gayn's partner] made friends with the *madame*, who was an officer's widow and a very charming woman, and from her we learned much of the way people thought and lived in this corner of Japan. "At one time," the *madame* said, "so many killers came from this district that no outsiders would marry our girls."[28]

Three days later, on September 29, Gayn met the head of Ibaraki Transportation Company. Takeuchi Yūnosuke, one of the major contributors to the construction of Inoue's former temple in Ōarai. Gayn described Takeuchi as "a small, thin, old man who looked like a tired shopkeeper."[29] Having received a letter from Inoue, Takeuchi was prepared for Gayn's arrival and immediately took Gayn and his partner by car to hot springs he owned more than a hundred miles to the north. After bathing, Gayn was treated to a tea ceremony followed by two separate feasts of fish and meat. All through dinner, Gayn probed Takeuchi for more information about Inoue, but each time his questions were deflected with a toast. None of this, however, prepared Gayn and his partner for what happened next.

After dinner, when Takeuchi had had a great deal to drink, he stood up and began to dance. His were not the smooth and slow movements of a typical Japanese dancer. This was a warrior's dance, violent and jerky. We were the enemy, and he lunged in our direction and slashed the air with an invisible sword. The long kimono was in the way, and he picked up the bottom ends and opened them, exposing his spindly legs encased in long white woolen drawers. The sight was grotesque, but it was never funny. This was an angry dance, done in premeditation and filled with meaning.

As abruptly as he began, Takeuchi returned to his seat on the floor, filled his cup and offered us a toast. His face was red and unfriendly. "You Americans talk of democracy. It doesn't suit us. Does it mean that the workers get a voice in the management of an industry? Do you have that in the United States? Does it mean that the workers can take over factories, as they have done in Japan? Does it mean that the unions can strike at a time of crisis like we're in now? Does it mean that men can criticize the emperor?"

His voice was sharp and high and angry. He spoke in long stretches and even while Roy [the interpreter] was still translating, Takeuchi began anew. He was getting out of hand, and I was beginning to get worried. Both of us, I knew, would lose face irreparably if I had to restrain him. When a pause came, I thanked him for the gracious reception, and Sally and I retreated to the hotel.[30]

Fortunately, not everyone Inoue had contacted on Gayn's behalf gave him such a rude reception. By the end of his three-day visit, Gayn felt he had gained a much better understanding of the Mito school. This led him to conclude: "It was not by accident that political terrorism sprang up here, for Mito has always been the cradle of extreme nationalism, and *Mito Gaku*, or the Mito school of Nationalist thought, had left an inerasable shadow on Japanese history."[31]

Although Inoue never met Gayn again, he was aware of how Gayn had described him, as well as the latter's meeting with Takeuchi, in his book, *Japan Diary*. None of this bothered Inoue, but he was unhappy that Gayn had failed to include the manner in which, during their first meeting, Gayn has been silenced by the logic of Inoue's rebuttals. "Gayn was half-baked," Inoue opined, "for the only thing he wrote about was how everywhere he went he got the better of the Japanese in arguments."[32]

POVERTY ONCE AGAIN

By September 1947 Inoue found himself, as so often in the past, "with no prospects for earning a living."[33] Moreover, he was in a poor state of health. "There was nothing left to do but commit suicide," he decided.[34] But then he had second thoughts, recalling the Chinese maxim, "All parts have a mission to fulfill toward the whole."[35] Based on this, he realized it would be inexcusable for him to give up his mission because he had grown tired. No matter how small, he decided, he still needed to contribute to the good of society.

With this in mind, in September 1948 Inoue wrote a short pamphlet, only seven pages long, entitled "Absoluteness" (*Zettai*). It described his sense of the unity of all things. However, under the Allied occupation, all writing was subject to censorship.

Thus, he first submitted the pamphlet for review by the occupation authorities, but it was not until December of that year that permission was granted. He was also instructed that, once available, one copy was to be submitted to ensure compliance.

Inoue believed there were two reasons why the occupation authorities took three months to approve his short pamphlet. In the first instance, it was because the authorities had been unable to understand what he meant by the pamphlet's title. Secondly, because, during his earlier interrogation, he had referred to the War Crimes Tribunal as a barbaric, extremely illegal act, the safest course of action was to prevent him from publishing anything until after the tribunal had handed down its verdicts, something it only did in November 1948.

Inoue found a publisher willing to print four thousand copies of his pamphlet. With these in hand, Inoue embarked on a program of speaking wherever he was invited. However, as part of his ban from holding public office, he wasn't allowed to make any political statements. This didn't bother him since, in his estimation, there weren't many Japanese, let alone occupation authorities, who were able to understand his message.

Despite the widespread devastation and poverty of postwar Japan, Inoue's message had not changed. He embraced the truth of a non-dualistic universe, rooted in the equality of all things, in contrast to a world still based on the distinction between one thing and another. Inoue claimed,

> Only those who have truly acquired the truth of a non-dualistic universe are qualified to be leaders. In the absence of such qualified persons, there can be no revival of Japan or new construction. However, as I survey the country at the moment, I find no such qualified political figures. Given this, we must look to the emergence of new leaders.[36]

Inoue added that the truth of a non-dualistic universe was not his creation but something revealed thousands of years ago in Mahāyāna Buddhist texts and even Japanese classics. Furthermore, the creation of an ideal country required this non-dualistic truth to be understood not only by political leaders but by every citizen of the nation. Inoue's role was to teach this truth to young and old, men and women. In other words, he was, once again, to become a sacrificial pawn dedicated to the renewal of Japan. A renewed Japan would then usher in the renewal of the entire world. Although still in the distant future, this would one day bring about the realization of a "world state" (*sekai kokka*), albeit only after an immense effort on the part of humankind.

As someone born in Japan, Inoue realized it was his responsibility to devote himself to Japan's renewal, the first step of which consisted in the conduct of a "thought campaign" (*shisō-undō*). Only after the concept of a non-dualistic universe was widely disseminated would it be possible to develop political and economic movements based on this truth. Further, concrete plans for implementing this truth must be developed in accordance with the time and place of their implementation. "Fanciful plans were of no use," he claimed, "no more than Marxist illusions."[37] Inoue's opposition to communism had not weakened in the least.

In accomplishing his mission, Inoue was well aware of his own limitations:

It's not that I lack proposals, but I'm not a specialist in either politics or economics. Therefore, rather than coming up with a shabby plan, it's better for interested specialists who have acquired a non-dualistic understanding of the universe, and guided by predecessors, to create a worthy organizational structure. No one can be expected to do everything inasmuch as there are none who are omnipotent. My role is that of a path-finder. Among the ninety million citizens of this country, there will certainly be those who will harvest the seeds now being planted.

I have struggled hard to apply the truth of a non-dualistic universe to the renewal of Japan for more than twenty years. In addition, my prior struggle to discover this truth lasted more than thirty years. Thus, I regard my whole life as one long struggle.[38]

LECTURING AT A ZEN TEMPLE

Given Inoue's promotion of a non-dualistic universe, it is unsurprising that a major, if unnamed, Zen monastery was one of the first places to invite Inoue to speak. Inasmuch as his audience was composed exclusively of senior priests and some thirty novice monks, Inoue decided to reveal his true feelings about the state of Zen in contemporary Japan.

First, however, Inoue noted that the monastery was being run as a de facto hotel, one that disguised its moneymaking activities by describing its guests as lay pilgrims. Both the monastic officials and novice monks served as the hotel staff, severely reducing their practice of *zazen* and study of the sutras to the little time they had left over. Inoue wrote, "Can this be said to be a religious training center for those taking upon themselves the sacred work of saving all sentient beings? It's clear this goes against the wishes of the great founders of Zen."[39]

According to Inoue, religious founders like Shakyamuni Buddha were interested, in the first instance, in investigating the true nature of all phenomena, thereby advancing from the realm of desire and pain to the realm of comfort. The ultimate purpose was to bring salvation to the whole world as well as individuals. Unfortunately, Shakyamuni's successors gradually became degenerate, failing to keep in mind their responsibility to save society and all sentient beings. Instead, they devoted themselves exclusively to a life of ease through securing donations from lay adherents. Inoue addressed the assembled monks as follows:

You, young novice priests assembled here, have no thought of faithfully and zealously applying yourselves to religious practice. Instead, you think that by training at this monastery for ten years or so you will get the credentials necessary to become the abbot of a first-class temple. This will qualify you to wear the purple robes of a high-ranking priest, something every priest would like to have. As for you, monastic leaders, you, too, have little interest in serious religious practice. Instead, you are content to use your lectures as a means of skillfully ingratiating yourselves with lay adherents.

When you eventually leave this hothouse of extreme degeneracy and become temple abbots, what will you do? You will lead a life of relative ease based on the donations received from lay adherents, not to mention the money received from a deceased adherent's family when you assign a posthumous Buddhist name upon a family member's death. Or the money you receive when conducting one of the numerous memorial services for deceased adherents. Further, even though postwar land reforms stripped temples of much of their agricultural land, there is still the income received from the remaining temple property, including both wet and dry fields plus forested lands. Thus, you will become a bunch of good-for-nothings whose lives have no purpose.

In other words, from the beginning of your entrance into the priesthood you had no intention of investigating the true nature of reality, let alone devoting yourselves to the salvation of society and all sentient beings. In effect, your minds are not even slightly different from those of the masses who are themselves in need of religious salvation. Despite this, you feel no shame in calling yourself a "Zen master" or a "Buddhist priest." On the one hand, you cower in the face of those with financial and political power while you act arrogantly toward ordinary people. There are no more wretched priests than you today, for you have lost all sense of shame.[40]

Needless to say, Inoue's harsh condemnation did not endear him to the assembled monks, young or old. The senior monks mumbled something and let their heads drop. Four or five of the young training monks listened with clenched fists, eyes flashing with anger and jaws tense. Inoue inwardly welcomed the angry reaction of these young monks, for he took it as a sign of their genuineness as opposed to the senior monks who simply sat sulking. When Inoue left the monastery that evening, one of the young monks accompanied him to the bus stop. Inoue found reason for hope in the young monk's parting words: "Some years have passed since I first entered this monastery, but never once have I accepted worldly favors. Nevertheless, it's just as you say, this is a hothouse, not a religious training center. I've had a change of heart and from now on will train earnestly."[41] Reflecting on this experience, Inoue shared his thoughts on what he considered the future of not just Zen but religion in general:

From my vantage point, I see religion gradually shifting its focus from the individual to all of humanity. This means that religion will gradually develop to the point it cannot help but seek the salvation of society as a whole and not only the individual. Won't this lead to discarding the main object of worship that now consists of a deity endowed with a human personality? Won't this mean that religious movements practiced heretofore will turn into thought movements?[42]

Although Inoue didn't touch on this, it's clear that were existing religious movements to turn into "thought movements," Inoue would be in an ideal position to play a leading role.

NATIONAL PROTECTION CORPS— REBIRTH OF THE RIGHT WING

With the end of the Allied occupation in April 1952, Japan regained its sovereignty. This brought an end to Allied censorship, and Inoue was finally able to publish the complete version of his memoirs, entitled *Ichinin Issatsu* (One Person Kills One [Person]), in October 1953. The title reflected the strategy his terrorist band adopted in carrying out their 1932 assassination campaign. At the same time, the Buddhist connection to his band's acts was clear through the phrase he had printed on the lower left-hand corner of his photo. The phrase, located on the book's inside cover, read: "Kill one that many may live" (*issatsu tashō*). Stephan Large informs us that Inoue had initially hoped to make this phrase the formal title of his book but was overruled by his publisher, Nihon Shūhōsha.[43] The Buddhist significance of the phrase on Inoue's photo will be discussed in chapter 14.

By April 29, 1954, Inoue was ready to act on his call for the "renewal" of Japan. It was on this day he joined other prewar ultrarightist leaders, including former band members, to form both the National Protection Corps (Gokokudan) and its subsidiary, the National Protection Youth Corps (Gokokudan Seinentai). Inoue was chosen to be the initial head. Surprisingly, in postwar Japan, the need for ultra-right-wing groups like his was, if anything, even more acute than it had been in the prewar years. This is because, due to reforms enacted in the early days of the Allied occupation, Japan was a far more liberal society than it had been in the prewar period. Women, for example, were granted the right to vote in December 1945.

In addition, major land reform measures were enacted. Approximately 38 percent of Japan's cultivated land was purchased from landlords under the government's reform program and resold at extremely low prices to the farmers who worked the land. By 1950, three million peasants had acquired land, dismantling a rural power structure long dominated by landlords. Further, the new constitution adopted in 1947 guaranteed fundamental human rights, strengthened the powers of the Diet (i.e., parliament), and reinstated government cabinets formed by one or more political parties commanding a majority of seats in the Diet. Police power was decentralized, and political prisoners, including communists, were released from prison.

Of particular concern to the postwar right wing was the Diet's passage, in 1945, of Japan's first-ever trade union law protecting the right of workers to form or join a union, organize, and strike. There had been prewar attempts to recognize labor unions, but none was successful until laws legalizing labor unions were passed under pressure from the Allied occupation. Even today, the trade union law passed in June 1949 remains in place. Coupled with the Labor Standards Act of April 1947, organized labor, typically left wing in orientation, exercised far greater power than in the prewar period.

However reluctantly on the part of some postwar Japanese political leaders, the state was now required to protect workers, including their right to organize and strike, rather than repress, jail, and torture them, as had occurred in the prewar period.

Inasmuch as the government could no longer be depended on to crush labor unions or control striking workers, Japanese business leaders were in need of someone to do their bidding. Unsurprisingly, such leaders, often with behind-the-scenes support from conservative politicians, became the patrons of resurgent right-wing groups like Inoue's National Protection Corps, relying on them to take "extralegal" action in the event of strikes. Inoue had, in fact, anticipated this development when in the last pages of his memoirs he noted, "The [postwar] age is one based on power. Expressed using the terminology of the Shinto-derived, three Imperial regalia, "this is not the age of the 'jewel' or the 'mirror,' but the 'sword.'"[44]

The National Protection Corps was at the forefront of those ultra-right-wing groups using the sword (i.e., violent tactics) in the postwar period. On the one hand, the National Protection Corps spoke highly of the emperor, describing him as the "center of the blood relationship that bound the race together," employing the ideas of the prewar period in which Japanese society was presented as one large family with the emperor at its head.[45]

Additionally, the corps pledged itself "to liberate the masses from the despotism of the rich and powerful."[46] While these sentiments reflected Inoue's long-held views, the reality was that, like fellow right-wing organizations, the National Protection Corps' actions consisted of repeated involvement in violent political incidents aimed at disrupting if not suppressing all forms of left-wing activities. It was, in short, as strongly anticommunist as its prewar predecessors. According to the postwar Metropolitan Police, the corps was nothing more than a violent organized crime group (*bōryokudan*).

The corps' major funding sources were Kodama Yoshio (1911–1984) and Sasakawa Ryōichi (1899–1995), both notorious prewar and postwar ultra-right-wing leaders and, like the now deceased Tōyama Mitsuru, influential behind-the-scenes fixers. Like Inoue, both men had been suspected of being war criminals by the occupation authorities. Unlike Inoue, both men were incarcerated in Sugamo Prison for three years while their wartime activities were investigated. However, again like Inoue, they ultimately escaped indictment and were released from prison in 1948. Not only that, in postwar Japan they both became extremely wealthy men, so much so that Sasakawa once claimed, "I am the world's richest fascist."[47]

It is also revealing that a lawyer and politician named Kimura Tokutarō was actively involved in recruiting corps members, who were often no more than petty hoodlums. Kimura served as justice minister in two postwar cabinets headed by Prime Minister Yoshida Shigeru (1878–1967). A conservative, Kimura successfully prevented the revival of trial by jury during his tenure. The corps's connection to powerful political figures like Kimura shows that, despite the many liberal changes that had taken place during the occupation, governance of the now independent country continued to reflect the prewar political agenda, at least domestically. The one major difference was that now, as Prime Minister Yoshida's policies demonstrated, Japan was highly subservient to the United States, especially in its foreign policy. On this point, Inoue remained strangely silent.

FINAL DAYS

By 1954 Inoue was already sixty-eight years old, too old to join younger members in battling leftists on the streets or disrupting political rallies and strikes. However, thanks to his prewar reputation, Inoue was now regarded as the grand old man of the Japanese right wing. As such, his name gave instant credibility to the National Protection Corps among right-wing factions. For his part, Inoue used his position as head of the corps to influence and support some of Japan's most important conservative postwar political leaders, including Ikeda Hayato (1899–1965), then secretary-general of the Liberal Democratic Party and later prime minister, who visited Inoue in the hospital when he was ill.

Inoue also met former Class A war criminal suspect Kishi Nobusuke (1896–1987) when the latter was still Japan's foreign minister, prior to him becoming prime minister. During his meeting with Kishi, Inoue informed him for the first time of secrets he knew about the wartime cabinet of Tōjō Hideki. Inoue was also interested in the political situation in Indonesia and met Indonesian Vice President Mohammad Hatta (1902–1980) when he visited Japan. This led to a proposal that Inoue take up permanent residence in Indonesia, where he would be responsible for certain unspecified aspects of Japan's relations with Southeast Asia. As in the 1940s, Inoue was once again operating in the wings of the highest echelons of the Japanese government.

However, before anything grew out of these plans, Inoue was struck down with diabetes, his sickness progressing to the point he was unable to function normally. This led to Inoue stepping down as head of the National Protection Corps in 1956. In one sense this was fortuitous because the postwar younger members of the corps were becoming increasingly dissatisfied with Inoue's leadership. Their dissatisfaction stemmed from his continued use of Buddhist terminology to explain his thinking. Inoue seemed out of step with the times because in the postwar era traditional Buddhism was relegated to the performance of funerary rites and, for the most part, no longer regarded as having solutions to society's varied problems.

Inoue effectively retired at this point and moved to Japan's ancient military capital, Kamakura, located some thirty miles southwest of Tokyo. With the financial support of Miura Gi'ichi (1898–1971), president of the Bank of Japan and prominent right-wing fixer, Inoue built a house for his mistress and himself. True to his former profligate lifestyle, his mistress was a former *geisha* from the Kagurazaka district of Tokyo. At the same time, and as at so many times in the past, Inoue left his wife, Toshiko, and their only daughter, Ryōko, to fend for themselves in Tokyo.[48]

Toshiko's longtime heart condition worsened and, no longer able to work as a nurse, she ended up an itinerant peddler. Distraught by this development, Ryōko attempted to retrieve her father from Kamakura but without success. As a consequence, Ryoko and her mother continued their longstanding life of poverty. However, Onuma Shō, Inoue Junnosuke's assassin, did provide them with some financial support. Onuma also assisted Inoue in founding the National Protection Corps and went on to become president of a major publishing company.

As for Inoue, even though retired and receiving medical treatment, his social activism continued unabated. Inoue proposed, for example, that the annual meeting of the recently formed World Peace Council be convened in Japan. However, before his proposal could be realized, Inoue suffered a severe stroke at the beginning of 1967. On realizing death was imminent, Inoue made a deep obeisance in the direction of the distant Imperial Palace.[49] Inoue died on March 4, 1967, aged eighty-one. His grave, together with that of his wife, is located at the large Rinzai Zen temple of Kichijōji, located in Kawaba village, his birthplace.

Today, a life-sized bronze statue of Inoue stands on a pedestal at the entrance to Risshō Gokokudō, the temple Inoue once headed in Ōarai. It was, however, only in the postwar period that this temple formally affiliated itself with the Nichiren sect. The village museum in Kawaba also has a corner dedicated to Inoue and his writings. While the National Protection Corps still exists, it is today located in shabby walk-up offices in central Tokyo, a shadow of its former self. However, as exemplified by Inoue's own life, the corps, like its sister right-wing organizations, remains ready to emerge from the shadows should Japan once again encounter serious social instability. Inoue may be gone, but the potential for a repeat of what he represented lives on.

Hungry children in Iwate prefecture in northern Japan eating uncooked white radishes (daikon), November 1934. Photo courtesy of Mainichi Shimbunsha

Girls from Yamagata prefecture in northeastern Japan arriving in Tokyo after having been sold into prostitution, October 1934. Photo courtesy of Mainichi Shimbunsha

Inoue Nisshō's childhood home in Kawaba village as it appears today. His home originally had a thatched roof without sliding window doors on the first floor.

Santoku-an hermitage in Kawaba village as it appears today. It is now used as a storage shed for the adjacent cemetery.

The grave for both Inoue Nisshō and his wife Shitsu (aka Toshiko). It is located at the Rinzai Zen Kichijō-ji Temple in Kawaba village.

Inoue Nisshō dressed as a neophyte Tendai priest in 1916. His priestly status was in name only. Photo courtesy of the Kawaba Village Museum

Inoue Nisshō in the prewar era, year unknown. Photo courtesy of the Kawaba Village Museum

Inoue Nisshō as the grand old man of the ultraright in postwar Japan. Photo courtesy of Mainichi Shimbunsha

Rinzai Zen master Yamamoto Gempō, Inoue Nisshō's Zen master. Photo courtesy of the Library of Congress

Inside of Shōinji's newly renovated meditation hall (zazendō), where Inoue Nisshō once trained.

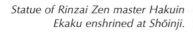

Statue of Rinzai Zen master Hakuin Ekaku enshrined at Shōinji.

Risshō Gokokudō Temple as it appears today. Inoue Nisshō headed this temple and trained his terrorist band here. It first became affiliated with the Nichiren sect in the postwar period.

A statue of Nichiren enshrined on the altar of Risshō Gokokudō Temple.

Emperor Meiji Memorial Hall, located adjacent to Risshō Gokokudō Temple.

Hishinuma Gorō at the time of his arrest in March 1932, following his shooting of Dan Takuma. Photo courtesy of Mainichi Shimbunsha

Ōnuma Shō at the time of his arrest in March 1932, following his shooting of Inoue Junnosuke. Photo courtesy of Kyōdō Tsūshin

Former finance minister Inoue Junnosuke. Photo courtesy of the National Diet Library

Director-General of Mitsui Dan Takuma. Photo courtesy of the National Diet Library

Prime Minister Inukai Tsuyoshi at the time he made a condolence call to the family of Dan Takuma in March 1932, not knowing that he, too, would soon be shot on May 15, 1932 (May 15th Incident). Photo courtesy of Mainichi Shimbunsha

Inoue Nisshō about to enter the courtroom for his trial in June 1933. Photo courtesy of Kyōdō Tsūshin

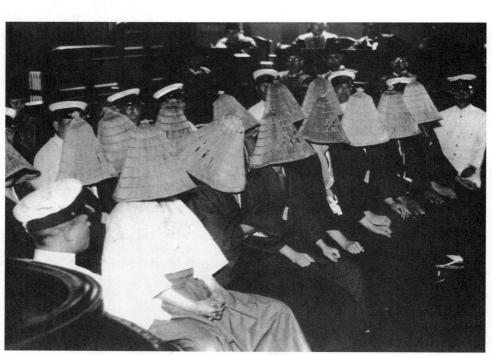

Fourteen defendants of the Blood Oath Corps wearing prisoners' straw hats. Photo courtesy of Mainichi Shimbunsha

Tōyama Mitsuru, fixer par excellence, in the 1930s. Photo courtesy of National Diet Library

Army General Araki Sadao, major leader of the Imperial Way Faction. Photo courtesy of National Diet Library

Prime Minister Konoe Fumimaro. Photo courtesy of National Diet Library

Army General and Prime Minister Tōjō Hideki. Photo courtesy of National Diet Library

Ōkawa Shūmei, ultranationalist writer and fixer. Photo courtesy of National Diet Library

Kita Ikki, ultranationalist activist close to the Young Officers' Movement.

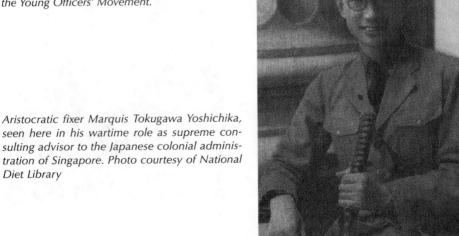

Aristocratic fixer Marquis Tokugawa Yoshichika, seen here in his wartime role as supreme consulting advisor to the Japanese colonial administration of Singapore. Photo courtesy of National Diet Library

Bronze statue of Inoue Nisshō with pagoda in background at Risshō Gokokudō Temple.

Close-up of bronze statue of Inoue Nisshō at Risshō Gokokudō Temple.

Grave of Patriots of the Shōwa Restoration at Risshō Gokokudō Temple. The Chinese character engraved on the black marble at the top of the pillar reads "Spirits."

13

Unraveling the Historical Matrix

In this chapter we return, at last, to the surface after our long sojourn in the netherworld. It is now time to make sense of what happened, first from a historical point of view and then, in the following chapter, from a religious standpoint. Let me stress, however, that the comments contained in this chapter are not meant to be a definitive history of the period. Instead, I hope to provide readers with a clearer understanding of the environment in which Inoue and his terrorist band operated. In addition, to the extent that conclusions are reached, they are not meant to be final but rather "possibilities" deserving of further exploration by future historians of this period.

With this in mind, the first thing to be said is that if this book were a detective novel, it would now be possible to simply stamp "case closed" and stop writing. After all, there can be no doubt that Onuma Shō, who shot politician Inoue Junnosuke, and Hishinuma Gorō, who shot business magnate Dan Takuma, were guilty of the crimes they readily confessed to. Additionally, Inoue Nisshō just as readily admitted being the leader of the terrorist band responsible for carrying out these killings as well as additional failed attempts. In short, if this were a "whodunit," there would be nothing more to write.

Yet there are many questions remaining to be answered. To begin with, it is clear that Inoue had powerful friends and benefactors behind the scenes. Who were these individuals and what led them to support Inoue and his band's terrorist acts? If Inoue were the puppeteer of his youthful band, is it possible that he himself was a puppet manipulated by far more powerful actors behind the scenes? In fact, the Japanese have a name for just such behind-the-scenes manipulators. They are called *kuromaku*, literally "black curtains," a term known in the West as a "fixer."

It can be argued that the Blood Oath Corps Incident wasn't all that significant. After all, only two men were killed initially and one later on, far fewer than are typically gunned down on America's streets every day. It is true, however, that in this case the victims were political and corporate leaders whose deaths had a substantial impact on Japanese society. Just how important these persons were, and the impacts their deaths had, clearly needs to be explored in more detail.

The possibility exists that Inoue and his band's actions might have been part of a much larger plot, a plot to end "Taishō Democracy," the last major barrier preventing Japan from coming under the direct control of the emperor and his advisors. This possibility gains further weight when the historical impact of the Blood Oath Corps Incident is considered in conjunction with its second phase, the May 15 Incident of 1932 that resulted in the death of Prime Minister Inukai Tsuyoshi.

The Blood Oath Corps Incident becomes even more significant in light of the importance attributed to it at the time by Japanese leaders at the zenith of Japanese society. For example, where else in the history of terrorism do we see a convicted terrorist leader leave prison not only a free man but with his entire conviction erased from the record? Where else has a convicted terrorist gone on to become the live-in adviser of his country's prime minister? These facts alone alert us that something strange, very strange, was going on behind the scenes.

THE HISTORICAL BACKGROUND OF ASSASSINATIONS

One indication of what was going on can be found in the long history of political assassinations in Japan. For example, one of Japan's earliest recorded assassinations occurred in 592, when Emperor Sushun (r. 587–592) was killed by a political rival. However, the 1889 assassination of statesman, diplomat, and Christian Viscount Mori Arinori (1847–1889) was distinctly different, for it marked the beginning of assassinations stemming from concerns beyond personal animosity or rivalry. On February 12, 1889, the day the Meiji Constitution was promulgated, Mori was stabbed by an ultranationalist and died the following day. At the time, rightly or wrongly, Christianity was perceived as an appendage of Western imperialism and therefore a threat to Japan's political and cultural integrity. Mori's assassin was outraged by the latter's failure to show proper respect to Amaterasu, the Shinto Sun goddess, during his visit to the Ise Shrine two years earlier. Specifically, on entering the shrine, Mori had failed to observe the custom of removing his shoes and, moreover, pushed aside a sacred veil with his Western walking stick.

A more politically charged assassination took place on October 26, 1909, when Prince Itō Hirobumi (1841–1909) was shot repeatedly at the Harbin Railway Station in Manchuria. The assailant, An Jung-geun, a Korean nationalist and independence activist, opposed Itō in his role as resident-general of Korea, then a Japanese protectorate but soon to become an outright colony. In the years immediately following, the struggle over Japan's role in Asia, as well as its domestic economy, became ever more acute.

Prime Minister Hara Takashi (1856–1921) was the next major political leader to fall to the hand of an assassin. On November 4, 1921, Hara was stabbed to death by a right-wing railroad switchman named Nakaoka Kon'ichi at Tokyo Station. In a harbinger of things to come for "patriotic" assassins, Nakaoka was released thirteen years after committing the murder. Hara's death resulted from the fact that he had tried, as Japan's first commoner prime minister, to steer a path between contending left- and right-wing forces, pleasing neither side. Ultranationalists acted in the face of what they regarded as Hara's weakness in attempting to quell unrest in Korea by granting it limited self-rule despite its colonial status.

As previously introduced in chapter 2, Japan enjoyed an economic boom as a result of war-related procurements by allied powers in Europe during World War I. Following the war's end, however, the country entered a period of ever-deepening recession. This was followed by the devastating 1923 Great Kantō Earthquake and the worldwide Great Depression of 1929. As a result, by the time Hamaguchi Osachi (1870–1931) became prime minister in 1929, he was convinced of the need to implement fiscal austerity measures, including curtailment of military spending by, for example, ratifying the London Naval Treaty of 1930. However, the antitreaty faction within the Japanese navy was outraged by his agreement to weaken the navy vis-à-vis the Western powers. Right-wing political parties and their supporters also opposed his decision since they believed in the need for a strong military in order to continue overseas expansion, especially on the Asian continent.

As opposition to Hamaguchi's policies mounted, he fell victim to an assassination attempt on November 14, 1930, when he was shot inside Tokyo Station by Sagoya Tomeo (1910–1972), another self-described patriot and member of the secret ultranationalist Aikoku-sha (Society of Patriots). Hamaguchi was seriously wounded and eventually died of complications on August 26, 1931. Sagoya claimed he had shot Hamaguchi because the latter was, among other things, interfering with the emperor's right of supreme command of the military. Although initially sentenced to death, Sagoya had his sentence steadily reduced until, like Inoue and his band members, he was released from prison in 1940 and resumed his right-wing activities. In the postwar period, he also collaborated with Inoue to form the Gokokudan (National Protection Corps) in 1954 and served as its head when Inoue stepped down.

Hamaguchi's death marked the first of an increasing number of assassinations of both political and financial leaders in 1930s Japan. Like previous assassinations, Hamaguchi's death served to reinforce the precedent that Japan's leaders, no matter how powerful, could be dispatched at the hands of ultranationalist assassins when the former failed to please powerful right-wing forces in Japanese society. The assassins always claimed to have acted out of patriotic motivations, and while their patriotic claims were not quite a "get out of jail free card," they certainly resulted in relatively short prison sentences given the gravity of their crimes. Thus, the stage was set for the emergence of Inoue and his terrorist band. But what had Inoue Junnosuke, Dan Takuma, and shortly thereafter Prime Minister Inukai Tsuyoshi done to deserve death?

VICTIMS OF THE BLOOD OATH CORPS
AND MARCH 15 INCIDENTS

Inoue Junnosuke was both a financier and a statesman. He first gained national prominence in 1919 when appointed governor of the Bank of Japan. In 1923 he became finance minister in the cabinet of Prime Minister Yamamoto Gonbee (1852–1933). The following year he was selected as a member of the House of Peers by imperial command. In 1927, he was reappointed governor of the Bank of Japan. In 1929, he became finance minister and lifted the gold embargo, creating a gold-backed yen. Junnosuke was then a member of the cabinet of Prime Minister Hamaguchi Osachi, who, as noted above, died in 1931 following an assassination attempt the year before. Junnosuke resigned as finance minister in 1931 and went on to become the administrator of the Constitutional Democratic Party (Rikken Minseitō).

The Constitutional Democratic Party advocated cooperation with the United States and protection of Japanese interests through diplomacy. For that reason, it opposed a full-scale military invasion of China. Further, as the Democratic Party's finance minister from 1929 to 1931, Junnosuke deliberately adopted a deflationary policy in order to eliminate weak banks and inefficient firms. He sought to restore the yen to gold convertibility at its old pre–World War I value. Coupled with this was a major campaign by the government to induce households to reduce their consumption. These policies caused severe depression in Japan, but Junnosuke refused to change course, making him highly unpopular with the general public. Combined with his party's long-standing opposition to military expansion abroad, these policies made him a target for assassination by Inoue's band.

Dan Takuma was a leading Japanese businessman who was director-general of Mitsui, one of the leading Japanese *zaibatsu* (family corporate conglomerates). He was also a graduate of the Massachusetts Institute of Technology. While leading Mitsui, Dan concurrently served in many executive posts in the financial world, including director of the Industry Club of Japan. In 1928, he was elevated to the rank of baron (*danshaku*).

Like Inoue Junnosuke, Dan favored closer relations between Japan and the Western powers. In 1921, for instance, he led a group of Japanese business leaders on a visit to the United States, Great Britain, and France. Their goal was to discuss bilateral economic issues and to promote personal ties with businesspeople in those countries. However, in the eyes of the ultranationalists, Dan was a symbol of the evil power of high finance in government. His ties with the West, combined with his leading role in what the ultranationalists regarded as corporations with little regard for the common people, made him a target.

Finally, the major cause of Prime Minister Inukai Tsuyoshi's assassination was a series of actions he took in an attempt to rein in the military, especially related to preventing further troop increases in China. He also favored entering into negotiations with the Chinese government to search for a diplomatic solution to outstanding issues between the two countries. Although more symbol than substance, this led him to initially withhold diplomatic recognition of the Japanese puppet state of Manchukuo (Manchuria) when it was formally established on March 1, 1932. He did this as a gesture of his displeasure at what he regarded as radical elements in the army as well as his concern for rapidly worsening relations with the United States.

REMAINING VICTIMS

The following are the names and positions of those persons who had not yet been assassinated by the Blood Oath Corps members at the time of their arrest. Nearly all those slated for assassination were known for their desire to find some kind of accommodation with the United States and other Western powers, coupled with their opposition to full-scale war with China though not necessarily opposition to Japan's control of the puppet state of Manchukuo. Inoue's band originally planned to kill a total of approximately twenty influential figures. According to Hugh Byas, when it was agreed to add a few more bankers and capitalists, "as nobody knew who should be chosen the extra names were not put down."[1]

- Baron Wakatsuki Reijirō (1866–1949), prime minister, initially on the list until resigning the premiership on December 13, 1931, prior to the time the Blood Oath Corps acted
- Baron Shidehara Kijūrō (1872–1951), foreign minister
- Dr. Suzuki Kisaburō (1867–1940), home minister
- Tokonami Takejirō (1866–1935), railway minister
- Prince Saionji Kinmochi (1849–1940), twice prime minister before becoming an elder statesman and Emperor Hirohito's highest political adviser
- Prince Tokugawa Iesato (1863–1940), president of the House of Peers
- Count Makino Nobuaki (1861–1949), Lord Keeper of the Privy Seal of Japan
- Ikeda Seihin (1867–1950), managing director of the Mitsui Bank in 1932, later governor of the Bank of Japan and, during the war years, a member of the Privy Council

TOWARD A THEORETICAL UNDERSTANDING

As noted above, there was ample historical precedent for transforming government by assassination in modern Japanese history, including assassinations based on ideological differences in prewar Japan. Yet how should these ideological assassinations be understood at the theoretical level, especially as Japan inched ever closer to becoming a totalitarian state? Maruyama Masao (1914–1996) was one of postwar Japan's first political scientists to attempt to explain this phenomenon.

Maruyama sought to contrast the rise of a totalitarian state in Japan with what had occurred almost simultaneously in Germany. He described the features of prewar and wartime Japanese society that clearly made it fascist in nature by identifying what he viewed as the three stages of fascism's development. (Note, as discussed in chapter 1, I prefer to use *totalitarian* instead of *fascist* to describe Japan's prewar and wartime society in order to distinguish it from its similar, but not entirely identical, German and Italian counterparts. In the following paragraphs, however, Maruyama's terminology is employed.)

According to Maruyama, the three stages of fascism's development in Japan were (1) the preparatory stage, between 1919 and 1931, when various fascist societies of civilians existed on the margins of Japanese politics; (2) the mature stage, from 1931 to 1936, when fascism manifested itself in acts of terrorism that were supported by young military officers; and (3) a stage of consummation, from 1936 to 1945, when fascism was adopted by Japan's ruling elite.[2] Maruyama also identified three distinct types of political personality involved in this process who "serv[ed] to formulate not only the fascist period but the entire political world of Imperial Japan." Designating these three as the "Shrine," the "Official," and the "Outlaw," Maruyama described their respective roles as follows:

> The Shrine represents authority; the Official, power; and the Outlaw, violence. From the point of view of their position in the national hierarchy and of their legal power, the Shrine ranks highest and the Outlaw lowest. The system, however, is so constituted that movement starts from the Outlaw and gradually works upwards. The Shrine is often a mere robot who affects other people by "doing nothing" ([Ch.] *wu wei*).
>
> The force that "holds aloft" the Shrine and that wields the real power is the Official (civilian or military). His rule over the powerless people is based on the legitimacy that descends from the Shrine. He, in turn, is being prodded from behind by the Outlaw.[3]

Needless to say, the "Outlaw" encompassed Japan's civilian ultranationalists like Inoue whose emperor-centric, fascist-promoting groups gathered steam in the 1920s and then, bolstered by their youthful military supporters, burst on the scene as terrorists in the 1930s. While not the only sanctioning body in Japanese society, Emperor Hirohito was nevertheless the ultimate "Shrine" who empowered the entire system ruled over by the "Official," both military and civilian. As Herbert Bix notes, Hirohito was *the reason* the system worked."[4]

Inoue, due to his right-wing affiliations in the 1920s and his involvement in terrorist violence in the 1930s, clearly falls into the Outlaw type. In evaluating the influence he and his followers had on turning Japan into a fascist state, it is important to remember "that movement start[ed] from the Outlaw and gradually work[ed] upwards." However, it is also true that in the biggest Outlaw act of them all, the February 26, 1936, Incident (Young Officers' Uprising), the Outlaws *appear* to have failed miserably. (For further details about the Young Officers' Uprising, see the appropriate section in appendix 3, "Historical Background Materials.")

Yet appearances can be deceiving, for as David Titus notes in *Palace and Politics in Prewar Japan*, "The Outlaw(s) of the unsuccessful Shōwa Restoration were instruments of pressure used to consolidate a bureaucratic monolith in government and then [they were] discarded."[5] More concretely, Herbert Bix adds,

> Interestingly, in their concept of total war, the thinking of the leaders [of the Young Officers' Uprising] and their senior commanders in the Army Ministry and the Army General Staff was strikingly similar: Both wanted state control of industrial production in order to fully mobilize the nation's resources. . . . The emperor and most of his advisers concurred with the demands of the Army and Navy for accelerated military buildup and state-directed industrial development.[6]

If military leaders, presided over by the emperor and his advisers, represented "fascism from above," it is equally important to recognize that for Maruyama the initial violence unleashed by the Outlaws represented "fascism from below" and, further, that in "suppressing fascism from below, . . . fascism from above made rapid progress."[7] As we have seen, despite his initial commitment to legal political activism, Inoue went on to align himself as completely with "fascism from above" as he had with "fascism from below." No doubt he was sustained in this by his Buddhist-related belief that "if one trains in Zen, one must do everything thoroughly and completely." And, of course, there was his equally firm belief that "with regard to their ultimate goals and aims, the sword and Zen are one."[8]

AN ALTERNATIVE POSSIBILITY

There is, however, an alternative explanation of Inoue's actions and statements, one that allows for a different understanding of what Maruyama described as "fascism from below." Namely, what appeared to be "from below" may have been orchestrated and supported *behind the scenes* by powerful players *from above* at an early stage, perhaps even from the beginning. For example, as early as 1873, Japan's political leaders seriously debated whether to invade Korea but decided against doing so *for the time being* because Japan was still modernizing and an invasion would be too costly to sustain. However, the desire to control Korea did not disappear and eventually led to the first Sino-Japanese War of 1894–1895 and, thereafter, the Russo-Japanese War of 1904–1905. Far from satisfying Japan's desire for territorial expansion, these wars only whetted the desire on the part of Japanese political and financial leaders for further expansion.

Two of Japan's most powerful nongovernmental "patriotic societies," the Genyōsha (Dark Ocean Society) and Kokuryūkai (Black Dragon Society), date from this period and actively agitated for, and abetted, the expansionist movement. (For further details concerning the important role played by both of these societies, see appendix 3.)

Suffice it here to state that in prewar Japan these two pioneering ultranationalist patriotic organizations both enjoyed a truly symbiotic relationship with the most important political, military, and economic leaders in Japan who also secretly funded them. This support is not surprising in that these groups often did the behind-the-scenes "dirty work" of their patrons, which the latter could not do publicly. Their hallmark was violent support for military expansion abroad while, at the same time, actively repressing both liberal and leftist movements at home.

To be sure, looking at only two of the scores of prewar ultranationalist groups cannot prove that "fascism from below" in 1930s Japan was, in actuality, "fascism from above," disguised to make it appear as if it were emerging from the "Outlaws." Yet the possibility exists that the Outlaws were, in fact, beholden to, if not manipulated by, their powerful patrons from early in Japan's modern history. This does not mean, however, that powerful actors in Japanese society were always in agreement with each other any more than that the multitude of patriotic organizations always had identical goals or adopted identical strategies for achieving their goals. Nevertheless, they were equally dedicated to promoting Japanese expansion abroad and suppressing the left wing at home.

WHO BENEFITS?

Still another method of understanding who was behind Inoue's actions is to ask a question that is key to legal and police investigations: "*Cui bono?*," Latin for "Who benefits?" This question is used to suggest either a hidden motive or indicate that the party responsible for something may not be who it first appears to be. In this instance, when someone like Tōyama Mitsuru or Prime Minister Konoe Fumimarō intervened, as they did, to aid Inoue on multiple occasions, it is possible they might have been acting, directly or indirectly, at the behest of the "Shrine," Hirohito and/or his close advisers. What historical evidence suggests this might be the case?

Before attempting to answer this question, it is important to remember that Tōyama and Konoe were far from the only influential Japanese Inoue interacted with. For example, there was Army Gen. Araki Sadao, who later became war minister under Inukai Tsuyoshi and education minister under Konoe, and Count Tanaka Mitsuaki, a former imperial household minister, among many other high-ranking positions he once held. Readers will recall it was Tanaka who chose Inoue to head the newly established Risshō Gokokudō Temple for the express purpose of training "patriotic youth." Konoe, among others, provided funds for the temple's construction. Beyond influential men like these who exercised great power, there were other fixers at work behind the scenes like Ōkawa Shūmei, the man who initially promised to secure pistols for Inoue's band and figured prominently in other abortive coup attempts.

There is no question that Tōyama Mitsuru was by far the most famous and powerful fixer in 1930s Japan. In the first place, this was due to his longtime leadership role in Japan's ultranationalist movement, including being one of the founders of the Genyōsha in 1881. In addition, Tōyama enjoyed a long-term, personal relationship with the emperor due to the assistance he had rendered the emperor when the latter was still crown prince. In 1920, Tōyama mobilized ultra-right-wing leaders to ensure (through intimidation) that the crown prince would be able to marry the woman of his choice, Princess Nagako Kuni (1903–2000), despite a history of color blindness in the princess's family.[9] This resulted in a lifelong relationship between the two men. Nakano Masao notes Tōyama grew so powerful that "when a new prime minister formed his cabinet, it was first necessary to secure Tōyama's approval of those he appointed."[10]

Thus, while Inoue may rightly be described as an "Outlaw," he was an amazingly *well-connected* Outlaw who greatly benefited from his connections to powerful and influential men, themselves connected to the shrine. Might one or more of these men have been the "voice of Heaven" who, Inoue claimed, directed his actions at pivotal moments in his life? This is just one of the many unsolved mysteries whose answers we may never know. (Additional details about these figures and more are contained in appendix 3.)

THE EMPEROR'S ROLE

Returning to the emperor, what might happen if the "system" of which he was the kingpin was in danger of *not* working? Would the emperor and his advisers remain silent? Would they say and do nothing?

It is important to understand that Hirohito grew up in the shadow of two men, his grandfather, Emperor Meiji, and his father, Emperor Taishō (1879–1926). Emperor Meiji was the titan who, together with his able advisers, led Japan into modernity and then transformed the nation into an empire by waging two major wars, the first Sino-Japanese War and the Russo-Japanese War. As a result, first Taiwan and then Korea became Japanese colonies during his reign. As a child, Hirohito was beguiled by tales of Emperor Meiji's greatness as told to him by his influential mentor, Count Nogi Maresuke (1849–1912), the army general, national hero, and accomplished Zen practitioner credited with having defeated Russia in the Russo-Japanese War.[11]

By contrast, Hirohito's father, Emperor Taishō, was completely bereft of Emperor Meiji's accomplishments and charisma. From childhood, he suffered from both physical and mental disabilities. His infirmities and eccentricities were so severe that they led to an increase in incidents of lèse-majesté (insulting the monarch) during his reign. Further, as his condition deteriorated, he took less interest in daily political affairs, and the ability of his close advisers to manipulate his decisions became common knowledge. Taishō's weakness was one of the factors providing the political space for the slow development of a party-based political system, with party-based cabinets working in tandem with popularly elected representatives. This system came of age following World War I and led to a shift in political power from the emperor and his advisers to Japan's Diet (parliament). Though far from perfect (e.g., women could not vote), these developments produced what came to be known as "Taishō Democracy."

When Emperor Taishō died on December 25, 1926, his eldest son, Hirohito, inherited a throne that remained constitutionally absolute in name but possessed only a vestige of the glory it previously possessed under Emperor Meiji. If things were allowed to continue as they were, there was a real danger that the throne might devolve to the point that the emperor would be little more than a constitutional monarch, as was the case with an increasing number of European kings and queens.

Hirohito and his advisers could not have been blind to the threat that Taishō Democracy's existence, let alone further growth, posed to his ability to shape events. A related concern was the emergence of a political theory that the emperor was no more than an "organ of the state" and therefore subservient to the state. This theory had been put forth by Minobe Tatsukichi (1873–1948), a statesman and constitutional law scholar. By contrast, ultranationalists, both in and out of the Diet, maintained that the emperor was, by definition, the very embodiment of the state and, as such, could not be held politically accountable for his actions, no matter how arbitrary they might be. By the spring of 1935, Minobe had lost the debate with the result that his most controversial writings were banned. He was subsequently forced to resign his posts, including his seat in the House of Peers, the upper house of the Diet.

At the same time, the denigration of political parties continued unabated. Governments with party-based cabinets were rapidly becoming a thing of the past, with political parties losing more and more of their ability to make government policy. As Herbert Bix notes, in the aftermath of the assassination of Prime Minister Inukai Tsuyoshi in the March 15 Incident of 1932, "Hirohito blamed party-based cabinets rather than insubordinate officers for the erosion of his own authority as commander-in-chief. More distrustful of representative parties than military insurgents, he would strengthen the power of the throne by weakening the power—indeed the very principle—of party government."[12]

Note that it was Hirohito who decided to place the major blame on party-based cabinets while distrusting representative parties more than military (and civilian?) insurgents. In other words, he could have decided differently. But what ambitious emperor wouldn't seek to increase his power by weakening contenders for that power, in this instance party-based government? Inukai's assassination, it should be remembered, was actually the second phase of Inoue's plan. Readers will recall that in chapter 11 Inoue made similar comments on exactly what had been wrong with party government: Inoue claimed that before Konoe took over the government of the day decided policy on its own and only then reported its decisions to the emperor as it saw fit. The result, Inoue claimed, was a lot of fabrication.

This is the state of affairs attributed to Taishō Democracy and exactly why it had to be eliminated, for the emperor had lost his right to initiate and control government policy. In addition, party cabinets gave civilians control over the military's budget. This is despite the fact that the Meiji Constitution placed the emperor in sole command of the military. What the Blood Oath Corps Incident, together with its second phase, the March 15 Incident, accomplished was, I suggest, to provide the *pretext* for the elimination of party-based governments, replacing them with prime ministers appointed directly by the emperor and his advisers. This effectively brought an end to Taishō Democracy, thereby disenfranchising the Japanese electorate and effectively excluding political parties from the decision-making process.

The result was that, by the time Konoe became prime minister on June 4, 1937, he, together with the emperor, could govern in the way they both believed proper. Inoue explained: "Once Konoe became prime minister, however, things changed. No matter what the issue, Konoe first sought the emperor's consent. It was only after the emperor gave his approval that a policy was implemented. Government administered directly by the emperor came about in this way."

The emperor was, of course, surrounded by influential advisers who undoubtedly played an important role in the emperor's decision-making process. But, in the end, Emperor Hirohito's decisions were his own, for better or for worse. While only two political and financial leaders died as a result of the first stage of the Blood Oath Corps Incident, when combined with Inukai's death in the second stage, there were sufficient grounds to justify (or mask) a process that brought an end to representative democracy. Yet, as influential as Inoue and his band's terrorist acts were, nothing had occurred that *compelled* the emperor to end representative democracy. Once again, this was his choice.

Those who seek to defend Emperor Hirohito from the charge that he and his advisers secretly colluded with, or used, ultranationalists like Inoue, point to the decisive role the emperor played in suppressing the Young Officers' Uprising of February 26, 1936. As soon as he was informed of the uprising on the morning of February 26, Hirohito personally ordered its immediate suppression.[13] Hirohito's supporters use this as an example of the emperor's antimilitarist, peace-loving stance. Although incarcerated at the time, Inoue, too, betrayed no sympathy for the uprising, even though, of all the many ultranationalist coup attempts, it clearly would have succeeded had the emperor endorsed it. Emperor Hirohito, however, resolutely and decisively opposed it from the outset.

YET ANOTHER QUESTION

This raises the question, might there be an alternative explanation for the emperor's decisiveness? Although he didn't explain when or how, readers will recall that Inoue became aware the radical Young Officer coup plotters intended, with the backing of those senior military leaders sympathetic to them, to enact their own social reform plans even if the emperor was unwilling to do so. For Inoue, ignoring the will of the emperor was utterly unacceptable. Thus, in the event the coup had been successful, bringing with it release from prison for Inoue and his band members, Inoue was determined that at the first cabinet meeting of the postcoup military government held in the emperor's presence, he would kill, with the aid of his band members, all of the military leaders present. Why? Because Inoue believed the coup sponsors (i.e., the senior leaders of the Imperial Way Faction) were prepared, if need be, to force their will on the emperor. This is a truly amazing statement coming from an alleged "ultranationalist" leader like Inoue, someone regarded even today as having been a fanatical supporter of the Imperial Way Faction.

If Inoue felt this way, would the emperor have been any happier to have his prerogatives ignored by the Imperial Way Faction? And if Inoue knew of the Imperial Way Faction's plans, is it possible the emperor or his close advisers would have been unaware of the faction's true motives in instigating the coup? The successful destruction of Taishō Democracy had brought with it the restoration of near total political power to the emperor and his advisers. In light of this, it is difficult to believe the emperor would have welcomed the prospect of once again losing political power, this time to a radical faction of the military with its national socialist–oriented agenda.

Adoption of national socialist policies would, moreover, have entailed, as in Nazi Germany, a degree of state control over large corporations, the *zaibatsu* in Japan's case. In his aptly named book *Imperial Zaibatsu (Tennō Zaibatsu)*, Yoshida Yūji notes that "the Imperial family's wealth was far greater than that of any other *zaibatsu*."[14] This fact was well known to the Young Officers, for as early as 1919, in his book *An Outline Plan for the Reorganization of Japan*, right-wing political theorist Kita Ikki had advocated limits be placed on the emperor's wealth.[15] The emperor could hardly have been enamored by this prospect.

When comparing Japan with Nazi Germany, it is noteworthy that Hitler, a civilian, was in command of the military, not vice versa. Seen in this light, the frequently used term "Japanese militarism" to describe wartime Japan is inaccurate, for it implies that during the war years Japan was under total control of the military. While it is true that Japan's military leaders sometimes acted on their own, and were very influential, the military was nevertheless ultimately under civilian control, that is, the control of the emperor.

It must be admitted that even if the emperor were sympathetic toward (or even supported) those ultranationalists involved in early domestic right-wing assassinations, at least up to the Young Officers' Uprising in 1936, there is no proof of his *direct* involvement. Yet, when it comes to evidence of his *indirect* involvement, we know, according to Inoue, that Konoe, acting on a request from Count Tanaka, approached the emperor regarding Inoue's release from prison. This occurred after Konoe became president of the House of Peers, sometime between 1933 and 1937.

Konoe continued his efforts to free Inoue after becoming prime minister in June 1937. Japanese historian Ota Beyūji informs us that Konoe had long wanted to free not just Inoue but all right-wing political prisoners. Konoe took his first concrete steps in this direction in July 1937, only one month after becoming premier. It was then that Marquis Tokugawa Yoshichika (1886–1976), yet another powerful right-wing fixer and aristocrat, requested Konoe arrange for the release of Blood Oath Corps band member Ōkawa Shūmei, imprisoned for his role in the May 15 Incident. Konoe agreed to this, and Ōkawa was freed in October 1937.[16] Ota continues, "At the time of [Konoe's] second premiership [from July 1940 to October 1941],

Konoe arranged for the release of everyone connected to the Blood Oath Corps Incident as well as Sagoya Tomeo [assassin of Prime Minister Hamaguchi Osachi in 1930]. Konoe was obsessed with the release of nationalists."[17]

While Inoue was not the only beneficiary of Konoe's actions, there was, nevertheless, a unique feature connected to his release. As previously indicated, Inoue was the recipient of a highly unusual, if not unprecedented, "special pardon" (*tokusha*), meaning that his original conviction was completely erased from the record. Inasmuch as Konoe was responsible for Inoue's release, the special pardon must have been his doing. But what would have led Konoe to take such an unusual step?

Although Ota doesn't touch on this point, one possibility is that Konoe wanted Inoue to be in a position where, with no criminal conviction on his record, he could assume an important post following his release, such as a prime minister's confidant. Readers will recall that it was Konoe who personally telephoned Inoue to ask for a meeting following the latter's release. But why would a prime minister want someone with Inoue's background to serve as his confidant?

According to an entry in the diary of Vice Minister of the Navy Admiral Sayamoto Yorio (1886–1965), by 1940 Konoe was living under threats to his life made by various ultranationalists who feared the prime minister might make too many concessions to the United States during negotiations to avoid war. The admiral claimed this was the reason Konoe sought to employ Inoue. As an ultranationalist with a peerless reputation, Inoue would make an excellent bodyguard, for who would dare attack Inoue in an attempt to kill Konoe? Although Inoue himself made no reference to this possibility, it is certainly one plausible explanation. Inoue did describe a series of meetings he arranged to promote understanding between Konoe and ultranationalist leaders like Tōyama. Additionally, he saved Hiranuma Kiichirō, Konoe's home minister, from assassination.

Whatever may have first drawn them together, it is clear from Inoue's frequent, even intimate, exchanges with Konoe that the two men grew close to one another. Even if Inoue exaggerated his own importance in their relationship, Konoe clearly valued Inoue's advice. While this is certainly a strange turn of events, it once again demonstrates how well-connected Inoue was. (See appendix 3 for further background information on Konoe Fumimarō.)

Let me express the hope that future historians will continue to investigate this matter, especially any role the emperor may have played in Konoe's actions or with prewar ultranationalists in general. However, it may well be that even if the emperor or his advisers did play a role, it is now so well hidden that it will never be known. Needless to say, contact with terrorists is not something Hirohito or his advisers are likely to have left a record of. Additionally, if such contact did occur, it would have been indirect, done with the aid of political figures like Konoe or fixers like Tōyama Mitsuru and Tokugawa Yoshichika. By nature, fixers, too, don't leave records of their activities. Thus, readers are left to ponder these questions and reach their own conclusions.

A RELATED QUESTION

The preceding discussion brings up another key question related to Inoue: how was it possible for him to have been so completely and unconditionally devoted to the emperor? Inoue appears to have believed that once the emperor was in complete political control, he would, of his own accord, initiate the reforms necessary to mitigate rampant poverty in the countryside; end the self-indulgent, luxurious lifestyle of the *zaibatsu*; and eliminate corrupt politicians. In short, how was it possible that Inoue had become what can only be called a "true believer" in the emperor?

Although not meant as a justification for Inoue's "imperial faith," it must be remembered that, like all Japanese of his era, Inoue had been taught from childhood that the emperor was the benevolent father of the Japanese people, all of whom were his "children." Moreover, the emperor was the divine descendant of the Shinto Sun goddess, Amaterasu. Thus, as a benevolent father of divine origin, why *wouldn't* the emperor do his best to ensure the happiness and well-being of *all* his children?

Inoue's absolute faith in, and subservience to, the emperor may rightly be seen as a form of "hero worship." Readers will recall from chapter 1 that hero worship is one of the major characteristics of a totalitarian state. Inoue and the members of his band took pride in the fact they embraced no fixed ideology. They were prepared to act as *sute-ishi* (pawns) and selflessly sacrifice themselves in order for "others" to bring about the ideal society they sought. For Inoue, as well as the members of his band, the "others" clearly began and ended with the emperor and those who faithfully carried out his wishes.

Even after Japan's defeat, Inoue continued to protect the emperor by asserting that the responsibility for the war lay not with the emperor but with those surrounding him, primarily military leaders like Tōjō Hideki. Inasmuch as Tōjō was a leader of the military's Control Faction (i.e., the Imperial Way Faction's bitter rival), it was a simple matter for Inoue to place the blame entirely on him. By blaming others, it was possible for Inoue, even in the postwar era, to state, "The emperor and the people of this country have always been one, differing only in their respective missions and stations in life. No matter what the organization, it is always made up of a center and its branches. The emperor is naturally at the center ruling over his subjects."

Although Inoue claimed to have no ideology, in reality he had one—"emperorism." An integral part of this ideology is that the end definitely justified the means, for neither Inoue nor his band ever expressed the least concern, let alone regret, for the victims they killed. However, in the postwar era, Inoue did say, "When asking whether it was good or bad to have undertaken 'direct action' [by killing someone], there's no question but that it was bad. No one wishes to participate in terrorism. I deeply desire the emergence of a society in which politics are conducted properly and no one thinks of things like terrorism."[18]

At the same time, readers will recall that at his trial, Onuma Shō testified, "In the process of destroying ourselves, it couldn't be helped if there were [other] victims. This was the fundamental principle of our revolution." True, like the good Bodhisattvas they claimed to be, Inoue and his band members were willing to sacrifice themselves in order to accomplish their goals, but they also felt "it couldn't be helped if there were [other] victims." As Onuma's mentor, if not his Buddhist master, there is no reason to doubt that Inoue shared this conviction at the time.

In light of this, it may be considered a major step forward that in postwar Japan, in the wake of immense wartime death and destruction, Chapter 1, Article 1, of the 1947 Japanese Constitution states, "The Emperor shall be the symbol of the State and of the unity of the People, deriving his position from the will of the people with whom resides sovereign power." This postwar conversion of the emperor into a constitutional monarch shorn of political power shows that men like Inoue and his band notwithstanding, human progress is possible, not to mention necessary. It is necessary because history records that when a single human being, whether emperor, king, queen, or dictator, is in power, without effective restraints, the blood of those below almost inevitably flows in torrents.

INOUE AND WORLD WAR II

The final question to be examined is whether, as British Naval Lt. Parsons charged, Inoue was responsible for having started World War II. Needless to say, most historians would readily dismiss this claim, noting, for example, that the Blood Oath Corps Incident occurred in the spring of 1932, years before World War II began in either Asia or Europe. Yet, as we have seen, it is true that the terrorist assassinations Inoue directed, including the assassination of Prime Minister Inukai, had an impact on Japanese society far out of proportion to the importance of the three men who were killed. The impact was no less than the demise of cabinet-led governments based on the political party or allied parties enjoying a majority in the Japanese Diet.

As imperfect and weak as Taishō Democracy was prior to the assassinations of 1932, it still possessed one powerful weapon that gave it significant control over the military—the power of the purse. Without adequate funding approved by both the cabinet and the Diet, the military could not have continued its military expansion throughout Asia, let alone gone to war with opposing Western powers, starting with the United States. Thus, the argument can be made that it was Japan's military leaders who were the most interested in ending Taishō Democracy and the financial restraints they were subject to. In Inoue's case, it is clear he initially worked together with such Imperial Way Faction leaders as Gen. Araki Sadao, as well as radicalized young naval officers, to eliminate Taishō Democracy and bring about a Shōwa Restoration. A Shōwa Restoration would not only restore complete power to the emperor but eliminate any democratic control whatsoever over the Japanese government and military.

Yet, in an abrupt about-face, Inoue subsequently indicated that he and his band were prepared to kill all of the military leaders who assumed political power in the wake of a successful coup leading to the Shōwa Restoration. What caused Inoue to take this momentous step? The reason, as discussed above, was because he had come to the realization that the coup leaders, together with their Imperial Way Faction–aligned senior military supporters, had their own agenda, an agenda influenced by the national socialist–oriented thinking of figures like Kita Ikki. In the event the emperor refused to implement their agenda, these leaders were prepared to coerce him to do so, perhaps even force him to abdicate and install one of his more amenable princely brothers in his stead.

Inoue's concern is not without historical basis, for Bix writes that at the time of the Young Officers' Uprising of February 26, 1936, Hirohito feared the rebels might recruit his younger brother, Prince Chichibu (1902–1953), to force him to step down in the event he failed to follow the rebels' directives.[19] Prince Chichibu, himself a military officer, was known to be sympathetic to the young officers and the Imperial Way Faction of which they were a part.[20] However, forcing the emperor to take a particular course of action was anathema to Inoue and his band.

It was for this reason that, when later undergoing questioning as a possible war criminal, Inoue could in good conscience claim that he was neither right wing nor left wing. In his mind, Inoue was convinced that such labels simply didn't apply to him because he had no political ideology, either right or left. Yet, as made clear above, Inoue had long ago embraced the ideology of emperorism—once the emperor was in complete control, he would undoubtedly do the right thing. This may not have been the ideology of the right or the left, but it is nevertheless a distinguishing characteristic of totalitarianism.

While Inoue and his band did not start World War II, they effectively provided the pretext, the excuse, to end any form of democratic control over the military in Japan. Had he wished to do so, the emperor could have clamped down on the military since Article 11 of the Meiji Constitution stated, "The Emperor has the supreme command of the Army and the Navy." However, as Herbert Bix makes abundantly clear, Emperor Hirohito had no interest in reining in the military so long as it was successful in expanding and enriching the empire. Hirohito's one, and essentially only, reservation was his fear of losing a war he had initiated, for doing so might endanger the continuity of imperial rule.

Inoue claimed that Emperor Hirohito was a man of peace, as demonstrated by the emperor's opposition to war with the United States. This claim is not as at odds with the historical record as it might seem, for Hirohito was well aware of the danger of going to war with a much larger, and much stronger, country like the United States. However, at the time, Japan enjoyed a military alliance with Nazi Germany and Fascist Italy, having joined the Tripartite Pact on September 27, 1940. The Tripartite Pact provided Japan with powerful allies, especially Nazi Germany.

In the fall of 1940, Germany appeared on the verge of defeating Great Britain, the last major unconquered European power. With powerful friends like these, how could Japan lose? Thus, the Japanese attack on Pearl Harbor was not as reckless as it appears in retrospect, especially since the war, as initially planned, was to be brought to a quick, negotiated end beneficial to Japan. As for Inoue, he was clearly satisfied with the way things turned out by 1940. No doubt he felt he and his band's actions had contributed to the favorable outcome. Readers will recall Inoue saying,

> Before Konoe took over, Japanese politics consisted of "politics by report." This meant the government of the day decided policy on its own and only then reported its decisions to the emperor as it saw fit. The result was a lot of fabrication. Once Konoe became prime minister, however, things changed. No matter what the issue, Konoe first sought the emperor's consent. It was only after the emperor gave his approval that a policy was implemented. Government administered directly by the emperor came about in this way.

In going to war with the United States, the emperor was aware that a Japanese defeat might imperil the continuation of the imperial system. Thus, when Konoe resigned and recommended Prince (and Army General) Higashikuni Naruhiko (1887–1990) succeed him as prime minister in October 1941, Hirohito rejected his advice. Instead, Hirohito chose Army Gen. Tōjō Hideki, stating,

> I actually thought Prince Higashikuni suitable as chief of staff of the army, but I think the appointment of a member of the imperial house to a political office must be considered very carefully. Above all, in time of peace this is fine, but when there is a fear that there may even be a war, then more importantly, considering the welfare of the imperial house, I wondered about the wisdom of a member of the imperial family serving [as prime minister].[21]

In choosing Tōjō, Hirohito made a fateful choice. Prince Takamatsu, Hirohito's younger brother, understood just how fateful it was, for he confided in his diary at the time, "We have finally committed to war and must now do all we can to launch it powerfully."[22] The powerful launch was, of course, the navy's December 7, 1941, attack on Pearl Harbor. As for Konoe, his chief cabinet secretary, Tomita Kenji, later recorded Konoe's feelings at the time of his resignation as follows: "I felt the emperor was telling me: My prime minister does not understand military matters. I know much more. In short, the emperor had absorbed the views of the Army and Navy high commands."[23]

On the home front, Konoe had already created the Imperial Rule Assistance Association (Taisei Yokusankai) in October 1940. As the association's first president, Konoe sought to create a single-party state to further enhance domestic support for Japan's war effort in China. As a result, following Japan's last wartime general election in April 1942, all members of the Diet were required to join the Imperial Rule Assistance Political Association (Yokusan Seijikai), effectively turning Japan into a one-party totalitarian state, lasting through 1945. The only role left open to the Japanese people was, as the association's name implied, to *assist* imperial rule, that is, the emperor, by giving their all, up to and including their lives, to the war effort.

Given this background, when in 1940 Inoue described the ideal form of government as "administered directly by the emperor," he may not have realized how deeply he implicated "peace-loving" Hirohito in the events that followed, including the latter's responsibility for war with the United States. In reality, I suggest Hirohito's love of peace only surfaced when there was a danger, as in the case of war with the

United States, that the imperial forces might be defeated. In China, Japanese aggression continued unabated through war's end in August 1945, at the cost of many millions of Chinese (and Japanese) lives. Although Japan's military leaders would have strenuously objected, Hirohito's position as the constitutionally mandated supreme commander of the imperial armed forces meant that it was within his power to end the military's aggression at any time.

Despite this, in postwar Japan, U.S. occupation forces chose to conceal Hirohito's war responsibility in order to enlist him in controlling Japanese society, especially in suppressing an increasingly powerful Japanese left composed of both socialists and communists. According to historian Awaya Kentarō, "The US tried to drive a wedge between the military, which it attacked, and the emperor and the people, which it did not attack. This continued as part of Occupation strategy and the political myth that 'the Emperor and the people were fooled by the military' permeated deeply throughout the population."[24] In this effort, General Douglas MacArthur and the occupation forces were eminently successful. However, with the recent emergence of carefully documented research like that of Awaya, Bix, and other historians, the emperor's active wartime role and responsibility are now undeniable.

INOUE IN THE POSTWAR ERA

In reflecting on Inoue's ongoing role in right-wing activities in the postwar era, especially the National Protection Corps, we must ask what, if anything, changed in the postwar years? The corps, like its prewar antecedents, outwardly took a critical position toward the rich and powerful, pledging to liberate the masses from their control. While such a pledge might seem left wing, given the corps's actual actions in suppressing all forms of left-wing activities, such words might best be described as, at most, a populist facade. Furthermore, the corps continued to speak highly of the emperor, describing him as "the center of the blood relationship that bound the race together." This was no different than in the prewar period when Japanese society was presented as one large, single family with the emperor as its head (and brain).

Whether in war or peace, in prewar or postwar Japan, the one constant running through the right wing was the need to preserve and protect the emperor and the imperial system. As in the prewar period, the right wing was prepared to use violence, including deadly violence, against anyone who dared criticize the emperor. For example, in December 1988, Motoshima Hitoshi, mayor of Nagasaki, publicly suggested that Hirohito, who was then dying, bore some degree of responsibility for the Asia-Pacific War. Motoshima stated, "If I look at the descriptions in Japanese and foreign histories, and reflect on my experiences in the military in the educational training of soldiers, in that regard I think the emperor has war responsibility. But based on the will of a majority of Japanese and Allied countries, the emperor escaped and became a symbol in the new Constitution, and we have to act under that understanding."[25]

As mild as his criticism was, it still resulted in multiple threats being made against the mayor's life. Nevertheless, the mayor refused to retract his comments and, on

January 19, 1990, was shot once in the chest as he left city hall by a right-wing youth who was later arrested. Although seriously wounded, Motoshima survived the attack. Nevertheless, the point had been made, to criticize the emperor was to risk death.

By comparison, Asanuma Inejiro (1898–1960), head of Japan's Socialist Party, was not so fortunate. Although Asanuma didn't publicly attack Hirohito, he did express his support for the Chinese Communist Party and criticized the Japan–U.S. Mutual Security Treaty. This was sufficient reason for another right-wing youth, seventeen-year-old Yamaguchi Otoya, to run Asanuma through with a samurai sword as he was speaking in a televised political debate in Tokyo on October 12, 1960. The right wing had by no means abandoned the use of Japanese youth to strike down those it deemed its enemies. As for Yamaguchi, he committed suicide less than three weeks later while being held in a juvenile detention facility. Before using his bedsheet to hang himself, Yamaguchi wrote on his cell wall, "Would that I had seven lives to give for my Emperor! Long live His Imperial Majesty, the Emperor!"[26]

Following Hirohito's death on January 7, 1989, Japan experienced the long and peaceful reign (not rule) of his son, Akihito, together with his commoner wife, Empress Michiko, and their children. Akihito was the very model of a constitutional monarch who, standing above the fray of partisan politics, embodied the country's concern for its citizenry, especially those who met with misfortune from the many natural, and sometimes human-made, disasters that visit Japan on a regular basis. For this reason, there exists today little criticism of either the emperor or the imperial system. Japan truly seems to have entered a new era.

The sense of having turned a corner in the history of Japan's emperor system was further reinforced by Akihito's abdication of the throne, due to retirement, on April 30, 2019. On assuming the throne on May 1, 2019, his son, Naruhito, stated in his first public pronouncement, "In accordance with the Constitution of Japan, I pledge to perform my duties as a symbol of the Japanese state and people."[27] He also pledged to devote himself to peace and staying close to the people. There is nothing to suggest that Oxford-educated Naruhito is any less sincere in fulfilling this role than his father was. Nevertheless, as noted in the previous chapter, should Japan once again undergo severe social instability as it did in the 1920s and 1930s, a return to totalitarianism cannot be ruled out.

Japan remains a strongly hierarchical society with leaders who are the descendants of prewar and wartime political dynasties.[28] The continued presence of right-wing organizations in Japan with close bonds to national leaders indicates the possibility of various forms of intimidation up to and including political violence. While Inoue and his ultranationalist peers are long gone, in the postwar era monuments have been built to commemorate, if not laud, their allegedly compassionate, selfless, and patriotic deeds. The monuments are made of bronze, stone, and concrete, but their deeds reside in the hearts and minds of their right-wing successors, ever ready to be repeated if deemed necessary. Or to paraphrase Inoue's words, ever ready to be repeated should their successors decide that "politics are conducted [*im*]properly."

14

Unraveling the Religious Matrix

Closely intertwined with the historical dimension of Inoue and his band's actions are questions relating to their relationship to religion, in particular, the Zen school of Buddhism. The first of these questions is why, up to this point, respected historians both inside and outside of Japan have almost universally considered Inoue to have been a Nichiren sect–affiliated Buddhist or a disciple of Nichiren nationalist Tanaka Chigaku, or even a Nichiren priest.[1]

For example, Ivan Morris, editor of Maruyama Masao's *Thought and Behavior in Modern Japanese Politics*, included a glossary in which Inoue is identified as "a Nichiren priest of extreme rightist beliefs who before turning to Buddhism had spent most of his life on the continent as a secret agent for the Japanese army."[2] In *Modern Japan: An Encyclopedia of History, Culture and Nationalism*, Inoue is described as "a native of Gumma Prefecture, [who] traveled to China and Manchuria during the early 1910s to gather intelligence for the Japanese army. Later, he became a militant Buddhist, converted to the Nichiren sect."[3] In *Revolt in Japan: The Young Officers and the February 26, 1936 Incident*, Ben-Ami Shillony writes that Inoue was a "Nichiren mystic."[4] These descriptions are despite the fact that in his court testimony Inoue clearly stated, "I reached where I am today thanks to Zen. Zen dislikes talking theory so I can't put it into words, but it is true nonetheless."[5]

More importantly, what did Inoue find in Zen that was so helpful in both justifying his terrorist ideology and informing his band's practice of meditation? If Inoue's understanding of Zen and Buddhism is a distortion of that tradition, just what was distorted and why? Was Inoue's distortion unique within Zen Buddhist history, or, on the contrary, did his acts stem from certain long-standing interpretations of Zen expressed, perhaps, in an "unconventional" manner?

Finally, if Inoue did distort Zen Buddhism, was he the only one to have done so? What about Inoue's Rinzai Zen master, Yamamoto Gempō? Did the latter accurately express Zen Buddhist ethics in his testimony at Inoue's trial? Did, as Gempō claimed, Shakyamuni Buddha justify killing "good men" who destroy "social harmony"?

NICHIREN

In discussing Inoue's putative relationship to the Nichiren tradition, it must be admitted there are reasons why nearly all previous authors, Japanese and non-Japanese alike, have alleged a connection between Inoue and the Nichiren sect, typically identifying him as a Nichiren priest. In the first instance, this is due to the central role the *Lotus Sūtra* plays in the Nichiren tradition, nearly to the exclusion of all other Buddhist teachings. To understand its importance, it is necessary to have at least an introductory understanding of the *Lotus Sūtra* (J., *Myōhō-renge-kyō*).

The *Lotus Sūtra* is believed to have been composed in India sometime in the first two centuries CE, or possibly earlier. It was translated into Chinese on numerous occasions, most notably by Kumārajīva in 406 CE, and came to exert a major influence on the development of Chinese Buddhism, and an even more influential role in Japanese Buddhism. Held to be the culmination of the historical Buddha's fifty years of teaching, the *Lotus Sūtra* claims to be superior to other sutras and states that full Buddhahood is only achieved through its teachings and skillful means. As Paul Williams notes, "For many East Asian Buddhists since early times the *Lotus Sūtra* contains the final teaching of the Buddha, complete and sufficient for salvation."[6] Moreover, there is a long tradition of understanding the title of this sutra as containing its essence.

However, despite its widespread influence on all Japanese Buddhist sects, it was only Nichiren (1222–1282) who adhered exclusively to this sutra and required his followers to do the same. It is for this reason that both Japanese and non-Japanese Buddhist scholars, as well as secular historians, immediately think of the Nichiren sect when they read about someone whose faith is centered on the *Lotus Sūtra*.

In Inoue's case, it was his Sōtō Zen master in Manchuria, Azuma Soshin, who informed Inoue that he would have liked to have had the opportunity to introduce him to the *Lotus Sūtra*. This is not surprising inasmuch as the *Lotus Sūtra* is also held in high regard in Zen temples, where sections of this sutra are chanted on a daily basis. Zen master Dōgen (1200–1253), founder of the Sōtō Zen sect in Japan, spent his last days reciting and writing the *Lotus Sūtra* in his room, which he named "The *Lotus Sūtra* Hermitage."[7] The great Rinzai Zen reformer Hakuin Ekaku achieved enlightenment while reading the third chapter of the *Lotus Sūtra*.[8]

Inoue would later encounter this same sutra in a vivid and life-threatening dream he had while still in China. However, none of Inoue's initial encounters with the *Lotus Sūtra* had any direct connection to the Nichiren sect. Yet, Inoue did begin to chant the mantra, *Namu-myōhō-renge-kyō* ("I take refuge in the Wondrous Dharma of the *Lotus Sūtra*") during his solitary training in the Santoku hermitage in his hometown of Kawaba village. And it is true that in Japan this mantra, incorporating the title of this sutra, is widely viewed as part of the Nichiren sect, where it is referred to by the abbreviated term *daimoku* (lit., title).

Buddhist historian Jacqueline Stone notes that the *daimoku* was chanted even prior to Nichiren's time, that is, prior to the Kamakura period (1185–1333). Its use, however, was neither uniform nor widespread.[9] Buddhist scholar Takagi Yutaka adds that the words "*Namu-myōhō-renge-kyō*," or similar expressions of devotion to the *Lotus Sūtra*, first appeared in Japan as early as 881 CE in formulaic expressions of devotion to the three treasures of Buddhism,[10] specifically devotion to the Dharma.[11]

Although not its creator, Nichiren stated his clear preference for what is today the standard formulation of this mantra, *Namu-myōhō-renge-kyō*. Additionally, Nichiren appears to be the first person to have popularized this mantra, holding it to be an exclusive practice with claims to universal validity. Those who chant the *daimoku*, Nichiren claimed, will never be dragged down by evil karma and worldly offenses into the lower realms of transmigration but are sure to attain Buddhahood in this very body or achieve birth in the Pure Land of Utmost Bliss.[12] Further, Jacqueline Stone notes that in the early Nichiren community, "the *daimoku* was at least occasionally taught as a meditative discipline."[13] This is unsurprising inasmuch as Nichiren began his career as a priest in the Tendai sect, where by the end of the Heian period (794–1185), the practice of chanting the *daimoku* was emerging as an adjunct or alternative to traditional Tendai meditative practices.[14]

While Inoue was probably unaware of the background to the *daimoku* as a meditative discipline, it is clear he chanted this phrase as a variant of seated, silent Zen meditation, *zazen*. However, it is unusual to chant the *daimoku* as a meditative practice in the Zen school even though it is a mantra (i.e., a sacred utterance believed to have psychological and spiritual powers). The *Oxford Living Dictionary* defines mantra as "a word or sound repeated to aid concentration in meditation."[15] In other words, it is a meditative aid because it helps develop not only mental concentration but tranquility as well. Consciously or not, it was for these reasons that Inoue chanted the *daimoku* at Santoku-an, for he had long been tormented, deeply tormented, about the standards for right and wrong. Nevertheless, Inoue's use of *daimoku* recitation as a meditative aid, to enter *samādhi*, did not signify his affiliation with the Nichiren sect, something Inoue clearly stated in his conversation with Chief Justice William Flood Webb, as recounted in chapter 12.

Nevertheless, it is true that at two points in his life Inoue was involved with the Nichiren sect and related organizations. In the first instance, Inoue made it clear he greatly admired Nichiren as a historical figure, including his devotion to the *Lotus Sūtra*, his steadfastness in the face of adversity, and his concern for Japan. As a consequence, Inoue went to train on Mount Minobu in Yamanashi prefecture, the spiritual center of the Nichiren sect and where Nichiren had spent his last days. However, once there, he found the Nichiren monks' early morning sutra chanting "unsatisfactory" and moved to a small temple adjacent to Nichiren's gravesite on the mountain, where he fasted and read. This, too, eventually proved unsatisfactory, and Inoue returned to Tokyo a few months later, never to return.

NICHIRENISM

As readers will recall, the second point of contact with Nichiren-related groups occurred when Inoue participated in a weeklong series of lectures in Shizuoka city at the beginning of 1925. These lectures were offered by Tanaka Chikaku, a lay Nichiren leader with a following numbering in the thousands, resulting from his promotion of a highly nationalistic interpretation of Nichiren's teachings known as "Nichirenism" (*Nichiren-shugi*).

While Nichirenism was based on Nichiren's teachings, Tanaka instilled them with decidedly modern and political interpretations, including advocacy of Japan's mission to first save Asia, and eventually the rest of the non-Western world, from Western imperialism. In this sense it can be said that Nichirenism as an ideology saw Japan as having no choice but to undertake a kind of "Yellow man's burden" or "civilizing mission" in the region. According to Tanaka, this was Japan's "heavenly task" (*tengyō*) that would lead to "world unification" (*sekai tōitsu*). Given this, it is not difficult to understand why this interpretation of Nichiren's thought found favor in an expansionist Japan of the 1930s. Yet Nichirenism, placing its faith exclusively in the *Lotus Sūtra*, remained as intolerant of other Buddhist sects as its traditional Nichiren sect predecessors.

Given Inoue's own nationalist leanings, it is not surprising to learn of his initial attraction to this modern-day, politically active version of Nichiren's teachings, especially given Tanaka's innovative use of print media to disseminate his message. Nevertheless, on personal inspection, Inoue found Tanaka's lectures full of nothing but theory and therefore as "unsatisfactory" as the traditional Nichiren sect. In his prison diary, Inoue wrote,

> The reason I chose Zen is that, while Nichirenism is all right, it is full of discussion and debate. Furthermore, this discussion is of a scholarly type in which putting theory into practice only comes later, if at all. . . . What the nation and our people need now, however, is not theory but actual reform. That is to say, implementation must come first and theory later. As far as I'm concerned, theory can be left up to those specialists who call themselves scholars. Given this and my own personality, which eschews both doctrines and creeds, I realized that Zen was the best for me.[16]

Inoue's attendance at Tanaka's lectures would mark the last direct connection he had with the Nichiren school, either traditional or modern.

An additional problem Inoue had with Nichiren-related groups was the same one that has long bedeviled, and ultimately marginalized, this sect of Buddhism in Japan. Namely, whether in the thirteenth or twentieth centuries, Nichiren-related groups always promoted their own sectarian agendas, each group claiming exclusive possession of the truth. Consequently, they demanded every other sect of Buddhism in Japan be destroyed as *jakyō* (false teachings), with little tolerance for each other as well. Every Nichiren-related group maintained that it alone could save Japan, though only after first eliminating all false Buddhist sects. Over the centuries, this exclusivity has been the Nichiren-affiliated groups' undoing since they could never muster sufficient power to eliminate Buddhism's other, allegedly heretical, sects.

Furthermore, Nichirenism had its own unique political program. Were it to succeed, even the emperor would be forced to follow its dictates. As previously discussed, Inoue was a "true believer" in the emperor, meaning the latter must be free to act without the least outside coercion from whatever source—military, political, or religious. As the literal father of all Japanese, the emperor would, once restored to power, definitely act benevolently toward his subjects—his children—just as any father would do. Thus, Inoue could never embrace any "ism," including Nichirenism, that threatened the emperor's prerogatives. Moreover, and perhaps most importantly, Inoue sought a spiritual faith that strongly favored action, not theory.

THE ZEN CONNECTION

Given this background, it is readily understandable why Zen would appeal to Inoue. First, it emphasized "pure action" based solely on intuition (allegedly transcending discursive thought, ethical considerations, and even history itself). In this it is difficult to claim that Inoue misunderstood Zen or twisted it into something it was not. For example, D. T. Suzuki, the well-known expositor of Zen in both Japan and the West, wrote,

> Zen did not necessarily argue with them [warriors] about immortality of soul, or about righteousness of the divine way, or about ethical conduct, but it simply urged to go ahead with whatever conclusion rational or irrational a man has arrived at. Philosophy may safely be left with intellectual minds; Zen wants to act, and the most effective act is, once the mind is made up, to go on without looking backward. In this respect, Zen is indeed the religion of the samurai warrior.[17]

In this quote, Suzuki is clearly addressing Zen's connection to warriors, not terrorists. No doubt, Suzuki defenders would vehemently deny his words could be applied to terrorists like Inoue. Defenders would argue that while warriors, like terrorists, did kill their opponents, this was done only after all peaceful means of avoiding conflict had been exhausted, and then only in an honorable manner, never in cowardly acts of terrorism. Further, inasmuch as Zen is a school of Buddhism, Buddhist ethical principles could never be used to justify terrorism.

The problem with this defense is that when it came to the "isms" Zen might be identified with, Suzuki, among others, would accept no limits:

> Zen has no special doctrine or philosophy with a set of concepts and intellectual formulas, except that it tries to release one from the bondage of birth and death and this by means of certain intuitive modes of understanding peculiar to itself. It is, therefore, extremely flexible to adapt itself almost to any philosophy and moral doctrine as long as its intuitive teaching is not interfered with. It may be found wedded to anarchism or

fascism, communism or democracy, atheism or idealism, or any political and economical [*sic*] dogmatism. It is, however, generally animated with a certain revolutionary spirit, and when things come to a deadlock which is the case when we are overloaded with conventionalism, formalism, and other cognate isms, Zen asserts itself and proves to be a destructive force.[18]

Here, the question must be asked, if Zen can be found wedded to *any* political and economic dogmatism whatsoever, fascism included, what is to prevent it from being wedded to terror-ism? Additionally, Suzuki informs us that Zen is "extremely flexible" in adapting itself to almost any philosophy and moral doctrine so long as its intuitive teaching is not interfered with. If so, what prevents Zen from being connected to the ethical proposition that Inoue and his band members employed, "killing one that many may live"?

Inoue wrote that he initially intended to train youth to be catalysts for legal, peaceful change throughout Japan. Later, however, he felt compelled to adopt terrorist tactics in the face of the perceived need for urgent social change, in other words, because Japanese society in the 1930s was effectively deadlocked. In this situation, what could be better suited than Zen to break this stalemate in light of its "revolutionary spirit" that "asserts itself and proves to be a destructive force"? In combination with the broader support nearly all Zen leaders gave to Japan's war effort, Zen's penchant for becoming a "destructive force" is undeniable.[19]

THE ZEN CONNECTION TO WARRIORS

It is important to recognize that Zen's penchant for destruction was not Suzuki's invention but had been an integral part of Zen from the time the first Zen temple was established in Japan in 1195.[20] The reason for this is because, from the outset, Zen was patronized and supported by Japan's warrior class, a class that had taken over governing Japan in 1185 at the outset of the Kamakura period (1185–1333). As the idiom cautions, "Don't bite the hand that feeds you." Given this, how could Zen have maintained its allegiance to Buddhist ethics, the very first precept of which requires abstinence from killing?

In this connection, one of the most revealing exchanges occurred at the time of repeated Mongolian invasions of Japan from 1274 to 1281. Japan was then ruled by the warrior class in the form of Hōjō Tokimune (1251–1284), the eighth regent of the Kamakura Shogunate. Warrior though he be, Tokimune was overcome by feelings of cowardice in the face of the expected Mongol invasion. Hoping to overcome his cowardice, he sought guidance from Zen master Bukko Kokushi (aka Mugaku Sogen, 1226–1286), an émigré priest from Song Dynasty China. Suzuki describes the conversation that is alleged to have taken place between the two men.

Tokimune: The worst enemy of our life is cowardice, and how can I escape it?

Bukko answered: Cut off the source whence cowardice comes.

Tokimune: Where does it come from?

Bukko: It comes from Tokimune himself.

Tokimune: Above all things, cowardice is what I hate most, and how can it come out of myself?

Bukko: See how you feel when you throw overboard your cherished self known as Tokimune. I will see you again when you have done that.

Tokimune: How can this be done?

Bukko: Shut out all your thoughts.

Tokimune: How can my thoughts be shut out of consciousness?

Bukko: Sit in cross-legged meditation [*zazen*] and see into the source of all your thoughts which you imagine as belonging to Tokimune.[21]

Tokimune followed Bukko's advice and thereafter devoted himself to the practice of *zazen* seated meditation. When he received reports that the Mongols were definitely on the way, he contacted Bukko once again.

Tokimune said, "The greatest event of my life is at last here."

Bukko asked, "How would you face it?"

Tokimune uttered "*Kwatsu!*" as if he were frightening away all his enemies actually before him.[22]

Bukko was pleased and said, "Truly, a lion's child roars like a lion."[23]

Suzuki praised this exchange in that it showed how Zen training was utilized to successfully defeat the Mongols, who attacked not once but twice.[24] Suzuki's defenders also point out that in this instance Zen had been invoked to defend Japan from foreign invasion. What could be wrong with that?

In reality, Tokimune viewed Zen practice as a method to ensure victory no matter who the enemy might be, domestic or foreign. Toward that end he had the major Zen monastic complex of Engakuji built in Kamakura. On the one hand, the temple was to serve as a memorial for the dead from both sides of the conflict. At the same time, the temple was to serve as a center to promote Zen practice among warriors. Tokimune wanted other samurai to learn how to incorporate Zen into their lives, in both war and peace.

In effect, Tokimune *instrumentalized* Zen in the cause of overcoming his cowardice, thereby enabling him to kill without hesitation and die fearlessly if need be. No longer was meditation a vehicle for self-awakening as formulated by Buddhism's founder, Shakyamuni Buddha, but was effectively a weapon for use on the battlefield. It is noteworthy that his "weaponization" of Zen was done while under the guidance of a Chinese Zen (Ch., *Chan*) master, suggesting (though not proving) that the origins of this phenomenon can be traced back to Buddhism in that country.

Be that as it may, subsequent Japanese history bears ample testimony to just how successful Tokimune was in promoting Zen practice among his warrior successors, for over the following centuries many of Japan's martial leaders became both Zen practitioners and patrons. While Japan never again faced foreign invasion until the modern era, its history is rife with domestic conflict, involving the samurai warriors of one feudal lord fighting against those of another feudal lord. The lords and their retainers sought to enhance their secular power, overcome their fear of death, and ensure victory through their Zen practice.

As for Japan's Zen masters, they acquiesced unconditionally to serving the needs of their warrior patrons. A good example is Zen master Hakuin Ekaku (1686–1768), the great revitalizer of the Rinzai Zen sect. He went so far as to identify the life of a warrior as superior to that of a monk.

> In my later years, I have come to the conclusion that the advantage in accomplishing true meditation lies distinctly in favor of the warrior class. A warrior must from the beginning to the end be physically strong. In his attendance to his duties and in his re-lationships with others, the utmost punctiliousness and propriety are required. . . . With this exact and proper deportment, true meditation stands forth with an overflowing splendor. Mounted on a sturdy horse, the warrior can ride forth to face an uncountable horde of enemies as though he were riding into a place empty of people. The valiant undaunted expression on his face reflects his practice of peerless, true, uninterrupted meditation sitting. Meditating in this way, the warrior can accomplish in one month what it takes a monk a year to do; in three days he can open up for himself benefits that would take a monk one hundred days.[25]

Nothing could be more important for a warrior than his ability to use his sword with consummate skill. Here, too, Zen in Japanese hands had something to offer, at least in terms of the warrior's requisite mental attitude. The famous Rinzai Zen master Takuan (1573–1645) wrote a letter to his warrior-patron, Yagyū Tajima no Kami Munenori (1571–1646). In it, Takuan described how the mind that has transcended discriminating thought, known as "no mind" (*mushin*) in Zen, could be applied to swordsmanship:

> "No-mind" applies to all activities we may perform, such as dancing, as it does to swordplay. The dancer takes up the fan and begins to stamp his feet. If he has any idea at all of displaying his art well, he ceases to be a good dancer, for his mind "stops" with every movement he goes through. In all things, it is important to forget your "mind" and become one with the work at hand.
>
> When we tie a cat, being afraid of its catching a bird, it keeps on struggling for free-dom. But train the cat so that it would not mind the presence of a bird. The animal is now free and can go anywhere it likes. In a similar way, when the mind is tied up, it feels inhibited in every move it makes, and nothing will be accomplished with any sense of spontaneity. Not only that, the work itself will be of a poor quality, or it may not be finished at all. Therefore, do not get your mind "stopped" with the sword you raise; forget what you are doing, and strike the enemy.[26]

An additional prerequisite for the warrior was unconditional loyalty. Once again, Takuan joined his Zen peers in emphasizing complete and "selfless" devotion to one's lord. He wrote,

> To be totally loyal means first of all to rectify your mind, discipline your body, and be without the least duplicity toward your lord. You must not hate or criticize others, nor fail to perform your daily duties. . . . If the spirit in which the military arts are practiced is correct, you will enjoy freedom of movement, and though thousands of the enemy appear, you will be able to force them to submit with only one sword. This is [the meaning of] great loyalty.[27]

What made it possible for Zen to so easily discard its ethical heritage? Was it nothing more than pure opportunism? Buddhist scholar Winston King sums up this centuries-long development as follows:

> For essentially Zen, with its slight regard for scripture and literary or ritual tradition, has no means of checking its "Buddhist" quality from time to time or maintaining a consistent witness to a good or holy life-pattern. In a word, it has no intrinsic ethical quality or inner monitor, but (to repeat) historically seems to be primarily a psychological technique for maximizing the visceral energies whatever their orientation.[28]

Given this background, it is hardly surprising that terrorists like Inoue and his band would have been attracted to Zen, a faith that, lacking any intrinsic ethical quality, truly aided its practitioners in maximizing their visceral energies. Not only that, unlike the military leaders of the Imperial Way Faction or Nichiren-affiliated groups, Zen never developed a religious, let alone secular, program or ideology that it sought to impose on others, most especially its powerful patrons. Lacking any "orientation" of its own, Zen can be said to have been truly "selfless" in serving the needs of anyone, terrorist or otherwise, who chose to employ it.

It was for this reason that at the outset of the Asia-Pacific War in 1937, Army Lt. Col. Sugimoto Gorō (1900–1937), a celebrated "god of war" (*gunshin*) wrote, "Through my practice of Zen I am able to get rid of my ego. In facilitating the accomplishment of this, Zen becomes, as it is, the true spirit of the Imperial military."[29] Viewed within the context of Zen's history in Japan, these words were not a distortion of that history but merely the latest expression of its usefulness on the battlefield. If this were true for the Japanese army, it was equally true for Inoue and his band's terrorist acts, especially as both groups were ultimately beholden to one and the same person—the emperor of Japan.

THE ZEN CONNECTION TO THE SUTRAS AND BUDDHIST ETHICS

If the picture of Zen promoted by Suzuki focused on intuitive action unencumbered with concern for Buddhist ethics, the same cannot be said for Inoue and his band.

As mentioned above, Inoue claimed to be motivated by the ethical doctrine of killing one so that many might live. Agree or disagree with this doctrine, it does possess a moral edge, but the question is, is it a *Buddhist* moral edge?

In seeking to answer this question it is important to note that the doctrine of killing one to save many is by no means limited to the Zen sect. In modern Japan its use can be traced back at least as far as 1883, when the Ōtani branch of the True Pure Land (Shin) sect employed this teaching in its statement of support for Japan's expansion abroad even prior to the First Sino-Japanese War of 1894–1895.[30] This usage is not surprising inasmuch as both the Shin and Zen sects are part of the much larger Mahāyāna tradition of Buddhism. Thus, any determination of the orthodoxy of this ethical doctrine must take into account its role in this larger tradition.

There is at least one Mahāyāna sutra that supports this doctrine, the *Upāyakauśalya Sūtra* (Skillful Means Sutra). It contains a story about Shakyamuni Buddha in a former life, when he was yet a Bodhisattva (Buddha-to-be) on his way to Buddhahood. As a ship's captain, named "Greatly Compassionate," Shakyamuni discerned there was a robber onboard whose intent was to rob and kill all five hundred of the passengers who were themselves Bodhisattvas. Although reluctant to take life, Shakyamuni ultimately decided to kill the robber. He did so, however, not only without ill will but, on the contrary, with compassion for both the would-be victims and even for the robber himself. Shakyamuni sought to prevent the latter from being reborn and suffering in hell as the karmic result of his evil deeds.

On the one hand, Shakyamuni's act of killing is presented in accordance with the view that acts of killing are instances of unwholesome karma, given the latter's universal and inescapable nature. Nevertheless, although the negative karma resulting from his killing of the robber should have accrued even to Shakyamuni, it did not, for, as he explained, "Good man, because I used ingenuity [skillful means] out of great compassion at that time, I was able to avoid the suffering of one hundred thousand *kalpas* of *samsāra* [the ordinary world of form and desire], and that wicked man was reborn in heaven, a good plane of existence, after death."[31]

In the Mahāyāna tradition, no less than in Theravāda, the intention with which an act is done is a key determinant in deciding whether it is ethical or not. Thus, this sutra has often been used by a wide variety of Mahāyāna adherents to support those who claim that a good Buddhist may kill if the act is done without ill will toward the victim. For example, the Dalai Lama, who identifies himself as a Mahāyāna, rather than an esoteric Vajrayāna, adherent, takes this position.[32] Despite his reputation as a champion of peace, the Dalai Lama defended the CIA-trained and -funded Tibetan guerillas who killed Chinese soldiers from 1957 to 1969. The Dalai Lama stated, "If the motivation is good, and the goal is good, the method, even apparently of a violent kind, is permissible."[33]

In the case of the Dalai Lama, the argument can be made that he approved the use of violence only in defending Tibet from Chinese invasion. However, it should be noted that when Chiang Kai-shek and his Nationalists were in control of China, the United States regarded Tibet as an integral part of China.[34] It was only after the communist takeover in 1949 that the United States recognized Tibet as an independent country and rallied to its defense as part of a larger anticommunist crusade.

In the case of Inoue and his band's terrorist acts, the two men killed, out of some twenty intended victims, could hardly be called foreign invaders. However, according to Zen master Yamamoto Gempō, they nevertheless deserved to die because the Buddha stated that "when there are those who destroy social harmony and injure the polity of the state, then even if they are called good men killing them is not a crime."

It is noteworthy that when Inoue and his band members referred to themselves as *sute-ishi* (pawns), fully prepared to sacrifice themselves in the course of assassinating their intended victims, they once again identified with a Mahāyāna Buddhist archetype, that is, Bodhisattvas, ever ready to selflessly and compassionately sacrifice themselves for the benefit of all sentient beings. Just how important a role Buddhist compassion played in Inoue's thinking is expressed in the following court testimony:

> Revolution employs compassion on behalf of the society of [our] nation. Therefore, those who wish to participate in revolution must have a mind of great compassion toward the society of [our] nation. In light of this there must be no thought of reward for participating in revolution. A revolution that does not encompass a mind of great compassion is not Buddhist. That is to say, revolution is itself the mind of great compassion.[35]

At least in their minds, Inoue's band members regarded themselves as no less compassionate than their master. Onuma Shō, assassin of Inoue Junnosuke, testified,

> Our goal was not to harm others but to destroy ourselves. We had no thought of simply killing others while surviving ourselves. We intended to smash ourselves, thereby allowing others to cross over [to a new society] on top of our own bodies. I think this is what our master Inoue meant when he told us that our goal was not to sacrifice personal affections on the altar of justice but to destroy ourselves. In the process of destroying ourselves, it couldn't be helped if there were [other] victims. This was the fundamental principle of our revolution. A mind of great compassion was the fundamental spirit of our revolution.[36]

And, of course, if the *Upāyakauśalya Sūtra* is to be believed, even the two victims of Inoue's terrorist band would be better off having been killed, for this sutra taught these allegedly wicked men would be "reborn in heaven, a good plane of existence, after death." By extension, even the terrorist perpetrators would, thanks to their great compassion, avoid the suffering of one hundred thousand *kalpas* of *samsāra*. In short, everyone should end up a "winner." Note, however, as Buddhist ethics scholar Peter Harvey points out, "If one's 'compassion' is set within a deluded perspective and wrong view, it is in an unwholesome mind state! In the Mahāyāna, wisdom and compassion need to support each other."[37]

THE ZEN CONNECTION TO SIMPLETONS

Whether in Japanese or English, Inoue Nisshō has consistently been portrayed as something of a tongue-tied simpleton because of his inability to adequately explain his political and religious thinking during the trial. For example, in his book *Government by Assassination*, British journalist Hugh Byas described Inoue as someone who professes "to be an ignorant man unable to answer deep questions."[38] Additionally, "The priest showed no signs of intellectual capacity at his trial."[39] And, of course, Inoue himself testified, "I reached where I am today thanks to Zen. Zen dislikes talking theory so I can't put it into words, but it is true nonetheless."

For Maruyama Masao, Inoue exemplified the extreme "fantasy, abstraction, and lack of a plan" characterizing early Japanese fascism or "fascism from below." He noted that Inoue "deliberately rejected any theory for constructive planning." To justify his opinion, Maruyama quoted a statement Inoue made at his trial: "I have no systematized ideas. I transcend reason and act completely upon intuition." In short, Maruyama used Inoue to illustrate the putative immaturity and lack of modern subjectivity defining what he described as Japanese fascism.

However, when we turn to Zen, at least according to D. T. Suzuki, we see Inoue's paucity of words in a different light. First, Suzuki wrote, "As intellection expresses itself in logic and words, Zen distains logic and remains speechless when it is asked to express itself."[40] Suzuki continued:

> From the philosophical point of view, Zen upholds intuition against intellection, for intuition is the more direct way of reaching the Truth. Therefore, morally and philosophically, there is in Zen a great deal of attraction for the military classes whose mind being comparatively simple and not at all addicted to philosophizing—and this is one of the essential qualities of the fighter—naturally finds a congenial spirit in Zen.[41]

Once again, it can certainly be argued that Suzuki didn't intend for his words to apply to a terrorist, only a "fighter." Nevertheless, Suzuki's claim that "Zen upholds intuition against intellection, for intuition is the more direct way of reaching the Truth" clearly refers to all Zen practitioners. Moreover, Suzuki failed to distinguish between intuition that is real wisdom arising from "Buddha-nature," that is, good depths of the mind, and intuition that merely serves to reinforce unthinking, ingrained bad habits. Finally, Suzuki urged practitioners to give up "intellection," the act or process of using the discriminating intellect. Given this, why wouldn't Zen have been as attractive to terrorists as it was to fighters, especially were one to believe that, like the military classes, terrorist minds were "comparatively simple and not at all addicted to philosophizing"?

In this connection, it should be noted that there is ample scriptural precedent in the Zen school for its emphasis on intuition. The *Laṅkāvatāra Sūtra*, for example, describes an exchange that took place primarily between Shakyamuni Buddha and a Bodhisattva named Mahāmati (Great Wisdom). Bodhidharma, the legendary Indian priest said to have introduced Zen (Ch., *Chan*) to China in the fifth or sixth century, gave a copy of this sutra to his chief Chinese disciple, Hui-k'e, in order to point out that the discriminating intellect can only be overcome if a complete "turning-about" takes place in the deepest seat of consciousness. The habit of looking outward, toward external objects, must be abandoned and a new spiritual attitude established by realizing truth or ultimate reality with the intuitive consciousness, that is, by becoming one with reality.

Suzuki described the importance of intuition in this sutra as follows:

> As [the *Lankāvatāra Sūtra*] is concerned with the highest reality or the ultimate truth of things, it is no superficial knowledge dealing with particular objects and their relations. It is an intuitive understanding which, penetrating through the surface of existence, sees into that which is the reason of everything logically and ontologically.
>
> The Lanka[*vatāra Sūtra*] is never tired of impressing upon its readers the importance of this understanding in the attainment of spiritual freedom; for this understanding is a fundamental intuition into the truth of Mind-only and constitutes the Buddhist enlightenment with which truly starts the religious life of a *Bodhisattva*.[42]

Whether Inoue's intuitive understanding genuinely allowed him to see into "that which is the reason of everything logically and ontologically" is certainly contestable. However, Zen's strong emphasis on the role of intuition must be understood as forming the backdrop if not the basis of his court testimony. Readers will recall that when Inoue was asked about the political ideology that informed his actions, he replied, "It is more correct to say that I have no systematized ideas. I transcend reason and act completely upon intuition." There can be little debate that both Inoue and his band did indeed "transcend reason."

No doubt it is difficult for a secular academic like Maruyama to understand the thinking of a Zen-trained layman like Inoue. In this case, Zen's dependence on intuition, and unwillingness to express itself in abstract or rational thought, was a perfect combination for Inoue and his band, who rejected the very idea of imposing their aspirations, let alone demands, on the emperor. As readers will recall, in postwar Japan, Inoue informed his American interrogator as follows:

> The relationship between the emperor and the people of this country is the same as the relationship between a parent and his children. If the emperor weren't our parent, why would he do his duty as a parent. It is for this reason we call him our "Great Parent." If we weren't the emperor's children, why would we do our duty as children? For this reason, we are called "His Majesty's children." Not only this, but as history reveals, the emperor and the people of this country have always been one, differing only in their respective missions and stations in life. No matter what the organization, it is always made up of a center and its branches. The emperor is naturally at the center ruling over his subjects. It is for this reason that following the introduction of writing from China the phrase "sovereign and subjects are one" has been used to express Japan's national body politic.

Once again, readers today may well be incredulous in encountering someone like Inoue who willingly rendered unconditional and absolute loyalty to another human being. Nevertheless, for many millions of his subjects, including Inoue and his band, Emperor Hirohito was such a personage, moreover a *divine* personage. It was Zen "egolessness" that provided the metaphysical foundation making this possible.

As introduced above, it was Lt. Col. Sugimoto Gorō who claimed, "Through my practice of Zen I am able to get rid of my ego," that is, achieve "egolessness." What this meant in practice was that Sugimoto, Inoue, and their like believed, having achieved this state, they acted not on the basis of what they personally determined to be right or proper but only on the basis of the "august mind" of the emperor.

THE ZEN CONNECTION TO MEDITATION

What was it, exactly, about Zen practice that made it so useful to Inoue and his band? The answer is the Zen form of meditation, *zazen*.[43] A key component of *zazen* is the experience of *samādhi* and the mental power associated with it. Without *samādhi*, Zen would be no more than a "mental health practice" instead of the basis for a profound realization of the true nature of the self. Did Inoue and his band members have an authentic experience of *samādhi* and the mental power associated with it? When they recited the *daimoku* over and over again, were they able to enter *samādhi*, technically known as *daimoku-zammai* (i.e., *daimoku samādhi*)?

Before attempting to answer this question, let us first examine *samādhi* and its associated mental power in more detail. *Samādhi* refers to a state of meditative consciousness. The term *samādhi* derives from the Sanskrit root *sam-ā-dhā*, which means "to collect" or "bring together" and is often translated as "concentration" or "unification of mind." In early Buddhist texts, *samādhi* is associated with the term *samatha* (calm abiding). In the Pali *suttas* (Skt., *sūtras*), *samādhi* is defined as one-pointedness of mind, a meditative absorption attained through the practice of meditation, that is, *jhāna* (Skt., *dhyāna*; Kor., *Seon*; J., *Zen*; Ch., *Chan*; Vietnamese, *Thiền*).

Jhāna/dhyāna, a core Buddhist practice commonly translated as meditation, is described as a state of "no mind" in the Chan/Zen school. It refers to a series of cultivated states of mind that lead to a state of perfect equanimity and awareness (Skt., *upekkhā-sati-pārisuddhi*). Upon entering into *samādhi* during meditation, the mind becomes still, without conscious thought, yet totally aware of the present moment. As such, *samādhi* also lies at the heart of the last of the eight elements of the Buddhist Noble Eightfold Path (i.e., right concentration).

Because "one-pointedness of mind" is an intrinsic and indivisible part of *samādhi*, the mental power produced by this concentrated state of mind is a potent force for understanding the true nature of the self in the hands of an experienced meditator. *Samādhi* and the psycho-spiritual power associated with *samādhi* are closely related to one another.

For those who have experienced a deep *samādhi*, it is a luminous experience that seems to the meditator to be beyond time and place, though it is definitely not a trancelike experience in which the meditator is transmitted to a supernatural realm. In fact, if anything, the meditator is more fully "present" in the "here and now" than ever before. The meditator may also subsequently experience a wonderful sense of "oneness" with his or her surroundings. Further, as will be discussed in more detail below, for *right* (as opposed to *wrong*) *samādhi*, one needs to suspend various spiritual hindrances, including aversion/ill will. Thus, to use *samādhi* to harm other sentient beings would appear, on the face of it, to be utterly impossible.

Nevertheless, before and during the Asia-Pacific War, Japanese Zen leaders, including D. T. Suzuki, often wrote about this meditation-derived mental power, emphasizing the effectiveness of *samādhi* power (J., *zenjōriki*) in battle.[44] On the military side, one of the first men to write about the importance of *samādhi* power was Vice Admiral Yamaji Kazuyoshi (1869–1963). Yamaji wrote a book titled *Zen no Ōyō* (The Practical Application of Zen), in which he described how he put his many years of Zen training to practical use during the Russo-Japanese War (1904–1905).

Yamaji discussed *samādhi* in a section of his book titled "The Realm of *Samādhi*" as follows:

> In Zen there is something called "*samādhi*." This is a realm where there is neither "self" nor "others," neither mountains nor rivers; the entirety of one's whole mind becomes the character *mu* (*muji*), [the sound of] one hand (*sekishu*).[45] If you do not endeavor to sit quietly in this realm, you will never realize enlightenment.
>
> At first, I was unable to unify my spirit by becoming the character *mu* or [the sound of] one hand for even three to five minutes. I was attacked by various illusory and worldly thoughts from the front, rear, left, and right. However, as I continued to practice, it gradually became easier to enter *samādhi*. And after sitting quietly in the realm of *samādhi*, I was finally able to penetrate my assigned *kōan*, achieve great peace of mind and experience a feeling of great exultation. It was then I realized the mental state where "throughout heaven and earth I alone am honored."
>
> In the midst of war, each time I sat quietly and entered *samādhi*, a wise plan would suddenly appear. Furthermore, the moment I saw the enemy, a countermeasure would emerge. Still further, when faced with various problems in daily life, I found my practice of *zazen* very helpful to their resolution.[46]

In this passage, we learn of the wide scope for the application of *samādhi* power. First, it allowed the vice admiral to devise a "wise plan" even in the midst of war. Additionally, when the enemy appeared, *samādhi* power facilitated "countermeasure[s]," measures to more effectively kill the enemy. And even in "daily life," *samādhi* power was a valuable resource for solving various problems. If not precisely a "man for all seasons," *samādhi* was definitely a "power for all seasons."

With the advent of the Asia-Pacific War, meditation-derived *samādhi* power became even more prominent, as demonstrated by the life and death of Zen adept and Army Lt. Col Sugimoto Gorō. Sugimoto died on the battlefield in China in 1937, and his Rinzai Zen master Yamazaki Ekijū (1882–1961) offered the following eulogy:

> A grenade fragment hit him in the left shoulder. He seemed to have fallen down but then got up again. Although he was standing, one could not hear his commands. He was no longer able to issue commands with that husky voice of his. . . . Yet he was still standing, holding his sword in one hand as a prop. Both legs were slightly bent, and he was facing in an easterly direction [toward the imperial palace]. It appeared that he had

saluted though his hand was now lowered to about the level of his mouth. The blood flowing from his mouth covered his watch. . . . From long ago, the true sign of a Zen priest had been his ability to pass away while doing *zazen*. Those who were completely and thoroughly enlightened, however, . . . could die calmly in a standing position. . . . This was possible due to *samādhi* power. . . . Although it can be said that his life of thirty-eight years was all too short, for someone who has truly obtained *samādhi* power, long and short are not important. The great, true example of Sugimoto Gorō was that of one who had united with emptiness, embodying true loyalty [to the emperor] and service to the state. I am convinced he is one of those who, should he be reborn seven times over, would reverently work to destroy enemies of the emperor (written on the 11th of February of the 2,598th year of the imperial reign) [1938].[47]

These descriptions by Yamazaki make it clear just how wide-ranging *samādhi* power was believed to be. It provided Sugimoto with the same power as that of ancient Zen masters, the power to choose one's posture at the time of death even when mortally wounded. Additionally, it facilitated a state of true loyalty to the emperor such that an early death on the battlefield was "not important." In fact, Sugimoto's death was regarded as no more than a prelude to his being reborn and repeatedly killed, seven times over, in loyal service to emperor and state.[48] Needless to say, Rinzai Zen master Yamazaki Ekijū expressed no concern for the "all too short" lives of the enemy soldiers Sugimoto killed.

It is important to note that these modern applications of *samādhi* power to the battlefield were not the first time this phenomenon had occurred in Japanese Zen history. For example, the retired samurai-turned-Zen-priest Suzuki Shōsan (1579–1655) wrote, "It's with the energy of Zen *samādhi* that all the arts are executed. The military arts in particular can't be executed with a slack mind. . . . This energy of Zen *samādhi* is everything. The man of arms, however, is in Zen *samādhi* while he applies his skill."[49] In light of all this, it should come as no surprise to learn that *samādhi* was a key part of Onuma Shō's preparations to assassinate Inoue Junnosuke:

> After starting my practice of *zazen*, I entered a state of *samādhi* the likes of which I had never experienced before. I felt my spirit become unified, really unified, and when I opened my eyes from their half-closed meditative position I noticed the smoke from the incense curling up and touching the ceiling. At this point it suddenly came to me—I would be able to carry out [the assassination] that night.

Onuma's comments make it clear that *samādhi* power, acquired through meditation, was what had made it possible for him to commit his terrorist act. Significantly, Onuma also testified that he had first recited four passages from the *Lotus Sūtra*, then repeated the *daimoku* four or five times, before sitting silently in *zazen*. Thus, *daimoku*-induced *samādhi* (i.e., *daimoku-zammai*) was an integral part of his practice.[50] Onuma's comments are not surprising in light of the fact that in the run-up to his own enlightenment experience, Inoue referred to his own fervent practice, day and night, of *daimoku-zammai*.[51] In short, *samādhi* power was as available to terrorists as it had once been to warriors and their soldier successors, for exactly the same reason—it enhanced their ability and determination to kill (and be killed).

WAS INOUE NISSHŌ "ENLIGHTENED"?

If Inoue were not a tongue-tied simpleton, but instead an accomplished Zen practitioner who understood the critically important role of intuition, the question naturally arises as to whether Inoue's enlightenment experience was authentic. Inoue certainly believed he had a genuine enlightenment experience while meditating at Santoku-an in his hometown of Kawaba village. Readers will recall Inoue described his enlightenment experience in the spring of 1924 as follows:

> I experienced a oneness in which the whole of nature and the universe was my [true] Self. I was overwhelmed with the feeling that "heaven and earth [and I] are of the same root," and "the ten thousand things [and I] are of one substance." This was something I had never felt before, a truly strange and mysterious state of mind. I thought to myself, "This is really weird!" And then I thought, let me examine my past doubts in light of the enlightened realm I had just entered. As I quietly reflected on these doubts, I was astounded to realize that my doubts of thirty years standing had melted away without a trace.

Although, as previously noted, it was unusual to recite the *daimoku* as a meditative technique, Inoue nevertheless employed classic Zen terminology to describe his breakthrough. As introduced in chapter 6, the two phrases Inoue quoted above are contained in the fortieth case of the *Blue Cliff Record* (J., *Hekiganroku*; Ch., *Biyan Lu*), the famous twelfth-century collection of one hundred *kōan* that is considered to contain the essence of Zen. In the case in question, the conversation partner of the famous Zen master Huairang (677–744) cites a passage from an earlier essay written by Sengzhao (384–414) describing the oneness of heaven, earth, and humanity. Significantly, Sengzhao is known for the deep influence Taoist thought and terminology exerted on his understanding of Mahāyāna philosophy, especially the Madhyamaka school's teaching of "emptiness" (Skt., *śūnyatā*; J., *kū*).

The connection between Inoue's enlightenment experience and terrorism is to be found in his determination of the standards for good and evil, right and wrong. Inoue continued:

> It is truly a case in which, from the very beginning, "good and evil do not differ [from one another]." Rather, when our thoughts and actions are in accord with the truth of a non-dualistic universe, this is good. When they are not, this is evil. . . . This said, concrete manifestations of good and evil do differ from one another according to the time, place, and those involved. Thus, there is no need to be attached to a particular concept [of good and evil] or think about what is right or wrong.

These are perhaps the most frightening words contained in this book, for if there is no need to "think about what is right or wrong," then, literally, any action is acceptable, especially when done intuitively, let alone compassionately. In other words, everything depends on context. Yet, without ethical values, how does one know how best to deal with a particular context?

While this mode of thinking seems unacceptable in light of Buddhism's strong emphasis on intentionality, it fit in perfectly with the thinking of Inoue's contemporary, D. T. Suzuki. As previously noted, Suzuki wrote,

> Zen did not necessarily argue with [warriors] about the immortality of soul, or about righteousness of the divine way, or about ethical conduct, but it simply urged to go ahead with whatever conclusion rational or irrational a man has arrived at. Philosophy may safely be left with intellectual minds; Zen wants to act, and the most effective act is, once the mind is made up, to go on without looking backward. In this respect, Zen is indeed the religion of the samurai warrior.[52]

With little to no concern for "ethical conduct," let alone the need for rational conclusions, why wouldn't Zen have been as ideal for a band of terrorists as it had once been for samurai warriors?

RINZAI ZEN MASTER YAMAMOTO GEMPŌ

In light of the terrorist acts committed by Inoue's band, Zen partisans would no doubt deny, vehemently deny, that Inoue could possibly have had a genuine awakening or enlightenment experience of any kind. To suggest otherwise would call into question the very foundation of the Zen school. Unfortunately for Zen partisans, Inoue's enlightenment experience was verified, as required by Zen tradition, by one of the greatest Zen masters of his day—Yamamoto Gempō. At his trial Inoue testified, "At the time I first met Zen Master Gempō, he said that I was enlightened. Reflecting on this now, I think what he said was truly remarkable. However, he added that I was not yet able to live an enlightened life. . . . 'Don't get discouraged,' he told me, 'I'm certain you'll be able to become fully enlightened' [J., *daigo*]."[53]

Needless to say, this is Inoue's recollection of events, and therefore must be treated with a degree of skepticism. However, as readers will recall, Gempō began his testimony at Inoue's trial as follows:

> The first thing I would like to say is that Inoue has engaged in spiritual cultivation for many years. This led him to a direct realization of the most important element in religion—the true nature of the mind, something Buddhism calls perfect wisdom. Perfect wisdom is like a mirror that reflects humans, heaven, earth, and the universe. Inoue further realized that the true form of humans, heaven, earth, and the universe is no different than the true form of the self. The manifestation of this truth of the universe is the Spirit of Japan, that is to say, the polity of Japan.[54] It is in these things that Inoue's spirit is to be found. . . .

> Although Inoue came to visit me in the midst of his spiritual training, I most definitely did not give him my sanction [i.e., confirming him as being fully enlightened] nor say that his practice was complete.

Within a Rinzai Zen framework, when Gempō stated that Inoue's many years of spiritual cultivation had led him "to a direct realization of the most important element in religion—the true nature of the mind," he was in fact confirming that—in his view—Inoue had experienced *kenshō* (lit., seeing one's nature), an initial enlightenment/awakening experience. It is probable that Gempō did not use the term *kenshō* because its meaning would have been unfamiliar to those outside the Zen school. In the Zen school, a practitioner relies on his teacher to authenticate and formally acknowledge his enlightenment, initial or complete.

Note, however, that Gempō added, "I most definitely did not give him my sanction nor say that his practice was complete." By this, Gempō meant that he had not yet granted Inoue *inka-shōmei* (lit., the legitimating seal of recognition), the ultimate sanction in Rinzai Zen. That is to say, in Gempō's eyes, Inoue had not yet completed his training and therefore was not fully enlightened (i.e., he had not yet fully realized Buddhahood).

Gempō's testimony would neither have surprised nor disappointed Inoue, for it was he who had taken the initiative to train under Gempō as part of his *post*-enlightenment training (J., *gogo no shugyō*). Inoue was well aware that Zen training in Rinzai Zen does not end with a *kenshō* experience. Instead, practice must be continued to deepen the initial insight and express it in daily life as would a Buddha.

Additionally, Hakuin, the great eighteenth-century reviver of Rinzai Zen, taught the purpose of post-enlightenment training was "to bestow the great gift of the Dharma, leading his fellow beings toward salvation in place of the Buddha patriarchs."[55] Thus, the question must be asked: by incorporating Zen into the training of his terrorist band, had Inoue led them toward salvation in place of the Buddha patriarchs?

It would be easy and comforting to answer this question in the negative. However, it should be recalled that Gempō testified:

> It is true that if, motivated by an evil mind, someone should kill so much as a single ant, as many as one hundred and thirty-six hells await that person. This holds true not only in Japan but for all the countries of the world. Yet the Buddha, being absolute, has stated that when there are those who destroy social harmony and injure the polity of the state, then even if they are called good men, killing them is not a crime.

Although Gempō failed to cite the source for his surprising if not shocking assertion, it is not difficult to identify the doctrinal basis for his assertion, namely the *Nirvāna Sūtra* (aka *Mahāparnirvāna-Sūtra*). Together with the *Lotus Sūtra*, this sutra has had the widest impact of any Mahāyāna writing in East Asia. Compare Gempō's claim with the following exchange between Shakyamuni Buddha and one of his disciples recorded in chapter 40 of the *Nirvāna Sūtra*:

"O World-honored One! Why is it that the *icchantikas* do not possess good?"

"O good man! Because the *icchantikas* are cut off from the root of good. All beings possess such five roots as faith, etc.[56] But the people of the *icchantika* class are eternally cut off from such. Because of this, one may well kill an ant and gain the sin of harming, but the killing of an *icchantika* does not [constitute a sin]."[57]

The question here is what is meant by the term *icchantika*? According to some Mahāyāna Buddhist scriptures, an *icchantika* is someone given over to total hedonism and greed, the most spiritually deluded of all types of being. This is, of course, exactly the way in which many Japanese in 1930s Japan, not just ultranationalists, viewed allegedly corrupt politicians in league with wealthy members of the *zaibatsu* financial conglomerates. In turn, it was the hedonism and greed of these two groups that was held to be responsible for destroying "social harmony" in Japan. Moreover, "sowing discord" in the Buddhist community (i.e., *Sangha*) is traditionally viewed as one of distinguishing wrongful acts of *icchantikas*.

From the generally accepted Mahāyāna doctrinal viewpoint, what is strange about the above reference to *icchantikas* is that it seems to run counter to, even deny, the message of hope embodied in the Mahāyāna belief in the universality of Buddha-nature. Buddha-nature affirms that the potential to realize Buddhahood exists in all sentient beings. Despite the assertion that *icchantikas* are "eternally cut off from [the root of good]," the status of an *icchantika* is typically understood to be a state of mind, not an unchanging karmic destiny. Thus, no matter how deluded a person may be, there remains the possibility of overcoming his or her hedonism and greed. Of course, it can be cogently argued that after having been killed, this possibility no longer exists. On the other hand, since no "sin" (i.e., karmic debt) is alleged to have been incurred by killing an *icchantika*, why should Gempō, or the killer, be concerned?

WAS YAMAMOTO GEMPŌ AN AUTHENTIC ZEN MASTER?

Gempō's controversial assertion raises the question of whether he was an authentic Zen master. If he were not, his assertions, let alone his acknowledgment of Inoue's initial enlightenment experience, would be invalid. No doubt many readers, especially those within the Zen school, would like to believe Gempō lacked the qualifications of a genuine Zen master. After all, how many Zen masters are known to have testified on behalf of terrorists in an attempt to justify their murderous actions?

In seeking to determine Gempō's legitimacy, it should be noted that Yamamoto was deeply admired by his fellow Rinzai Zen masters. Among other things, this is reflected by the fact that he was selected to head the entire Rinzai Zen sect in 1947. In addition, he was the head priest of two of Rinzai Zen's most distinguished temples, Ryūtakuji and Shōinji, both famous for their association with the great Hakuin Ekaku. Thus, Yamamoto remains widely recognized as one of the Rinzai sect's greatest Zen masters of the twentieth century.

To further understand Gempō, it may be helpful to know that he came from an unusual background, beginning from his childhood. Readers interested in learning more about his background are invited to read Gempō's entry in appendix 3. Suffice it here to state that, like his lay disciple Inoue, Gempō was closely connected to the pinnacles of power in wartime Japan. This is hardly surprisingly, for as I noted in *Zen at War* and *Zen War Stories*, Gempō was no different in his unconditional, fervent support of Japanese aggression than any of his fellow Zen masters, whether affiliated with the Rinzai or Sōtō Zen sects.

Although in the postwar years both the Rinzai and Sōtō Zen sects have apologized for their support of Japan's war effort, no one, in either sect, has ever questioned, let alone criticized, Gempō, or denied his assertion that "the Buddha, being absolute, has stated that when there are those who destroy social harmony and injure the polity of the state, then even if they are called good men, killing them is not a crime."[58] While Gempō never assassinated anyone, he certainly made his contribution to the spiritual foundation justifying terrorism and overall Japanese aggression on behalf of the "well-being of all the colored races."[59] The fact that even today, seventy-five years after the war's end, the Zen school in Japan, both Rinzai and Sōtō, finds it impossible to criticize Zen masters like Gempō by name, or refute their violence-affirming teachings, reveals a profound sickness in this tradition, one that shows no prospects of being overcome anytime soon.

CONCLUSION

On the one hand, it is clear Zen Buddhism did not serve to motivate Inoue or his band to undertake their terrorist-related actions. At least in this regard, Zen cannot be designated as an intrinsically fanatical or murderous practice. On the other hand, it is equally clear that Zen can be and was used to justify or *enable* acts of terrorism. Inoue testified at his trial, "I reached where I am today thanks to Zen. Zen dislikes talking theory so I can't put it into words, but it is true nonetheless."

In addition, Inoue made it abundantly clear that he selected Zen both because it eschews intellectual musings and because it concentrates, instead, on action. As we have seen, Suzuki supported Inoue's position when he wrote, "Philosophy may safely be left with intellectual minds; Zen wants to act, and the most effective act is, once the mind is made up, to go on without looking backward."[60] Suzuki was, of course, talking about the relationship of the samurai to Zen. Yet, if as Suzuki claims in the same quotation "ethical conduct" also need not be considered, what is there to prevent Zen from becoming connected to terrorism?[61]

Furthermore, it cannot be denied that, once their minds were made up, Inoue and his band did "go on without looking backward."[62] Even though band members initially managed to kill only two of some twenty intended victims, their murderous acts, combined with the subsequent assassination of Prime Minister Inukai Tsuyoshi, were quite effective in providing the pretext, the excuse, for bringing

Taishō Democracy to an end. In so doing, Inoue and his band made a substantial contribution to Japan's transformation into a totalitarian state under the ultimate control of a single individual, the emperor.

Zen had two further contributions to make to Inoue's terrorist acts. One was the practice of meditation, *zazen*. It was as a result of his meditation practice, specifically his initial enlightenment experience, that Inoue concluded "there is no need to be attached to a particular concept [of good and evil] or think about what is right or wrong."

A second contribution to Zen-enabled terrorism was the provision of meditation-derived *samādhi* power. As noted above, it was Onuma Shō who testified:

> After starting my practice of *zazen*, I entered a state of *samādhi* the likes of which I had never experienced before. I felt my spirit become unified, really unified, and when I opened my eyes from their half-closed meditative position I noticed the smoke from the incense curling up and touching the ceiling. At this point it suddenly came to me—I would be able to carry out [the assassination] that night.

Previous discussion of *samādhi* power makes it clear that this power was as available, and as useful, to the samurai as it was to the modern Japanese military. To that list must now be added terrorists. Once Buddhist ethics were stripped from meditation, as had already occurred in feudal Japan, the resulting *samādhi* power was available for anyone to use as they saw fit. After all, there was no need to think about "right or wrong." As Suzuki was fond of saying, "Good fighters are generally ascetics or stoics, which means to have an iron will. When needed Zen supplies them with this."[63] It is true that without Buddhist ethics, *samādhi* power can unquestionably produce an iron will—an iron will to kill.

It should be noted, however, there is a scriptural reference in the Mahāyāna corpus that disavows the use of *samādhi* to kill others. Chapter 35 of the *Nirvāṇa Sūtra* contains the following verse:

> How does one practice *samādhi*? If, when practicing *samādhi*, one does it to enlighten one's own self, for profit, not for the sake of all beings, not for the practicing of *Dharma*, but out of greed, for defiled food, for sexual reasons, because of the impurities of the nine holes, for disputes, for beating, and *for killing others*, anybody who practices *samādhi* thus is not one who practices *samādhi*.[64] (emphasis mine)

Despite the seminal role the *Nirvāṇa Sūtra* played in East Asian Buddhism, there is no evidence to indicate that, at least in Japan, this disavowal of killing was ever employed to discourage, let alone oppose, the samurai class from employing *samādhi* power in their bloody profession. Nor, of course, did this passage lead any modern Zen masters, including Yamamoto Gempō, to oppose the use of *samādhi* power on either the battlefield or in terrorist incidents.

The southern Theravāda tradition of Buddhism also rejects taking Buddhist meditation as value neutral and specifically warns against the misuse of *samādhi*, describing it as *micchā* (wrong)-*samādhi*. As Peter Harvey points out, in both Theravāda and Sarvāstivāda Abhidharmas, *samādhi* is a mental quality that can be found in both wholesome and unwholesome states of mind.[65] For example, when angry, one can be very focused on the object of one's anger. The Theravāda Abhidharma also sees Pāli *viriya* (Skt., *vīrya*; i.e., energy, vigor, mental strength) as something that can be an ingredient in either wholesome or unwholesome states of mind. Hence the qualities that can empower spiritual practices include ones that are ethically variable. As a result, those who have experienced the power of these qualities may then use this power to bad ends, supported by attachment to some distorted view. The key problem is the presence of hindering defilements in the human mind, which can use good things for bad ends.[66]

In the *Ganaka-Moggallāna Sutta*, Ananda, one of Shakyamuni Buddha's chief disciples, pointed out to Vassakara, the chief minister of the country of Magadha, that Shakyamuni did not praise every form of meditation:

> What kind of meditation, brahman, did the Lord not praise? As to this, brahman, . . . He dwells with his thought obsessed by ill-will, overcome by ill-will, and he does not comprehend as it really is the escape from ill-will that has arisen; he, having made ill-will the main thing meditates on it, meditates absorbed, meditates more absorbed, meditates quite absorbed. . . . The Lord does not praise this kind of meditation, brahman.[67]

Whether speaking of soldiers on the battlefield or terrorists, killing the designated "other" *without ill will* would seem to be a dubious proposition at best. In Onuma Shō's case, the question must be asked as to why only after entering a state of *samādhi*, the likes of which he had never previously experienced, was he able to carry out the assassination of Inoue Junnosuke.

Yet readers may interject, Inoue and his band did embrace a form of Buddhist ethics—killing one so that many may live. This is a form of ethics contained in the *Upāyakauśalya Sūtra*. The premise of this sutra is that Bodhisattvas are ever ready to sacrifice themselves in order to kill one or more evil doers in order to benefit the many. This is clearly a powerful motif, one that was embraced by *all* of Japan's traditional Buddhist sects up through Japan's defeat in August 1945.

For example, following Japan's full-scale invasion of China on July 7, 1937, institutional Buddhist leaders from each of the major sects signed a proclamation in support of Japan's war actions only five days later, on July 12, 1937. This proclamation was issued by a pan-Buddhist organization known as the Myōwa-kai and contained the following paragraph:

> In order to establish eternal peace in East Asia, arousing the great benevolence and compassion of Buddhism, we are sometimes accepting and sometimes forceful. We now have no choice but to exercise the benevolent forcefulness of "killing one in order that many may live" [*issatsu tashō*]. This is something which Mahāyāna Buddhism approves of only with the greatest of seriousness.[68]

However, Mark Tatz, the translator of the *Upāyakauśalya Sūtra*, informs us this sutra is likely to have been composed in the first century BCE.[69] If he is correct, this sutra is highly unlikely to represent the original teachings of Shakyamuni Buddha concerning the use of violence. In fact, Damien Keown, a noted scholar of Buddhist ethics, has gone so far as to label this sutra the place "where it all started to go horribly wrong for the Mahāyāna."[70]

Whether or not things went "horribly wrong for the Mahāyāna," as far as condoning the use of violence is concerned, is a highly contentious topic, one that exceeds the confines of this book. Yet there is another seminal Buddhist text that must be considered, the universally recognized collection of sayings attributed to Shakyamuni Buddha known as the *Dhammapada*. Verses 129–30 of chapter 10 of this work state,

> All men tremble at punishment, all men fear death; remembering that thou art like unto them, do not strike or slay.
>
> All men tremble at punishment, all men love life; remember that thou art like unto them, do not strike or slay.

In light of this injunction, it is difficult, if not impossible, to believe the ethic of killing one to save many can ever be justified on the basis of the teachings of Shakyamuni Buddha, whether applied to the actions of soldiers, let alone terrorists. Moreover, when "egolessness" is used to turn over one's own thought processes to another, including determinations of right and wrong, the following admonition attributed to Shakyamuni Buddha in the *Kālāma Sutta* has been violated in the extreme:

> Do not go upon what has been acquired by repeated hearing; nor upon tradition; nor upon rumor; nor upon what is in a scripture; nor upon surmise; nor upon an axiom; nor upon specious reasoning; nor upon a bias towards a notion that has been pondered over; nor upon another's seeming ability; nor upon the consideration, "The monk is our teacher." Kalamas, when you yourselves know: "These things are good; these things are not blamable; these things are praised by the wise; undertaken and observed, these things lead to benefit and happiness," enter on and abide in them.[71]

The reference to "good" in this paragraph refers to states free of the "three poisons" in Buddhism, that is, greed, hatred, and delusion, for these states do not lead to such unethical actions as killing. It is in words like these that the true spirit of Buddhism is to be found.

15

Trilogy Conclusion

This chapter is written to provide an overall conclusion to the three-part study of the close, supportive relationship between the Zen school in Japan, both Sōtō and Rinzai sects, and Japanese imperialism abroad as well as totalitarianism at home. As previously noted, the first two volumes of this study were titled *Zen at War* and *Zen War Stories*.

AN ETHICS-LESS ZEN

If there is a single, overwhelming conclusion to be derived from my three books on this topic, it is that Zen, at least in its Japanese form, is essentially "ethics-less." Or more precisely, it is largely bereft of *Buddhist* ethics, having been replaced centuries ago by Confucian and especially Neo-Confucian social ethics. A key element in this process was the introduction to Japan of the Neo-Confucian doctrines of Zhu Xi (aka Chu Hsi, 1130–1200). D. T. Suzuki emphasized Zen's close connection to Neo-Confucianism in Japan as follows:

> During the Ashikaga period [1336–1568], the position of the Chu Hsi philosophy as upholding the orthodox doctrine of Confucianism was generally recognized and the Zen monks began to pursue its study with more than a zeal of sheer learning. They know where their Zen was most needed and where the Sung philosophy proved its most practical usefulness. They thus became its real official propagators, and their influence radiated from Kyoto as centre out into the remoter parts of the country.[1]

Whereas in China, Neo-Confucianism developed in opposition to, and as a critique of, Buddhism, in Japan it was Zen monks who transmitted and promoted its doctrines to their warrior patrons up to the sixteenth century. At that point it became an

221

independent school and was soon adopted as the official guiding philosophy of the Tokugawa Shogunate (1603–1867). Tokugawa military rulers recognized in Neo-Confucian doctrines an effective ideology for imposing what amounted to a rigid, class-based "straitjacket" on society. They sought the creation of a society in which all religious, philosophical, and ethical systems were dedicated to upholding the regime's objective—that of establishing a hierarchically controlled social and political entity that no one would dare challenge.

Neo-Confucianism's independence from Zen, however, did not lessen Zen's embrace of Neo-Confucianism, for during the centuries it had been harbored in Zen temples, its social ethics effectively replaced, at least *in practice*, those of Buddhism. Zen monks promoted its teachings in order to provide a religious sanction for the existing social order. They taught, in accordance with Neo-Confucian dictates, that the ideal of social harmony was established by a reciprocal relationship of justice between superiors, who ought to be benevolent, and subordinates, who are required to be loyal to their superiors.

In the hands of the samurai class, the Zen school's patrons, this became the ideal of absolute, self-sacrificing and unconditional loyalty to one's feudal lord from the Kamakura period onward. However, following the Meiji Restoration of 1868, the object of absolute and unconditional loyalty was changed to the emperor, who was held to be the father of the nation. For their part, the Japanese people were his "children," who had a filial obligation to obey him unconditionally. Zen monks steadfastly supported these developments, for as D. T. Suzuki noted above, they truly understood "where their Zen was most needed" in both premodern and modern Japan.

To be sure, Neo-Confucian ethics is capable of producing the long-cherished Confucian ideal of a "harmonious society" but only on the condition that subordinates loyally follow their superiors' directives *without question*. Thus, Japanese Zen did have a form of ethics, but it was essentially an ethics of unquestioning loyalty unto death, the very antithesis of Buddhist ethics. This helps explain why a Zen master like Yamamoto Gempō could so readily defend Inoue Nisshō, claiming that "those who destroy social harmony" deserved to die. Similarly, Zen training combined with Neo-Confucianism made it possible for Rinzai Zen master Yamazaki Ekijū to eulogize his "god of war" disciple, Lt. Col. Sugimoto Gorō, as follows: "The great, true example of Sugimoto Gorō was that of one who had united with emptiness, embodying total loyalty [to the emperor] and service to the state."[2] In short, Zen "emptiness," "total loyalty," and "service to the state" were fused together into one indissoluble entity.[3]

However, while the terms *total loyalty* and *service to the state* can be attributed to Neo-Confucianism, the Zen (Buddhist) term *emptiness* demonstrates not all of Japanese Zen's ethics-less character is derived from that school of thought. As quoted in the previous chapter, Winston King, in his 1993 book *Zen and the Way of the Sword*, identifies the fundamental problem to be that "Zen has no intrinsic ethical quality or inner monitor, but (to repeat) historically seems to be primarily a psychological technique for maximizing the visceral energies whatever their orientation."[4]

While King's statement concerned Zen's relationship to the warrior class, King was also aware of the way Zen had been used during the Asia-Pacific War, writing, "Many in Zen circles gave their blessing to the new Japanese militarism of the first half of the twentieth century."[5] In this connection, King criticized D. T. Suzuki's interpretation of Zen "selflessness" or "egolessness":

> Only when one becomes a depersonalized, unthinking set of warrior techniques, actions, and reactions has one overcome the "ego" and totally unified oneself with action—the highest of Zen excellences. Such "selflessness," says [D. T.] Suzuki, makes the killing sword into a "life-giving" instrument of "righteousness." (To whom? It might be asked.) To be sure, most moments of intense action are mindless in one sense; personal identity—sense, time, place—all these are temporarily forgotten in the heat of action, and necessarily so. But to speak of this as egolessness in an ethical sense, as the height of holy realization, is a definition the Western world will find impossible to accept.[6]

Suzuki's defenders, including Satō Gemmyō Taira, Gary Snyder, and Nelson Foster, continue to justify or mitigate Suzuki's references to the sword, claiming he was referring exclusively to a "life-giving sword," the sword as an instrument of righteousness or, alternatively, as a sword that cuts through illusory thought in the mind of the practitioner. In any event, Suzuki is said to have been speaking metaphorically when he referred to the connection between Zen and the sword. Suzuki's supporters further assert he simply sought to emphasize the important role "intuition" plays in Zen. In addition, they point to what they regard as Suzuki's strong opposition to both war and violence based on his embrace of Buddhist compassion.[7]

In reality, in making these claims, Suzuki's defenders simply reveal their ignorance, willful or otherwise, of what Suzuki really stood for. As early as 1904, Suzuki wrote an essay in English titled "A Buddhist View of War." Inasmuch as this essay is available in its entirety on the web, there is no need to repeat its entire contents here.[8] It will suffice to introduce its key points. First, Suzuki tells us, as any honest observer would, that "war is abominable, and there is no denying it." However, he then goes on to point out:

> But it is only a phase of the universal struggle that is going on and will go on, as long as one breath of vitality is left to an animate being. It is absurdity itself to have perpetual peace and at the same time to be enjoying the full vigor of life. We do not mean to be cruel, neither do we wish to be self-destructive. When our ideals clash, let there be no flinching, no backsliding, no undecidedness, but for ever and ever pressing onwards. In this kind of war there is nothing personal, egotistic, or individual. It is the holiest spiritual war.

According to Suzuki, Buddhists view war as only "a phase of the universal struggle" that will go on "as long as one breath of vitality is left to an animate being." For this reason, "it is absurdity itself to have perpetual peace" should one wish "to be enjoying the full vigor of life." The result? So long as "there is nothing personal, egotistic, or individual" in the war being fought, "it is the holiest spiritual war."

Building on his concept of the "holiest spiritual war," Suzuki concludes his essay as follows:

> Let us then shuffle off the mortal coil whenever it becomes necessary, and not raise a grunting voice against the fates. From our mutilated, mangled, inert corpse will there be the glorious ascension of something immaterial which leads forever progressing humanity to its final goal. Resting in this conviction, Buddhists carry the banner of Dharma over the dead and dying until they gain final victory.

Given the year of publication, the occasion for this essay was clearly the Russo-Japanese War of 1904–1905. The war began when Japan launched a surprise naval attack against Port Arthur, a Russian naval base in China, on February 8, 1904. The Russian fleet was decimated. Two days later, Suzuki, then resident in the United States, commented to a friend in a letter written in English: "The Chicago papers this morning published two naval battles fought at Port Arthur and Chemulpo, in both of which the Japanese seem to have won a complete victory. This is a brilliant start & I hope that they would keep on this campaign in a similar manner till the end."[9]

It is noteworthy that this letter was written six years after Suzuki had his initial enlightenment experience (*kenshō*) in December 1896. He claimed his initial enlightenment had taken place at the time he participated as a layman in an intensive meditation retreat (*sesshin*) at Engakuji in Kamakura. This experience immediately preceded his departure for more than a decade-long period of study and writing in the United States (1897–1908). Suzuki's subsequent war-related statements make clear that, his *kenshō* experience notwithstanding, Suzuki saw no contradiction in encouraging Buddhist soldiers to "carry the banner of Dharma over the dead and dying until they gain final victory." At the same time, he urged soldiers to "shuffle off the mortal coil whenever it becomes necessary, and not raise a grunting voice against the fates." Why wouldn't soldiers do this when, according to Suzuki, they were selflessly fighting in the "holiest spiritual war"?

While Suzuki's words may be shocking to some, they are hardly surprising in light of the fact that Suzuki's Rinzai Zen master, Shaku Sōen (1860–1919), Engakuji's abbot, was also a strong supporter of Japan's war effort. In fact, Shaku's support of Japan was so strong that during the Russo-Japanese War he volunteered to serve as a military chaplain in Manchuria. Shaku explained, "I also wished to inspire, if I could, our valiant soldiers with the ennobling thoughts of the Buddha, so as to enable them to die on the battlefield with the confidence that the task in which they are engaged is great and noble."[10]

Once Japan had defeated Imperial Russia, its expansionist rival, it immediately forced Korea to become a Japanese protectorate in November 1905. This was followed by Japan's complete annexation of Korea in August 1910, thereby cementing the expansion of the Japanese empire onto the Asian continent. For his part, Suzuki avidly supported Japan's takeover of Korea as revealed by comments he made in 1912 about that "poor country," Korea, as he traversed it on his way to Europe via the Trans-Siberian Railroad:

They [Koreans] don't know how fortunate they are to have been returned to the hands of the Japanese government. It's all well and good to talk independence and the like, but it's useless for them to call for independence when they lack the capability and vitality to stand on their own. Looked at from the point of view of someone like myself who is just passing through, I think Korea ought to count the day that it was annexed to Japan as the day of its revival.[11]

Suzuki's comments reveal not only his support for Japanese colonialism but also his dismissal of the Korean people's deep desire for independence. For Suzuki, a better future for poverty-stricken Korea depended on Japanese colonial beneficence. In this, he was no different from the leaders, both secular and religious, of many Western imperialist nations. This includes, of course, the United States, which had forcefully annexed the Philippines in 1898, precipitating Filipino resistance in the Philippine–American War of 1899–1902.

Significantly, Suzuki's support for Japanese aggression against Korea and other Asian countries by no means ended with the Russo-Japanese War and its aftermath. To give but one example, in June 1941, when Japan was in the fourth year of its full-scale invasion of China, Suzuki wrote an article that appeared in the Japanese army's officers journal, *Kaikō Kiji* (Kaikō Association Report). Although not formally a government organization, the parent *Kaikō-sha* (lit., "let's join the military together") body had been created in 1877 for the purpose of creating army officers who were to be of "one mind and body." In an article titled "Makujiki Kōzen" (Rush Forward without Hesitation), Suzuki wrote,

I think that most scholars and informed persons will agree that Zen thought is one of the most important factors forming the basis of Japanese culture. Although Zen originally came from India, in reality it was brought to fruition in China while its real efficacy was achieved to a great extent after coming to Japan.

The reason for this is that there are things about the Japanese character that are amazingly consistent with Zen. I think the most visible of these is rushing forward to the heart of things without meandering about. Once the goal has been determined, one goes directly forward to that goal without looking either to the right or to the left. One goes forward, forgetting where one is. I think this is the most essential element of the Japanese character. In this, I think, Zen is one of the strongest factors allowing the Japanese people to rush forward. . . .

Be that as it may, the character of the Japanese people is to come straight to the point and pour their entire body and mind into the attack. This is the character of the Japanese people and, at the same time, the essence of Zen.[12]

The assertion that the character of the Japanese people, let alone the essence of Zen, is to "pour their entire body and mind into the attack" is certainly debatable. Yet it is clear that whether we are talking about Inoue and his band members or the millions of Japanese soldiers on the battlefields of the Asia-Pacific War, they all attempted to go directly forward toward their goal, looking neither to the right nor left, forgetting where they were.

It is noteworthy that following Japan's attack on Pearl Harbor on December 7, 1941, Suzuki no longer wrote articles supporting or encouraging the Japanese military. In fact, Suzuki publicly warned against war with the United States in September 1941. The unlikely occasion was a guest lecture Suzuki delivered at Kyoto University titled "Zen and Japanese Culture." Upon finishing his lecture, Suzuki initially stepped down from the podium but then returned to add, "Japan must evaluate more calmly and accurately the awesome reality of America's industrial productivity. Present-day wars will no longer be determined as in the past by military strategy and tactics, courage and fearlessness alone. This is because of the large role now played by production capacity and mechanical power."[13]

As his words reveal, Suzuki's warning against war with the United States had nothing to do with his Buddhist faith or a commitment to peace. Rather, having previously lived in the United States for more than a decade, Suzuki knew Japan had no chance of winning a conflict with such a large and powerful nation. When coupled with subsequent private writings, it is clear that Suzuki remained personally opposed to war with the United States up through Japan's defeat in August 1945. Suzuki's supporters have seized on his opposition to war as proof that, based on his Buddhist faith, Suzuki was a true man of peace. In reality, Suzuki had only learned what little boys typically learn on the school playground by the age of seven or eight—don't pick a fight with someone much bigger than you are.

Further proof of my viewpoint is to be found in the fact that there is no record of Suzuki having spoken out against Japan's full-scale invasion of China beginning in July 1937. As demonstrated by his "post-enlightenment" strong support for the earlier Russo-Japanese War, coupled with the "Buddhist View of War" he penned at the time, Suzuki's Buddhist faith had nothing to do with peace but was, on the contrary, evoked in support of his prowar stance. Apart from his opposition to war with the United States, Suzuki's pre-1941 writings are supportive of Japan's foreign aggression and colonial policies. In this, he was similar to many other wartime Zen leaders, like Yasutani Haku'un, Harada Sōgaku, Sawaki Kōdō, and thousands of Zen priests who, whatever personal reservations they may have had, invoked their faith in publicly and unconditionally supporting Japanese aggression despite the massive death toll, to friend and foe, it entailed.

DAMIEN KEOWN'S VIEWPOINT

Perhaps the most comprehensive, if not strongest, critique of an ethics-less Zen comes from Damien Keown, emeritus professor of Buddhist ethics at the University of London. In a seminal quotation, Keown challenges us to examine this question from within the context of both the Theravāda and Mahāyāna traditions:

> Ethics is a very subversive subject, for once you start asking ethical questions you can be led to some challenging conclusions. Coming at this particular issue from a Theravāda

point of view, it is psychologically impossible to have an *arhat* or the Buddha break the precepts. They would never do it because ethical conduct is a fundamental part of their enlightenment. In important respects it's what constitutes their enlightenment.

In Theravāda Buddhism, enlightenment is not just a kind of knowledge. It is not a mystical intuition, or *satori*, or intellectual grasp of metaphysical truth. Enlightenment is also a personal moral transformation, an emotional as much as intellectual experience. You become enlightened because you have both understood something and implemented that knowledge—which includes an understanding of moral principles—in your daily life. If you went against the precepts you would be going backwards: it would be a retrograde step that would mean that you could not be regarded as having achieved the goal. This is why we never see the Buddha doing anything immoral, not telling a lie, certainly not killing anybody, and never breaking any precepts. It's said in the Pāli canon that it's simply impossible for those things to happen.

Things shifted in the Mahāyāna where it becomes possible to conceive of breaking the precepts for two main reasons. First of all, out of compassion. Compassion becomes almost the supreme ethical principle, and anything is allowed if done out of compassion. This line of thought begins with the *Upāyakauśalya Sūtra*, and from there on an important strand of the Mahāyāna takes the view that a *Bodhisattva* who acts from compassion can do no wrong.

The other strand is a metaphysical one based on the doctrine of emptiness. The idea here is that nothing has any real essence and so all phenomena are relative. This applies to notions like good and evil, and we are told by sources that to make a distinction between them, or to assume they really exist, is the sign of a deluded mind.

In the Mahāyāna these two streams come together and reinforce one another, and that's a powerful combination. On this basis justifications are offered for all kinds of breaches of the precepts, particularly the first precept against taking life. There are plenty of examples in the literature from the *Upāyakauśalya Sūtra* onwards. To take a modern example, during the Korean War, Chinese monks defended all sorts of atrocities on the basis of these two very dubious propositions.

As noted, this represents a significant departure from early Buddhist teachings, which see ethical conduct (defined at a minimum as respecting the precepts) as integral to the enlightenment experience. By contrast, the enlightenment of certain Zen masters—at least as can be seen from their conduct—seems to be an incomplete awakening. For the Theravāda at least, complete enlightenment must include the perfection of ethics, otherwise it is not an authentically Buddhist attainment.[14]

Keown states that the enlightenment of at least certain Zen masters "seems to be an incomplete awakening." Why? Because early Buddhist teachings regarded ethical conduct "as integral to the enlightenment experience." In the Theravāda tradition "complete enlightenment must include the perfection of ethics." Many contemporary Zen leaders, both in Japan and the West, would readily dismiss these claims, especially when applied to the wartime conduct of the Zen masters in their own spiritual heritage (aka Dharma lineage). However, in light of everything presented in my three books, a facile dismissal of Keown's criticism is not the answer.

It is also noteworthy that Keown places his criticism of Zen's ethical shortcomings within the larger context of a critique of the Mahāyāna tradition as a whole.

Keown identifies this tradition as one in which "compassion becomes almost the supreme ethical principle," leading to the belief that "a *Bodhisattva* who acts from compassion can do no wrong." Further, when the metaphysical doctrine of emptiness is added, concepts like good and evil become relative, resulting in a situation where "to make a distinction between them, or to assume they really exist, is the sign of a deluded mind."

Readers will recall that at the time of his alleged enlightenment, Inoue realized, "there is no need to be attached to a particular concept [of good and evil] or think about what is right or wrong."[15] Subsequently, Inoue taught his band members that "those who wish to participate in revolution must have a mind of great compassion toward the society of [our] nation."[16] It could hardly be clearer that when these two threads of Keown's critique are applied to Inoue and his band's actions, they fit perfectly.

Moreover, in recalling Zen master Yamamoto Gempō's defense of Inoue, it is hard to deny Keown's charge that in the Mahāyāna tradition "justifications are offered for all kinds of breaches of the precepts, particularly the first precept against taking life." Readers will recall that Yamamoto testified:

> It is true that if, motivated by an evil mind, someone should kill so much as a single ant, as many as one hundred and thirty-six hells await that person. This holds true not only in Japan but in all the countries of the world. Yet the Buddha, being absolute, has stated that when there are those who destroy social harmony and injure the polity of the state, then even if they are called good men, killing them is not a crime.[17]

It is almost as if Yamamoto, Inoue, and his band members are "poster children" for Keown's insight that when the Mahāyāna understanding of compassion and emptiness are joined together, "justifications are offered for all kinds of breaches of the precepts, particularly the first precept against taking life."

THERAVĀDA BUDDHISM

My only reservation concerning Keown's critique concerns what seems to be an underlying assumption that the southern tradition of Theravāda Buddhism has a solid grasp of Buddhist ethics. At a theoretical or doctrinal level (i.e., in the Pāli Canon), Keown's assumption is certainly correct. As Bhikkhu Bodhi, American Theravāda monk and translator of the Pāli Nikāyas, notes, "The *suttas* [Skt., *sutras*], it must be clearly stated, do not admit any moral justification for war. . . . One short *sutta* even declares categorically that a warrior who dies in battle will be reborn in hell, which implies that participation in war is essentially immoral."[18]

Unfortunately, neither Keown nor Bhikkhu Bodhi's comments take into account Theravāda Buddhist *practice*. The historical reality is that, canonical or not, the Theravāda tradition has also found a way to condone killing, that is, by denying the humanity of the Other. For example, the noncanonical but still highly influential

Mahāvamsa (Great Chronicle), written in the fifth century CE, contains a description of a war fought between the Sinhala Buddhist King Dutthagamani (r. 161–137 BCE) and Tamil King Elara (204–164 BCE). The claim is made that Dutthagamuni deeply regretted the loss of life the war entailed. This regret led to the following conversation between the king and his Buddhist monk advisors:

> How shall there be any comfort for me, O venerable sirs, since by me was caused the slaughter of a great host numbering millions?" [One monk advisor replied]: "From this deed arises no hindrance in thy way to heaven. Only one and a half human beings have been slain here by thee, O lord of men. The one had come unto the (three) refuges, the other had taken on himself the five precepts [of Buddhism]. Unbelievers and men of evil life were the rest, not more to be esteemed than beasts. But as for thee, thou wilt bring glory to the doctrine of the Buddha in manifold ways; therefore cast away care from thy heart, O ruler of men!"[19]

This denial of the humanity of "unbelievers and men of evil life" within Theravāda Buddhism has been used down through the centuries to justify killing, even to the present day. For example, in mid-1970s Thailand, there was increasing domestic unrest, with demonstrations by farmers, laborers, and students. Senior Thai Buddhist monk Kittiwutto Bhikkhu was a coleader of the psychological warfare unit Nawapol, a legacy of CIA counterinsurgency operations in that country. He taught that "communists were the national enemy" and therefore "non-Thai." These supposed non-Thai communists should be killed: "Because whoever destroys the nation, the religion or the monarchy, such bestial types [*man*] are not complete persons. Thus we must intend not to kill people but kill the Devi [*Māra*]; this is the duty of all Thai."[20]

In Sri Lanka, during the twenty-six years of civil war ending in 2009, many Buddhist leaders and laity also invoked the *Mahāvamsa*, using it to justify the Sri Lanka military's use of deadly force to defeat the Tamil Tiger insurgency. Even more recently, on October 30, 2017, Sitagu Sayadaw, a high-ranking monk in Myanmar, gave a speech to military officers urging them not to fear the karmic consequences of taking human life. He said, "Don't worry . . . it's only a little bit of sin. Don't worry, even though you killed millions of people, they were only one and a half real human beings. Now I'm not saying that, monks from Sri Lanka said that." He then went on to add, "Our soldiers should bear this [story] in mind."[21]

Needless to say, Sitagu was also referring to the *Mahāvamsa*, and the killing he alluded to was, first and foremost, the Myanmar military's use of force against the Muslim (non-Buddhist) Rohingya. Just how revered and influential Sitagu is can be seen in the fact that in 2018 he was awarded the title "Honorable, Excellent, and Great Teacher of Country and State" by the government of Aung San Suu Kyi. Suu Kyi, a Nobel Peace Prize laureate, has long been a Buddhist hero for her many admirers, myself included, as she struggled relentlessly for the restoration of democracy in Myanmar. Thus, it is exceedingly disappointing to see the manner in which she has acceded to the ethnic cleansing of, and violence inflicted upon, the Muslim Rohingya minority by the Myanmar military and its Buddhist supporters, both monks and laity.

In this connection, reference must also be made to United States Army Captain Somya Malasri, a former Thai Theravāda monk and yet another American Buddhist military chaplain. On the one hand, Thai ecclesiastical authorities required Malasri to formally disrobe in order to become a military chaplain. At the same time, the same authorities raised no objection to his becoming a military chaplain, for Buddhist chaplains are also present in the Thai army. Malasri explained the Buddhist rationale for warfare as follows:

> A lot of people ask if a Buddhist can be a soldier because the first precept is no killing. The answer is yes. You can protect yourself or sacrifice yourself to do the righteous thing. You can sacrifice yourself to protect your country because if there's no country, there's no freedom and you cannot practice your religion. In Buddhism, if you go to war and kill others, it's your duty, not your intention to kill other people. If a person dies of your intention, and you have anger, that is wrong in Buddhism. When soldiers go to war, they don't have any intention to kill others and they don't have hatred in their minds.[22]

Whether by coincidence or not, it is eerie how closely Malasri's words echo those of the Dalai Lama, who in 2010 addressed soldiers as follows:

> I have always admired those who are prepared to act in the defense of others for their courage and determination. In fact, it may surprise you to know that I think that monks and soldiers, sailors and airmen have more in common than at first meets the eye. Strict discipline is important to us all, we all wear a uniform and we rely on the companionship and support of our comrades.
>
> Although the public may think that physical strength is what is most important, I believe that what makes a good soldier, sailor or airman, just as what makes a good monk, is inner strength. And inner strength depends on having a firm positive motivation. The difference lies in whether ultimately you want to ensure others' wellbeing or whether you want only to do them harm.
>
> Naturally, there are some times when we need to take what on the surface appears to be harsh or tough action, but if our motivation is good our action is actually non-violent in nature.[23]

In reading the Dalai Lama's words "if our motivation is good our action is actually non-violent in nature," it is clear they are an extension of his earlier defense of the actions of the CIA-trained and -funded Tibetan guerillas as described in chapter 14. In short, so long as your motivation is "good," killing is not a problem, for after all, such apparently harsh or tough action "is actually non-violent in nature."

As much as Buddhists, East and West, may seek to deny it, Buddhism has a long history of justifying killing, one way or the other. In the case of the northern Mahāyāna tradition, this justification may be based on canonical sources or, in the case of Zen, grounded in "emptiness" (J., *kū*), "no-self" (J., *muga*), life-giving swords, and the like. At least doctrinally speaking, the southern Theravāda tradition seems less bellicose, but it has nevertheless found a way, based on denying the humanity of the enemy, or denying the intent to kill, to make violence acceptable if not sacred, allegedly in accord with the teachings of the Buddha. In making excuses for the use of violence, the northern and southern traditions of Buddhism diverge less than many of their adherents care to admit. Buddhist author Barbara O'Brien addressed this divergence as follows:

> Buddhists through the ages have debated whether it's morally acceptable to kill one being to save the lives of many, or whether the Dharma requires us to stand aside and let events take their course rather than break the First Precept. My understanding is that Theravāda tends to come down on the "hands off" side of the argument, whereas Mahāyāna takes a more interventionist position.[24]

The historical reality is that whether one takes a "hands off" or more intervention-ist approach, the result is always the same—death. Yet, although this book has been unable, due to space limitations, to explore them thoroughly, Buddhists have ample teachings refuting any and all justifications for killing—*if they choose to follow them.*

NOT JUST BUDDHISM

Following the publication of *Zen at War* in 1997, I came across a number of Chris-tian websites that made reference to this book. However, instead of attacking the book, these websites use the war-affirming statements made by Zen masters before and during the Asia-Pacific War to demonstrate that Buddhism is not the religion of peace so many in the West believed it to be. Instead, they used the debunking of a pacific Buddhism in order to promote belief in Christianity.

In an article published on the website for *World Magazine* titled "Zen Violence: War and Peace in Buddhism," Marvin Olasky wrote,

> Zen priest Brian Victoria's *Zen at War* (Rowman & Littlefield, 2nd edition, 2006) and Zen War Stories (RoutledgeCurzon, 2003) bravely revealed how Zen leaders in the 1930s applauded killing. . . . Brian Victoria shows how that doctrine hardened Japanese soldiers with Buddhist training. . . . Buddhism gets a great press in the United States, but it is one more man-made religion that reflects our naturally sinful natures. Murderers and adulterers all need Christ.[25]

On the one hand, I do not object to the use of my research to promote faith in other religions. The right to criticize other faiths, hopefully accurately, is an important as-pect of religious freedom. At the same time, the following biblical injunction comes to mind: "Why do you look at the speck of sawdust in your brother's eye and pay no attention to the plank in your own eye?"[26]

This is said without any intention to defend Zen, or Buddhism as a whole, from the charge of having supported killing and war in the past, let alone the present. But in light of such events as the medieval Christian Crusades, this is an undeniable historical fact that applies to all religions. Sadly, there is no major organized religion existing today whose adherents have not, at one time or another, employed their religious faith in support of killing others. In short, the adherents of all faiths must face with honesty that in this matter we are truly "all in the same boat." Given this, no faith can save the blood-soaked boat called "religion" without first admitting, and then working to end, its own contribution to this commonly shared legacy.

Fortunately, there are hopeful signs that this reckoning is occurring. For example, Roman Catholic historian Paul Johnson revealed that the religious justification given for the Crusades, to free the Holy Land from Muslim control, was not born out of religious conflict. Instead, it was little more than a cloak for something far less noble: "The Crusades were not missionary ventures, but wars of conquest and primitive experiments in colonization; and the only specific Christian institutions they produced, the three knightly orders, were military."[27]

It is noteworthy that Johnson identifies the Crusades, then deemed "holy wars," to have been, in reality, "wars of conquest and primitive experiments in colonization." In other words, Christianity per se was not the true cause of the Crusades but was invoked to disguise, to justify, the early colonial efforts of European powers. This does not mean, however, that Christian faith didn't also serve to motivate the knightly participants. Chiefly, however, the secular powers of the day, with the blessing of the Roman Catholic Church, used religion as a powerful motivational tool to enhance their power. In comparing this with Inoue's use of Zen to restore complete political power to the emperor, the question must be asked, has anything changed?

Despite the hopeful beginnings seen in the writings of Christian historians like Johnson, the reality is that when it comes to the modern-day wars waged by nations identifying themselves as Christian, there is, as of now, much less reflection on the way Christianity has been used to valorize warfare. For example, when the United States entered World War I in 1917, Rev. Randolph McKim of the Episcopal Church of the Epiphany in Washington, DC, proclaimed, "It is God who has summoned us to this war. It is his war we are fighting. . . . This conflict is indeed a crusade. The greatest in history—the holiest. It is in the profoundest and truest sense a Holy War. . . . Yes, it is Christ, the King of Righteousness, who calls us to grapple in deadly strife with this unholy and blasphemous power [Germany]."[28]

On the German side, Lutheran pastor Dietrich Vorwerk reworked the Lord's Prayer to say, in part,

> Our Father, from the height of heaven, / Make haste to succor Thy German people. / Help us in the holy war. . . . In thy merciful patience, forgive / Each bullet and each blow / That misses the mark. / Lead us not into the temptation / Of letting our wrath be too gentle / In carrying out Thy divine judgment. . . . Thine is the kingdom, / The German land. / May we, through Thy mailed hand / Come to power and glory.[29]

When it comes to bellicosity, the Roman Catholic Church showed it could match, if not surpass, its Protestant rivals. This was especially apparent in the homeland of the most monstrous regime of modern times—Nazi Germany. In the midst of the Nazis' failing invasion of Russia, the church's Office for Military Affairs in Germany provided a series of sermon outlines for its approximately ten thousand Catholic military chaplains. The sermon outline for the 1942 Christmas season contained the following passage:

> God gave the German people a noble mission in this war—reordering Europe. This reconstruction should be done in the name of Christ. Communism means a Europe without God, and without and against Christ. The front of young nations led by Germany wants a Europe with God, with Christ. . . . So we celebrate the birth of Christ very purposely. Christianity is after all not just a workshop for the highest spiritual culture but also a construction site for national greatness and power.[30]

In describing Nazi Germany's "noble mission" in the war, the Catholic Church, or at least its German military affairs office, had by 1942 already witnessed the Nazis' very public and ruthless suppression of German Jews, such as in the infamous November 1938 anti-Jewish pogrom known as the "Night of Broken Glass" (G., *Kristallnacht*). As revealed in the following passage of Hitler's *Mein Kampf*, first published in 1925, anti-Semitism combined with Christianity was an integral part of Nazi anti-communist ideology:

> If the Jew with his Marxist catechism triumphs over the peoples of the world, his crown will be the dance of death for mankind, and as once before, millions of years ago, this planet will again sail empty of all human life through the ether. . . . I believe that I am today acting according to the purpose of the Almighty Creator. In resisting the Jew, I am fighting the Lord's battle.[31]

Following Hitler's assumption of power in 1933, the Catholic Church in Germany neither publicly challenged nor denied Hitler's words.

When we speak of Inoue's allegedly compassionate killing of one in order to save many, we see it is matched by the words of Christians in support of deadly strife against an unholy and blasphemous power and the deadly struggle to reconstruct Europe under Nazi control in the name of Christ. From time immemorial, Buddhism, Christianity, and other faiths have been invoked to provide the doctrinal, organizational, *and emotional* support for killing the evil/inhuman Other. This is both the most frightening aspect of religion's alliance with killing and war and, at the same time, explains why this relationship plays such a crucial role—it provides the belligerents, especially soldiers in the field, with the belief that their actions, no matter how cruel, are both just and moral.

Recognizing this reality, peace activist and Jesuit Daniel Berrigan forthrightly admitted,

> Everybody has always killed the bad guys. Nobody kills the good guys. The Church is tainted in this way as well. The Church plays the same cards; it likes the taste of imperial power too. This is the most profound kind of betrayal I can think of. Terrible! Jews

and Christians and Buddhists and all kinds of people who come from a good place, who come from revolutionary beginnings and are descended from heroes and saints. . . . Religion becomes another resource for the same old death-game.[32]

Should anyone wonder why Berrigan included Jews in this list, it is only necessary to read the following comments of Rabbi Ovadia Yosef (1920–2013), Sephardi chief rabbi of Israel from 1973 to 1983 and the founder of Israel's ultra-Orthodox Shas Party. During a sermon preceding the 2001 Passover holiday, Rabbi Ovadia Yosef exclaimed, "May the Holy Name visit retribution on the Arab heads, and cause their seed to be lost, and annihilate them. . . . It is forbidden to have pity on them. We must give them missiles with relish, annihilate them. Evil ones, damnable ones."[33]

As for Islam, the words and deeds of terrorists in the Mideast who identify themselves as Muslims are only too well known:

"The only reward for those who make war on Allah and on Muhammad, his messenger, and plunge into corruption, will be to be killed or crucified or have their hands and feet severed on alternate sides, or be expelled from the land," the man says. With that, the two gunmen flanking the executioner shout *"Allahu akbar!"* (God is Great), drop their Kalashnikovs and tumble Mr. Fawazi face down on the ground. The killer pulls his knife from behind a magazine belt on his chest, grabs Mr. Fawazi by the hair, severs his head, holds it up briefly to the camera, then places it between his rope-tied hands on his back.[34]

If the adherents of today's organized religions were placed together on a single ship, that ship would be overflowing with the blood of the innocent and not so innocent. Given this, one can but ask, is there nothing that can be done? Needless to say, I am far from the first person to ask this question about either religion as a whole or Buddhism and Zen in particular. The response is worthy of a book in itself and is therefore beyond the scope of this study. Thus, solutions offered here must necessarily be confined to suggested avenues for future exploration, especially regarding Buddhism. However, as Lao Tzu, the founder of Taoism, is recorded as having said, "A journey of a thousand miles starts from beneath your feet."[35]

TOWARD SOLUTIONS

Let us begin with two somewhat contradictory statements. First, there appears to be no "magic bullet" or ready solution to bring an end to the relationship between religion and violence. Yet this does not mean there are no solutions. However, I suggest the solutions must come from within each of the world's major faiths. In saying this, I am reminded of the final words attributed to a dying Shakyamuni Buddha in the *Mahā-Parinibbāna Sutta*: "Work out your salvation with care."[36]

Applied to this case, these words indicate that it is up to the adherents of each faith to address those elements/teachings that have been used to justify, even encourage, the use of violence. In order to do so, however, it is first necessary for adherents to honestly admit that such teachings/practices/interpretations exist, however painful that may be. This may well call for a new type of religious adherent, someone dedicated to a critical investigation of the doctrines and historical practice of their own faith.

There is, of course, need for "outsiders," non-adherents of a particular faith, to criticize any and all inhumane religious doctrines, especially those that directly or indirectly support the use of violence. Typically, however, such criticisms by outsiders provoke defensive, dismissive, and all too often angry reactions among believers, seldom leading to serious reflection or change on the part of those criticized. It is therefore far more important for critiques to come from within a faith, from adherents who clearly wish to create a brighter and more humane future for their faith.

Given that I remain a (Zen) Buddhist, I would like to believe my writings, however imperfect, model the painful honesty that a critical investigation requires not just of scholars of a particular faith but of all those who identify with that faith, lay and cleric alike. If, for example, today's Zen Buddhists don't like the "ethics-less" form of the Buddhism they've inherited from their Japanese ancestors, they have every right—no, *duty*—to change it if they are sincere in their claim to follow the teachings of the Buddha.

Vietnamese Zen/Thiền monk Thich Nhat Hanh places strong emphasis on the importance of both ethics and nonviolence, demonstrating the potential the Zen school has to make a contribution to genuine peace.[37] In the meantime, however, the first step is to admit that change is necessary for much of what passes as "Zen" today—in other words, to admit that a restoration of truly Buddhist ethics is *critically important* to the overall Zen school, especially for those in, or descended from, the Japanese Zen school. As Jesus is recorded as having said, it is a case of "Physician, heal thyself."[38]

This is not simply a case of becoming a "critic," for behind honest and sincere criticism is a commitment to something that, fortunately, all of the world's major faiths hold in common—the universal identity of all humankind and beyond. Rabbi David Gordis, president of the Hebrew College of Boston, expressed this shared ideal as follows:

> More than ever before . . . independent religious communities and cultures must come to terms with the reality of the interdependence of all humanity. Prior to our identity as Jew, Christian or Muslim [or Buddhist], prior to our identity as male or female, as Indian, British or American, is *our fundamental human identity*. Both the nobility and the tragedy of human experience are universal. They cross religious and national lines. This must be part of the religious insight and teaching of all religious traditions. *Our very survival on this planet is dependent on our successfully navigating this [terrain].*[39] (emphasis mine)

There are no better words with which to end this trilogy. And also no better words to challenge adherents of all religions to work together to create a truly just and peaceful world, free of the scourge of religious violence. However, in seeking to change the "world," the first step is to engage in an honest examination of the "self," at both the individual and *collective* level. The latter, in particular, requires a recognition of those elements in one's own faith that have been, and too often continue to be, used to support violence against the Other. If "charity begins at home," then so does the struggle for the birth of religions divorced from violence and wholly devoted to the promotion of genuine peace, based on mutual understanding, respect, and social justice.

Finally, for those who find this final section of "solutions" all too short, it is done deliberatively, for, as Gordis points out, our survival is truly dependent on our collective efforts across all religions and cultures. Now is the time to get to work. *All* of us.

Written for the good of the many, for the happiness of the many. With palms pressed together, head bowed, in *gasshō*.

Epilogue

Lessons to Be Learned

If the terrorist acts described in this book, together with their religious underpinnings, were simply "one-off" affairs, unlikely to be repeated, they could be ignored. But, all too sadly, religion-related terrorism, far from being a phenomenon of the past, remains a deadly reality. Although the terrorist acts of substate actors currently receive the most attention, it should not be forgotten that states, too, invoke religion, or at least religiously tinged language, when seeking to justify taking military action. For example, following the attacks on the United States of September 1, 2001, President George W. Bush stated, "This is a new kind of—a new kind of evil. And we understand. And the American people are beginning to understand. This crusade, this war on terrorism is going to take a while."[1]

While President Bush's reference to a "crusade" against terrorism passed largely unnoticed in the United States, it rang alarm bells in Europe, the cradle of the medieval Crusades. It raised fears that the terrorist attacks could spark a "clash of civilizations" between Christians and Muslims, sowing fresh winds of hatred and mistrust. France's Foreign Minister Hubert Vedrine noted, "We have to avoid a clash of civilizations at all costs. . . . One has to avoid falling into this huge trap, this monstrous trap."[2] Given this, are there any lessons for the present to be learned from the Zen-affiliated terrorism described in this book? In particular, are there lessons to be learned that might lead to a more effective response, especially in terms of *preventing* future terrorist acts?

Fortunately, there is a growing body of literature that has employed the "life-story method" to examine terrorist acts as described by the terrorists themselves. For example, in 2018 Murat Haner published *The Freedom Fighter: A Terrorist's Own Story*. By allowing one Kurdish PKK terrorist to describe himself in his own words, Haner provided valuable insight into what leads a person to become a terrorist (or "freedom fighter" in their own eyes). Moreover, the account provides extensive information on the PKK, including the group's recruitment, ideological and military training, as well as armed strategies, internal structures, and code of ethics. It also facilitates an understanding of what leads "normal people" to become involved in terrorist organizations. In short, like this book, Haner's work is a further example of the advantages of using the life-story method to better understand terrorism and its perpetrators.

In seeking to identify lessons to be learned, I am keenly aware of the danger of reaching overly broad or definitive conclusions based on the small number of terrorist acts described in this book. Thus, the conclusions presented here are no more than hypotheses whose validity can only be determined by further analysis within a much larger pool of similar incidents. Nevertheless, these hypotheses are shared with the hope they will contribute to the work of unravelling the complex web of causal factors leading to terrorism. If proven true, these hypotheses may even contribute, over the long term, to the eradication of terror itself.

HYPOTHESES ON THE NATURE OF TERRORISM

(1) Starting with the least controversial, the first hypothesis is that terrorism is essentially a tactic employed by the weak against the strong for the simple reason that terrorists, at least substate terrorists, lack the means (heavy weapons, artillery, navy, air force, etc.) to employ any other method. As we have seen, Inoue initially had no intention of engaging in terrorist acts. Instead, he hoped to train a cadre of youthful activists dedicated to the drastic reform of Japanese society through legal and peaceful means. It was only after he, and those around him, concluded that social reform couldn't wait—the immediate need was too great—that he embraced terrorism.

Thus, to believe, as many governments do, that it is possible to "stamp out" or "eradicate" terrorism by killing every terrorist they find is akin to believing, in the case of an air force, that aerial bombardment as a tactic of warfare can be permanently eliminated if every living bombardier (or drone operator) is killed. Desperate situations inevitably give rise to desperate measures, and those who were not terrorists in the beginning come to embrace terrorism even at the cost of their lives. Terrorists cannot be killed out of existence. So long as desperate situations exist, there will always be more.

While Inoue never expressed remorse for his and his band's terrorist acts, he nevertheless admitted they had been "bad." In chapter 13 Inoue said, "When asking whether it was good or bad to have undertaken 'direct action' [i.e., killing someone], there's no question but that it was bad. No one wishes to participate in terrorism. I deeply desire the emergence of a society in which politics are conducted properly and no one thinks of things like terrorism." Yes, Inoue admits, terrorism is bad, but his words also provide justification for what he and his band did. In essence, Inoue claimed that terrorism arises when politics are *not* conducted properly. Inoue is but one example of the reality that when legal, nonviolent methods of addressing social injustice are unavailable, there will always be those ready to employ terrorism to accomplish their goals.

(2) Closely connected with the first hypothesis is that terrorism is not simply an isolated product of crazed or fanatical religious adherents. Instead, there are nearly always underlying political, economic, and social causes associated with terrorist acts. As we have seen, Japan in the 1930s was a deeply socially and economically unjust society. It was, for example, a society in which many poor tenant farmers were forced to sell their daughters into a lifetime of prostitution and degradation. Additionally, many of the political leaders, corrupted by their ties with *zaibatsu* business conglomerates, showed little concern for the welfare of the majority of the Japanese people. It is not surprising that the economic disparity between rich and poor led to attempts, increasingly violent, to enact major social reform. When it becomes clear that peaceful means are ineffective, terror seems to some to be the only possibility remaining.

(3) Terrorists do not view themselves as hate-filled, bloodthirsty monsters motivated by the desire to kill for the sake of killing. Instead, as incongruous as it may seem, the terrorists introduced in this book were motivated by nothing less than "compassion," that is, what they regarded as their deep concern for compatriots. This led Inoue and his band to adopt the Buddhist motto "kill one that many may live." They convinced themselves their actions were motivated by compassion and concern for the well-being of the majority of the exploited and oppressed in Japan, especially the rural poor. For them, the ends justified the means; a few must die if the majority were to flourish under the benevolent rule of the emperor, to whom absolute power was to be restored.

Religion-related terrorists typically care so much about protecting or rescuing those compatriots in perceived need that they are prepared to sacrifice their own lives in the process of carrying out their terrorist acts. Inoue and his band, it will be recalled, regarded themselves as no more than expendable "pawns" (*sute-ishi*) in the struggle to reform Japan. It was this conviction that allowed them (and those sympathetic to them) to view themselves as Buddhist Bodhisattvas, ever ready to sacrifice their own welfare for the sake of others. Needless to say, such self-sacrifice resonates with the tenets of other religious faiths, allowing terrorists (and their supporters) to regard themselves as not only ethical but even unselfish exemplars of their faith.

A similar ethic is at work among so-called Islamic fundamentalists, who are convinced their terrorists acts are dedicated to *protecting the Ummah* or the Islamic community from the oppression and corrupting influence of nonbelievers, even when the "nonbelievers" claim to be Muslims yet belong to a heretical sect (in the eyes of the terrorists). It's this view of themselves as essentially "good," "pure," and "self-sacrificial" that allows many terrorists to commit their heinous acts, secure in the belief, however mistaken, that they are acting ethically and according to the highest dictates of their faith.

Thus, to demonize terrorists, turning them into evil incarnate, is to fail to recognize their most salient characteristic. No matter how twisted and inhumane, their

acts are nonetheless moral in the eyes of the terrorists themselves and their supporters, by virtue of their concern for others, their willingness to sacrifice themselves
on their (or God's) behalf. Thus, depending on the context, they regard themselves
(and are regarded by those sympathetic to them) as "freedom fighters," "heroes of the
faith," or more typically "matryrs."

In this connection, it is helpful to recall the words of Richard Koenigsberg: "Those
who make war are not driven by a hate need, but by a love need. They feel they must
accept the need for self-sacrifice so that their love objects might live. Men see war
as a duty toward their love object. What is at stake in war is not so much the safety
of the individual as the safety of the collective love object."[3] Koenigsberg wrote the
above in a review of Franco Fornari's book *The Psychoanalysis of War*.[4] Obviously,
Koenigsberg, like Fornari, is referring to the "love need" of soldiers in this quote,
not terrorists. Yet, if one were to substitute "terrorist acts" for "war," this description
would fit perfectly with Inoue and his band's motivations. If so, it should come as
no surprise that terrorists affiliated with other religions, or even no religion, view
themselves in a similar positive light.

As much as many adherents of today's major organized religions might wish to
deny it, each of their faiths, over its long history, has developed mechanisms, whether
regarding acts of war or acts of terrorism, to allow adherents to believe sacrificing
themselves "so that their love objects might live" is not only moral and just but also
sacred, no matter how injurious to others their acts might be.

(4) The prevailing sentiment throughout the world—at least in non-Islamic
countries—is that Islam, or at least some aspects of "Islamic extemism," are chiefly if
not solely responsible for religion-related terrorist acts. The proferred "solution" (or
demand) is that Muslims change their terror-prone religion into a religion of peace
by abandoning doctrines like *jihad*. The unstated assumption is, of course, that the
world's other major religions lack such violence-affirming doctrines and are completely peaceful. However, as Inoue and his band reveal, Buddhism, especially in its
Zen formulation, is quite capable of serving as an "enabling mechanism" to kill even
those whom Zen master Yamamoto Gempō referred to as "good men."

In reality, no religion is free of having committed terrorist acts or providing the
doctrinal/ethical justification for terrorism. For example, we need only look at the
Christian faith (both Roman Catholic and Protestant) of terrorists in Northern
Ireland in recent years, or the Jewish faith of the Lehi militant group (aka Stern
Gang) involved in anti-British terrorist acts leading to the formation of the state
of Israel. In the summer of 1943, an article in the Lehi underground newspaper
Hehazit (The Front) argued,

> Neither Jewish ethics nor Jewish tradition can disqualify terrorism as a means of combat.
> We are very far from having any moral qualms as far as our national war goes. We have
> before us the command of the *Torah*, whose morality surpasses that of any other body of
> laws in the world: "Ye shall blot them out to the last man." We are particularly far from
> having any qualms with regard to the enemy, whose moral degradation is universally

admitted here. *But first and foremost, terrorism is for us a part of the political battle* being conducted under the present circumstances.[5] (emphasis mine)

Placed in historical context, today's "Islamic terror" is no more, religiously speaking, than the "flavor of the day," the immediate problem. This is certainly not to deny that Islam-related terror is a deadly serious issue, but it is also a Buddhist, Christian, Jewish, and Hindu issue. Simply placing the blame on the "other" religion, Islam in this instance, is not the solution. On the contrary, doing so effectively blocks a solution since it prevents mutual understanding and leads to an unfounded self-righteous attitude on the part of adherents of non-Islamic faiths.

(5) As the preceding Jewish-related quotation indicates, religion-linked terrorism is, first and foremost, a form of *political* (not religious) violence. One of the least understood, yet critically important, elements of such terrorism is that terrorists are often, consciously or not, manipulated and supported by much bigger players behind the scenes to accomplish the latters' political goals. This is not to deny the existence of individual "lone-wolf" acts of religion-linked terrorism committed by unaffiliated individuals on sudden impulse, personal animosity, or mental illness. But lone-wolf acts, in terms of accomplishing major political goals, typically have but limited impact.

As introduced in chapter 1, there is now no question that it was the CIA that initiated the first terrorist acts against the Soviet-supported, left-wing, but secular Afghanistan government. In connection with the emergence of Osama bin Laden in Afghanistan, Robin Cook, UK foreign secretary from 1997 to 2001, wrote, "Bin Laden was, though, a product of a monumental miscalculation by western security agencies. Throughout the '80s he was armed by the CIA and funded by the Saudis to wage *jihad* against the Russian occupation of Afghanistan."[6]

As Cook writes, the claim can be made that arming Bin Laden was a "monumental miscalculation" on the part of the CIA. Or phrased in CIA terminology, it ultimately led to devastating "blowback," the unintended consequences of a particular CIA operation. Whether Cook's description is completely accurate or not, this episode reveals the willingness of a major player, the United States and its allies in this case, to enlist the self-sacrificial religious devotion to a form of *jihad* on the part of Islamic fundamentalists to attain its decidedly secular geopolitical goals in Afghanistan.

The argument can be made, of course, that these terrorist acts were justifiable since the resistance to the Soviet Union's intervention in Afghanistan ultimately contributed to the former's collapse. This way of thinking, however, comes close to providing a justification for terrorist acts in the event of having a "good cause," with the terrorists recast as "freedom fighters." But who is entitled to make the decision to support terrorism and on what basis? The reality, of course, is that not only groups but many nations have been, and remain, secretly willing to support terrorism if such support is determined to be in the "national interest" and the supporting nation is sufficiently powerful to withstand the "blowback."

It has been suggested that the large-scale terrorist acts in Sri Lanka on Easter Sunday, April 21, 2019, may have enjoyed significant support from important behind-the-scenes actors. Journalist Satya Sagar wrote,

> In the times we live in, where smoke and mirrors are the world's two chief weapons of war, fiction is a better guide to contemporary events than "facts" presented by governments and media. A case in point are the horrific Easter Sunday bombings in Sri Lanka, that killed over 250 and maimed scores of people, and has sparked fears of the dreaded Islamic State's growing presence in the region. . . .
>
> As details emerge and reactions from key players, the terrorist attacks in Sri Lanka follow a pattern from several other similar operations over the last couple of decades. Yes, a handful of fanatics do carry out the actual attacks, but they are pawns in the hands of other very powerful forces, who monitor and even aid their actions, for various political and strategic purposes. . . .
>
> Sri Lanka is scheduled for a general election before end of 2019—one in which Gothabaya Rajapaksa, former Defence Minister, is likely to be a frontrunning candidate. He and his brother, former President Mahinda Rajapaksa, are both venerated by Sinhala nationalists for their "tough on terrorism" position and for leading the country to victory against the LTTE [Tamil Tigers].
>
> Not surprisingly, within a week of the Easter Sunday bombings Gothabaya has already announced that, if elected President, he would stop the spread of Islamist extremism by rebuilding the intelligence service and increasing surveillance of citizens. Several Sri Lankan commentators have noted Gothabaya as the biggest beneficiary of the terrorist attack—in political terms—as they have hugely boosted his chances of becoming the next President.
>
> One does not have to be a crazy conspiracy theorist to suspect the mainstream narrative of what the Easter Sunday bombings were all about. A very obvious reason [for] suspicion is the truly strange fact that Sri Lanka's topmost political leaders and security officials did nothing to stop the bombings despite having very detailed information about these Islamist radicals, their identities, intentions and targets.[7]

The problem with comments like these is that the author presents very little in the way of hard evidence to demonstrate his assertions. Many knowledgeable commentators have, for example, dismissed out of hand the possibility that former defense minister Gothabaya Rajapaksa had any connection to the terrorist acts. Thus, there can be no question Sagar's comments are highly speculative in nature.

At the same time, it is true that successful terrorist acts, especially preparations for them, inevitably take place in a "twilight zone" where the actions of behind-the-scenes enablers, if any, are effectively hidden from view. Further, should such behind-the-scenes enablers exist, they would undoubtedly go to great lengths to conceal their involvement, including attempting to shift blame to other parties. The author of the preceding comments appears to be well aware of this possibility, for he suggests that mainstream commentators readily dismiss analysis like his as being no more than that of "a crazy conspiracy theorist."

In the case of Inoue and his band, however, it is impossible to deny they enjoyed behind-the-scenes connections to, if not support from, some of Japan's most powerful political and military figures. Significantly, this support continued even after their arrests and was especially effective during the subsequent trial, imprisonment, and postincarceration. From beginning to end, Inoue and his band's terrorist acts would have been unthinkable without this support. To give but one example, what other "terrorist leader" has ever had his very court conviction erased from the legal record, only to then become a live-in advisor to his country's prime minister? Nevertheless, there is no definitive evidence indicating exactly who Inoue and his band's powerful patrons were.

While Inoue's case may be seen, in Maruyama's words, as an extreme case of "support from above," it's certainly not the only example, as we have already seen in the case of Afghanistan. A more recent example involves the role of outside parties in the long and bitter conflict in Syria. One observer of this conflict, Flemish Father Daniël Maes (aged seventy-eight), lives in the sixth-century Mar Yakub (St. Jacob) Monastery in the city of Qara, ninety kilometers north of the Syrian capital, Damascus. Father Maes writes,

> The idea that a popular uprising took place against President Assad is completely false. I've been in Qara since 2010, and I have seen with my own eyes how agitators from outside Syria organized protests against the government and recruited young people. That was filmed and aired by *Al Jazeera* to give the impression that a rebellion was taking place. Murders were committed by foreign terrorists, against the Sunni and Christian communities, in an effort to sow religious and ethnic discord among the Syrian people. . . .
>
> When thousands of terrorists settled in Qara, we became afraid for our lives. They came from the Gulf States, Saudi Arabia, Europe, Turkey, Libya, there were many Chechens. They formed a foreign occupation force, all allied to *al-Qaeda* and other terrorists. Armed to the teeth by the West and their allies with the intention to act against us, they literally said: "This country belongs to us now." Often, they were drugged, they fought each other, in the evening they fired randomly. We had to hide in the crypts of the monastery for a long time. When the Syrian army chased them away, everybody was happy: the Syrian citizens because they hate the foreign rebels, and we because peace had returned. . . .
>
> It's the Americans who have a hand in all of this, for pipelines and natural resources in this region and to thwart Putin. Saudi Arabia and Qatar want to establish a Sunni state in Syria, without religious freedom. Therefore, Assad must go.[8]

While the accuracy of Father Maes's description may be questioned, his words are those of an independent observer unaffiliated with any side of the conflict. Additional support for Father Maes's description is provided by investigative journalist Max Blumenthal:

> By June 2012, CIA operatives had set up shop on the southern Turkish border with Syria, in the city of Adana, home to the American air base Incirlik. From there, the *New*

York Times reported, "automatic rifles, rocket-propelled grenades, ammunition and some antitank weapons, [were] being funneled mostly across the Turkish border by way of a shadowy network of intermediaries including Syria's Muslim Brotherhood and paid for by Turkey, Saudi Arabia and Qatar."

To justify the arms shipments, Washington conjured up the label "moderate rebels," stamping it on an umbrella organization of Syrian army defectors and former Muslim Brotherhood cadres that called itself the Free Syrian Army (FSA). The Obama administration and a collection of pundits, many housed in Gulf-funded think tanks in Washington, zealously promoted the FSA as the best hope for combating ISIS. Douglas Laux—acknowledged by the CIA as the lead member of its Syrian Task Force and a key figure behind the plan for then-agency director David Petraeus to topple the Syrian government with insurgent proxy forces—later acknowledged what few of the FSA's promoters in the West ever would: "There were no moderates."[9]

With no moderates in its midst, it did not take long for FSA and ISIS to become allies in Syria. For example, when FSA finally took over the Syrian military's Menagh airbase in mid-2013, following a ten-month siege, it was only able to do so due to aid from ISIS fighters. Following victory, the two sides held a joint press conference characterized by the *New York Times* as follows: "a mix of jihadist and Free Syrian Army leaders, who stood together, each praising his men, like members of a victorious basketball team."[10]

It was another American luminary, this time Vice President Joseph Biden, who addressed the result of this coalition. Speaking at the Harvard Kennedy School of Government in October 2014, Biden first singled out Turkey and Saudi Arabia and said,

> Our biggest problem is our allies. They were so determined to take down Assad and essentially have a proxy Sunni–Shia war; what did they do? They poured hundreds of millions of dollars and thousands of tons of weapons into anyone who would fight against Assad. Except that the people who were being supplied were Al-Nusra and Al Qaeda and the extremist elements of *jihadis* coming from other parts of the world.[11]

In the aftermath of this admission, Blumenthal notes that Biden was forced to embark on the equivalent of an international apology tour the same month, issuing "a formal clarification" to Turkey's Erdoğan and thanking Saudi Arabia's foreign minister for his country's supposed cooperation in the fight against ISIS. Thereafter, scarcely anyone in Washington, whether in "government, the world of think tank experts, or in the press corps, dared to openly confront America's core Middle Eastern allies for their backing of Al Qaeda and ISIS."[12]

The point here is not to prove that the United States and its allies are behind every major terrorist group in the world, for there are many terrorist groups who have little or no connection to the United States. However, Blumenthal's comments once again demonstrate there is often more behind terrorist groups and their heinous acts than appears on the surface or in news reports. Diving down the rabbit hole into America's very own "Wonderland" (aka "Horrorland"), one often finds a subterranean world that is the inverse of above-ground rhetoric. Be that as it may, what is undeniable is that *someone* is funding (and often arming) the terrorists, especially when they are numerous, well organized, and well equipped.

As previously discussed in chapter 13, in seeking to understand acts of terrorism, the question "who benefits?" must always be asked. The historical record reveals that governments, or at least parts of governments, are willing to support terrorism if it advances what their political leaders consider to be in the national (or their own) interest. Thus, it is not unusual for powerful, behind-the-scenes players, up to and including governments, to serve as "enablers" of terrorism through funding, supply of weapons, suggested targets, and so on. While religious fervor may motivate individual terrorists, especially in their willingness to sacrifice themselves, their movement as a whole is open to manipulation by fixers who may themselves be funded by still more powerful actors.

(6) If the ethical blindness of terrorists is to be condemned, as it should be, this does not mean there are no ethical questions to be asked of those (typically governments and their militaries) who seek to kill terrorists. The foremost of these questions is, in the absence of a fair and impartial judicial process, what gives a government the right (other than brute force) to become judge, jury, and executioner of those it deems to be terrorists or sometimes merely suspects of being terrorists?

However imperfect it may have been, Inoue and his band were given a public trial at which they had the right to defend themselves, including lengthy explanations of their motives and goals. In addition, the public, thanks to newspaper coverage, was afforded the opportunity to understand what had happened and even write letters supporting or opposing Inoue and his band's actions. Stephan Large reports that by November 1934 the desks in the Tokyo District Court, where the trial was held, "were piled high with petitions from all over Japan demanding leniency for the defendants."[13] Okamura Ao adds that these petitions, numbering some three hundred thousand in all, came from "a wide range of citizens, especially those in debt, suffering from poverty, and farmers tormented by starvation."[14]

In the current fight against terrorism, terrorists, let alone the public, are seldom if ever afforded similar opportunities. Instead, governments and their militaries exercise the sole right to determine who should die, without the need for a trial or making public any evidence whatsoever. Needless to say, citizens of a country that kills terrorists in such an arbitrary manner would object if their government treated fellow citizens similarly, no matter how heinous their crimes. Yet are suspected foreign terrorists any less deserving of the same degree of legal protection simply because they are foreign?

It's hardly surprising that "extrajudicial" killings of terrorists, especially those merely *suspected* of being terrorists in so-called signature strikes, often create additional terrorists seeking revenge for the deaths of their loved ones.[15] Further, as previously mentioned, there are instances when a government ostensibly fighting terrorism is, behind the scenes, secretly enabling or abetting terrorism, especially when the terrorists and the government in question share a common foe.[16] Thus, the possibility exists that by killing terrorists, the government involved is attempting to destroy incriminating evidence (or lack of evidence) that might be revealed if the suspected terrorists were ever tried in an open court of law.[17]

CONCLUSION

Once again, it is admittedly dangerous to use a study of limited acts of terrorism by members of only one religion to draw blanket conclusions about all acts of terrorism on the part of adherents of a variety of religions. Nevertheless, it's fair to ask whether a study of limited acts of terrorism may suggest avenues of approach, or provide hints, leading to a broader understanding of this phenomenon. In this regard, Inoue and his band offer a variety of instructive insights. These insights, moreover, may prove helpful to future studies of religion-related terrorism, especially because, in this instance, the study does *not* involve the "flavor of the day," Islamic terrorism.

In fact, this is the purpose of the next book I intend to write, tentatively titled *Holy War Unmasked: The Universal Characteristics of Religious Violence*. The hope is to either confirm, or disprove, one of the major conclusions of this book, that religion-related terrorism is *not* primarily a religious phenomenon. Instead, as religious studies scholar Karen Armstrong noted, "Terrorism is fundamentally and inherently political, even when other motives—religious, economic, or social—are involved. Terrorism is always about power—acquiring it or keeping it."[18] Agreement with Armstrong's assertion does not, however, lessen the importance of religion's role in terrorism, for it is equally true that all religions can (and have) been used by powerful behind-the-scenes actors as enabling mechanisms, serving to justify, or at least facilitate, the death of both the Other (i.e., victims of terror) as well as oneself (the terrorists).

In Inoue's case, it is clear there would have been no terrorist acts in the absence of deep-seated economic and social malaise in Japan. Given this, it's also true that one, if not the chief, method of fighting terrorism is to "drain the swamp." However, in this instance, draining the swamp does not mean seeking the impossible (i.e., attempting to kill everyone identified as a real or potential terrorist). Aside from the inhumanity of doing so, it is an impossible goal so long as severe social and economic distress exists in society. In such situations, there will always be those, especially the young, willing to take matters into their own hands. When religious fervor/ethical justification is added to the mix, you have a combustible mixture ever ready to explode (and open to manipulation by outside actors). Terrorism is the one violent tactic available to both those who otherwise have no means of fighting back and those behind-the-scenes supporters who find it convenient to fund terrorists for their own ends.

If the preceding description is accurate, the true "solution" to terror is one that is seldom if ever discussed, and even less often acted upon. Namely, the solution to all but so-called lone-wolf acts of terror is the establishment of socially and economically just societies, no matter how difficult that may be.[19] Where oppression exists, resistance is inevitable, and religion is one of the most readily available means of organizing, and typically justifying if not making sacred, that resistance, especially by the otherwise powerless.

It is equally, if not more, important to expose those state and substate political forces who seek to maintain, or even enhance, their own power by secretly funding and supporting terrorists, capitalizing on the religious fervor of believers, especially the latters' willingness to sacrifice themselves. Both the fixers and those who employ them must be exposed, tried, and sentenced for the self-seeking aggrandizers they are. Terrorism, at least on a large scale, could not exist without their support and funding.

At the same time, those who believe in the salvific power of religion, of whom I am one, must honestly acknowledge how easily their religion's highest ideals can be, and have been, hijacked by those seeking to enhance their worldly power. In the absence of critical self-reflection on the part of religious adherents, the cycle of religion-affiliated terrorism will never be broken. Tragically, as the following words attributed to French scientist Blaise Pascal (1623–1662) inform us, "Men never do evil so completely and cheerfully as when they do it from religious conviction."[20] If nothing else, this is the lasting legacy, and lasting warning, Inoue and his terrorist band have left us.

Appendix 1

The Assassination of General Nagata Tetsuzan

As this book has revealed, the growth of Japanese totalitarianism, like its German counterpart, took place in concert with the repression of domestic dissent, including dissent within the military itself. In addition to Inoue Nisshō and his band, there were other Zen leaders who played active roles in curbing domestic resistance to Japan's expansion onto the Asian continent and beyond.[1] This is in addition to the even more widespread role Zen (and other Buddhist) leaders played in supporting Japanese military aggression abroad.

In stating this, the claim is not made that Zen was the *cause* of either terrorism at home or Japanese aggression abroad. Instead, Zen served as an "enabling mechanism," making it possible for Zen practitioners, both military and civilian, to commit their heinous acts, all the while believing they were acting justly, engaged in what they described as "compassionate killing" while ever ready to sacrifice their own lives. As D. T. Suzuki noted, "Good fighters are generally ascetics or stoics, which means to have an iron will. When needed, Zen supplies them with this."[2] In the examples that follow, Zen clearly supplied the terrorist protagonists with an iron will.

As mentioned in chapter 1, inasmuch as the ultimate goal of the individual "assassinations" described in appendices 1 and 2 were carried out in the name of achieving a much larger goal, that is, a Shōwa Restoration, they are collectively referred to as terrorist acts. Readers are advised that in order to provide the fullest possible context for what follows, there is some duplication of earlier material.

The first example describes the role played by one prominent Sōtō Zen master, Fukusada Mugai (1871–1943), in the assassination of a major military leader, Army General Nagata Tetsuzan (1884–1935). While Mugai neither pulled the trigger of an assassin's pistol nor wielded an assassin's sword, he was nevertheless convinced, like his terrorist disciple Army Lt. Colonel Aizawa Saburō, that Zen Buddhism justified killing his fellow Japanese in the name of the Buddhist-inspired phrase "destroying the false and establishing the True" (*haja kenshō*).[3]

BRIEF HISTORICAL INTRODUCTION

As previously described, the Manchurian Incident of September 1931 set off a chain of events that led to the establishment of the Japanese puppet state of Manchukuo in February 1932 and eventually to Japan's full-scale invasion of China in July 1937. Japanese aggression abroad, however, did not imply unanimity of opinion at home, for widely diverse groups of civilian political leaders, including the emperor, as well as ultranationalists, leftists, and military officers of various ranks, continued their attempts to bend domestic and foreign policy to their particular viewpoints and ideologies. In short, in the early to mid-1930s, Japan was still some distance away from the monolithic emperor-centric, military-dominated society it would become by the end of the decade.

In seeking to understand how the emperor, military, and sympathetic bureaucrats, with their corporate allies, ultimately emerged triumphant in Japanese society, it is crucial to understand the role played by the domestic assassinations of both civilian and military figures. Although assassination is the ultimate form of political intimidation, in the Japan of the 1930s (and before) right-wing-inspired violence rarely resulted in anything more than a short prison sentence for the "patriotic" perpetrator(s) involved, at least, that is, up through the major military insurrection staged by a group of young military officers and their troops on February 26, 1936. This uprising succeeded in killing three leading cabinet ministers, wounding a fourth, and injuring a number of others, some critically, before it was finally suppressed.[4] It is also noteworthy that no matter how disparate the views of the assassins were, the one thing they and their supporters always agreed on was their deep concern for the "welfare of the nation."

One of the military assassins active during this period was Lt. Col. Aizawa Saburō of the Forty-First Regiment in Fukuyama, a member of a group of relatively young army officers who, at least in their own eyes, were characterized by their complete and total devotion to a uniquely divine emperor. Appropriately, they designated themselves, as previously mentioned, the Young Officers' Movement (Seinen Shōkō Undō) and willingly identified themselves with the larger Imperial Way Faction (Kōdō-ha) within the army, which included some of Japan's top-ranking military officers.

Imperial Way Faction members further attached the pejorative label Control Faction (Tōsei-ha) to those officers of any rank who, by refusing to join them, stood in the way of the realization of their goals. It should be noted, however, that the military's leadership was also split on the basis of such things as age, educational and family background, and even former clan affiliation. In addition, there was fierce rivalry, especially for funding but also on strategy, between army and navy leaders.

This rivalry was typically won by the navy in that the construction of modern war-ships was a very expensive endeavor. With less money available for the army, the relatively inexpensive, and Zen-influenced, "spiritual education" (*seishin kyōiku*) of soldiers became ever more important.

As advocates of a Shōwa Restoration, the Imperial Way Faction sought to bring about the direct rule of the emperor, something they believed would result in land reform; overthrow of the corrupt, "privileged classes"; and a more equitable distri-bution of the nation's wealth through the nationalization of big business. In theory at least, their goals shared much in common with national socialism, and like the Nazis they were fully prepared to employ violence, especially political assassina-tion, to bring about a government to their liking. As for foreign policy, they were strongly anticommunist and therefore regarded the Soviet Union, rather than the United States, Great Britain, and other Western powers, as the chief threat to the Japanese Empire, especially to growing Japanese economic interests in Manchuria and neighboring Mongolia.

By comparison, members of the Control Faction were generally more accepting of the status quo, at least at home. They accepted a basically capitalist society but wanted the government to intervene more actively in the private sector to ensure their military-related, economic goals were achieved. Believing that it was possible to advance the military's interests through close cooperation with Japan's leading finan-cial combines (*zaibatsu*) and government bureaucrats, they were generally opposed to political assassination, at least domestically. In the foreign policy arena, however, they advocated ever greater advancement onto the Asian continent, including further encroachments on a divided and militarily weak China. They also came to favor proposals for the forcible acquisition of strategic raw materials, especially oil and rubber, from the colonized countries of Southeast Asia, even at the risk of war with the Western rulers of these countries.

Both military factions, it must be stressed, were equally committed to the main-tenance and, if possible, the expansion of Japan's own colonial empire. In this sense, the struggle within the military was not one of "good guys" versus "bad guys," or even "moderates" versus "radicals." In the end, however, what may be termed the more realistic, if not opportunistic, stance of the Control Faction meant that its leaders eventually gained the upper hand in the military (and then the government), gradually purging members of the Imperial Way Faction from positions of leadership beginning as early as January 1934.

Predictably, this purge of leaders produced a strong backlash, especially among those younger and more radical officers associated with the Young Officers' Move-ment within the Imperial Way Faction. Having been one of the few high-ranking officers to oppose the ongoing purge, Gen. Mazaki Jinsaburō, then inspector-general of military training, was a hero (or "savior") to the Young Officers, among them Lt. Col. Aizawa Saburō. Thus, when in July 1935 Aizawa learned that General Mazaki had himself been purged, the former took it upon himself to seek revenge. As a midranking officer, Aizawa later claimed that he acted in order to save still younger officers from ruining their careers by taking matters into their own hands (as some of them nevertheless did on February 26, 1936).

The man Aizawa chose for assassination was Maj. Gen. Nagata Tetsuzan, director of the Military Affairs Bureau at the War Office. Nagata was known not only for his brilliant mind but equally for his attention to detail and the calm and thoughtful manner in which he reached decisions. None of these, however, were qualities that appealed to the deeply felt yearnings of Aizawa and his comrades for a swift and thoroughgoing restructuring of Japanese society even though they were unsure of the particulars. In the first instance, possession of a detailed plan for social reform would have impinged on the prerogatives of the emperor, something that was unthinkable for loyal subjects (although not necessarily for the highest-ranking officers of the Imperial Way Faction). Inasmuch as Nagata actively opposed their call for a Shōwa Restoration, he had to be eliminated.

On July 19, 1935, Aizawa, then forty-six, called on Nagata for the first time, verbally demanding that the general step down for his role in ousting Mazaki. Nagata not only refused to do so but in retaliation arranged for Aizawa to be transferred to Taiwan. This in turn prompted Aizawa to consider more drastic action, for he realized that once in Taiwan he would no longer be able to influence the course of events at home.

At approximately 9:20 a.m. on August 12, 1935, Aizawa entered the War Ministry from the rear and went to the first-floor office of an old friend, Lieutenant General Yamaoka Shigeatsu (1882-1954), head of army maintenance. Ostensibly, he had come to inform the general of his imminent departure for Taiwan. After sharing tea, Aizawa asked Yamaoka if Nagata was in his office on the second floor. Informed that he was, Aizawa excused himself and, at 9:45 a.m., burst in on Nagata, sword in hand.

Nagata did not immediately realize what was about to happen, for he was deep in conversation with Colonel Niimi Hideo, chief of the Tokyo Military Police. Ironically, the topic of their conversation was what to do about the growing discontent in the army.[5] Quickly coming to his senses, Nagata jumped up and headed for the door, successfully dodging Aizawa's first blow. He was, however, unable to escape the next, a thrusting blow from the back that momentarily pinned the general to the door. Not yet dead, the general was then given a final blow to the head by Aizawa as the former lay outstretched on the floor.

Although unarmed, Col. Niimi initially attempted to aid Nagata but suffered a disabling cut to his left arm. For his part, Aizawa, a former swordsmanship instructor at the military academy, later confessed to having been embarrassed by the manner in which he had dispatched the general. "I failed to kill Nagata with one blow and as a fencing master I felt deeply ashamed," he said.[6] Ashamed or not, Aizawa calmly left the general's office and returned to Gen. Yamaoka's office, where he informed his startled friend what had taken place. Noticing that Aizawa was bleeding, Yamaoka arranged for the colonel to be taken to the ministry's medical dispensary. There, while being treated for a minor cut to his left wrist, Aizawa was arrested by the military police.

AIZAWA AND ZEN

Aizawa first encountered Zen at the Rinzai temple of Zuiganji located near Matsu-shima in Miyagi prefecture. At the time, Aizawa was a twenty-six-year-old second lieutenant attached to the Twenty-Ninth Infantry Regiment headquartered in the northern Honshū city of Sendai. On a Monday morning in the spring of 1915, Aizawa's company commander, Prince Higashikuni Naruhiko (1887–1990), paternal uncle to Emperor Hirohito, addressed the assembled company officers: "Yesterday I visited Zuiganji in Matsushima and spoke with the abbot, Matsubara Banryū [1848–1935]. He informed me that Buddhism was a religion that taught exerting oneself to the utmost in service to the country."[7] As simple as this statement was, it nevertheless proved to be the catalyst for Aizawa's Zen practice, for as he later related, "I was troubled by the fact that I knew so little of what it meant to serve the country."[8]

Aizawa decided to personally visit Banryū to hear more. Banryū related the well-known example of Kusunoki Masashige (1294–1336), a loyalist samurai leader at the time when the imperial system was divided into two parts, known as the North-ern and Southern Courts Period (1336–1392), each court with its own emperor. Defeated in battle and facing death, Masashige is said to have vowed to be reborn seven times over in order to annihilate the enemies of the Southern emperor. Banryū went on to inform Aizawa that, if he truly wished to acquire a spirit like that of Kusunoki, he "must study the Buddha Dharma and especially practice Zen medita-tion."[9] Inspired by these words, Aizawa determined to do exactly that, though he first encountered the practical problem that Zuiganji was located some distance from Sendai, making it impossible for him to meditate there on a daily basis.

The result was that Aizawa sought out an equally well-known Sōtō Zen master resident in the city of Sendai itself, Fukusada Mugai (1871–1943), abbot of the large temple complex of Rinnōji. Similar to the way Yamamoto Gempō treated Inoue Nisshō when the two first met, Mugai initially refused to accept Aizawa as his lay disciple. "If you're just coming here for character-building, I don't think you'll be able to endure [the training]," Mugai told him.[10] Refusing to be dissuaded, Aizawa eventually gained Mugai's acceptance. In fact, shortly after Aizawa began his training, Mugai granted him, in a highly unusual gesture, permission to board in the priests' quarters just as if he were an *unsui* (novice monk).

Some months later, Aizawa encountered yet another barrier to his Zen practice when his regimental superiors decided it was improper for him to actually live at the temple. Hearing this, Mugai set about finding alternative living quarters for his military disciple. It was in this way that Aizawa came to board with Hōjō Tokiyoshi (1859–1929), then president of Tōhoku University and yet another of Mugai's lay disciples. With this arrangement in place, Aizawa continued to train under Mugai through the spring of 1917.

As to what he gained from his Zen training, Aizawa later testified at his pretrial hearing, "The result of [my training] was that I was able to deeply cultivate the con-viction that I must leave my ego behind and serve the nation."[11] When, during the court-martial itself, the judge specifically asked which one of Mugai's teachings had influenced him the most, Aizawa immediately replied, "Reverence for the emperor [is] absolute."[12] As for Mugai's attitude toward his military disciple, one of Aizawa's close officer friends described it as "just like the feelings of a parent for his child."[13]

Unsurprisingly, Aizawa felt the same about Mugai. This is revealed, among other things, by the fact that even after his imprisonment, Aizawa arranged for medicine to be sent to Mugai upon hearing of his master's illness. In fact, it was this illness that prevented Aizawa from realizing his final wish—that Mugai be present to witness his execution. Having failed in this, Aizawa's last message to Mugai read, "I pray that you will fully recover from your illness just as quickly as possible."[14]

Given the closeness of the master–disciple relationship between Aizawa and Mugai, it is not surprising that Mugai was the second person to visit Aizawa in prison after the latter's arrest on September 4, 1935. Mugai subsequently visited him once again on September 10. The entries in the prison's visitor log describe Mugai as Aizawa's "teacher to whom is owed a debt of gratitude" (*onshi*). The purpose of the visits was recorded as a "sympathy call" (*imon*).

COURT-MARTIAL

Aizawa's public court-martial began on January 28, 1936, at the headquarters of the First Division in Tokyo and received wide press coverage. Testifying on the general background to his act, Aizawa stated,

> I realized that the senior statesmen, those close to the throne, and powerful financiers and bureaucrats were attempting to corrupt the Army for the attainment of their own interests; the Army was thus being changed into a private concern and the supreme command [of the emperor] was being violated. If nothing were done I was afraid the Army would collapse from within. The senior statesmen and those close to the throne are indulging in self-interest and seem to be working as the tools of foreign countries who watch for their chance to attack Japan.[15]

It should be noted that the "[right of] supreme command" referred to in this passage meant that the military was, constitutionally speaking, not subject to the control of the civilian government. Rather, at least in theory, it was under the emperor's direct command (and that of his designated representatives). In practice, this meant that anyone (other than the emperor) who sought to interfere with or restrict the military in any way could be charged with "violating" not simply the military's prerogatives but the right of command of the emperor himself—a charge akin to treason.

In light of this, why did Aizawa choose to assassinate another military man, indeed his lawfully appointed superior officer? Was he not thereby violating the very right of supreme command he claimed to be defending? To this charge, Aizawa replied,

> I marked out Nagata because he, together with senior statesmen, financial magnates and members of the old Army clique like Generals Minami and Ugaki, were responsible

for the corruption of the army. The responsibility for the Army rested on Nagata, the Director of the Military Affairs Bureau. He was the source of the evil. If he would not resign there was only one thing to do. I determined to make myself a demon and finish his life with one stroke of my sword.[16]

Aizawa also testified about the spiritual dimension, or motivation, behind his act, stating,

> The emperor is the incarnation of the god who reigns over the universe. The aim of life is to develop according to His Majesty's wishes, which, however, have not yet been fully understood by all the world. The world is deadlocked because of communism, capitalism, anarchism, and the like. As Japanese, we should make it our object to bring happiness to the world in accordance with His Majesty's wishes. As long as the fiery zeal of the Japanese for the Imperial cause is felt in Manchuria and other places, all will be well, but let it die and it will be gone forever. Democracy is all wrong. Our whole concern is to clarify Imperial rule as established by Emperor Meiji.[17]

Although the above words appear to leave little room for a "Zen connection" to the incident, readers will recall the phrase "The world is deadlocked . . ." is pregnant with the "flavor" of Zen, at least as understood by D. T. Suzuki. More to the point is the following short yet key comment Aizawa made in describing his state of mind at the moment of the assassination itself: "I was in an absolute sphere, so there was neither affirmation nor negation, neither good nor evil."[18]

Is this a manifestation of the Zen spirit? As we have seen, Inoue Nisshō certainly identified it as such. Additionally, in postwar years the well-known Western exponent of Japanese culture and Zen Reginald Blyth (1898–1964) wrote, "From the orthodox Zen point of view, . . . any action whatever must be considered right if it is performed from the absolute."[19]

MUGAI'S DEFENSE

Mugai appeared as a witness for the defense at the ninth hearing held on February 22, 1936. Following his court testimony, Mugai returned to the witness waiting room, where he told a reporter for the *Yomiuri Shimbun*,

> Although I don't intend to discuss the incident itself, I would like to say that I have known Aizawa's parents for the past thirty years. For this reason, there is no one better acquainted with Aizawa's childhood and character than I am. While it is true that Aizawa's Zen practice is still immature in some respects, I think that the decisive action he took in accomplishing his great undertaking transcended both life and death. Even should he receive the death penalty, Aizawa will be satisfied, for as long as his ideas live on, life and death are of no concern to him.[20]

If the preceding comments leave some doubt as to what Mugai really thought of his disciple and his "great undertaking," Mugai later clarified his position in a pamphlet entitled *A Glimpse of Lt. Colonel Aizawa* (*Aizawa Chūsa no Hen'ei*). In a section labelled "Comments by Fukusada Mugai-rōshi," Mugai wrote,

> Aizawa trained at Rinnōji for a period of three years starting when he was still a lieutenant. In applying himself to his practice with untiring zeal, he acted just as if he were a Zen priest, something quite impossible for the ordinary person to do. His character was honest and pure, and from his youth he had, through his Zen training, continually strengthened his resolve to "destroy the false and establish the True" as he sought the Buddha Way. I believe the recent incident was truly a reflection of the purity of mind he had acquired over a period of more than twenty years since having been a young officer. That is to say, he was burning with his ideal of destroying the false.[21]

If the preceding comments still strike readers as relatively vague, especially as regards Mugai's assessment of Aizawa's motive in killing General Nagata, Mugai was prepared to be more specific, including his own estimation of the problems facing Japan. He wrote,

> Aizawa frequently lamented the existing state of corruption in our country. Military morale, he noted, had deteriorated to the point that he was concerned about the nation's safety. Whenever Aizawa came to Sendai, he visited me without fail, and in addition frequently wrote me letters overflowing with his intense concern for the welfare of the nation. Especially in the last two or three years, he spoke of his inconsolable sorrow. In this regard, I felt the same as he did.[22]

And finally, Mugai was ready to tell his readers just how truly wonderful his disciple was. Mugai praised Aizawa's "superb spirit" coupled with his "resolute and steadfast faith":

> It is clear that Aizawa thought day and night of how to break the deadlock facing the nation in the present emergency. I believe Aizawa felt compelled to express his spirit as he did. He intended to sacrifice himself from the outset in hope of single-handedly purifying the military through eradicating the source [of the problem]. I recognize, however, that many of those who today think only of their own personal advancement find his action difficult to understand. For my part, I fully understand why he acted as he did.
>
> Aizawa's act was definitely not one of madness. Without discussing whether it was right or wrong, I know that, prior to acting, he repeatedly gave the matter serious thought. His was not a rash undertaking, nor one, as many now say, of seeking fame for himself. Neither, I'm convinced, was it one of simple blind faith. There is no doubt that, given Aizawa's purity of character and self-sacrificing devotion, he felt compelled to do what he did in the face of present-day corruption.
>
> I believe in Aizawa. The consistency of Aizawa's character lies in his readiness to serve sovereign and country on the basis of a resolute and unshakable faith that enabled him to transcend life and death. I am certain this is not a question of placing too much confidence in him, for I know that many of his former classmates [at the military academy] also recognize the nobility of his spirit.[23]

EXECUTION

In light of Mugai's admiration for his disciple, it was only natural that the close relationship between these two lasted even beyond the grave. Thus, following Aizawa's execution by the military authorities on July 3, 1936, Mugai bestowed on his disciple a posthumous Buddhist name (*kaimyō*) consisting of nine Chinese characters, numerically speaking the highest honor a deceased Japanese Buddhist layman can receive. The meaning of the characters also reveals the esteem Mugai had for his disciple: "Layman of loyalty and thoroughgoing duty [residing in] the temple of adamantine courage."

Mugai bestowed this auspicious posthumous name on Aizawa in spite of the fact that a general order had been issued that forbade both elaborate memorial services and the erection of shrines or monuments in his memory. Thus, by honoring a man the army had branded a "traitor to the nation" (*kokuzoku*), Mugai himself became the subject of an investigation by the military police. Although hospitalized at the time, upon being informed of the investigation, Mugai said, "Are there any traitors in the realm of the dead? . . . If they [the military police] have any complaints, tell them to have the Minister of the Army come here and lodge them in person!"[24]

Aizawa had yet a second connection to Zen following his death. A portion of his cremated ashes were retained in Tokyo and interred in a common grave for all twenty-two former officers and civilian sympathizers who were executed for their part in the February 26, 1936, Incident, described in detail in appendix 2. The grave site is located at the Sōtō Zen temple of Kensōji in Azabu, Tokyo, founded in 1635 by the Nabeshima family, the former feudal lord of Hizen (present-day Saga prefecture).

It was only in the postwar years that relatives of the deceased were allowed to openly hold memorial services at Kensōji. In 1952, these relatives erected a tombstone over the common grave that included the names of the deceased together with the following inscription: "Grave of the Twenty-Two Samurai." In 1965, this same group erected a statue of the Bodhisattva of compassion, Avalokiteśvara (*Kannon*), at the spot in Yoyogi, Tokyo, where the executions took place. This statue was dedicated to the memory of both the executed rebels and their victims. Even today, memorial services are held yearly at Kensōji on February 26 and July 12 (the day on which most of the victims were executed).

The organizational name chosen by the relatives for their undertakings is Busshinkai (Buddha Mind Association). One is left to ponder the connection between "Buddha mind" and the terrorist acts of the perpetrators. Their terrorist acts were dedicated to the restoration of complete political power to the emperor via a military coup, that is, the Shōwa Restoration.

CONCLUSION

In evaluating the above, it should be noted that Mugai was far from the first modern Zen master to heap lavish praise on a military disciple. The noted Meiji period

Rinzai Zen master Nantembō (1839–1925), for example, praised his own famous disciple, Army General Nogi Maresuke (1849–1912) as follows:

> I have no doubt that Nogi's great accomplishments during the Sino-Japanese and Russo-Japanese Wars were the result of the hard [Zen] training he underwent. The ancient Zen patriarchs taught that extreme hardship brings forth the brilliance [of enlightenment]. In the case of General [Nogi] this was certainly the case. . . . All Zen practitioners should be like him. . . . A truly serious and fine military man.

And Nantembō added, "There is no *Bodhisattva* practice superior to the compassionate taking of life."[25]

Mugai, however, was certainly unique in praising a military man who had been labelled a traitor to his country though it is abundantly clear he didn't regard Aizawa as such. On the contrary, he was convinced, as was Aizawa himself, that such acts were necessary in order to "break the deadlock facing the nation in the present emergency." Although the historical validity of this statement is questionable, what is of interest here is the almost uncanny resemblance between Mugai's thought and that of D. T. Suzuki. As previously noted, it was only two years later, in 1938, Suzuki would claim, "[Zen] is, however, generally animated with a certain revolutionary spirit, and when things come to a deadlock—as they do when we are overloaded with conventionalism, formalism, and other cognate isms—Zen asserts itself and proves to be a destructive force."[26]

Readers will recall that in the same paragraph Suzuki also claimed that Zen was "extremely flexible" and able to adapt itself "almost to any philosophy and moral doctrine as long as its intuitive teaching is not interfered with."[27] In supporting the actions of an assassin, it can be said that Mugai demonstrated just how extremely flexible Japanese Zen of the 1930s was in adapting itself to almost any philosophy and moral doctrine. In this context, the question must be asked if there was anything in Suzuki's interpretation of Zen that would have argued against Mugai's endorsement of his disciple's action.

I suggest there is nothing. In other words, the type of Zen advocated by Suzuki, Mugai, and other Zen leaders of that period was, under the right conditions, just as amenable to supporting assassination at home as it was to supporting Japan's aggression abroad. Readers will recall yet another of Suzuki's statements:

> Zen did not necessarily argue with them [warriors] about the immortality of the soul or righteousness or the divine way *or ethical conduct*, but it simply urged *going ahead with whatever conclusion rational or irrational a man has arrived at*. Philosophy may safely be left with intellectual minds; Zen wants to act, and the most effective act, once the mind is made up, is to go on without looking backward. In this respect, Zen is indeed the religion of the samurai warrior.[28] (emphasis mine)

Whether Aizawa's act was rational or not is yet another contestable point, but for both Suzuki and Mugai the question of "rationality" was, in any case, of little or no consequence. Furthermore, like Suzuki, Mugai did not wish to consider "whether [his disciple's act] was right or wrong," that is, whether it was ethical or not. For both Suzuki and Mugai, there was only one direction for the Zen practitioner to proceed—straight ahead "without looking backward."

Pointing out the similarity in thought between Mugai and Suzuki is not to suggest these two men were either acquaintances or directly influenced each other's thinking. Nevertheless, it is interesting to note the existence of an indirect link between the two in the person of Hōjō Tokiyoshi. As noted above, Mugai had arranged for Aizawa to reside in Hōjō's home during the period he trained at Rinnōji. Not only was Hōjō then president of Tōhoku University, he was also the same man who, as D. T. Suzuki's former high school mathematics teacher, first introduced Suzuki to Zen.

One indication of Hōjō's own Zen orientation is that he originally trained as a layman under the noted Rinzai Zen master Imakita Kōsen (1816–1892), abbot of Kamakura's Engakuji monastic complex. In the 1870s Kōsen was a leading figure in promoting reverence for the emperor and unquestioning loyalty to the state by virtue of his role as a "national evangelist" for the Meiji government's ill-fated Ministry of Doctrine. No doubt it was Hōjō's influence that led Suzuki to train at Engakuji beginning in 1891, first under Kōsen until the abbot's death the following year, and then under Kōsen's successor, Shaku Sōen.

Be that as it may, Suzuki's connection to Hōjō did not end in high school, for the latter eventually resigned his university presidency to become head of the prestigious Gakushūin (Peers' School) in Tokyo in June 1917. It was at Gakushūin that Suzuki once again found himself under Hōjō's tutelage, for Suzuki had been an English teacher at this same school following his return to Japan from the United States in 1909.

Although there is no evidence indicating this indirect link is anything more than coincidence, it nevertheless reveals something about the intellectual climate within Zen circles of that era. It was perfectly acceptable to represent Zen as being a "destructive force" as long as that destruction was in the service of some alleged greater good, especially in the service of the state and its policies. Although it was unusual for this destructiveness to be directed against representatives of the state, even this was not unprecedented. As we have seen, Inoue and his band were already deeply involved in the assassination of two civilian government and financial leaders, plus a prime minister, in early 1932, with plans to assassinate many more.

Borrowing Suzuki's words once again, it can be argued that this was the inevitable price Japanese Zen in the 1930s had to pay for its willingness to be found "wedded to anarchism or fascism, communism or democracy, atheism or idealism, or any political or economic dogmatism."[29] Did Suzuki forget to mention terror-ism?

Appendix 2

Zen in the February 26, 1936, Incident

The second example consists of the Zen connection to the previously introduced February 26, 1936, Incident, aka the "Young Officers' Uprising, the largest military insurrection in Japan's modern history. Similar to Zen's role in the Blood Oath Corps Incident, as well as the assassination of Gen. Nagata Tetsuzan, Zen once again served as an enabling mechanism, this time in the form of Ōmori Sōgen (1904–1994), a Zen-trained layman in prewar Japan who became a well-known Rinzai Zen master in postwar Japan. To this day, Ōmori remains lauded, at least by his disciples, as the "greatest Zen master of modern times," whose very life is "worthy to be considered a masterpiece of Zen art."[1]

As extravagant as these claims sound, Ōmori was unquestionably an accomplished master of the traditional arts of swordsmanship (*kendō*) and calligraphy (*shodō*), not to mention a prolific author of books and articles on Zen. In the postwar era, he also served as president of the Rinzai Zen sect–affiliated Hanazono University and was the founder of Chōzenji International Zen Dōjō (Training Center) in Honolulu, Hawaii. Like Inoue Nisshō, Ōmori claimed Buddhist enlightenment as his own, having had his initial enlightenment experience at age twenty-nine while still a lay disciple of another highly regarded Rinzai Zen master, Seki Seisetsu (1877–1945).

Yet, as will be detailed below, Ōmori was also an ultranationalist who, like Inoue, shared a close connection to Tōyama Mitsuru, the ultimate ultranationalist fixer.[2] At the same time, Ōmori personified what D. T. Suzuki, among others, held to be a Zen ideal—the "unity of Zen and the sword" (*Zenken ichinyo*). In fact, when in 1958 Ōmori published a book promoting this unity, Suzuki praised it, saying, "I was enthralled by Mr. Ōmori's *Zen to Ken* (*Zen and the Sword*). . . . With this, for the first time, we can speak of *Ken* and Zen as one."[3]

Ōmori began his practice of *kendō* (the way of the sword) at the age of fourteen or fifteen and subsequently trained under some of Japan's best-known masters, including Maeno Jisui (1870–1940), Oda Katsutarō, and Yamada Jirōkichi, fifteenth-generation head of the Jikishin Kage school of swordsmanship. Further, Sōgen studied calligraphy under Yokoyama Setsudo (1884–1966) of the Jubokudō school. In time, the two of them founded their own school of calligraphy known as the Hitsuzendō (Way of Brush and Zen).

Ōmori's connection to Zen was no less illustrious than his mastery of the above arts. He commenced his Zen training at age nineteen under Maeno Jisui, who, like so many teachers of swordsmanship, was also an experienced lay Zen practitioner in the Rinzai tradition. Ōmori explained why he took up Zen as follows:

> Honestly speaking, the reason I entered the Way of Zen from the Way of the Sword had nothing to do with any lofty ideals on my part. Instead, being short, I realized that I had no hope of standing up to opponents taller than me if I couldn't compensate for their physical advantage by acquiring superior spiritual power. In short, I entered the Way of Zen due to the fear experienced when sword fighting. I hoped to overcome this fear.[4]

Subsequently, in the late spring of 1925, Ōmori met Seki Seisetsu, head of the Tenryūji branch of the Rinzai Zen sect. Ōmori continued his training under this distinguished master for the next twenty years, until the latter's death in October 1945. It was in 1933, following eight years of intensive struggle with the *kōan* "*mu*," that Ōmori had his initial enlightenment experience. Ōmori related his "breakthrough" as follows: "I finished *zazen* and went to the toilet. I heard the sound of the urine hitting the back of the urinal. It splashed and sounded very loud to me. At that time, I thought, 'Aha!' and understood. I had a deep realization."[5]

Ōmori added that thanks to his breakthrough, he realized that he was at the center of absolute nothingness (*zettai-mu*) as well as at the center of the infinite circle. "To be at the center of the infinite circle in this human form," he claimed, "is to be BUDDHA himself."[6]

ŌMORI AS AN ULTRANATIONALIST

As an ultranationalist, Ōmori joined his first right-wing organization, the Kinki-kai (Imperial Flag Society), in May 1927 at age twenty-three. The Kinki-kai had just been formed for the purpose of pushing for the creation of a totally emperor-centric society. Among other things, this entailed the abolishment of political parties and the transfer of the nation's wealth, especially industrial wealth, from the private sector to the emperor for disposal as befits a "benevolent father."

The justification for restoring the nation's wealth to the emperor was described in the first tenet of the Kinki-kai as follows: "We believe that Japan is one sacred, indivisible body consisting of the emperor, our benevolent father and a living god, and we the masses, his loyal retainers and children."[7] At its peak, the Kinki-kai had some seven hundred members and published its own organ, *Japanese Thought* (*Nihon Shisō*).

Not content with mere membership in a right-wing organization, Ōmori helped found the Kinnō Ishin Dōmei (League for Loyalty to the Emperor and the Restoration) on February 11, 1932. Inasmuch as Ōmori served as the league's secretary-general, its three founding principles may rightly be seen as reflecting his thinking, at least at the time:

1. Taking the establishment of our nation as a matter of first importance, we march forward in a movement dedicated to making a prosperous country through the historic [Shōwa] Restoration (of total political power to the emperor).
2. We cry out for the nation's democratic financial machinery to be restored to the emperor as the second phase of the Meiji Restoration.
3. Restoring the spirit of the Taika Reforms [of 645 CE], we eagerly await the placing of all private production under the emperor's firm control as well as the completion of the Japanization of all aspects of the nation, including its politics, economy, culture, etc.[8]

Significantly, Ōmori did more than merely participate in, or found, emperor-centric organizations. Utilizing his prowess as a master swordsman, Ōmori was also willing to both support, and personally engage in, violence to achieve his political goals. This is most clearly demonstrated by his involvement in a July 1933 anti-government plot known as the Sacred Soldiers Incident (*Shinpeitai Jiken*).

SHINPEITAI INCIDENT

The aim of this attempted coup d'état was to bring about the oft-discussed Shōwa Restoration. In this version, the restoration was to be accomplished through the creation of a cabinet composed of members of the imperial family. Toward this end, a group of mostly civilians drawn from various right-wing organizations intended to assassinate the entire existing cabinet, the presidents of the two major political parties, the superintendent-general of the Metropolitan Police, and other leading politicians and financial magnates. Though none of the radical young officers in the army were directly involved, Navy Commander Yamaguchi Saburō was scheduled to bomb the cabinet from his plane.

The scale of this plot was unprecedented, as demonstrated by the subsequent police arrest of a total of ninety-five people armed with ninety-eight swords as well as some four hundred armbands to identify the participants. Interestingly, one of the arrested plot leaders was Maeda Torao. Readers will recall that in chapter 12 Inoue introduced Maeda as "one of my comrades" with whom he had worked in Manchuria. Although the fact that both Ōmori and Inoue shared a close connection to Maeda does not prove the former two men were linked in some way, it does suggest, at the very least, an affinity between them.

Be that at it may, the conspirators also prepared a large number of leaflets, some of which were to be scattered from Com. Yamaguchi's plane, to justify their actions. The leaflets contained three main principles, the third of which read, "The sacred soldiers will annihilate the financial magnates, political parties, and traitors surrounding the sovereign together with their watchdogs, who continue to block the development of the basic principles of our imperial state." This statement was followed by the following five slogans:

1. Establish politics by the emperor!
2. Establish an economy in accordance with the Imperial Way!
3. Long live the restoration of the Imperial Way!
4. Exterminate the communist movement!
5. Annihilate financial magnates and political parties![9]

As for the perpetrators, there should by rights have been ninety-six arrestees instead of ninety-five, together with one additional sword. Ōmori was the additional arrestee, but he successfully managed to avoid the police:

> The police were looking for me as one of the top leaders in the affair. I was on the list of people to arrest. I had to hide, so I left for Nagoya with only the kimono I was wearing and my short sword. In Nagoya I was caught in a police cordon and searched, but my sword was carefully hidden under my arm. The detective did not find it. . . . From then on, I went from place to place and hid.[10]

The fact that Ōmori had time, before being stopped by the police, to get as far away as Nagoya, more than three hundred kilometers to the southwest of Tokyo, reveals an important fact about his involvement in this incident. Namely, Ōmori had decided, albeit at the last minute, against participating in the plot and was therefore not present when the main body of conspirators was arrested. Ōmori explained what led him to drop out as follows: "One of the leaders of this incident, Mr. Suzuki [Zen'ichi], asked me to join them. But after listening to what he said, there were several points I could not agree with. One of their targets was General Araki [Sadao], a man whom I respected."[11]

General Araki was then minister of war, a position he held in two successive cabinets, beginning in December 1931. Ōmori objected to killing Araki because, together with Gen. Mazaki Jinsaburō, he was regarded as the leader of the Imperial Way Faction in the military. Araki was highly respected by the young officers for the premium he placed on military spirit as expressed in the *Bushidō* code. He was also responsible for the Japanese military's redesignation as the "imperial (or emperor's) military" (*Kōgun*).

Nevertheless, Araki's performance since assuming the position of minister of war was, from the point of view of Japan's ultranationalists, far from satisfactory. The civilian-dominated governments of which Araki was a part consistently blocked his moves to significantly increase military expenditures, let alone put into effect the political and economic reforms required of a Shōwa Restoration. The dissatisfaction with Araki's lack of effectiveness reached the point that the leadership of the Sacred Soldiers was ready to kill him together with the other despised civilian cabinet members. Ōmori, on the other hand, perhaps because of his close ties to members of the Young Officers' Movement, viewed Araki's assassination as unwarranted.

Japanese historian Hori Yukio reports that an additional factor influencing Ōmori was his belief that "the time was not yet ripe."[12] This may account for Ōmori's own statement that he found himself in disagreement with "several points" of the plot. Here too, Ōmori's opinion may have been influenced by supporters of the Young Officers' Movement, specifically his close friend Nishida Mitsugi (1901–1937), a former military officer. In the fall of 1933, Nishida is known to have counseled patience to a different group of plotters composed of young officers, noncommissioned officers, soldiers, and civilians. In Nishida's opinion, the timing for such an uprising was "premature."[13]

Whatever its causes, Ōmori's decision to drop out of the plot at the last minute was clearly fortuitous, for otherwise he would have been arrested alongside his fellow conspirators. Yet it must not be forgotten that Ōmori, literally sword in hand, had been prepared to take part in a terrorist act comprising the mass assassination of at least the civilian members of the cabinet, plus many other political and financial leaders, with no apparent objection to the murderous nature of their task. As previously noted, Japan's civilian politicians, primarily because of their power over the budget, were still able to exercise a degree of control over the military. It was exactly for that reason, together with their ongoing support of the capitalist status quo, that they had to be eliminated.

In short, while Ōmori may have disagreed with his fellow conspirators over tactics, he had no quarrel with them over ultimate goals or the use of violence to achieve those goals. As a master swordsman, Ōmori was fully prepared to wield his sword in his self-appointed role as judge, jury, and executioner of those whom he saw as preventing the implementation of his political ideals. Neither should it be forgotten that this incident occurred in the same year that Ōmori had his first enlightenment experience. That is to say, it occurred in the year he realized, "To be at the center of an infinite circle in this human form is to be BUDDHA himself."

JIKISHIN DŌJŌ

Despite having narrowly avoided arrest, Ōmori quickly resumed his right-wing activities. On January 1, 1934, Ōmori opened the Jikishin Dōjō (lit., "Direct Mind" Training Hall) in the Koishikawa district of Tokyo. The *dōjō* was created with the support of a number of right-wing activists aligned with the Imperial Way Faction, especially the Young Officers' Movement, and included such men as Nishida Mitsugi, Kobayashi Junichirō (1880–1963), and yet another former officer, Shibukawa Zensuke (1905–1936). In the role of *dōjō* "advisor" was Tōyama Ryūsuke, the sickly eldest son of Tōyama Mitsuru.

Appropriately, Ōmori headed the new *dōjō*, appropriately that is, because the *dōjō* incorporated all of his skills and interests. Namely, under one roof it became possible to practice Zen, *kendō*, *jūdō*, and calligraphy, all in preparation for the realization of the Shōwa Restoration. Given the nature of its program, it is not surprising that right-wing historian Arahara Bokusui described the *dōjō* as "giving the impression of having been the inner citadel of the Imperial Way Faction among all the patriotic organizations of the day."[14] This impression was given concrete expression in the *dōjō*'s founding statement:

> Based on our respect for the Founder of the Empire [i.e., mythical Emperor Jimmu], we reverently seek to promote the prosperity of our glorious imperial throne by respectfully revealing the fundamentals of statesmanship and investigating through our own persons the essentials of governance. The spread of the emperor's work is the national policy of Japan, while the mission of the people is to assist in this endeavor. It is for this reason that we have taken it upon ourselves, first of all, to aid each other in cultivating divine justice. Therefore, we have established the Jikishin Dōjō in order to resolutely promote the true practice of the Way of the warrior.
>
> We pray that by hiding nothing, we will encounter excellence; by exerting ourselves to the utmost, we will foster our talents; and by pointing directly at the source of the mind received from our ancestors, we will encounter our divine, immortal native spirit. Furthermore, we have made the reverent accomplishment of the [Shōwa] Restoration a pledge of steel in which mundane, personal interests have no place.[15]

An ordinary day at the *dōjō* began with wake-up at 6 a.m., followed by cleaning and then approximately forty-five minutes of *zazen*, the time required for one stick of incense to be consumed. This in turn was followed by a morning worship service consisting of the recitation of Shinto prayers (not Buddhist sutras) before the hall's main altar, on which was enshrined a large tablet of the Sun goddess, mythical progenitor of the emperor. To the left of the main altar were three rows of photographs of Japan's greatest military heroes and right-wing civilian leaders. To the right was an alcove in which, together with a flower arrangement and traditional Japanese swords, was hung a large scroll reading, "Enemy Countr[ies] Surrender!" (*Tekikoku Kōfuku*).

From 4 to 6 p.m. every afternoon, there was martial arts practice. *Jūdō* was taught on Monday, Wednesday, and Friday, while *kendō* was on Tuesday, Thursday, and Saturday. Thursday afternoon was reserved for study circles, while calligraphy was practiced on Sunday afternoon. In addition, from the fifteenth of every month there was a five-day period of intensive Zen meditation (i.e., *sesshin*), commencing at 4 a.m. and lasting until 10 p.m. each day. The purpose of the *sesshin* was described as "the realization of our great pledge [to achieve the Shōwa Restoration] by acquiring an indestructible and adamantine body of indomitable resolve through introspection and Zen practice."[16] Further, in justifying this rigorous training schedule, Ōmori wrote, "In *Bushidō*, as a traditional Way transmitted from ancient times, a person throws his mind and body into *Bushidō*. Forgetting himself and becoming one with the Way, he completely transforms the small self into the Way of the warrior. He then lives the Great Life."[17] For *dōjō* students, the "Great Life" clearly entailed a great deal of right-wing political activism, activism that would eventually bring imprisonment or death to many of its participants. Initially, however, the *dōjō's* political activism took the form of publishing right-wing organs, the first of which was a monthly magazine entitled *Essence* (*Kakushin*). The initial issue was published on September 18, 1934, with the lead article titled "Destroy the False and Establish the True—Risk Your Life in Spreading the Dharma—the Great Essence of the Shōwa Restoration." The article contained the following call to action:

> The [Shōwa] Restoration is a holy war to destroy the false and establish the True [Buddha Dharma] and applies equally to [Japan's] domestic and foreign affairs. The *Essentials of Combat* [*Sentō Kōyō*] states: "The essence of victory lies in integrating various combat elements, both material and immaterial, so as to concentrate and give full play to power superior to that of your enemy at a strategic point."
>
> In this instance, "various combat elements, both material and immaterial" refer to the unity in speech and action of all military and civilians involved in the Restoration Movement and other patriotic activities. The "enemy" refers to the enemy amongst us, that is to say, today's ruling powers who, with the backing of various financial cliques and elder statesmen, command the services of bureaucrats, big and small, as well as the police. The basis of power superior to this enemy is the force of all those dedicated to destroying the false and establishing the True. This force is to be found in the great unity of the people's forces composed of the civilians and military of this imperial land. . . .
>
> As a practical matter, we recognize that the Restoration can only be put into effect through the realization of a new cabinet of national unity centered on a unified army and navy. We must therefore support and promote the army and navy as the main force backing the Restoration while reverently seeking the promulgation of an imperial order that will promptly disperse the black clouds engulfing us. This is the proper duty of all citizens who cooperate with, and support, imperial policy.
>
> Duty is heavier than mountains while death is lighter than feathers. Given this, how is it possible that the epoch-making, great undertaking [of the Shōwa Restoration] can be accomplished without the valiant, dedicated spread of the Dharma at the risk of your life?[18]

The Buddhist influence on this article is as unmistakable as its political extremism. In addition to the call for the "dedicated spread of the Dharma," the phrase "destroy[ing] the false and establish[ing] the True" first appeared in a famous Chinese Buddhist treatise entitled *San-lun-hsüan-i* written by the Sui Dynasty priest Chi-ts'ang (643–712). It forms one of the fundamental tenets of the San-lun (Three Treatises; J., *Sanron*) school of Buddhism based on the Madhyamika philosophy of Nāgārjuna. However, the "destruction" called for in this school originally had nothing to do with taking the lives of other sentient beings. Instead, it referred to "destroying" the *mind of attachment*, such "destruction" being in and of itself the establishment of the True [Dharma].

Needless to say, doctrinal subtleties of this nature were of no interest to Ōmori and his associates, for they sought to employ Buddhism as a means of bolstering their claim that the movement for a Shōwa Restoration was part of a "holy war." Not only that, by calling on their readers to risk their lives on behalf of the restoration, the article's unspoken assumption was that killing the "enemy amongst us" was a necessary part of the process. This last point was not lost on police censors, who impounded the magazine's first issue only two days after its publication.

CONNECTION TO AIZAWA SABURŌ

Despite ongoing police interference, the *dōjō* added a second magazine, *Imperial Spirit* (*Kōki*), to its list of publications and then, on November 23, 1935, established a monthly newspaper, *Great Essence* (*Taiganmoku*). As Arahara noted, "Under the guidance of Nishida Mitsugi and other Young Officers, and using their sharp editorial style, this newspaper made propaganda for the Pure Japanism Movement."[19] Unsurprisingly, this newspaper also strongly supported Lt. Col. Aizawa, introduced in appendix 1, who was then awaiting court-martial for the assassination of Gen. Nagata in August 1935. Although Aizawa was not directly associated with the *dōjō*, his "direct action" against a man seen as the leader of the despised Control Faction was eagerly embraced as a further step on the road to the Shōwa Restoration. Israeli historian Ben-Ami Shillony describes the *dōjō*'s role at this time as follows:

> The ex-military activists of the Young Officers' Movement, Nishida Mitsugi, Shibukawa Zensuke, Muranaka Kōji, and Isobe Asaichi, became the "brain trust" of Aizawa's defense, trying hard to make the most of it for their cause. They founded a special organization, the *Jikishin Dōjō* (Sincere Spirit Seminary), for propagating "the ideals of Aizawa" and wrote articles in Nishida's *Taiganmoko*, which hailed the defendant as a forerunner of the Shōwa Restoration.[20]

On the one hand, it must be pointed out that Shillony's description contains two errors, the first being his claim that the Jikishin Dōjō was founded specifically to support Aizawa. In fact, the *dōjō* had been in existence for more than a year and a half prior to Nagata's assassination. Secondly, while it is theoretically possible to translate the *dōjō*'s name as "Sincere Spirit Seminary," this translation misses the traditional Zen meaning of the title, fully expressed in Sino-Japanese as "pointing direct(ly) at the human mind, seeing one's nature, [and] becoming Buddha" (*jikishi ninshin, kenshō jōbutsu*). No doubt, Shillony, like so many historians of modern Japan, was simply unaware of the Buddhist, especially Zen, background to terms like these.

Nevertheless, Shillony is quite correct in identifying the *dōjō* as being at the heart of the movement seeking to create popular support for Aizawa and his "ideals." This is hardly surprising since not only did these men share a similar political agenda, but they were personal friends as well. For example, Aizawa had stayed at Nishida Mitsugi's house the night before he assassinated Gen. Nagata. The morning of the attack, Nishida told Muranaka and Isobe, "Aizawa stayed with me last night after arriving in Tokyo from Fukuyama. This morning he said he was going to the Ministry of War to see Nagata. Knowing what kind of person Aizawa is, I think he may do something."[21]

The *dōjō* published a number of leaflets on Aizawa's behalf, some anonymously, in which the Zen emphasis on "transcendence" played an important role. One of these leaflets described Aizawa's actions as stemming from his desire to "clarify the national polity, cleanse the military, and bring about the [Shōwa] Restoration revolution." The leaflet also identified ongoing support for capitalism and the rule of law as two of the elements then present in Japan that were "opposed to the national polity" and thus had to be eliminated. Significantly, the "rule of law" was held to be synonymous with "individualism and liberalism" (*kojinshugi-jiyūshugi*), both of which were regarded in right-wing circles as "un-Japanese" imports from the West.[22]

The strong attack on the rule of law is also unsurprising in that a successful Shōwa Restoration would have meant the end of any semblance of the rule of law, at least as contained in the Meiji Constitution of 1889. Thus, all political parties were to be dissolved and, accordingly, policy debate would become not only unnecessary but a sign of disloyalty. Instead, the emperor, aided by his (mostly military) advisors, would rule directly as the "benevolent father" he was held to be. While it can be argued that there was an element of government "for the people" in the proposed Shōwa Restoration, there was not the slightest hint of a government "of the people," let alone "by the people."

More to the point, in Aizawa's case, the rule of law had to be ended if he were to escape the death penalty, for in killing a superior officer he was clearly guilty of committing a capital offense. Thus, the same leaflet contained the following demand: "The fate of those parties who, having transcended the law, have sacrificed themselves for the Restoration that also transcends the law, must itself transcend the law."[23]

FEBRUARY 26, 1936, INCIDENT

As noted above, one of the *dōjō*'s demands, that Aizawa's court-martial be open to the public, was successful, and the first hearing was held on January 28, 1936. Yet by this time Aizawa's trial was no longer the main focus of the *dōjō*'s activities. Rather, the time for large-scale action had come at last, and on the evening of the trial's opening, *dōjō* activists Isobe Asaichi and Muranaka Kōji met with their active military counterparts to plan what would become the largest military insurrection in modern Japanese history—the Young Officers' Uprising of February 26, 1936. Although Nishida Mitsugi initially felt that the time was still not ripe, he was eventually won over, and all of the *dōjō*'s activists devoted themselves to the uprising's success.

Just how important the role played by these activists was is revealed by the fact that the uprising was planned by only five men, three ex-military civilians and two officers. All three civilians, Nishida, Isobe, and Muranaka, were also key figures in the Jikishin Dōjō.[24] Further, Isobe and Muranaka were two of the three members of the committee that drew up the political demands to be submitted to the minister of war once the uprising was underway. At a more practical level, Shibukawa Zensuke and his wife spent the night of February 23 at a Japanese inn located in Yugawara, Kanagawa prefecture, to observe the movements of Lord Keeper of the Privy Seal Count Makino Nobuaki (1863–1949), one of the "evil advisors" surrounding the throne slated for assassination.

What Ōmori's exact role was in all this is unknown. It may well have been limited inasmuch as the uprising's leaders made a conscious decision to exclude civilians, at least those who were not former military officers, from the initial phase of operations. Shillony suggests this decision was made because "civilian terrorists were held in lower public esteem than military officers and their involvement could impair the heroic image that the rebels wished to create."[25] As for Ōmori himself, he later admitted that "during the February 26 Incident, the persons involved in the incident had come to me for advice." Yet he also claimed, "I said, 'Now is not the time. You must wait a little longer,' and opposed the action."[26] Once again, we find Ōmori opposed to the *timing* for terrorist assassinations, not their use.

Ōmori's associates, however, had no such reservations. For example, Isobe and Muranaka once again donned their military uniforms to help lead the insurrection. In addition, on the uprising's first day, Nishida, Shibukawa and other civilians gathered at the home of another and much better known Buddhist supporter of the Young Officers, Kita Ikki. Kita was better known because, inspired by the teachings of the *Lotus Sūtra*, he was one of the chief ideologues to whom the Young Officers turned for guidance concerning the nature of an emperor-centric, yet national socialist–oriented, Shōwa Restoration.

During the four days of the insurrection, the civilian supporters used Kita's house as a liaison center between the twenty-one rebel officers and the more than 1,400 men they commanded. These supporters provided the rebels with encouragement and advice as well as information from the outside world. They also published three issues of a *Shōwa Restoration Bulletin* (*Shōwa Ishin Jōhō*), in which they appealed to the people of Japan to join them and to sympathetic officers stationed outside of Tokyo to commit their units in support of the "glorious uprising in the capital."[27] Before any of these things could occur, however, the insurrection was bloodlessly suppressed, apart from two officer suicides, on February 29.

As previously discussed, the insurrection collapsed for one key reason. Despite support for its goals from Imperial Way Faction generals like Araki Sadao, and especially Mazaki Jinzaburō, Emperor Hirohito was dead set against it from the outset. Awakened in the early morning of February 26 and informed of what had taken place, Hirohito told his chief aide-de-camp, "They have killed my advisors and are now trying to pull a silk rope around my neck. . . . I shall never forgive them, no matter what their motives are."[28] By a "silk rope" the emperor acknowledged that the insurrection was taking place in his name, but that, if successful, he would become hostage to the leaders of the Imperial Way Faction and their national socialist reform agenda.

Shortly after the insurrection's collapse, Hirohito insisted on special courts-martial to try those involved. In the end, a total of thirteen officers, together with *dōjō* activists Isobe, Muranaka, Shibukawa, and Nishida, and including civilian Kita Ikki, faced a military firing squad. As American historian Herbert Bix notes, it was Hirohito's resolute decisiveness that "abruptly ended the period in which alienated 'young officers' had tried to use him as a principle of reform to undermine a power structure they could not successfully manipulate."[29]

As for Ōmori, this time he was unable to avoid arrest and, together with four additional hall members, was held at the Otsuka Police Station on suspicion of having fanned the insurrection. Ōmori described one of his interrogation sessions as follows:

> The prosecuting attorney said that I had agitated the emperor's army. I asked, "Do you really think that an ordinary citizen like myself could agitate the soldiers of the emperor? If you think that, you are really showing contempt for the army." When I said that, the prosecuting attorney began to tremble.
>
> I continued, "During the February 26 Incident, you called them (those who participated in the Incident) revolutionary soldiers, in other words, you were calling them the enemy. If that is so, according to military law, in the event that the general staff office is occupied by enemy forces, even if just temporarily, the person in charge must be punished. Was the commander-in-chief, Naninnomiya [an aristocrat], punished? If he has not yet been punished, he should be punished before me."
>
> When I said that, the prosecutor's face turned blue.[30]

Unbowed, Ōmori was finally released after two months in detention, the police having been unable to amass sufficient evidence to convict him of any offense. By this time, however, the trials of both the military and civilian rebels had begun. Given that all the military court hearings related to these cases were now closed to the public, there was a strong likelihood that the accused would be sentenced to death. Furthermore, because martial law was still in effect, including strict censorship provisions, direct appeals to the public on behalf of men whom the emperor himself had condemned as "mutineers" (*bōto*) were out of the question. This, however, did not stop Ōmori from trying.

Specifically, Ōmori and two of his students from the *dōjō*, Kuroda Sueo and Kaneko Nobuo, got their hands on a number of memoranda written by Isobe Asaichi that had been smuggled out of prison by his wife when she visited him. One read in part, "Appeal to the patriots of Japan. Help us destroy the members of the military clique in power [i.e., the Control Faction] which is the enemy of the true Restoration. . . . Annihilate them in order that the Restoration may be realized. I shall fight to the end!"[31]

Ōmori and his students proceeded to mimeograph these memoranda and mail copies throughout Japan. Not content with this, they hit on a unique method of distributing them to the larger public. According to a postwar Allied intelligence report titled "The Brocade Banner," Ōmori and Kuroda "distributed the appeals like Gideon

Bibles in the toilet compartments of the Tōkaidō Line trains."[32] Given his earlier spiritual "breakthrough" in a urinal, it is almost comical to picture Ōmori making his way from one toilet compartment to the next armed with nothing more than leaflets.

The police, however, were not amused by Ōmori and Kuroda's activities. Eventually both of them were arrested together with fifty-eight other rightists who had engaged in similar acts. They were convicted and sentenced to prison, where Ōmori remained for one year before being placed on probation for three years. Later, in 1940, he received a full pardon. Like Inoue, Ōmori found his time in prison quite beneficial, both mentally and spiritually: "A solitary cell in a prison is a great convenience. Everything can be done in one room: the toilet is there; you can eat there; you can even study there. While I was there, I didn't think that I should read all the time, so during the day I read books, and at night I did *zazen*."[33]

Ōmori was later gratified to find that his Rinzai Zen master, Seki Seisetsu, approved of his conduct.[34] On the day of his release from prison, Seisetsu visited Ōmori at the *dōjō* and said, "You had a long *sesshin* [intensive meditation period]. You had much hardship, but you did well."[35] Seisetsu then took his disciple out to dinner. Ōmori summed up his prison experience as follows: "Since there is no other place where one can study so leisurely, everyone should do the right thing and get into prison."[36] In light of Ōmori's actions up to that point, one can only express surprise that he hadn't succeeded in "do[ing] the right thing" earlier.

WAR YEARS

Not long after his release from prison, Ōmori resumed his right-wing activities although what had previously been "right wing" was now official government policy. Thus, Ōmori became a loyal supporter of Japan's military actions in China and throughout Asia. In August 1940, he helped found the Youth League for the Construction of the [Imperial Rule] Assistance Structure (Yokusan Taisei Kensetsu Seinen Renmei). When the participants in this group couldn't agree on a common agenda, Ōmori left to form yet another new organization, the Japanism Youth Council (Nipponshugi Seinen Kaigi), established in September 1940. Finally, in July 1944, Ōmori took up an administrative position in the [Imperial Rule] Assistance Manhood Group (Yokusan Sōnen Dan).

This last organization was a service group of the Imperial Rule Assistance Association (IRAA), a government-sponsored mass organization modeled on the Nazi Party that had been established in October 1940. Like its Nazi counterpart, its purpose was to replace all political parties and factions and create one united, war-affirming body, based on the slogan "100 million [subjects of] one mind" (*ichi-oku isshin*). However, as noted in "The Brocade Banner," the IRAA and its supporting organizations were beset from the outset with internal policy and organizational differences, not to mention petty personal jealousies, all of which combined to reduce their effectiveness in rousing and sustaining the people, especially after it became clear that

Japan was losing the war. Nevertheless, they did succeed in "regimenting and herding the populace behind the war effort" even if the old struggles for power remained as active as ever.[37] Whatever reservations he may have had, there can be no doubt that Ōmori was an integral part of this effort.

A KONOE CONNECTION

In mid-1940 Ōmori made direct contact with Prime Minister Konoe Fumimarō, then in the midst of forming his second cabinet. Ōmori repeatedly pleaded with him to choose either General Ugaki Kazushige or Mazaki Jinzaburō as his new minister of war. Konoe, however, refused Ōmori's advice and eventually stopped inviting him to his advisors' meetings. For Ōmori, his failure to sway Konoe became a source of lifelong regret. As he later wrote, "I should not have given up. I should have persevered and even used intimidation if necessary."[38] Whether Ōmori was acquainted with Inoue at this time is unknown.

Ōmori further claimed that his plea to Konoe had been motivated by his earnest desire "to prevent the war."[39] Inasmuch as Japan had already been engaged in full-scale warfare with China since July 1937, it is reasonable to assume that what Ōmori meant was preventing war with the United States. This is in accord with the Imperial Way Faction's unwavering belief that Japan's primary enemy was Russia and its communist ideology. Additionally, Ōmori may genuinely have wanted to prevent an attack on a powerful country like the United States. In this, Ōmori appears to have shared a common viewpoint with Inoue.

However, even had Ōmori been successful, this would have done nothing to save the colonized peoples of Taiwan, Korea, and Manchuria, for Generals Ugaki and Mazaki's careers reveal that they were as dedicated to the maintenance and, if possible, expansion of the Japanese Empire as any of Japan's other military leaders. Ugaki, for example, had willingly accepted appointment as governor-general of Korea in 1931.[40] Further, neither Ōmori's writings nor those of the many right-wing organizations of which he was a part contain the slightest hint of opposition to Japanese imperialism. For geographical, historical, and ideological reasons, Russia, not the United States, was seen as the chief threat to the maintenance and expansion of the Japanese Empire. Thus, Ōmori's effort "to prevent the war" was in reality an effort to prevent war *with the wrong enemy*.

Significantly, even Ōmori's postwar disciples admit that their master had a change of heart once Japan launched its attack on the United States. Hosokawa Dōgen, one of Ōmori's Dharma successors and later abbot of Hawaii's Chōzenji, notes that Ōmori was determined to see the war through to the end. "Winning or losing was not the point. He [Ōmori] felt that something that had been started should be carried through to the end," Dōgen wrote.[41] In light of the many millions of lives lost in seeing the war "through to the end," this must surely be one of the inanest justifications for the mass slaughter of human beings ever written.

Ōmori's total commitment to Japan's war effort is further demonstrated by his attempt to preempt the emperor's pre-recorded radio broadcast scheduled for noon on August 15, 1945. "Since I wanted to resist till the end," Ōmori stated, "I was going to obstruct the emperor's broadcast [in which he would announce Japan's surrender]. For that reason, I often went to the Imperial Headquarters to incite the soldiers."[42] Needless to say, Ōmori would have had to be very well connected indeed to even know that such an unprecedented broadcast was planned.[43]

Had Ōmori and others like him succeeded in preventing Japan's surrender, an Allied invasion of Japan would have been inevitable. An almost unimaginable carnage would have resulted, especially for those millions of Japanese civilian men and women of all ages required to fight the Allied invaders armed with the only weapons remaining—awls and sharpened bamboo spears. But that was of no concern to Ōmori, for whether one was trying to prevent a war or fight it, he claimed that "if one trains in Zen, one must do everything thoroughly and completely."[44]

IN THE POSTWAR ERA

During the war years, Ōmori had primarily supported himself and his family as a civilian instructor of swordsmanship. The year 1945, however, dealt a double blow to Ōmori, for not only did Japan lose the war but his own Zen master, Seki Seisetsu, passed away. These events, especially Japan's surrender, became the catalyst for Ōmori's decision to formally enter the Rinzai Zen priesthood. "The first half of my life ended when Japan lost the war," he explained, "[so] according to the samurai code, I became a Buddhist priest."[45]

Seki was succeeded by his chief disciple, Seki Bokuo (1903–1991). In 1946, Ōmori, at age forty-two, entered the priesthood as Bokuo's disciple. In little more than two years, he completed the *kōan* training he had started as a layman and received *inka-shōmei*, a certificate attesting to his full enlightenment in the Rinzai Zen sect. Bokuo then directed Ōmori to become the abbot of Kōho-in, a small temple located in Tokyo's Higashi-Nakano district.

Kōho-in might be called the perfect temple for someone like Ōmori, for though it had been founded as recently as 1943 it was built on land where Yamaoka Tesshū (1836–1888) once lived. Yamaoka was not only one of the Meiji period's best-known practitioners of swordsmanship, calligraphy, and Zen, but he contributed to the relatively bloodless transition from the Tokugawa Shogunate to the new Meiji government. Thus, what Kōho-in lacked in terms of institutional history was made up for by the character and accomplishments of the man who had lived in its precincts. In Ōmori's eyes, Yamaoka was the "very model of a Japanese."[46]

Life at postwar Kōho-in, however, was far from easy, for, like Inoue's temple in Ōarai, as a new temple it lacked traditional parishioners to support it. Thus, Ōmori was forced to turn elsewhere for his primary source of income and eventually became a civil magistrate in Tokyo, serving in this position for some twenty years. He did, however, find time to write, and as mentioned above, it was through his books that he became acquainted with D. T. Suzuki. Suzuki thought so highly of Ōmori that when he was asked by a high government official to recommend a Zen teacher for then Crown Prince Akihito (later Emperor Heisei), Suzuki reportedly said, "Mr. Ōmori would be the best."[47]

In 1970 Ōmori became a professor at Hanazono University in Kyoto, where he taught a course titled "The Practice of Zen." The core of the course was the practice of *zazen* coupled with lectures on such Zen classics as the *Hekigan-roku* (*Blue Cliff Record*) and the *Roankyō* (*Donkey-Saddle Bridge*). He went on to serve as the university's president from 1978 to 1982. During these years, he led a Wednesday evening *zazen* club that was started on behalf of the members of the university's *kendō* club but grew in popularity to take in members of other martial arts clubs, the all-male pep squad, and the general public.

It was also during these years that Ōmori commenced a series of visits to the West, most especially Hawaii, initially at the invitation of the Japanese-American Rinzai Zen master Tanoue Tenshin (1938–2003). In 1972, this led to the establishment of Chōzenji, International Zen Dōjō, in Honolulu as "a place of Zen training where persons of any race, creed, or religion who are determined to live in accordance with Buddha Nature (the Inner Self or the Way) may fulfill this need through intensive endeavor."[48] In Japan, Ōmori founded Seitaiji, a Zen training center for both clerics and lay people, in 1975.

Until suffering a debilitating stroke in December 1988, Ōmori carried on a busy schedule of lecturing, Zen instruction, and martial arts demonstrations that seldom saw him at his primary residence in Kōho-in for more than a few days at a time. Prior to his stroke, in August 1979, he visited Europe as part of a spiritual exchange titled "The Fount of East–West Culture." This visit was made possible by the well-known authority on Japan Trevor Leggett of the BBC and Father Kadowaki, a Catholic priest who had practiced Zen under Ōmori's guidance. Had he not fallen ill during the tour, Ōmori would have had an audience with the pope.

In October 1979 Ōmori elevated Chōzenji, now located on two and a half acres of land in Hawaii's Kalihi Valley, to the position of a *Daihonzan* (great main temple), thereby creating a new line of Zen with Tanoue Tenshin as its head. Ever faithful to his belief in the unity of Zen and the sword, Ōmori included the following paragraph in the canon for Chōzenji: "Zen without the accompanying physical experience is nothing but empty discussion. Martial ways without truly realizing the 'Mind' is nothing but beastly behavior. We agree to undertake all of this as the essence of our training."[49] After six years of laying bedridden at Kōho-in, Ōmori died on the afternoon of August 18, 1994.

POSTWAR RIGHT-WING ACTIVISM

Ōmori's distinguished postwar Zen career by no means signaled the end of his career as a right-wing activist. This is because when Japan finally surrendered on August 15, 1945, Ōmori's first impulse had been to commit suicide. Surprisingly for someone schooled in *Bushidō*, Ōmori had no intention of using a sword to slowly and painfully disembowel himself in the traditional manner (i.e., commit *seppuku*). Instead, "I had decided to kill myself instantly with a pistol," he explained.[50] However, early on the morning of the appointed day, his old calligraphy teacher, Yokoyama Setsudo, dropped by the *dōjō*, now relocated in Tokyo's Setagaya district. Yokoyama also intended to kill himself because in his opinion, "These days all Japanese have become hopeless cowards." Yet Yokoyama subsequently had a change of heart and, after waking Ōmori, said, "The reason we lost the war is because there was some weak point. . . . It won't be too late to die after we completely investigate the reason." Ōmori replied, "I agreed right away, but if he hadn't come, I would have committed *seppuku*."[51]

As previously noted, Ōmori stated that after Japan's defeat he had decided to enter the Rinzai Zen priesthood "according to the samurai code." What he neglected to mention, however, was that as a practical matter, apart from suicide, he had very few other options. In the first place this was because his prominent role in Japan's ultranationalist movement brought him to the attention of the Allied occupation authorities. While the Allies did not indict him as a war criminal, they did, as with Inoue, include his name on a list of persons purged from public life, including employment even as a schoolteacher. In addition, as the practice of the martial arts was also proscribed, Ōmori's career as an instructor came to an abrupt end. Practically speaking, the Zen priesthood was one of the few remaining positions open to someone with his interests.

Priestly status, however, had no influence on Ōmori's right-wing activism. Thus, on April 1, 1952, four weeks prior to the formal end of the Allied occupation, Ōmori held a meeting with ten other former right-wing leaders to discuss rebuilding the right in a soon-to-be-independent Japan. Subsequently, this group met regularly for about a year under the name of the East Wind Society (Tōfū-kai). Ōmori and his associates felt that in its weakened state the right could only influence events if it spoke with a united voice.

With the goal of creating a united right, Ōmori became one of the founders, and first committee chairman, of the Kantō District Council of the [Shōwa] Restoration Movement (Ishin Undō Kantō Kyōgi-kai), founded in July 1953. Similar to the prewar years, the goals of this new umbrella organization included the creation of an "ethnic state" (*minzoku kokka*), the ousting of the Communist Party and its allies, and the purging of corrupt political parties, financial magnates, and government bureaucrats.

Despite Ōmori's best efforts, the prewar internal rivalries soon reappeared, and by May 1954 it became necessary to create yet another umbrella organization fostering right-wing unity—the General Federation of Citizens for the Salvation of the Nation (Kyūkoku Kokumin Sōrengō). Once again, Ōmori served as the committee chairman of this group. Nevertheless, by December 1956, so many of the constituent right-wing organizations in the federation had dropped out that a further name change became necessary. The end result was simply called the General Federation of Citizens (Kokumin Sōrengō).

Never one to give up, in January 1958, Ōmori became a permanent director of the New Japan Council (Shin-Nippon Kyōgi-kai). As its name suggests, this was the most mainstream of the many right-wing organizations of which Ōmori had been a part. In fact, it has been described as a "vehicle for the unification of the right wing with Japan's financial circles and the Liberal Democratic Party (LDP)."[52] The LDP, of course, is the conservative (and corruption-prone) political party that has ruled Japan on an almost uninterrupted basis from the end of the Asia-Pacific War to today.

On the one hand, Ōmori was now aligned with men like Takasugi Shin-ichi (1892–1978), chairman of the board of directors of Mitsubishi Electric Company and council finance chairperson. On the other hand, Ōmori's longstanding anticommunism was reflected by the following tenet of the council's charter: "This council will endeavor to expel communism, defeatism, and all plots by foreign countries that threaten the peace and freedom of our citizens."[53] In this context, the council was particularly critical of the left-leaning Japan Teachers' Union (Nikkyōsō) and demanded that education be "normalized" (*seijō-ka*) in accord with what it called the "proper ethics for teachers."[54]

In addition, the council demanded that Japan's postwar "peace" constitution be revised in order that Japan might once again maintain a full-fledged military. This was coupled with a demand for the maintenance of the Japan–United States Mutual Security Treaty that came up for renewal in the face of strong left-wing opposition in 1960 and again in 1970. In the face of this opposition, the council also called for the establishment of a law to "preserve public peace and order," thereby enhancing the power of police to control antitreaty demonstrations. As Hori Yukio commented, "In the final analysis, the council became the mouthpiece for the ideology of [Japan's] political and financial circles who sought to steer Japan to the right by creating a sense of crisis."[55]

This is not to say that Ōmori cut himself off from his ultranationalist roots altogether, for in October 1961 he became a director of the postwar version of the infamous (and deadly) Black Dragon Society, now renamed as the Black Dragon Club (Kokuryū Kurabu). As readers will recall, the original Black Dragon Society had been created in 1901 to block Russian penetration into the Far East on the one hand and promote Japanese advancement onto the Asian continent, especially Manchuria, on the other. The postwar Black Dragon Club sought to "succeed to the spirit of the [prewar] Black Dragon Society and promote the [Shōwa] Restoration." It also aimed at "comforting and exalting the spirits of the society's former members."[56] Although the club never attracted more than 150 members, Ōmori no doubt felt more at home there than he did in the New Japan Council, where he sat alongside the corruption-prone politicians and financial magnates he had so long opposed.

Finally, Ōmori is the only Zen master to have a fifteen-line entry in the 1991 Japanese publication *Dictionary of the Right Wing* (*Uha Jiten*), including the notation that he eventually became president of the Rinzai Zen–affiliated Hanazono University. While at first glance this appears unconnected to Ōmori's right-wing activism, in reality it was not, for it had been Ōmori's right-wing reputation that brought him to the university in the first place. In 1970, left-wing student activism was on the rise throughout Japan, centered on opposition to the extension of the Japan–United States Mutual Security Treaty and a demand for an increased student voice in campus affairs. Hosokawa Dōgen describes the circumstances under which Ōmori was asked to teach at Hanazono University as follows: "During this time [1970] there was unrest at universities all over Japan. Hanazono University was no exception. Along with Ritsumeikan University, it was a well-known base for the students in the Japanese Red Army. Within the university there was strife. . . . As a result, [Ōmori] Roshi became a professor at that university."[57]

Although he had dropped out of university as a youth, who better than Ōmori to suppress left-wing student activism. Ōmori could not, of course, accomplish this task on his own, so he reached out to a group of students he knew from past experience would readily support him, that is, martial arts students. Even today martial arts students at Japan's universities regard themselves as the embodiment of the wartime "Spirit of Japan" (*Yamato-damashii*) and are decidedly right wing in their political orientation. Ōmori therefore began a weekly *zazen* club, initially for members of the *kendō* club but then expanded to include the karate and *kenpō* clubs as well as the all-male pep club. Since these students were more than willing to use their martial arts skills to intimidate left-wing students, it did not take long for university "strife" to end.

With the strong backing of these right-wing students, Ōmori the university dropout became Ōmori the university president in 1978. It would appear Ōmori had learned something from his earlier failure to intimidate Prime Minister Konoe after all. Nevertheless, it must not be forgotten that from the 1920s onward Ōmori had been an active participant in the ultraright's agenda to eliminate parliamentary democracy through terrorist assassinations at home while promoting Japan's imperialist aims abroad. Like Inoue, Ōmori was a man willing to kill all who stood in the way of his political agenda, even while claiming the enlightenment of the Buddha as his own.

Appendix 3

Historical Background Materials

SELECTED MAJOR RIGHT-WING ORGANIZATIONS (IN ALPHABETICAL ORDER)

Genyōsha

As one of Japan's earliest ultranationalist and expansionist "patriotic societies," Genyōsha (Dark Ocean Society), founded in 1881, was involved in domestic assassinations almost from its beginning. However, its main goal was the promotion of Japanese military expansion and conquest on the Asian continent. The society's agenda was reflected in its name, *Genyōsha*, taken from the name of the Genkainada Strait separating Japan from Korea. In a harbinger of things to come, Genyōsha began as a terrorist organization attracting figures involved in organized crime to assist in its campaigns of violence and assassination against both foreigners and liberal politicians.

In 1889, for example, Genyōsha strongly criticized the weakness of a plan by Foreign Minister Ōkuma Shigenobu (1838–1922) to revise Japan's unequal treaties with Western powers. As a consequence, a Genyōsha member threw a bomb that blew off Ōkuma's right leg but failed to kill him. However, if Genyōsha could oppose the government, it could also support it. In the election of 1892, Genyōsha conducted a campaign of intimidation and violence to influence the election outcome, enjoying the tacit support of the government of Prime Minister Matsukata Masayoshi (1835–1924). This is but one example that demonstrates Genyōsha not only operated with the support of certain powerful figures in government but was sufficiently influential to demand concessions from the government, including a promise of a strong foreign policy from the Matsukata cabinet.

On the continent, Genyōsha provided funds and weapons to secret societies in China seeking to overthrow the Qing Dynasty. In addition, Genyōsha established a large network of brothels across China (and later throughout Southeast Asia) to provide meeting locations, and also to gather information. Among other things, this information was used for the later blackmail or subversion of patrons. Genyōsha-operated schools provided brothel prostitutes with the training and skills necessary to extract information from their clients.

Another sphere of Genyōsha activity was Korea. Genyōsha secretly prepared detailed topographical survey maps of Korea in anticipation of a future Japanese invasion. Genyōsha also actively supported the Donghak Peasant Movement of 1894, assuming correctly that this uprising would lead to war between China and Japan, both of whom had interests in Korea they wished to protect. The assassination of Queen Min of Korea in 1895 is also believed to have been conducted by Genyōsha members, bolstered by the direct involvement of the Japanese minister in Seoul, former army lieutenant general Miura Gorō (1847–1926).

During the first Sino-Japanese War of 1894–1895 and the Russo-Japanese War of 1904–1905, both the Japanese army and navy found Genyōsha's extensive intelligence-gathering network throughout East Asia invaluable. Genyōsha's network was also useful for the military in conducting sabotage activities behind enemy lines. After Korea became an outright Japanese colony in 1910, Genyōsha continued to support efforts toward Japan-dominated pan-Asianism. On the domestic front, it formed a political party called the Dai Nippon Seisantō (Greater Japan Production Party) to counter the influence of socialism in trade unions, thereby gaining the support of corporate *zaibatsu* leaders. Thus, by the 1930s, Genyōsha evolved to the point where it had almost become a member of mainstream Japanese politics.

A number of cabinet ministers and members of the Japanese Diet were known members of Genyōsha, including Hirota Kōki (1878–1948), who served as both Japan's foreign minister and later prime minister. The Anti-Comintern Pact with Nazi Germany and Fascist Italy was signed during Hirota's premiership in November 1936. Following the war, Hirota was arrested as a Class A war criminal and tried by the Tokyo War Crimes Tribunal. He offered no defense and was sentenced to death by hanging. Prior to being hung, Hirota stated he simply wished to return to "nothingness" (*mu*).[1] As previously introduced, *mu* is a key Zen expression. Hirota's use of this term is not surprising in light of the fact that his personal name, *Kōki* (broad strength), was the name Hirota acquired when he became a Rinzai Zen priest in his youth, a status he maintained until his death.

Kokuryūkai

Kokuryūkai, better known by its English name, Black Dragon Society, properly refers to the Amur River (Ch., *Heilongjiang*). It was founded in 1901 as a successor to Genyōsha with the public goal of keeping Russia north of the Amur River and out of East Asia. Initially, Kokuryūkai tried to exclude the criminal elements of its predecessor, Genyōsha. As a result, its membership included cabinet ministers and high-ranking military officers as well as professional secret agents. However, as time passed, and like so many of its sister patriotic groups, it found the use of criminal activities to be a convenient "means to an end" for many of its operations.

Kokuryūkai published a journal and operated a training school for spies who were dispatched to gather intelligence on Russian activities in Russia, Manchuria, Korea, and China. It also pressured Japanese politicians to adopt a strong foreign policy. Like its predecessor, Kokuryūkai also supported pan-Asianism, and provided financial support to Chinese revolutionary Sun Yat-sen (1866–1925) and his Filipino counterpart, Emilio Aguinaldo (1869–1964).

During and after the Russo-Japanese War of 1904–1905, the Japanese army made use of the Kokuryūkai network for espionage, sabotage, and assassination. Manchurian guerrillas were organized to fight against the Chinese, the most important of whom was Marshal Chang Tso-lin. Kokuryūkai waged a very successful psychological warfare campaign in conjunction with the Japanese military, spreading disinformation and propaganda throughout the region. It also provided interpreters for the Japanese army. Still further, Kokuryūkai formed close contact and even alliances with those Japanese Buddhist sects active in missionary work in China and other Asian countries.

Once again, like its predecessor, by the 1920s and 1930s Kokuryūkai became more of a mainstream political organization, publicly attacking both liberal and leftist thought. It enjoyed close ties to leading members of the government as well as military and business leaders, giving it a power and influence far greater than most ultranationalist groups.

As the above demonstrates, these two "founding members" among ultranationalist, patriotic organizations in prewar Japan both enjoyed a symbiotic relationship with the most important political, military, and economic leaders in Japan, who also secretly funded them. This support is not surprising in that these groups often did the behind-the-scenes "dirty work" that their patrons could not do publicly. Their hallmark was violent support for expansion abroad and repression of both liberal and leftist movements at home.

MAJOR INOUE-RELATED FIGURES
(IN ALPHABETICAL ORDER)

Araki Sadao

Army General Sadao Araki (1877–1966) was certainly the most powerful military leader Inoue was close to. Again, this is not surprising inasmuch as Araki was, aside from his military position, one of the principal nationalist right-wing political theorists in Japan. In particular, he was regarded as the leader of the radical, albeit informal, faction within the army known as the Kōdō-ha (Imperial Way Faction).

The Kōdō-ha considered the Soviet Union, with its communist government, Japan's principal enemy. In addition, this faction emphasized military and national spirit as superior to material force, something that became army doctrine from the

Russo-Japanese War onward.[2] It was this emphasis on spirit as the key to victory that led to a close relationship between Zen and Kōdō-ha adherents, especially the young officers. The Kōdō-ha was also loosely associated with the movement for a Shōwa Restoration that would, in theory, restore total political and military power to Emperor Hirohito.

Like so many officers, Araki came from a samurai family and rapidly rose through the ranks following service in the Russo-Japanese War. He was promoted to major in November 1909, to lieutenant colonel in August 1915, and was assigned to the Kwantung Army stationed in Manchuria. Promoted to colonel in 1918, Araki served as a staff officer at Expeditionary Army Headquarters in Vladivostok between 1918 and 1919 during the Japanese Siberian Intervention against the Bolshevik Red Army. He also carried out secret missions in the Russian Far East and Lake Baikal areas.

Araki was promoted to lieutenant general in July 1927 and then became commandant of the Army War College in August of the next year. By the time Inoue secretly met with Araki on the southern island of Kyūshū in December 1930, Araki was commander of the Sixth Division, headquartered in Kumamoto. According to Inoue, Araki expressed his preparedness to rebel, stating that once he heard an uprising had started, he would lead the Sixth Division to Tokyo to ensure its success.

The precipitating uprising never occurred, and on December 31, 1931, Araki was appointed minister of war in the cabinet of ill-fated prime minister Tsuyoshi Inukai. Ill-fated because in the May 15 Incident of 1932, Inukai was assassinated by ultranationalist naval officers, army cadets, and right-wing civilian elements. As previously noted, this assassination was in reality the second, delayed phase of the Blood Oath Corps Incident. Unsurprisingly, Araki supported the assassins, calling them "irrepressible patriots."[3] Later, he would, like Emperor Hirohito himself, support General Ishii Shirō and his infamous biological warfare research and development project in Manchuria, Unit 731.[4]

Araki remained as the war minister in the following government of Prime Minister and Navy Admiral Saitō Makoto (1858–1936). From September 1932 onward, Araki became more outspoken in promoting totalitarianism, militarism, and expansionism. In a September 23 news conference, Araki publicly mentioned the philosophy of Kōdō-ha for the first time, combining the emperor, people, land, and morality into one indivisible entity. Araki also strongly promoted highly Zen-influenced *seishin kyōiku* (spiritual training) within the army. Its basic doctrine emphasized adherence to the *Bushidō* code, with its call for absolute loyalty unto death. This, it claimed, would ensure victory over any enemy no matter how well materially equipped they might be.

The young officers affiliated with the Kōdō-ha launched their insurrection in the Young Officers' Uprising of February 26, 1936. Due to the emperor's direct intervention, the rebellion failed, and this time, unlike in the past, nineteen rebel leaders, including two civilian supporters, were all sentenced to death and executed almost immediately. In addition, Kōdō-ha generals were purged from the army, including

Araki. He was forced to retire in March 1936. Surprisingly, however, this did not end Araki's public career.

In 1938, Prime Minister Konoe Fumimarō appointed Araki as education minister despite his having been purged from the military. This was an ideal position for Araki, for it allowed him to instill his spirit-first ideals into the national education system and beyond to the general populace. Araki also promoted the incorporation of the *Bushidō* code into the national education system, using the official academic text *Kokutai no Hongi* (Fundamentals of the National Polity), and the *Shinmin no Michi* (The Path of Subjects), as an effective catechism on national, religious, cultural, social, and ideological topics.

Araki continued to serve as education minister when Konoe was succeeded as prime minister by Hiranuma Kiichirō (1867–1952) in 1939. In this position he revitalized the National Spiritual Mobilization Movement through sponsorship of public rallies, radio programs, printed propaganda, and neighborhood discussion seminars. When Konoe came to power for a second time in 1940, Araki continued as education minister. Thereafter he served as a government advisor through the end of the war. After the war, he was convicted of war crimes and given a life sentence but released, due to ill health, in 1955.

Hirohito (Emperor)

Needless to say, an entire book could be written about Emperor Hirohito (1901–1989), whose wartime responsibility was never seriously pursued by the Tokyo War Crimes Tribunal. Instead, in the postwar years, Hirohito was portrayed as a helpless figurehead, a puppet if not himself a victim of the Japanese military's leadership. The military leadership, especially Gen. Tōjō Hideki, who would be executed by the War Crimes Tribunal, was held responsible for having initiated the war.

Fortunately, this mistaken view has now been corrected, first and foremost by the meticulous scholarship of Herbert Bix in his groundbreaking book *Hirohito and the Making of Modern Japan*. We now know that Hirohito was at the very heart of decision making in wartime Japan. As for Hirohito's domestic role prior to the war, the following heated exchange between Hirohito and his younger brother, Prince Chichibu, is revelatory. It clearly shows how starkly divergent the two brothers' thinking was when it came to addressing the dire domestic situation Japan faced. The exchange occurred at the end of 1931 in the aftermath of two failed military coup attempts in March and October of that year.

Chichibu: I think it's necessary to have a government administered directly by the emperor.

Hirohito: What do you mean by that? What is it you wish to say?

Chichibu: If necessary, I respectfully request the [Meiji] constitution be suspended. Under the banner of a government administered directly by the emperor, I would like you to suspend the constitution, restrain the *zaibatsu* financial conglomerates, improve the lives of farmers, promote industry on behalf of workers, and improve the foundation of the lives of ordinary people.

Hirohito: Prince, where did you get all that? I never would have imagined a military man would suggest things like suspending the constitution. Aren't you a member of the imperial family? You clearly know nothing about the duties of an imperial family member, let alone the responsibilities of an imperial soldier! You should ask yourself what your duty is, including the appropriateness of making suggestions about the constitution that Emperor Meiji established, protected, and nurtured.

Chichibu: Your Majesty, you speak about imperial soldiers, but their reality has no substance. The wretched condition of the soldiers and their families is beyond description. While serving in the military, their older and younger sisters end up being sold as barmaids and *geisha*. Is there any greater hypocrisy or deceit than asking soldiers who have experienced these hellish conditions to die for their country?

Your Majesty, can you bear a deceitful situation like this? I can't. I can't bear it when I think of the genuine army soldiers who are prepared to give their lives for the Great Empire of Japan. I can't bear it even if my body were to be cut up into eight, nine, or ten pieces!

Hirohito: I'm aware of this situation. It is the result of my lack of virtue. Truly, I have no words to express my regrets to the ancestors of the imperial dynasty.

Chichibu: It's not a question of imperial ancestors! Instead, it's a question of today's soldiers and ordinary people. It's a question of soldiers and citizens who are alive now, who sweat as they work, of soldiers who are prepared to shed their blood. It's a question of men and women. Please make a firm decision. Please help them. The people of this country are awaiting your decision.

Hirohito: Prince, you talk about government administered directly by the emperor. However, according to the provisions of the constitution, I'm already in charge of making broad policies and presiding over their administration. What more do you want me to do?

Chichibu: . . . (frustrated, Chichibu bowed slightly and left the room).[5]

Commenting on this exchange, historian Fukuda Kazuya notes that Prince Chichibu was a captain in the Third Azabu Regiment stationed in Tokyo. The young officers in his unit were deeply influenced by the national socialist–oriented writings of Kita Ikki and formed the nucleus of the Young Officers' Uprising. Through his contact with these officers, Chichibu had come to share many of their concerns as reflected in the requests he made of his older brother. However, beyond regret, Hirohito showed little sympathy for Chichibu's requests.

In light of the above exchange, and as pointed out in chapter 13, it is clear why Hirohito almost immediately expressed his disapproval of the Young Officers' Uprising of February 26, 1936. In addition to his opposition to their demands for radical social change, Hirohito had ample reason to fear that a successful uprising would lead to his replacement by his younger brother. Summarizing the brothers' quarrel, Fukuda writes,

The exchange between them was fierce. Never before in the history of the imperial family since the Meiji Restoration had two influential members engaged in such a stormy debate. The intensity of the disagreement was the result of conflict over the state of the country and the path it should follow. At the same time it symbolized the divisions in public opinion and [the country's] uncertain future.[6]

On the one hand, Japan's uncertain future would come to an end with its full-scale invasion of China beginning on July 7, 1937. On the other hand, the uncertainty would be replaced by something far worse—a war that would cost tens of millions of lives and end in the destruction of the Japanese Empire.

Konoe Fumimarō

Prince Konoe Fumimarō (1891–1945) was Japan's thirty-fourth, thirty-eighth, and thirty-ninth prime minister. Japan's full-scale invasion of China in July 1937 began only one month after Konoe became prime minister for the first time. Konoe vigorously prosecuted the war but resigned in January 1939, stating that he was tired of being dictated to by the military. While Konoe may not have directly opposed the military, he was unwilling to be its puppet.

Konoe's second term as prime minister began on July 16, 1940. During his tenure, he continued to prosecute the full-scale invasion of China while maintaining that Japan's aggression was part of a plan to create a Greater East Asia Co-Prosperity Sphere. At the same time, he encouraged Japan to join the Axis alliance even as he sought to avoid war with a militarily powerful United States. When he realized war with the United States was unavoidable, he resigned his post on October 16, 1941, less than two months before Pearl Harbor.

Konoe was undoubtedly the most powerful politician with whom Inoue was directly connected. He was also what may be termed the most mainstream if not solidly establishment figure Inoue knew. The emperor trusted Konoe because he was a member of the ancient Fujiwara clan that had loyally served the imperial family for more than one thousand years. Additionally, Inoue felt close to him, a feeling that, if Inoue is to be believed, Konoe reciprocated. Konoe's aristocratic background makes it even more surprising that a convicted and confessed leader of a band of terrorists like Inoue was freed only to quickly become Konoe's live-in confidant. To better understand this, a more detailed understanding of both Konoe and his times is necessary.

Konoe's Family Background

In addition to being a true aristocrat, Konoe was also the heir to the politically powerful Konoe family in Tokyo. Konoe's father, Atsumaro, had organized the Anti-Russia Society in 1903. In 1904, Atsumaro's death left Konoe, at age twelve, with the title of prince, endowing him with plenty of social standing but not much money since, in the aftermath of the Meiji Restoration, the aristocracy no longer possessed landed estates. Surprisingly, given his aristocratic background, Konoe spent his student days studying Marxist economics at Kyoto University, a fact that left him with lifelong left-wing sympathies. Readers will recall the following exchange after Inoue charged Konoe with possessing a "split personality":

> When you were a student at Kyoto University, you had socialist ideology instilled in you by the likes of Kawakami Hajime [1879–1946] and other professors. Even today, at an intellectual level, you are still inclined to affirm socialism. At the same time, the intuitively antisocialist spirit of Japan pulsates through your blood just as it did that of your ancient [Shintō] ancestor Ama-no-Koyane-no-mikoto. Thus, you have a split between your intellect and your intuition that results in your indecisiveness in the face of problems you encounter. That's what I call a split personality.

Hearing this, Konoe recovered his composure and said, "It's just like you say. That's why I'm so troubled."[7]

His left-wing sympathies notwithstanding, Konoe, due to his hereditary title, automatically became a member of House of Peers in 1916. One of his first acts as a peer was lobbying to be part of the Japanese delegation to the Paris Peace Conference of 1919. In 1918, prior to the conference, he published an essay titled "Reject the Anglo-American-Centered Peace." At the conference, Konoe was one of the Japanese diplomats who supported the Racial Equality Proposal for the Covenant of the League of Nations. When the Racial Equality Clause came up before the committee, eight member nations voted in favor, but American President Woodrow Wilson overturned the vote by declaring that the clause needed unanimous support. As a representative of a non-Caucasian nation, Konoe was upset by the rejection of the Racial Equality Clause and felt that Japan had been humiliated.[8]

In 1925, Konoe gained the support of the Japanese public by endorsing a bill that would extend suffrage to all males aged twenty-five and over. In 1933, he was elected president of the House of Peers and became prime minister for the first time in June 1937. However, after only a month in office, Japanese troops clashed with Chinese troops near Peking in the Marco Polo Bridge Incident. On the one hand, Konoe responded by dispatching three divisions of troops to the area. On the other hand, he directed the military not to escalate the conflict. Nevertheless, within three weeks the army launched a general assault. In reality, the military's General Headquarters was completely autonomous from the civilian government and responsible solely to the emperor. The headquarters ordered its forces in China to drive toward Nanjing, the Chinese capital. Nanjing was captured in December 1937, after which the Japanese army committed the infamous Nanjing massacre, killing as many as three hundred thousand noncombatants.[9]

At this point, Gerhard Weinberg writes that Konoe chose to further escalate the war and push for "total victory" over China.[10] This included passage of a National Mobilization Law in the Diet that effectively nationalized strategic industries, the news media, and labor unions, in preparation for total war with China. Additionally, Japan stationed troops in French Indochina in September 1940 following the fall of

France to the Nazis. On September 27, 1940, the Tripartite Pact was signed, aligning Japan, Germany, and Italy. Yet, at the same time, Konoe attempted to pursue peace with the United States, including a proposal for a personal meeting between himself and American President Franklin D. Roosevelt.

Konoe's peace proposals notwithstanding, on July 28, 1941, Japanese forces occupied all of French-controlled Indochina. This caused Roosevelt to immediately freeze Japanese assets in the United States. Great Britain and the Dutch East Indies government did the same. Roosevelt also placed an embargo on oil exports to Japan. Inasmuch as over 80 percent of Japan's oil needs were being met through American imports, on July 31 the navy informed the emperor that Japan's oil stockpiles would be completely depleted in two years. While Konoe had been counting on the navy to restrain the army from further aggressive actions, Navy Chief of Staff Osami Nagano (1880–1947) now argued that if war with the United States was inevitable, it should be fought as soon as possible, while Japan still had oil reserves.

For his part, Konoe continued his efforts to avert war with the United States but without success. In a cabinet meeting on October 14, 1941, then army minister Tōjō Hideki stated that inasmuch as all of Konoe's peace proposals had failed, Japan had no choice but to declare war on the United States. This led Konoe to resign the premiership on October 16, 1941. Two days later, Hirohito chose Tōjō to succeed him. Six weeks after that, and with Emperor Hirohito's explicit approval, Japan attacked Pearl Harbor and declared war on both the United States and the British Empire.

Konoe took no active part in military decision making during the war. However, he continued to play an active role in the Imperial Rule Assistance Association (Taisei Yokusankai) that he had founded in October 1940. Note that Inoue and his band members were all released from Kosuge Prison on October 17, 1940, just five days after Konoe inaugurated this body. The release was justified as part of a general amnesty to promote national unity.

Initially, the association was to be a reformist political party designed to unite government bureaucrats with politicians and the military. However, it was subsequently expanded to mobilize the entire population. The November 6, 1940, issue of *Shashin Shūhō* (Weekly Photographic Report) explained, "The *Taisei Yokusankai* movement has already turned on the switch for building a new Japan and completing a new Great East Asian order which, writ large, is the construction of a new world order. The *Taisei Yokusankai* is, broadly speaking, the New Order movement which will, in a word, place One Hundred Million [Subjects of the Empire] into one body under this new organization that will conduct all of our energies and abilities for the sake of the nation."[11]

When Japan's defeat became increasingly likely in the fall of 1944, Konoe took an active role in bringing about the fall of the Tōjō government. Further, in February 1945, he advised Emperor Hirohito to begin negotiations to end the war, but according to Grand Chamberlain Fujita Hisanori, Hirohito first wanted to achieve at least one great victory and firmly rejected Konoe's recommendation.[12] Hirohito wanted a major victory in order to enter peace negotiations from a position of strength rather than weakness. However, despite the horrific losses inflicted on both military and civilian participants in battles on Saipan, Okinawa, and elsewhere, Hirohito failed to secure what he so desperately wanted. At the same time, Hirohito's decision to continue fighting cost the lives of tens of thousands of both Japanese soldiers and civilians, not to mention Allied troops.

At the beginning of the American occupation, Konoe served in the cabinet of Prince Higashikuni Naruhiko, the first postwar government and the first government to be headed by a member of the imperial family. Konoe, however, refused to collaborate with American army officer Bonner Fellers in "Operation Blacklist." Fellers headed an effort to clear the emperor and imperial family of any war responsibility because the United States had decided Hirohito would be useful in controlling Japan. It was at that time that Konoe came under suspicion of war crimes. In December 1945, facing a call by the Americans for alleged war criminals to turn themselves in, Konoe instead took potassium cyanide poison and committed suicide. Readers will recall that Inoue tried, unsuccessfully, to prevent him from doing so.

Konoe and Inoue

In reviewing Konoe's career in government, beginning with his peerage in 1916 and extending through 1941 and later, it is clear that he was an active, if not always successful, participant in everything that transpired. Given the degree of power he possessed, it would have been quite possible for him to serve as one of, if not the main, behind-the-scenes patrons of Inoue and his band. Written temple records indicate, for example, that Konoe was one of the major donors to the construction of Risshō Gokokudō Temple in 1928. More importantly, who but Konoe, among Inoue's known acquaintances, would have had the power to (1) arrange for sympathetic judges to replace the initial unsympathetic judges at Inoue and his band's trial, (2) inform Tōyama Mitsuru that Inoue would only have to serve three years of his life sentence before being released, (3) have Inoue's entire conviction erased from the record upon release from prison, and (4) hire the former head of a band of terrorists to serve as a live-in aide?

Needless to say, it is only the answer to the last of these four questions that can definitely be connected to Konoe. Yet when the question is asked who was in a position of influence when these highly unusual events occurred, the answer cannot help but point to Konoe even if his responsibility cannot be proven conclusively. Even if it were true that he was the one who interfered in the judicial process, the question is, why would he have done so? Was it, as Adm. Sayamoto alleged in chapter 13, simply because Konoe wanted Inoue to act as his bodyguard? This is certainly possible, but given all the other factors involved, it seems too simple an answer. In any event, to answer these questions, we cannot help but return to the role of that most mysterious and controversial character in this drama—Emperor Hirohito. When we return to his role, we realize we can go no further.

Ōkawa Shūmei

Ōkawa Shūmei (1886–1957) was certainly the best educated ultranationalist Inoue came in contact with. Ōkawa was a graduate of prestigious Tokyo University, where he studied Vedic literature and classical Indian philosophy. He became well known for his publications on Indian philosophy, philosophy of religion, Japanese history, and colonialism. Further, he had a sound knowledge of German, French, English, Sanskrit, and Pali. Following graduation in 1911, his first employment was doing translation work for the Japanese Army General Staff.

During his college years, Ōkawa had been interested in socialism, but in the summer of 1913 he read a copy of Sir Henry Cotton's *New India, or India in Transition* (1886, rev. 1905) which dealt with the political situation in British-occupied India and Asia generally. This led him to become a pan-Asianist and briefly house the pioneer Indian independence leader Rash Behari Bose (1886–1945). Ōkawa became convinced that the solution to Japan's pressing social and political problems lay in an alliance with Asian independence movements. He further advocated a revival of premodern Japanese philosophy coupled with a renewed emphasis on *kokutai*, the national polity of Japan.

In 1918, Ōkawa went to work for the East Asian Research Bureau of the South Manchurian Railway Company. In the 1920s, he became an instructor of history and colonial policy at Takushoku University, where he was also active in the creation of anticapitalist and nationalist student groups. In 1926, Ōkawa published his most influential work, *Japan and the Way of the Japanese* (*Nihon oyobi Nihonjin no Michi*), which became so popular that it was reprinted forty-six times by the end of the war.

Ōkawa's connection to Inoue was but one example of his involvement in a number of attempted coups d'état in the early 1930s by both civilians and members of the military. Ōkawa's ability to provide substantial funding to coup plotters is significant in that Ōkawa was not independently wealthy, meaning that he, too, was the beneficiary of well-off behind-the-scenes patrons. Nevertheless, readers will recall that Ōkawa failed to deliver the promised pistols to Inoue on time. While Ōkawa did not directly participate in the initial Blood Oath Corps Incident, he was a part of the subsequent March 15 Incident.

Despite being part of the incident that killed the prime minister, Ōkawa was sentenced to only five years in prison in 1935 and released two years later. He briefly rejoined the South Manchurian Railway Company before accepting a post as a professor at Hosei University in 1939. During the war, he continued to promote the war effort through numerous books and articles, popularizing the idea that a "clash of civilizations" between East and West was inevitable. It was Japan's destiny, he claimed, to assume the mantle of liberator and protector of Asia against the United States and other Western nations.

After the war, Ōkawa was prosecuted as a Class A war criminal. Of the twenty-eight persons indicted on this charge, he was the only one who was not a military officer or government official. The Allies described him to the press as the "Japanese

Goebbels" and claimed that he had long agitated for a war between Japan and the West. However, during the trial, Ōkawa behaved so erratically (e.g., dressing in pajamas, sitting barefoot, etc.) that he was judged unfit to stand trial and committed to a mental hospital. His mental instability seemed clear when, sitting behind Tōjō Hideki in the prisoners' dock, he stood up, slapped Tōjō on his bald head, and shouted in German, "Inder! Kommen Sie!" (Come, Indian!).

It is not surprising that, over the years, a number of observers have come to the conclusion that Ōkawa's mental illness was a sham.[13] This suspicion was strengthened by the fact that before being released from his mental hospital in 1948, he completed the first Japanese translation of the entire *Quran*. Ōkawa spent the final years of his life writing a memoir, *Anraku no Mon* (Gateway to a Carefree Life), reflecting on how he had found peace in a mental hospital.

In reflecting on Ōkawa's role in prewar Japan, it can be said he had a dual identity. On the one hand, he played the role of a not so dependable fixer as far as his relationship with Inoue was concerned. Yet he was an active participant in the May 15 assassination of Prime Minister Inukai. Since Ōkawa was not independently wealthy, it seems likely he had a hidden funding source. We learned in chapter 13, for example, that the very wealthy, aristocratic ultranationalist Marquis Tokugawa Yoshichika (see entry below) arranged for Ōkawa to be released from prison after serving only two years of an already short five-year sentence.

Yoshichika's concern for Ōkawa is readily understandable in light of the fact the two of them had a long-standing relationship, dating back to their joint involvement in the formation of an early ultranationalist organization, the Taika-kai, in 1920. Thereafter the two men were involved in a number of right-wing groups, with Yoshichika serving as both a leader and a funder. Given their close relationship, it seems likely that Yoshichika was at least one of Ōkawa's financial supporters, perhaps even his main supporter. Yet there is no definitive proof of this.

Tanaka Mitsuaki (Count)

Readers will recall it was Count Tanaka (1843–1939) who in April 1927 invited Inoue to serve as abbot of the soon-to-be-constructed Risshō Gokokudo Temple in Ōarai. Significantly, Tanaka was even more closely associated with Emperor Hirohito than Tōyama. Following a distinguished career as a judge and army major general, Tanaka served as chief secretary of the cabinet and member of the Chamber of Elders in 1885. In 1890 he was selected as a member of the House of Peers and appointed a court councilor in 1891. In 1898 he became the imperial household minister in the third Ito cabinet, a post held until 1909. In short, Tanaka was the ultimate court insider who served both Emperor Meiji and his successor, Emperor Taishō.

By the time Hirohito became emperor in 1926, Tanaka was in his eighties. Given this, it might be thought that he had lost his influence at court. On the contrary, Tanaka was entrusted with a matter of life and death for the continuation of the imperial institution. Namely, by late 1932, Empress Nagako had yet to give birth to a male heir to the throne, having previously given birth to only girls, three of whom survived. The solution appeared to be for Hirohito to fulfill his monarchical duty by fathering a male heir with a concubine. Tanaka was entrusted with the delicate task of finding a suitable mate and in due course selected a total of ten princess candidates. However, by then, Nagako had become pregnant again and, on December 23, 1933, gave birth to Prince Akihito, thus eliminating the need for a concubine. Despite his age, one can hardly imagine a more discreet, behind-the-scenes fixer than Tanaka. Nor was there anyone whom Hirohito trusted more.

As for Tanaka's relationship to Inoue, Inoue made clear their common antipathy to communism as well as their dedication to eradicating the corruption they saw in the political parties and *zaibatsu* financial leaders of the day. Tanaka's opposition was so strong he remained able, he claimed, "to cut down three to five men" of those he held to be responsible. That someone so close to successive Japanese emperors, including Emperor Hirohito, was personally willing to kill those he deemed corrupt suggests the importance Tanaka placed on Inoue's mission. Although the question cannot be answered definitively, this raises the issue of whether, in seeking Inoue's aid, Tanaka was acting alone or on behalf of powerful actors in the imperial institution. Had he, perhaps, been entrusted with yet another mission critically important to the throne?

Tokugawa Yoshichika (Marquis)

Marquis Tokugawa Yoshichika (1886–1976) was the biological son of Matsudaira Shungaku, last head of the Echizen feudal domain. However, in 1908 he was adopted by Tokugawa Yoshikatsu and became the nineteenth head of the Owari branch of the Tokugawa clan. The Tokugawas, of course, were the last feudal rulers of Japan prior to the Meiji Restoration of 1868. Following the restoration, many Tokugawa family members continued to enjoy leadership positions in modern Japan. Significantly, Yoshichika was also Emperor Hirohito's second cousin.

Like Hirohito, Yoshichika was educated at the prestigious Gakushūin (Peers' School) for children of the aristocracy. From there he attended the equally prestigious Tokyo Imperial University for his undergraduate education before going on to pursue graduate studies in botany in 1911. In that same year, Yoshichika became a member of the House of Peers and was on friendly terms with Hirohito due to their mutual interest in the natural sciences. Significantly, they were on such friendly terms that Yoshichika was able to meet Hirohito privately inside the Imperial Palace without going through the normally time-consuming protocol required for audiences with the emperor. This was possible because, as Nakano Masao explains, "They could meet whenever the emperor was in his [palace] laboratory."[14]

Surprisingly for someone of his aristocratic status, Yoshichika was actively involved in ultranationalist activities from the 1920s onward, especially in the 1930s. For example, although the exact amount is still subject to debate, Yoshichika donated what was then a large sum of money, somewhere between two hundred thousand

and five hundred thousand yen, in support of an ultimately unsuccessful military coup set for March 1931.[15] However, thanks to his position, he was never charged for his involvement. Five years later, he was involved with the Young Officers' Uprising of 1936 but, once again, escaped punishment. On the contrary, he later secured an influential (and safe) government position from 1942 to 1944, serving as the supreme consulting advisor to the Japanese colonial administration of Singapore. In the postwar era, Yoshichika, like Inoue, was interrogated by the Tokyo War Crimes Tribunal but never charged or put on trial.

In Yoshichika we find a politically powerful and wealthy aristocrat who provided substantial funding for ultranationalist activities over many years, all without being penalized for his support. The ultranationalist activities Yoshichika funded in the 1930s took place at the same time he enjoyed private access to the emperor. And as previously noted, Yoshichika worked closely with Ōkawa Shūmei, who in turn supported Inoue Nisshō. Did Yoshichika and Inoue ever meet?

The answer is they did, for Yoshichika and Inoue were in direct contact at least once. This occurred at the time Inoue and his band members were released from prison in 1940. Yoshichika invited Inoue and his newly released band members to take part in an unspecified plot in support of the Strike South military strategy (J., *Nanshin-ron*) then being advocated by the navy. Yoshichika was himself a longtime supporter of the Strike South strategy, which was, however, opposed by many army leaders even after the failed Young Officers Uprising in February 1936. These army leaders continued to promote a Strike North strategy (J., *Hokushin-ron*) since they viewed communism in the form of the Soviet Union as Japan's primary enemy. However, the army's decisive defeat by Soviet forces at the time of a months-long border conflict (J., *Nomonhan Jiken*) in Manchuria in 1939 resulted in an overall shift toward the Strike South faction. A military strike south would make it possible for Japan to procure colonial resources, especially oil, in Southeast Asia. This brought with it the imperative to neutralize the threat posed by Western naval forces, primarily those of the United States, in the Pacific.

The nature of the plot that Yoshichika asked Inoue and his band members to participate in, as well as their reactions to his invitation, is unknown. Inoue never mentioned having received the invitation nor his reaction to it. Instead, as we have seen, Inoue accepted Konoe's request to become his live-in advisor. It is also unknown whether Yoshichika's invitation represented the first direct contact between the two men. Once again, questions far outnumber answers.

As for Yoshichika, until he took up his high-ranking civilian position in Singapore in 1942, he continued to enjoy access to Hirohito in his palace laboratory, almost at will. Given the nature of Yoshichika's political activities, and the tumultuous nature of everything going on around them, it beggars belief that Yoshichika and Hirohito talked exclusively about their biological research when they met in private. In short, could this be the connection between ultranationalists and the throne we have been searching for? Circumstantial evidence strongly suggests it is, but, frustratingly, we lack conclusive evidence.

Tōyama Mitsuru

Readers will instantly recall the name of Tōyama Mitsuru (1855–1944) inasmuch as Inoue's numerous references to him make it clear that this patriarch of ultranationalism exerted a deep influence on his life, and not merely politically. This is hardly surprising in light of the fact that Tōyama was one of the founders of the Genyōsha in 1881. By 1889, he was implicated in the attempted assassination of Foreign Minister Ōkuma Shigenobu described previously.

Immediately prior to the start of the First Sino-Japanese War in 1894, Tōyama organized Tenyūkyō (Society of Heavenly Salvation [for the Oppressed]), a secret society and paramilitary force that operated in Korea prior to the arrival of the Japanese army. Tenyūkyō made detailed topographic maps, scouted out Chinese and Korean military installations and deployment, and arranged logistic support for the army. In cooperation with Genyōsha operatives in Korea and Manchuria, Tenyūkyō provided interpreters and guides to the regular Japanese army following their invasion.

Tōyama was a strong advocate of Japanese control of Manchuria. He also supported Chinese republican revolutionaries against the Qing Dynasty and gave considerable support to the future president of the Republic of China, Sun Yat-sen. When the Chinese revolution began in 1911, he went to China to personally oversee Genyōsha activities and provided financial assistance to Sun.

Following the success of the Chinese revolution, Tōyama officially retired and does not appear to have played an active role in the Black Dragon Society (Kokuryūkai) that he also helped create. Despite his retirement, Tōyama continued to play an important role behind the scenes as a fixer in Japanese politics up through his death in 1944. It is therefore not surprising that Inoue sought his assistance in hiding from the police in the immediate aftermath of the Blood Oath Corps Incident. Yet it must be said that, by hiding in a facility operated by such a well-known ultranationalist, Inoue was actually hiding "in plain sight" of the police, suggesting that Inoue fully expected to be apprehended.

Somewhat surprisingly, one of the best descriptions of Tōyama's influence is provided by a leading Nazi propagandist, Ernst Meunieur, in the January 15, 1942, Munich edition of the Nazi Party's national newspaper, *Völkischer Beobachter* (People's Observer):

> Tōyama is almost ninety years old. He holds no public office, he even has no occupation, he is neither politician, scholar, nor speaker. And yet there is no man of decisive importance in Japan who does not visit Tōyama to seek his advice prior to making major decisions. Tōyama is the living conscience of Japan.
>
> In his long life, Tōyama has experienced the unique development of his nation out of its medieval shadow existence into a modern empire. In his person, the old ties itself to the new, the traditional to the present. This man, who represents the old Japan like no other, is simultaneously the most modern of Japanese. For the past forty to fifty years, Tōyama has fought to establish Japan's dominant position in East Asia. This has made him the protecting spirit of Japanese politics and endowed him with a mysterious force

that he exercises without office or power over his people and which endows his personality with a mythical splendor while still alive.

Every morning, summer or winter, Tōyama, who is almost ninety years old, walks to Meiji Shrine, an hour away, whether in rain or snow. Without either a hat or coat, he sits on the stone tiles in front of the holy shrine and engages in a lengthy conversation with the great Emperor Meiji's soul. Upon returning home, visitors from all walks of life await him, even visitors from throughout the world, to whom he—and this is his single task—announces his views. Yet his views always express the essence of Japanese politics; they are a reflection of the Japanese race-soul. Here a wonderful life is already fulfilled in earthly existence and transfigured.[16]

In playing this role, Tōyama was viewed by a large section of the Japanese public, including the military, as a super patriot, the embodiment of the Spirit of Japan (*Yamato-damashii*). Although Tōyama was never more than a private citizen throughout his life, he became known as the "Shadow Shōgun," "Spymaster," and "The Boss of Bosses," due to his tremendous covert influence on nationalist politics as well as the *yakuza* crime syndicates. Inasmuch as Tōyama was never independently wealthy, it would have been impossible for him to exercise his influence without close relationships to very powerful patrons. Just how well connected Tōyama was is demonstrated, among other things, by his ability to inform Inoue's father that his son, sentenced to life imprisonment, would only have to spend three years in prison.[17]

While the names of Tōyama's powerful patrons remain a mystery to this day, Tōyama was known to have had personal ties with court officials even before Hirohito ascended the throne.[18] In what became known as the "certain grave incident at court" of 1920, Tōyama mobilized ultranationalist leaders to ensure the crown prince would be able to marry the woman of his choice, Princess Nagako Kuni (1903–2000). Tōyama's assistance was needed due to a history of color blindness in the princess's family. Because of this, one of the most powerful senior statesmen of the day, Field Marshall Yamagata Aritomo (1838–1922), opposed the marriage, claiming the imperial bloodline should not be endangered by genetic defects. In light of Emperor Taishō's many maladies, Yamagata's concerns are understandable, but political rivalries also appear to have played a major role. It is noteworthy that as early as 1920, Tōyama and his fellows were sufficiently powerful to silence a major political figure like Yamagata and others opposed to the marriage. They used what was, and would be, their modus operandi—harassment, threats of assassination, and charges of a lack of patriotism.

Hirohito, far from being angered by Tōyama's interference, was so grateful that he arranged for him to be invited to his marriage ceremony. Thus, even before becoming emperor in 1926, Hirohito was aware that Tōyama and the ultraright could be used to carry out extralegal activities on his behalf. As Herbert Bix ominously notes, "From this seemingly minor episode in the history of the imperial house emerges the prototype of 1930s-style right-wing terrorism."[19] If it were the emperor and his advisors' intention to manipulate right-wing figures like Inoue behind the scenes, they could not have had a better, more effective, or more willing accomplice than Tōyama.

Finally, it is possible Tōyama was, at least on occasion, the "voice of heaven" whose directions played a critical role in Inoue's decision-making process. After all, one of Tōyama's favorite expressions was "Love those [who] respect Heaven" (*keiten aijin*).[20] Was Inoue trying to protect Tōyama, or perhaps another benefactor, by disguising their role in his decision-making process? It is difficult to believe the "voice of heaven" was capable of being so specific as, for example, to direct Inoue, in July 1924, to "travel to the southeast on September 5."[21] Or is it possible the "voice(s)" Inoue heard on multiple occasions were a symptom of underlying mental illness, hallucinations perhaps? Or were they simply an outgrowth of "intuition," so celebrated in the Zen tradition? We will probably never know.

Yamamoto Gempō (Rinzai Zen master) and Those around Him

Abandoned as a newborn baby, Yamamoto Gempō (1866–1961) was adopted by an abusive father. His mother, however, was a warm and caring woman, and Gempō loved her deeply. Unfortunately, she died when Gempō was only twelve, leading him to a life of drug addiction and dissipation. In an attempt to curb Gempō's delinquent behavior, his father arranged an early marriage for his nineteen-year-old son. Just one year into the marriage however, Gempō was diagnosed with an eye disease, and doctors predicted he would eventually go blind.

On a visit to Sekkeiji Temple in Tosa in 1889, Gempō met the priest Yamamoto Taigen, who encouraged him to become a Buddhist priest like himself. The following year Gempō divorced his wife and entered Sekkeiji as a novice monk, taking the name Yamamoto Gempō (Mysterious Peak). Despite his determination and dedication to training, Gempō faced unusual difficulties because of his lack of education, compounded by increasingly poor eyesight. Nevertheless, when Taigen died in June 1903, Gempō succeeded him as the head monk of Sekkeiji. At this time, Gempō was also invited to pay his respects to Shoun (aka Sohan Gempō, 1848–1922) at Empukuji Temple during a meeting on national defense.

Gempō formed an immediate affinity with Shoun and decided to resign his position at Sekkeiji in order to continue his Zen training under Shoun. Gempō trained at Empukuji with Shoun from 1908 to 1915, when he received Shoun's seal of recognition (*inka*) affirming his full enlightenment at the age of forty-nine. This formal recognition of Gempō's enlightenment is extremely important in establishing Gempō's credibility as an authentic Zen master within the Rinzai Zen sect. Thus, he was fully credentialed to determine the validity of Inoue's initial enlightenment experience.

In the spring of 1915, the temple Ryūtakuji in Mishima, Shizuoka prefecture, was in need of a resident priest, and Gempō was recommended for the position. Closely associated with the illustrious Rinzai Zen reformer Hakuin, the temple had fallen into a state of extreme disrepair. When Gempō arrived, there was nothing—no bedding, not even the simple bowls needed for the altar. Nevertheless, Gempō succeeded in attracting many monks and lay followers to his cause and was successful in restoring this historically important temple.

Beginning in 1923, Gempō made several trips abroad, including visits to the United States, England, India, and China. In September 1932, Japan created the puppet state of Manchukuo. This violation of Chinese sovereignty led to growing anti-Japanese sentiment on the part of the Chinese government and people. In response, the Japan–China Buddhist Research Association dispatched, in June 1935, an eleven-member delegation, including Gempō, to counter this animosity by using the shared Buddhist faith of the two countries as a means to promote acceptance of Manchukuo within the framework of pan-Asian solidarity. With this goal in mind, Gempō and his fellow priests visited some of China's most famous temples and met many prominent Buddhist leaders.

In July 1935, prior to returning to Japan, Gempō decided to visit Hsinking (J., Shinkyō; present-day Changchun), the newly created capital of Manchukuo. Upon arrival, the Manchurian government's vice minister of foreign affairs held a dinner banquet on his behalf. His host, Vice Minister Ōhashi Chūichi, was not Manchurian but Japanese. This was no accident, for Japanese vice ministers, aided by a staff of Japanese secretaries, stood immediately behind, and in control of, all native Manchurian cabinet ministers.

Among the dinner guests was the adjutant-general of the occupying Japanese Kwantung Army, the local branch head of the Mitsubishi financial combine, the vice president of the central bank of Manchuria, a judge of the Manchurian Supreme Court, other senior military officers and business leaders, and government officials and legislators, numbering more than twenty in all. As it turned out, these leaders had more on their minds than simple hospitality, for their goal was to ensure "the proper exaltation of the spirit of both the Japanese military and other Japanese residents of Manchuria."[22] They believed this could be accomplished if Gempō would agree to create a branch temple in Hsinking of Rinzai Zen sect–affiliated Myōshinji.

Gempō immediately accepted their request, though he first had to return to Japan to secure permission from the head of Kyoto-based Myōshinji, headquarters of the largest branch of the Rinzai Zen sect. With permission in hand, construction began quickly and Gempō's personal residence was completed on July 7, 1936, while the dedication ceremony of the new *zendō* (meditation hall) was held on November 29 of the same year. This ceremony was attended by no less a figure than Chang Chung-hui, prime minister of Manchukuo, together with his cabinet ministers, the mayor of Hsinking, and of course a bevy of Japanese government vice ministers, Japanese embassy personnel, and other local leaders.

Although no Japanese military officers were present at the opening ceremony, the Japanese Kwantung Army had played a key role in the temple's actual construction, especially of Gempō's living quarters and the meditation hall. In addition, Hanaya Tadashi (1894–1957), Kwantung Army staff officer and youthful instigator of the Manchurian Incident of 1931, donated the first five hundred yen toward the temple's construction. The total construction cost more than fifty thousand yen, a large sum in those days, but with the military taking the lead, the remaining funds were readily raised from various Japanese companies doing business in Manchuria, notably the quasi-governmental South Manchuria Railroad Company.

The naming of the new temple turned out to be a contentious issue, for the temple's major patrons, the officers of the Kwantung Army, did not want the new temple to have the word *temple* (J., *-ji*) in its title. Instead, they favored calling it a "spiritual training hall" (*shūyō dōjō*). However, as far as Gempō and his superiors at Myōshinji were concerned, the new temple was definitely meant to be a subordinate of the head temple and should be designated as such. By this, they meant its Rinzai Zen Buddhist affiliation should be clear.

A solution acceptable to both parties was eventually worked out: the new temple would have two signboards, one identifying it as a spiritual training center, another identifying it as a subordinate temple (i.e., Myōshinji Shinkyō Betsuin). Gempō managed to unite these two positions when he later created a temple stamp engraved with both names and centered on the figure of Bodhidharma, the Indian priest whom legend credits with having introduced Zen (Chan) to China in the sixth century.

Gempō's best-known military acquaintance was Army General Yamashita Tomoyuki (1888–1946). While Yamashita would later earn the title "Tiger of Malaya" for his successful campaign in February 1942 to capture Singapore, the years 1936–1937 saw him serving as a brigade commander in Seoul, Korea. As important as his position was, his transfer from Tokyo nevertheless represented a relatively mild form of punishment for having sympathized with the abortive Young Officers' Uprising of February 26, 1936.

Gempō met General Yamashita on his way back to Manchuria from Japan for a second time. Yamashita, honored by his visit, asked Gempō for a calligraphic specimen on which he wanted him to inscribe Yamashita's favorite phrase: "Do your best and leave the rest to fate." Gempō readily acceded to the general's request but suggested a slight alteration to the latter part of the text in order to eliminate its passive character. The text now read: "Do your best and act in accordance with fate." Yamashita found the altered text even more to his liking and thereafter kept Gempō's calligraphy wrapped around his stomach as a kind of good luck charm.[23] While he survived the war unscathed, Yamashita was nevertheless executed as a war criminal in February 1946 for having been in command at the time of the sacking of Manila and other atrocities committed during the final days of Japan's occupation of the Philippines.

Gempō's call on Yamashita had been no accident; for the former was appointed, on August 21, 1937, by Myōshinji officials as the superintendent-general (*sōkan*) of a delegation of five Rinzai priests who were to pay "sympathy calls" (*imon*) on members of the military stationed on the continent. For this purpose, it was necessary for Gempō to take off his Buddhist robes and put on the plain, military-style uniform, including a billed hat, that was rapidly becoming standard wear for all civilians, regardless of occupation, in wartime Japan.

Nakagawa Sōen

Gempō was accompanied on his travels by Nakagawa Sōen (1907–1984), who in the postwar period became a well-known Zen master in the West. Although Sōen's

Western disciples have attempted to portray him as opposed to the war, in reality he was an active supporter. This is demonstrated by the fact that Sōen was much more than Gempō's wartime attendant. He was also responsible for making the rounds of various Japanese enterprises in Manchuria to urge employees, then designated as "industrial warriors" (*sangyō senshi*), to continuously increase production on behalf of the war effort. Sōen described both his and his master's efforts as having been motivated by "the spirit of eight corners of the world under one roof" (*hakkō ichiu*), the ubiquitous wartime slogan used to justify Japan's attempt to bring Asia, if not the world, under its control.[24]

Sōen also visited the Manchurian Mining Company, a major producer of such strategically important raw materials as gold, copper, zinc, and molybdenum. This company, with headquarters in Hsinking and mining operations throughout Manchuria, was owned and operated by the Nissan financial combine (*zaibatsu*) from 1937 onward. More importantly, it was well known, if not infamous, for its utilization of slave labor made up of Chinese peasants, prisoners of war, and criminals, all subject to inhuman living and working conditions, resulting in a large number of deaths.

Yamada Kōun

One of the company officials responsible for directing the labor force at the Manchurian Mining Company was Yamada Kōun (1907–1989). Yamada served as the company's personnel manager in 1941 and later became the deputy director of the General Affairs Department in 1945. Yamada was also Sōen's former schoolmate and a lay Zen practitioner, initially training under Gempō's successor at Myōshinji Betsuin during the war years.

Following repatriation to Japan at war's end, Yamada trained under Rinzai Zen master Asahina Sōgen (1891–1979), Sōtō Zen master Harada Sōgaku (1870–1961), and finally Yasutani Haku'un, whose chief Dharma heir he became in 1961. In 1967 Yamada succeeded to the leadership of the Sambōkyōdan (Three Treasures Association), an independent, lay-oriented Zen sect created by Yasutani in Kamakura in 1954. Significantly, the common thread uniting all of Yamada's Zen teachers was their fervently held ultranationalism, both during the war and even after it.[25] Asahina Sōgen, for example, was one of the founders of the Society for the Protection of Japan (Nihon o mamoru Kai) in 1974. In the face of an alleged loss of patriotism among postwar Japanese, the society advocated that the emperor should be restored to the center of national life.

As with Sōen, Kōun's wartime activities have largely been unacknowledged in both Japan and the West. This is particularly significant in light of the influence this Zen organization played in the spread of Zen to the United States as well as Europe, including among Catholic clerics. Yasutani Haku'un, its founder, long enjoyed a reputation in the West as an enlightened Zen master who restored vitality to the Sōtō Zen sect by emphasizing the importance of having a *kenshō* (initial enlightenment) experience. In reality, however, Haku'un was one of the most fervent, fanatical supporters of Japanese aggression. Moreover, he also made a series of anti-Semitic statements.[26] According to Haku'un, "We must be aware of the existence of the demonic teachings of the Jews who assert things like [the existence of] equality in the phenomenal world, thereby disturbing public order in our nation's society and destroying [governmental] control."[27]

Gempō Returns to Japan

In the aftermath of Japan's attack on Pearl Harbor, Gempō's efforts, like those of Sōen, were no longer limited exclusively to the military. He, too, was expected to enhance the patriotic spirit of the many Japanese civilian residents of Manchuria. One form this took was the construction of a memorial hall on the grounds of Myōshinji Betsuin Temple for all those Japanese who had died in the process of creating Japan's puppet state. The impetus for this memorial came from a delegation of civilians who first came to see Gempō shortly after the new temple's construction. They said, "The reason we are able to live in this foreign country without any fear or want is due to the more than ten thousand heroic spirits [*eirei*] who earnestly sacrificed themselves in order to preserve and pacify our country. For this reason, we would like to build a memorial hall to pray for their repose."[28] Although the initial steps were taken for the construction of this memorial, work eventually came to a halt due to the worsening war situation.

Gempō not only suffered from poor eyesight but had been ill much of his life. At age seventy-four, he contracted an ear disease that led to his resignation as abbot of Myōshinji Betsuin in January 1940 and subsequent return to Japan. It did not, however, lead to any lessening of his close relationship with the Japanese military. Among other things, Gempō turned over most of his home temple of Ryūtakuji for military use. The Buddha Hall, for example, became an army hospital for the seriously wounded, while the bell tower was used as a food warehouse for an army regiment stationed in Mishima. Further, for the benefit of his lay parishioners, Gempō had a special Rinzai Zen sutra booklet printed in 1942 that ended with the following words: "I pray for victory in the Great East Asian War. . . . Gempō."[29]

If there was anything that distinguished Gempō's war support from his contemporaries', it was his relatively early recognition that Japan was losing the war. When Tokyo came under air attack for the first time in 1943, Gempō reportedly told one of his disciples, "Well, Japan is really done for now." Yet, when asked what might be done to stop the war, Gempō cautioned patience, pointing out, "Events have their own momentum and direction. If you try to oppose that momentum or change direction before the time is ripe, you will accomplish nothing. When people are running to the east, you must run to the east with them. When they are running west, you must do likewise."[30]

Gempō clearly followed his own advice, for he never publicly spoke out against the war. Yet by April 1945, with Tokyo and other cities being progressively reduced to ashes by Allied firebombing, Gempō reached the conclusion that the time to act, if only indirectly, had come. Accordingly, when seventy-seven-year-old Adm. Suzuki Kantarō (1867–1948) sought his advice on whether or not to end the war, Gempō replied,

In terms of sumo, Japan is like a champion wrestler [*ōzeki*]. When a champion loses, he
loses like a champion—in a dignified way. Given the present state of affairs, Japan must
figure out how to win by losing. Today you are the only person capable of accomplishing
this great task. Although I know that a person of your pure and unblemished character
is not suited for politics, I nevertheless hope that you will, even at the risk of your life,
render this final public service.[31]

Adm. Suzuki may well have taken Gempō's advice to heart, for only a week later he
accepted Emperor Hirohito's request to become the next prime minister. Just how
deeply touched the admiral was by Gempō's words is revealed by the fact that early
on the morning of August 12, 1945, he sent a special messenger to inform Gempō
of Japan's imminent surrender three days later. Aware of the difficult situation Suzuki
found himself in, Gempō immediately gave the messenger a note of encouragement
to be delivered to Suzuki.

Gempō's note contained phraseology that was, in part, identical with the emperor's
famous and unprecedented radio broadcast of August 15, 1945, announcing Japan's
surrender. Gempō's note contained the following words: "Your true public service is
set to begin from this point onward. Please be careful of your health and work for the
reconstruction of our country while enduring what is hard to endure and practicing
what is hard to practice."[32] Based on this, Gempō's disciples later maintained that the
following passage of the emperor's radio address was influenced by Gempō's note:

> The hardships and sufferings to which Our nation is to be subjected hereafter will be
> certainly great. We are keenly aware of the inmost feelings of all ye, Our subjects. How-
> ever, it is according to the dictate of time and fate that We have resolved to pave the way
> for a grand peace for all the generations to come while tolerating what is hard to tolerate
> and enduring what is hard to endure.[33]

In addition to the possible influence of Gempō's words on this key wartime docu-
ment, what is revealing about the preceding incident is just how well connected
this Rinzai Zen master was to some of Japan's most powerful figures, including the
emperor. Once again, Inoue was closely connected to someone (i.e., his Zen master)
who had powerful connections.

Young Officers

The first thing to note about the Young Officers, and their not-so-young supporters in the upper echelons of the army, is that they were not ideologically unified
beyond their commitment to a somewhat nebulous Shōwa Restoration in which the
emperor would, in theory, reign supreme. In fact, it can be argued it was exactly
their commitment to an all-powerful emperor that prevented them from embracing
a unified ideological stance, for doing so would have demonstrated their preparedness to infringe on the prerogatives of the emperor, something that could not be
broached *in theory*.

This does not mean, however, that the Young Officers were unconcerned about the actions that the emperor would take once full political power had been restored to him. In the first instance, this is explained by the fact that Japanese military officers were the product of a meritocracy, especially at the lower levels. This meant that many officers of the greatly enlarged wartime officer corps were themselves from rural areas and well acquainted with the impoverishment found there, often personally so. Even if they came from comparatively well-off backgrounds in the cities, officers were aware of the pain their enlisted subordinates experienced when, for example, their sisters were sold into prostitution, families lost their land, or fathers their employment. As the allegedly benevolent father of all Japanese, the person of the emperor was the object of great expectations among the Young Officers, who believed, once freed from the control of corrupt political and business leaders, he would take strong measures to address society's multiple injustices. Nevertheless, it was not their place as loyal subjects to force any course of action or ideology on the emperor.

As the 1930s progressed without any visible social progress, some right-wing officers became increasingly frustrated. They looked for a clear program that could be implemented once the Shōwa Restoration had been accomplished. Readers will recall that the leaders of the Young Officers' Uprising of February 26, 1936, were particularly attracted to the national socialist–oriented writings of Kita Ikki, especially his book *Outline of a Plan to Reorganize Japan* (*Nihon Kaizō Hōan Taikō*). In it, Kita continued to advocate land reform together with bringing an end to the oligarchic rule of Japan by *zaibatsu* financial combines and corrupt politicians. This, he believed, would enable a true union of the people with their sovereign, something that remained of prime importance to the Young Officers.

In this context, Inoue's reaction to the increasingly ideological nature of the Young Officers and their supporters is of interest. On the one hand, Inoue described how close he felt to Kita, not least of all due to their shared Buddhist faith and devotion to the *Lotus Sūtra*. Yet at the same time, he wrote that in attempting to usurp power from the nation's leaders, whether they were rich *zaibatsu* heads or corrupt politicians, the coup plotters were enveloped in the same divisive worldview based on discriminatory thought as their opponents. As a result, Inoue could not support their actions.

Readers will recall that Inoue's plan was to wait until one or another of the attempted coups succeeded, and then, at the first cabinet meeting of the resulting military government held in the emperor's presence, he and his band members would kill those generals who had secretly backed the coup and subsequently taken over the reins of government from the Young Officers. This is truly startling information inasmuch as it reveals the deep divisions within the Shōwa Restoration movement. It also reveals that Inoue had only one goal, the complete and unconditional return of political power to the emperor. This was a much different vision of Japan's future than that of the military, especially the senior leaders of the Imperial Way Faction (Kōdō-ha), who effectively sought to empower themselves *in the name of* the emperor.

Notes

PREFACE

1. Brian Victoria, *Zen at War*, 2nd ed. (Lanham, MD: Rowman & Littlefield, 2006), and *Zen War Stories* (London: RoutledgeCurzon, 2003).

2. Mark Twain, *Autobiography of Mark Twain*, vol. 2 (Berkeley: University of California Press, 2013), entry for December 2, 1906, p. 301, http://www.marktwainproject.org/xtf/view?docId=works/MTDP10363.xml;style=work;brand=mtp;chunk.id=dv0073.

3. Suzuki, *Zen and Japanese Culture* (Princeton, NJ: Princeton University Press, 1959), 59.

4. See, for example, (1) "The 'Negative Side' of D. T. Suzuki's Relationship to War," *Eastern Buddhist* 41, no. 2: 97–138; (2) "Zen as a Cult of Death in the Wartime Writings of D.T. Suzuki," *Asia-Pacific Journal* 11, iss. 30, no. 4; (3) "D.T. Suzuki, Zen and the Nazis," *Asia-Pacific Journal* 11, iss. 43, no. 4; "A Zen Nazi in Wartime Japan: Count Dürckheim and His Sources—D.T. Suzuki, Yasutani Haku'un and Eugen Herrigel," *Asia-Pacific Journal* 12, iss. 3, no. 2. All of these articles, plus various rebuttals of my research, are available at http://www.thezensite.com/MainPages/critical_zen.html.

5. For details of the apologies on the part of the Myōshinji and Tenryūji branches of the Rinzai Zen sect, see Victoria, *Zen at War*, ix–x. Additionally, in the spring of 2001, Kubota Jiun, head of the Sanbō-kyōdan, apologized for the wartime "errant words and actions" of the organization's founder, Zen Master Yasutani Haku'un. For further details concerning Yasutani, see Victoria, *Zen War Stories*, 66–91.

6. For an introduction to Yasutani's wartime writings, see Victoria, *Zen War Stories*, 66–91.

7. Yasutani Haku'un, *Dōgen Zenji to Shūshōgi* [Zen Master Dōgen and the *Shūshōgi*] (Tokyo: Fuji Shobō, 1943), 245–46.

8. Yasutani Haku'un, *Dōgen Zenji*, 19.

9. Quoted in Victoria, *Zen War Stories*, 82.

10. Victoria, *Zen at War*, 191.

11. The July 2010 YouTube video of Lt. Dyer providing meditation instruction to U.S. soldiers stationed at Camp Taji, Iraq, is available at http://www.youtube.com/watch ?v=5GbFGBDFiNo.

12. Capt. Dyer's 2012 explanation of Zen and Buddhism is available at https://www.you tube.com/watch?v=jc-UAumSVL8.

13. Quoted in Vince Little, "Army's First Buddhist Chaplain Serving 11th Engineer Bn.," U.S. Army, December 15, 2011, https://www.army.mil/article/70976/armys_first_buddhist _chaplain_serving_11th_engineer_bn.

14. Associated Press, "Chaplains Lead Spiritual Fight," August 29, 2004.

15. Quoted in Victoria, *Zen at War*, 221.

16. "USAF Academy Buddhist Chapel Dedication," *Buddhist Military Sangha*, November 1, 2007, https://buddhistmilitarysangha.blogspot.com/2007/11/usaf-academy-buddhist -chapel-dedication.html.

17. Quoted in Victoria, *Zen at War*, 37.

CHAPTER 1. INTRODUCTION

1. For example, although now a hackneyed expression, there is still truth to the assertion that one group's "terrorist" is another group's "freedom fighter."

2. The background and full text of this resolution is available at http://en.wikipedia.org/ wiki/United_Nations_Security_Council_Resolution_1566.

3. Andrew Silke, "Research on Terrorism: A Review of the Impact of 9/11 and the Global War on Terrorism," in *Terrorism Informatics: Knowledge Management and Data Mining for Homeland Security*, ed. Hsinchun Chen, Edna Reid, Joshua Sinai, and Andrew Silke (New York: Springer, 2008), 101.

4. Norman Cohn, *Warrant for Genocide: The Myth of the Jewish World Conspiracy and the Protocols of the Elders of Zion* (London: Serif, 1998), 18.

5. Lewis Carroll, *Alice's Adventures in Wonderland*, chap. 6, http://www.gutenberg.org/ files/11/11-h/11-h.htm.

6. The formal name of the Tokyo War Crimes Tribunal was the International Military Tribunal for the Far East (IMTFE). It was a military trial convened on April 29, 1946, to try the leaders of the Empire of Japan for joint conspiracy to start and wage war (categorized as Class A crimes), conventional war crimes (Class B), and crimes against humanity (Class C). The tribunal was adjourned on November 12, 1948.

7. For readers interested in gaining a sense of wartime Japanese totalitarianism, I strongly recommend *The Human Condition* (J., *Ningen no jōken*), an epic film trilogy based on the six-volume novel published from 1956 to 1958 by Gomikawa Junpei. The film was directed by Kobayashi Masaki and follows the life of Kaji, a Japanese pacifist and socialist, as he tries to survive in the totalitarian and oppressive world of wartime Japan. The film is 9 hours and 47 minutes long and is available through the Criterion Collection. For further details, see https:// en.wikipedia.org/wiki/The_Human_Condition_%28film_series%29.

8. Quoted in Max Blumenthal, *Management of Savagery: How America's National Security State Fueled the Rise of Al Qaeda, ISIS, and Donald Trump* (London: Verso, 2019), 7.

9. Blumenthal, *Management of Savagery*, 16.

10. Quoted in Blumenthal, *Management of Savagery*, 7.

CHAPTER 2. SETTING THE STAGE:
JAPAN FROM THE 1860s THROUGH THE 1930s

1. I wish to express my appreciation to Herbert Bix for allowing me to include his insightful description of Emperor Hirohito from his article "War Responsibility and Historical Memory: Hirohito's Apparition," *Asia-Pacific Journal—Japan Focus* 6, no. 5 (May 2008).

2. The Manchurian Incident (aka Mukden Incident) was an event staged by Japanese military personnel as a pretext for the Japanese invasion in 1931 of northeastern China, known as Manchuria. On September 18, 1931, Lt. Kawamoto Suemori of the Independent Garrison Unit detonated a small quantity of dynamite close to a railway line owned by Japan's South Manchuria Railway near Mukden (today's Shenyang). The explosion was so weak it failed to destroy the track, and a train safely passed over it only minutes later. Nevertheless, the Japanese army accused Chinese dissidents of having sabotaged the rail line and used it as an excuse for a full-scale invasion that led to the occupation of Manchuria and the creation, six months later, of the puppet state of Manchukuo.

CHAPTER 3. A TROUBLED YOUTH

1. Inoue Nisshō, *Ichinin issatsu* [One Person Kills One Person] (Tokyo: Nihon Shūhō-sha, 1953), 20.
2. Inoue, *Ichinin*, 26.
3. Inoue, *Ichinin*, 37.
4. Inoue, *Ichinin*, 38.
5. Inoue, *Ichinin*, 42.
6. Inoue, *Ichinin*, 43.
7. Inoue, *Ichinin*, 43.
8. Inoue, *Ichinin*, 44.
9. Inoue, *Ichinin*, 45.
10. Inoue, *Ichinin*, 45–46.
11. Inoue, *Ichinin*, 46.
12. Inoue, *Ichinin*, 50.
13. Inoue, *Ichinin*, 62.
14. Inoue, *Ichinin*, 64.
15. Inoue, *Ichinin*, 65.
16. Inoue, *Ichinin*, 66.
17. Inoue, *Ichinin*, 68.
18. Inoue, *Ichinin*, 69.
19. Inoue, *Ichinin*, 70.
20. Inoue, *Ichinin*, 80.
21. Inoue, *Ichinin*, 81–82.
22. Inoue, *Ichinin*, 84.
23. Inoue, *Ichinin*, 88.

CHAPTER 4. AN ADVENTURER IN CHINA

1. Inoue Nisshō, *Ichinin issatsu* [One Person Kills One Person] (Tokyo: Nihon Shūhō-sha, 1953), 89.

2. Inoue, *Ichinin*, 91–92.

3. Inoue, *Ichinin*, 93–94.

4. Azuma Soshin was the disciple and adopted son of Azuma Daishin, abbot of Fukudaji in Ogi city, Saga prefecture.

5. Inoue, *Ichinin*, 94.

6. Inoue, *Ichinin*, 95–97.

7. Inoue, *Ichinin*, 98.

8. Quoted in Azuma Tōzen, "Ashikarichō to Ketsumeidan Jiken," *Ogi no Rekishi*, No. 65, May 19, 1997, 3. Azuma states that the exact date of their meeting is uncertain.

9. Inoue, *Ichinin*, 99.

10. Inoue, *Ichinin*, 101.

11. Inoue, *Ichinin*, 103–4.

12. Inoue, *Ichinin*, 108.

13. Inoue, *Ichinin*, 109. Note that during World War I Japan was allied to both Great Britain and the United States in their war against Germany and its allies.

14. Inoue, *Ichinin*, 119.

15. Inoue, *Ichinin*, 119.

16. Inoue, *Ichinin*, 119.

17. Inoue, *Ichinin*, 120.

18. Inoue, *Ichinin*, 120.

CHAPTER 5. FIGHTING IN WORLD WAR I

1. Inoue Nisshō, *Ichinin issatsu* [One Person Kills One Person] (Tokyo: Nihon Shūhō-sha, 1953), 120. As previously noted, Japan actually declared war on August 23, 1914, not August 3.

2. The Japanese military presence in Tianjin dates back to 1900 and the victory of seven major Western powers, plus Japan, over the Boxer Rebellion (1899–1901). Subsequent to their victory, the Eight-Nation Alliance forced China to allow them to garrison Tianjin in order to ensure open access to Beijing. The British maintained a brigade of two battalions in Tianjin, while Japan, Italy, France, Germany, Russia, and Austro-Hungary maintained understrength regiments.

3. Inoue, *Ichinin*, 121.

4. Inoue, *Ichinin*, 121–22.

5. Inoue, *Ichinin*, 123.

6. Inoue, *Ichinin*, 123.

7. Inoue, *Ichinin*, 126.

8. Inoue, *Ichinin*, 128.

9. Inoue, *Ichinin*, 135.

10. An abnormal downward displacement of the stomach frequently causing digestive symptoms and constipation.

11. Inoue, *Ichinin*, 156.

12. Inoue, *Ichinin*, 159.

13. Inoue, *Ichinin*, 161.

14. If this scenario seems somewhat unlikely, even far-fetched, it should be remembered that when, on July 7, 1937, the Japanese military launched its full-scale invasion of China

proper in the Marco Polo Bridge Incident, the disappearance of one of its soldiers, Pvt. Shimura, in the vicinity of the Marco Polo Bridge near Beijing, served as the pretext. The Chinese side received a message from the Japanese demanding permission to search for the missing soldier in areas under its control, but the Chinese refused. Although Pvt. Shimura later returned to his unit, the Japanese invaded nonetheless.

15. Inoue, *Ichinin*, 172.

16. Inoue, *Ichinin*, 174.

CHAPTER 6. THE WINDING ROAD TO ENLIGHTENMENT

1. Inoue Nisshō, *Ichinin issatsu* [One Person Kills One Person] (Tokyo: Nihon Shūhō-sha, 1953), 175.

2. Inoue, *Ichinin*, 175.

3. Inoue, *Ichinin*, 177.

4. Inoue, *Ichinin*, 177.

5. Inoue, *Ichinin*, 178.

6. Inoue, *Ichinin*, 178.

7. Inoue, *Ichinin*, 178.

8. Inoue, *Ichinin*, 178.

9. Buddhism contains various formulations of the content of the "three virtues." One formulation refers to the benevolent functions of sovereign, teacher, and parent that a Buddha is said to possess. The virtue of the sovereign is the power to protect all living beings, the virtue of the teacher is the wisdom to instruct and lead them to enlightenment, and the virtue of parent is the compassion to nurture and support them. A second formulation refers to the three attributes of a Buddha: Dharma body, wisdom, and emancipation. The Dharma body means the truth the Buddha realized, or the true aspect of all phenomena; wisdom is the capacity to realize this truth; and emancipation means the state of being free from the suffering of birth and death. There is a correspondence between the three virtues, the three truths, and the Buddha's three bodies: the Dharma body (of the three virtues) corresponds to the truth of the Middle Way and to the Dharma body (of the three bodies), wisdom to the truth of non-substantiality and to the reward body, and emancipation to the truth of temporary existence and to the manifested body. There are additionally several other sets of three virtues attributed to Buddha, such as, for example, the virtue of wisdom to perceive the nature of all things, the virtue of eradicating earthly desires, and the virtue of benefiting living beings.

10. Inoue, *Ichinin*, 183.

11. Inoue, *Ichinin*, 184.

12. Inoue, *Ichinin*, 185.

13. Inoue, *Ichinin*, 186.

14. Inoue, *Ichinin*, 187.

15. Inoue, *Ichinin*, 187.

16. Inoue, *Ichinin*, 188.

17. Inoue, *Ichinin*, 188.

18. *The Analects of Confucius*, trans. A. Charles Muller, 4.8, http://www.acmuller.net/con-dao/analects.html.

19. Inoue, *Ichinin*, 189.

20. Inoue, *Ichinin*, 190.

21. Inoue, *Ichinin*, 191.

22. Inoue, *Ichinin*, 192.

23. Inoue, *Ichinin*, 193.

24. Inoue, *Ichinin*, 194.

25. Inoue, *Ichinin*, 194.

26. Inoue, *Ichinin*, 197.

27. Heinrich Dumoulin, *Zen Buddhism: A History*, vol. 1, *India and China* (New York: Macmillan, 1988), 249. Note that D. T. Suzuki employed these same phrases to illustrate "Zen aestheticism" in *Zen and Japanese Culture* (Princeton, NJ: Princeton University Press, 1959), 352–54.

28. Sengzhao's essay, "The Namelessness of Nirvāna," was the fourth of four essays contained in the *Zhao Lun* (Treatises of Zhao). For further details on Sengzhao's life and the influence he exerted on the development of Zen (Chan) in China, see Dumoulin, *Zen Buddhism*, vol. 1, 70–74.

29. Inoue, *Ichinin*, 198.

30. Inoue, *Ichinin*, 208.

31. Inoue, *Ichinin*, 201–2.

32. Inoue, *Ichinin*, 202.

33. Inoue, *Ichinin*, 203.

34. Inoue, *Ichinin*, 204.

CHAPTER 7. THE VOICE OF HEAVEN

1. Inoue Nisshō, *Ichinin issatsu* [One Person Kills One Person] (Tokyo: Nihon Shūhō-sha, 1953), 209.

2. Inoue, *Ichinin*, 209.

3. Inoue, *Ichinin*, 209.

4. Inoue, *Ichinin*, 210.

5. Inoue, *Ichinin*, 211.

6. Inoue, *Ichinin*, 213.

7. Inoue, *Ichinin*, 213.

8. Inoue, *Ichinin*, 213–14.

9. Inoue, *Ichinin*, 219.

10. Inoue, *Ichinin*, 219.

11. Inoue, *Ichinin*, 220.

12. Inoue, *Ichinin*, 221.

13. Inoue, *Ichinin*, 221.

14. Inoue, *Ichinin*, 166.

15. Inoue, *Ichinin*, 224.

16. Inoue, *Ichinin*, 224.

17. Inoue, *Ichinin*, 227.

18. Inoue, *Ichinin*, 229–30.

19. Inoue, *Ichinin*, 231.

20. Inoue, *Ichinin*, 231.

21. Inoue, *Ichinin*, 233.

22. Inoue, *Ichinin*, 233.

23. Inoue, *Ichinin*, 234.
24. Inoue, *Ichinin*, 235.

CHAPTER 8. THE BLOOD OATH CORPS INCIDENT

1. Inoue Nisshō, *Ichinin issatsu* [One Person Kills One Person] (Tokyo: Nihon Shūhō-sha, 1953), 242.

2. Inoue, *Ichinin*, 242.

3. Note that Nichiren was not the only, or even the first, Japanese Buddhist priest to be concerned about the well-being of Japan. Among the reasons for Buddhism's acceptance in Japan in the mid-sixth century from Korea was its alleged ability to "protect the nation" (J., *gokoku Bukkyō*). Buddhism had previously been accepted in both China and Korea for the same reason. In Japan, the founders of both the Rinzai and Sōtō Zen sects, that is, Eisai and Dōgen, respectively, also wrote treatises on how Zen Buddhism had the same ability. Eisai wrote *Kōzen Gokoku-ron* (A Treatise to Protect the Nation through Promoting Zen), and Dōgen wrote *Gokoku Shōbōgi* (The Meaning of the True Dharma to Protect the Nation). Shakyamuni Buddha, however, did not make this claim for his teaching.

4. The connection to Nichiren is also clear from the temple's name, in that one of Nichiren's most famous treatises was titled *Risshō ankoku ron* (Treatise on [Securing] a Peaceful Land through establishing the True [Dharma]).

5. A *mandala* in Buddhism is a sacred graphic symbol of the universe. The most prominent feature of a Nichiren *mandala* as found on a *Gohonzon* is the phrase *Namu-myōhō-renge-kyō*, written down the center in bold calligraphy. This phrase is called the *daimoku*. Right below, also in bold, Nichiren wrote his name followed by his seal, signifying Nichiren's conviction that his life had manifested the essence of the *Lotus Sūtra*. On the scroll's top row can be found the names of Gautama Buddha and Prabhutaratna and the four leaders of the Bodhisattvas of the Earth. The names of deities believed to protect the Buddha land, called the Four Heavenly Kings (Bishamonten, Jikokuten, Kōmokuten, and Zōjōten), further occupy the four corners, and Sanskrit characters depicting Aizen Myō-ō and Fudō Myō-ō are situated along the left and right outer edges. Within this frame are the names of various Buddhas, Bodhisattvas, historical and mythological figures in Buddhism, personages representing the ten realms, and deities drawn from Vedic, Chinese, and Japanese traditions, arranged hierarchically. Each of these names represents some aspect of the Buddha's enlightenment or an important Buddhist concept.

6. Inoue, *Ichinin*, 247.

7. For example, James Huffman describes Inoue as follows: "A native of Gumma Prefecture, [Inoue] traveled to China and Manchuria during the early 1910s to gather intelligence for the Japanese army. Later, he became a militant Buddhist, converted to the Nichiren sect" (*Modern Japan: An Encyclopedia of History, Culture and Nationalism* [London: Routledge, 1997], 94). Ben-Ami Shillony (*Revolt in Japan: The Young Officers and the February 26, 1936 Incident* [Princeton, NJ: Princeton University Press, 1973], 18) describes Inoue as a "Nichiren mystic."

8. The word *daimoku* literally means "title" and refers to the title of the *Lotus Sūtra* as contained in the mantra *Namu-myōhō-renge-kyō*.

9. Inoue, *Ichinin*, 248–49.

10. Inoue, *Ichinin*, 249.

11. Women did not have the right to vote until the end of 1945 during the Allied occupation of Japan.

12. Inoue, *Ichinin*, 253.

13. Inoue, *Ichinin*, 253.

14. Inoue, *Ichinin*, 256, for this and preceding quotations.

15. For further details concerning his departure, see Inoue's testimony in Onuma Hiroaki, *Ketsumeidan Jiken Kōhan Sokki-roku* [The Stenographic Record of the Public Trial of the Blood Oath Corps Incident] (Tokyo: Ketsumeidan Jiken Kōhan Sokki-roku Kankō-kai, 1963), vol. 1, 117–18.

16. Although Yotsumoto would be sentenced to fifteen years of imprisonment for his role in the Blood Oath Corps Incident, he nevertheless went on to become the private secretary of two wartime prime ministers, Konoe Fumimarō and Suzuki Kantarō. In postwar Japan, Yotsumoto became an advisor and confidant to no less than nine prime ministers, including Nakasone Yasuhiro, a noted Zen practitioner who was particularly fond of Zen master Dōgen's masterwork, the *Shōbōgenzō* (Treasury of the Essence of the True Dharma). Further comments on the strange career of this and other "terrorists" will be made in chapter 13. Yotsumoto did later express regret for having participated in the incident.

17. Inoue, *Ichinin*, 258.

18. Shillony, *Revolt in Japan*, 18.

19. Inoue, *Ichinin*, 258.

20. Inoue, *Ichinin*, 259.

21. See George Wilson, "Kita Ikki's Theory of Revolution," *Journal of Asian Studies* 26, no. 1 (November 1966): 92.

22. Inoue, *Ichinin*, 261.

23. Inoue, *Ichinin*, 262.

24. Inoue, *Ichinin*, 262.

25. Quoted in Inoue, *Ichinin*, 264.

26. Inoue, *Ichinin*, 264.

27. Inoue, *Ichinin*, 267.

28. Inoue, *Ichinin*, 272.

29. Inoue, *Ichinin*, 271.

30. Inoue, *Ichinin*, 271.

31. Inoue, *Ichinin*, 272.

32. Inoue, *Ichinin*, 272.

33. Interestingly, Buddhism also played a role in the First Shanghai Incident. Two Japanese Nichiren sect Buddhist priests and three lay followers, all resident in Shanghai, were beaten by a group of Chinese factory workers on January 18, 1932, near Shanghai's Sanyou Towel Factory. The factory workers had been paid by Japanese army agents in order to provide a casus belli to justify further military action in China. Three of the group were seriously injured, including one of the priests, who died six days later. This attack subsequently became the pretext for a major Japanese attack on Chinese troops stationed in Shanghai that began on January 28. In 1956, Major General Tanaka Ryūkichi (1893–1972) admitted that he had been responsible for secretly arranging the attack when he was still a major attached to the Japanese legation in Shanghai as a military attaché.

34. For a discussion of the various military members who supplied Inoue with pistols, see Onuma, *Ketsumeidan*, vol. 1, 262–66. Nakano Masao states that at some point Inoue also received five pistols and 125 rounds of ammunition, as well as six thousand yen, from Ōkawa

Shūmei. See Nakano Masao, *Kakumei wa Geijutsu nari: Tokugawa Yoshichika no shōgai* (Tokyo: Gakugei Shorin, 1977), 132.

35. Inoue, *Ichinin*, 275.

36. Inoue, *Ichinin*, 277–78.

37. Inoue, *Ichinin*, 280.

38. Inoue, *Ichinin*, 389.

39. Inoue, *Ichinin*, 281.

40. Inoue, *Ichinin*, 282. Amano Tatsuo would later become best known for his role as a leader of another failed uprising, the Heavenly Soldiers Incident (*Shinpeitai Jiken*). The police learned of the plot before it could be carried out in July 1933 and arrested some fifty would-be participants.

41. Inoue, *Ichinin*, 282.

42. Inoue, *Ichinin*, 283.

43. See Inoue's testimony in Onuma, *Ketsumeidan*, vol. 1, 415.

CHAPTER 9. PATRIOTS ON TRIAL

1. Inoue Nisshō, *Ichinin issatsu* [One Person Kills One Person] (Tokyo: Nihon Shūhō-sha, 1953), 285.

2. Inoue, *Ichinin*, 286.

3. Inoue, *Ichinin*, 285.

4. Inoue, *Ichinin*, 288.

5. Inoue Nisshō, *Ume no Mi*, 124–25.

6. Hugh Byas, *Government by Assassination* (London: Bradford & Dicken, 1943), 29.

7. Herbert P. Bix, *Hirohito and the Making of Modern Japan* (New York: HarperCollins, 2000), 252.

8. For a detailed examination of Emperor Hirohito's role at this time see "The Man-churian Transformation," chap. 7 of Bix, *Hirohito and the Making of Modern Japan*, 235–78.

9. Quoted in Maruyama Masao, *Thought and Behaviour in Modern Japanese Politics*, ed. I. I. Morris (London: Oxford University Press, 1963), 67.

10. Inoue, *Ichinin*, 289.

11. The term *Pure Land* is contrasted with the ordinary world, which is tainted with suffering and desire. Amida Buddha's Pure Land is claimed to be blissful and free from impurity.

12. *Nembutsu* literally means to meditate on a Buddha. It was later interpreted to mean reciting the name of Amida Buddha as embodied in the phrase *Namu Amida Butsu* ("Homage to Amida Buddha" or "I take refuge in Amida Buddha"). This phrase is recited by followers of the Pure Land school in Japan, who believe that one can attain rebirth in the Pure Land of Amida Buddha by simply chanting this phrase. In the subsequent *True* Pure Land sect, however, *nembutsu* recitation is understood as an expression of gratitude to Amida Buddha. The belief behind this is that rebirth into the Pure Land is assured the moment one first has faith in Amida and not something one acquires by virtue of *nembutsu* recitation, i.e., through one's own efforts.

13. In the Pure Land school, Primal Vow (aka Original Vow) indicates the eighteenth vow of Amida Buddha, who is said to have promised to enable all people who invoke his name to be reborn in the Pure Land of Perfect Bliss in the West.

14. Shan-tao (613–681) was a Chinese patriarch of the Pure Land school who equated contemplation on Amida Buddha with the chanting of that Buddha's name.

15. In Japan, Hōnen (1133–1212) was revered by his followers as Shan-tao reborn. He refuted all practices other than *nembutsu* and spread the single practice of chanting the name of Amida Buddha.

16. Taitetsu Unno, trans., *Tannisho: A Shin Buddhist Classic* (Honolulu: Buddhist Studies Center Press, 1984). A complete translation, including chap. 2, is available at https://web .archive.org/web/20121018113404/http://www.livingdharma.org/Tannisho/TannishoChap tersI-X.html.

17. *Muga* is a term designating that the "self," i.e. my sense of "I," has no independent or permanent existence of its own. This is true not just of one's "self" but of all things.

18. Inoue, *Ichinin*, 291.

19. See n. 12 above for a discussion of the term *nembutsu*. The term *zammai* (aka *sammai*; Skt., *samādhi*) refers to an intensely concentrated state of mind, or meditation, said to produce inner serenity. *Sammai* is translated as meditation, contemplation, or concentration. Within the Zen school, the practice of *zazen* is used to cultivate, or enter into, this concentrated state of mind. Importantly, however, there are additional methods that can be used for this purpose. In this case, Inoue refers to the recitation of the *nembutsu* as a method of cultivating *sammai*. The recitation of the *daimoku* can also be used for this purpose. This latter point will be explored in further detail in chapter 14 of this book.

20. In the Zen school, it is standard practice for a Zen master to give the first Chinese character of his Buddhist name to a disciple together with a second Chinese character the master selects on the basis of the disciple's character. Thus, the *gen* (lit., mystery) in Inoue's lay name came from the first character in Yamamoto's priestly name, while Yamamoto selected the character *tetsu* (lit., piercing) based on his assessment of Inoue's character.

21. Yotsumoto shared this information with me during an interview held on January 20, 1998, at the Tokyo offices of the Sankō Industrial Construction Company, then headed by the still active Yotsumoto. Note that Ryū-un-in Temple is also known as Hakuzan Dōjō (training center) due to its location in the Hakuzan area of Tokyo's Bunkyō ward.

22. Civil Intelligence Section, General Headquarters, U.S. Far East Command, "The Brocade Banner: The Story of Japanese Nationalism," unpublished report issued September 23, 1946, p. 43.

23. Okamura Ao, *Ketsumeidan jiken* [The Blood Oath Corps Incident] (Tokyo: San-ichi Shobō, 1989), 326.

24. Quoted in Onuma Hiroaki, *Ketsumeidan Jiken Kōhan Sokki-roku* [The Stenographic Record of the Public Trial of the Blood Oath Corps Incident] (Tokyo: Ketsumeidan Jiken Kōhan Sokki-roku Kankō-kai, 1963), vol. 1, 368.

25. Onuma, *Ketsumeidan*, vol. 1, 369.

26. Quoted in Maruyama, *Thought and Behaviour in Modern Japanese Politics*, 53.

27. Daisetz T. Suzuki, *Zen and Japanese Culture* (Princeton, NJ: Princeton University Press, 1959), 36–37.

28. Quoted in Onuma, *Ketsumeidan*, vol. 1, 87–88.

29. Quoted in Onuma Hiroaki, *Ketsumeidan Jiken-jōshinsho-gokuchū Shuki* [The Blood Oath Corps Incident–Written Statements–Prison Diaries] (Tokyo: Ketsumeidan Jiken Kōhan Sokki-roku Kankō-kai, 1971), 30.

30. For a discussion of Onuma Shō's conception of Inoue's band as so many *sute-ishi*, see Onuma, *Ketsumeidan*, vol. 3, 187.

31. *Go* is a Japanese board game played with black and white stones, the object being to surround the opponent's stones.

32. Quoted in Onuma, *Ketsumeidan*, vol. 3, 184.

33. The term *shakubuku* refers to a method of expounding Buddhism aimed at the suppression of others' illusions and subduing their attachment to error. Concretely, it refers to refuting erroneous views and eliminating attachment to false opinions. Thus, the practice of *shakubuku* is a means of correcting the false views of others and awakening them to the truth of Buddhism. On the one hand, it is true that Nichiren employed this method of propagation, describing it in his 1272 treatise *The Opening of the Eyes*. However, it is not an exclusively Nichiren sect methodology since it was already described in earlier works like the *Shrīmālā Sūtra* and the *Great Concentration and Insight* treatise by the Chinese patriarch T'ien-t'ai (538–597). Needless to say, in its original Buddhist formulation, *shakubuku* has no connection to the taking of life.

34. Quoted in Onuma, *Ketsumeidan*, vol. 1, 358–59.

35. Quoted in Onuma, *Ketsumeidan*, vol. 1, 389.

36. Quoted in Byas, *Government by Assassination*, 61.

37. Quoted in Onuma, *Ketsumeidan*, vol. 3, 1151.

38. Quoted in Onuma, *Ketsumeidan*, vol. 2, 12.

39. Quoted in Onuma, *Ketsumeidan*, vol. 2, 25.

40. Quoted in Onuma, *Ketsumeidan*, vol. 2, 25.

41. Quoted in Onuma, *Ketsumeidan*, vol. 2, 13.

42. Quoted in Onuma, *Ketsumeidan*, vol. 2, 25.

43. Quoted in Onuma, *Ketsumeidan*, vol. 2, 29.

44. Quoted in Onuma, *Ketsumeidan*, vol. 2, 101.

45. Quoted in Onuma, *Ketsumeidan*, vol. 2, 114.

46. Quoted in Onuma, *Ketsumeidan*, vol. 2, 114.

47. Quoted in Onuma, *Ketsumeidan Jiken-jōshinsho-gokuchū Shuki*, 259.

48. Quoted in Onuma, *Ketsumeidan*, vol. 2, 149.

49. Quoted in Onuma, *Ketsumeidan*, vol. 2, 122.

50. Quoted in Onuma, *Ketsumeidan*, vol. 2, 203–4.

51. Quoted in Onuma, *Ketsumeidan*, vol. 3, 188.

52. Quoted in Onuma, *Ketsumeidan*, vol. 3, 187.

53. Quoted in Onuma, *Ketsumeidan*, vol. 3, 403.

54. The term *rōshi*, lit., "old teacher," is a term of respect for a Zen priest recognized as a "Zen master."

55. Quoted in Onuma, *Ketsumeidan*, vol. 3, 192.

56. Quoted in Tamaki Benkichi, *Kaisō—Yamamoto Gempō* [Reminiscences of Yamamoto Gempō] (Tokyo: Shunjū-sha, 1970), 40.

57. Although there is some variation in the content of the categories, the four individuals/ groups to whom gratitude is owed are typically identified as (1) one's parents, (2) all sentient beings, (3) one's sovereign, and (4) the Three Treasures of Buddhism (i.e., Buddha, Dharma, and *Sangha*). The Ten Good Practices are typically identified as (1) not killing, (2) not stealing, (3) not engaging in improper sexual conduct, (4) not lying, (5) not speaking deceitfully, (6) not speaking ill of others, (7) not using flowery language, (8) not coveting, (9) not getting angry, and (10) not holding false views.

58. Quoted in Onuma, *Ketsumeidan*, vol. 3, 737.

59. Quoted in Maruyama, *Thought and Behaviour in Modern Japanese Politics*, 53.

CHAPTER 10. IMPRISONMENT:
THE ZEN OF PASTING ENVELOPES

1. Inoue Nisshō, *Ichinin issatsu* [One Person Kills One Person] (Tokyo: Nihon Shūhō-sha, 1953), 292.

2. Inoue, *Ichinin*, 293.

3. Inoue, *Ichinin*, 293.

4. Inoue, *Ichinin*, 305–7.

5. Inoue, *Ichinin*, 295.

6. Chaen Yoshio, *Zusetsu Ni-niroku Jiken* (Tokyo: Nihon Tosho Center, 2001), 27.

7. Inoue, *Ichinin*, 317.

8. While the Control Faction was also anticommunist, they had been chastened by a military encounter with the Soviet Union known in Japan as the Nomonhan Incident. In 1939, the Japanese Sixth Army stationed in Manchuria had been decisively defeated in an undeclared border conflict with the Soviet Union and Mongolia. For further details on this incident and its effect on Japan, see the related *Wikipedia* entry: https://en.wikipedia.org/wiki/Battles_of_Khalkhin_Gol.

9. Inoue, *Ichinin*, 317.

10. Inoue, *Ichinin*, 288.

11. Inoue, *Ichinin*, 288.

12. Inoue, *Ichinin*, 318–19.

13. Inoue, *Ichinin*, 298–99.

14. Inoue, *Ichinin*, 313–14.

15. Brian Victoria, *Zen War Stories* (London: RoutledgeCurzon, 2003), 240, n. 17.

16. See review by Jooeun Noh of Yamada Shōji's 2011 book *The Great Kantō Earthquake, the Korean Massacre and Its Aftermath: The Responsibility of the Japanese Government and People* (Tokyo: Sōshisha). Available at https://www.harvard-yenching.org/the-great-kanto-earthquake.

17. For further details of this incident, including an introduction to the life and thought of Uchiyama Gudō, see Brian Victoria, *Zen at War*, 2nd ed. (Lanham, MD: Rowman & Littlefield, 2006), 38–48.

18. Inoue, *Ichinin*, 315.

19. Inoue, *Ichinin*, 319.

20. Stephen S. Large, "Nationalist Extremism in Early Showa Japan: Inoue Nissho and the 'Blood-Pledge Corps Incident', 1932," *Modern Asian Studies* 35, no. 3 (2001): 562.

CHAPTER 11. FROM PRISON CELL
TO PRIME MINISTER'S ESTATE

1. Yokochi Shō. *Shōwa no Genten: Ichinin Issatsu ni ikita Inoue Nisshō* [The Beginnings of Shōwa: Inoue Nisshō who lived One Person Kills One Person]. Tokyo: Gyōsei Tsushinsha, 1971, 240.

2. Inoue Nisshō, "Ketsumeidan Hiwa" [An Unknown Episode of the Blood Oath Corps], *Bungei Shunjū Magazine* 32, no. 11 (July 1954): 48.

3. Inoue Nisshō, *Ichinin issatsu* [One Person Kills One Person] (Tokyo: Nihon Shūhō-sha, 1953), 323.

4. Inoue, *Ichinin*, 324.

5. Ama-no-Koyane-no-mikoto is a male Shinto deity, one of the chief deities enshrined at Kasuga Shrine in Nara, Japan. He is considered to be an ancestor of the Nakatomi clan and,

hence, its most famous branch—the Fujiwara clan. The Konoe family is a direct descendant of the Fujiwara clan, which long enjoyed a direct historical connection, through marriage, to the imperial family.

6. Inoue, *Ichinin*, 324.

7. Inoue, *Ichinin*, 324.

8. Inoue, *Ichinin*, 325.

9. Inoue, *Ichinin*, 326.

10. Inoue, *Ichinin*, 326.

11. Inoue, *Ichinin*, 326–27.

12. Inoue, *Ichinin*, 327.

13. Inoue, *Ichinin*, 327.

14. Inoue, *Ichinin*, 328.

15. Yokochi Shō. *Shōwa no Genten: Ichinin Issatsu ni ikita Inoue Nisshō* [The Beginnings of Shōwa: Inoue Nisshō who lived One Person Kills One Person]. Tokyo: Gyōsei Tsushinsha, 1971, 300.

16. Inoue, *Ichinin*, 328.

17. Inoue, *Ichinin*, 340.

18. Inoue, *Ichinin*, 336.

19. For more on Yamamoto Gempō's relationship with General Yamashita, see Brian Victoria, *Zen War Stories* (London: RoutledgeCurzon, 2003), 96. For Yamashita's own Zen training, see Brian Padair Farrell and Sandy Hunter, eds., *Sixty Years On: The Fall of Singapore Revisited* (Ann Arbor, MI: Eastern Universities Press, 2002), 190.

20. Inoue, *Ichinin*, 337.

21. Inoue, *Ichinin*, 338.

22. Inoue, *Ichinin*, 339.

23. Inoue, *Ichinin*, 330.

24. Inoue, *Ichinin*, 331.

25. Inoue, *Ichinin*, 331.

26. Inoue, *Ichinin*, 335.

27. Inoue, *Ichinin*, 331.

28. Inoue, *Ichinin*, 331.

29. Inoue, *Ichinin*, 331.

30. Inoue, *Ichinin*, 332.

31. Inoue, *Ichinin*, 332.

32. Inoue, *Ichinin*, 334.

33. Inoue, *Ichinin*, 342.

34. Inoue, *Ichinin*, 342.

35. The Imperial Rule Assistance Association was created at Prime Minister Konoe's direction on October 12, 1940. Its purpose was to create a totalitarian one-party state in order to maximize the efficiency of Japan's total war effort, initially in China.

36. Yokochi Shō. *Shōwa no Genten: Ichinin Issatsu ni ikita Inoue Nisshō* [The Beginnings of Shōwa: Inoue Nisshō who lived One Person Kills One Person]. Tokyo: Gyōsei Tsushinsha, 1971, 306.

37. Inoue, *Ichinin*, 342.

38. Inoue, *Ichinin*, 343.

39. Inoue, *Ichinin*, 343.

40. Inoue, *Ichinin*, 345.

41. Inoue, *Ichinin*, 345.

42. Inoue, *Ichinin*, 346.

43. Yokochi Shō. *Shōwa no Genten: Ichinin Issatsu ni ikita Inoue Nisshō* [The Beginnings of Shōwa: Inoue Nisshō who lived One Person Kills One Person]. Tokyo: Gyōsei Tsushinsha, 1971, 308.

44. Estimates vary according to source. For further discussion of this raid and the ensuing damage, see https://en.wikipedia.org/wiki/Bombing_of_Tokyo.

45. Inoue, *Ichinin*, 348.

46. Inoue, *Ichinin*, 349.

47. Inoue, *Ichinin*, 349.

48. Inoue, *Ichinin*, 349.

CHAPTER 12. AN ULTRANATIONALIST IN POSTWAR JAPAN

1. As noted in chap. 1, Inoue records his conversation with Parsons, whom he describes as a British naval lieutenant, but he doesn't give his first name, age, or any other details about him. See Inoue Nisshō, *Ichinin issatsu* [One Person Kills One Person] (Tokyo: Nihon Shūhō-sha, 1953), 350.

2. Inoue, *Ichinin*, 352.

3. Inoue, *Ichinin*, 352–53.

4. Inoue, *Ichinin*, 353.

5. Inoue, *Ichinin*, 354–55.

6. Inoue, *Ichinin*, 358.

7. Inoue, *Ichinin*, 360.

8. Inoue, *Ichinin*, 360–61.

9. Inoue, *Ichinin*, 362–63.

10. Inoue, *Ichinin*, 367.

11. Inoue, *Ichinin*, 371.

12. Inoue, *Ichinin*, 371.

13. Inoue, *Ichinin*, 371.

14. Inoue, *Ichinin*, 372–73.

15. Inoue, *Ichinin*, 374–75.

16. Inoue, *Ichinin*, 374.

17. Inoue, *Ichinin*, 375.

18. Inoue, *Ichinin*, 376.

19. Inoue, *Ichinin*, 376.

20. Inoue, *Ichinin*, 379–83.

21. Inoue, *Ichinin*, 384.

22. Inoue, *Ichinin*, 384.

23. Inoue, *Ichinin*, 385–86.

24. Inoue, *Ichinin*, 386.

25. Inoue states that he was told "Kenna" was the eldest son of an English aristocrat. The only "Kenna" involved with the tribunal I have been able to locate is "Lee M(ountcastle) Kenna." See Inoue, *Ichinin*, 387.

26. Inoue, *Ichinin*, 388.

27. Inoue, *Ichinin*, 388.

28. Mark Gayn, *Japan Diary* (New York: William Sloane, 1948), 312–13.

29. Gayn, *Japan Diary*, 320.

30. Gayn, *Japan Diary*, 321.

31. Gayn, *Japan Diary*, 319–20.

32. Inoue, *Ichinin*, 391.

33. Inoue, *Ichinin*, 391.

34. Inoue, *Ichinin*, 391.

35. Inoue, *Ichinin*, 392.

36. Inoue, *Ichinin*, 394.

37. Inoue, *Ichinin*, 396.

38. Inoue, *Ichinin*, 396.

39. Inoue, *Ichinin*, 413.

40. Inoue, *Ichinin*, 414.

41. Inoue, *Ichinin*, 415.

42. Inoue, *Ichinin*, 416.

43. Stephen S. Large, "Nationalist Extremism in Early Showa Japan: Inoue Nissho and the 'Blood-Pledge Corps Incident', 1932." *Modern Asian Studies* 35, no. 3 (2001): 539, n. 15.

44. Inoue, *Ichinin*, 397.

45. Eiko Maruko Siniawer, *Ruffians, Yakuza, Nationalists: The Violent Politics of Modern Japan, 1860–1960* (Ithaca, NY: Cornell University Press, 2008), 159–60.

46. Large, "Nationalist Extremism in Early Showa Japan," 563.

47. Quoted in Tom Burghardt, "Drugs, Guns and Nukes: Iran as the New 'Dope, Incorporated,'" Global Research, March 18, 2012, http://www.globalresearch.ca/drugs-guns-and -nukes-iran-as-the-new-dope-incorporated/29839.

48. Inoue Nisshō's daughter informs us that her father referred to her as "Ryōko," but she identifies herself as simply "Ryō." See Inoue Ryō, "Chichi: Inoue Nisshō ga kataru Nankin to Genbaku" [My Father, Inoue Nisshō, Spoke about the Nanking Incident and the Atomic Bombing], *Bungei Shunjū Magazine* 85, no. 11 (September 2007): 291.

49. Yokochi Shō. *Shōwa no Genten: Ichinin Issatsu ni ikita Inoue Nisshō* [The Beginnings of Shōwa: Inoue Nisshō who lived One Person Kills One Person]. Tokyo: Gyōsei Tsushinsha, 1971, 310.

CHAPTER 13. UNRAVELING THE HISTORICAL MATRIX

1. Hugh Byas, *Government by Assassination* (London: Bradford & Dicken, 1943), 59.

2. Described in Ben-Ami Shillony, *Revolt in Japan: The Young Officers and the February 26, 1936 Incident* (Princeton, NJ: Princeton University Press, 1973), 216–17. For a more complete discussion, see Maruyama Masao, *Thought and Behaviour in Modern Japanese Politics*, ed. I. I. Morris (London: Oxford University Press, 1963), 26–33, 65.

3. Quoted in David Titus, *Palace and Politics in Prewar Japan* (New York: Studies of the East Asian Institute, Columbia University, 1974), 275.

4. Herbert P. Bix, *Hirohito and the Making of Modern Japan* (New York: HarperCollins, 2000), 302–6.

5. Titus, *Palace and Politics in Prewar Japan*, 287.

6. Bix, *Hirohito and the Making of Modern Japan*, 305.

7. Quoted in Bix, *Hirohito and the Making of Modern Japan*, 285.

8. Ōmori Sōgen, *Sanzen Nyūmon* (Tokyo: Kōdan-sha, 1986), 69.

9. For further details, see Bix, *Hirohito and the Making of Modern Japan*, 96–99.

10. Nakano Masao, *Kakumei wa Geijutsu nari: Tokugawa Yoshichika no shōgai* (Tokyo: Gakugei Shorin, 1977), 135.

11. For an introduction to General Nogi's Zen practice, see Brian Victoria, *Zen at War*, 2nd ed. (Lanham, MD: Rowman & Littlefield, 2006), 36–37.

12. Bix, *Hirohito and the Making of Modern Japan*, 254.

13. For a complete discussion of this incident, see Bix, *Hirohito and the Making of Modern Japan*, 295–305.

14. Yoshida Yūji, *Tennō Zaibatsu* (Tokyo: Gakkyū, 2011), 4.

15. For further details concerning Kita Ikki and his proposals for the reorganization of Japan, see https://en.wikipedia.org/wiki/Ikki_Kita.

16. Ota Beyūji, *Tokugawa Yoshichika no Jūgo-nen Sensō* [Tokugawa Yoshichika's Fifteen-Year War] (Tokyo: Aoki Shoten, 1988), 86.

17. Ota, *Tokugawa Yoshichika*, 126.

18. Inoue Nisshō, "Ketsumeidan Hiwa" [An Unknown Episode of the Blood Oath Corps], *Bungei Shunjū Magazine* 32, no. 11 (July 1954): 49.

19. Bix, *Hirohito and the Making of Modern Japan*, 299.

20. See Peter Wetzler, *Hirohito and War* (Honolulu: University of Hawai'i Press, 1998), 189.

21. Terasaki Hidenari, *Shōwa Tennō Dokuhakuroku* [Record of Emperor Hirohito's Monologue] (Tokyo: Bungei Shunjū, 1991), 118. Prince Higashikuni was an uncle-in-law of Emperor Hirohito twice over as well as the uncle of Empress Nagako.

22. Quoted in Bix, *Hirohito and the Making of Modern Japan*, 419.

23. Quoted in Bix, *Hirohito and the Making of Modern Japan*, 419.

24. Awaya Kentarō, "The Tokyo Tribunal, War Responsibility and the Japanese People," trans. Timothy Amos, *Asia-Pacific Journal—Japan Focus* 4, no. 2 (2006), https://apjjf.org/-Awaya-Kentaro/2061/article.html.

25. Quoted in David E. Sanger, "Mayor Who Faulted Hirohito Is Shot," *New York Times*, January 19, 1990, https://www.nytimes.com/1990/01/19/world/mayor-who-faulted-hirohito-is-shot.html.

26. The phrase "seven lives to give for my Emperor" refers to a pledge made by the brother of Kusunoki Masashige (1294–1336), a loyal fourteenth-century samurai who fought and died defending Emperor Go-Daigo (1288–1339).

27. Quoted in the *Okinawa Times*, https://www.okinawatimes.co.jp/articles/-/415491. Like all Japanese emperors, Naruhito will be addressed within Japan by the name of his reign era, Emperor Reiwa. Similarly, Akihito was Emperor Heisei, and Hirohito was Emperor Shōwa. Japanese emperors do not have family names, as they are, according to imperial myth, the progenitors of all Japanese.

28. To give but one example, Abe Shinzō, one of postwar Japan's longest serving prime ministers, is the grandson of Kishi Nobusuke (1896–1987). Kishi was known for his brutal rule of the Japanese puppet state of Manchukuo. Interestingly, however, Kishi had begun his political career in the prewar era as a follower of Kita Ikki. Following Japan's defeat, Kishi was imprisoned for three years as a Class A war crime suspect. Nevertheless, the U.S. government released him because they considered Kishi to be the best man to lead postwar Japan in a pro-American direction. He went on to become Japan's fifty-sixth and fifty-seventh prime minister, serving from February 1957 to June 1958. Kishi also favored, but was unable to bring about, the restoration of political powers to the emperor. Kishi was once again prime minister at the time of massive street demonstrations in 1960 opposing the renewal of the Japan–U.S. Security Treaty. He successfully supported the renewal though it cost him the premiership.

CHAPTER 14. UNRAVELING THE RELIGIOUS MATRIX

1. See, for example, Richard Storry, *The Double Patriots: A Study in Japanese Nationalism* (London: Chatto & Windus, 1957), 103, or the more recent monograph by Stephen S. Large,

"Nationalist Extremism in Early Showa Japan: Inoue Nissho and the 'Blood-Pledge Corps Incident', 1932," *Modern Asian Studies* 35, no. 3 (2001): 559.

2. Charles A. Morris, ed., *Thought and Behavior in Modern Japanese Politics* (London: Oxford University Press, 1963), 303.

3. James Huffman, *Modern Japan: An Encyclopedia of History, Culture and Nationalism* (London: Routledge, 1997), 94.

4. Ben-Ami Shillony, *Revolt in Japan: The Young Officers and the February 26, 1936 Incident* (Princeton, NJ: Princeton University Press, 1973), 18.

5. Quoted in Onuma Hiroaki, *Ketsumeidan Jiken Kōhan Sokki-roku* [The Stenographic Record of the Public Trial of the Blood Oath Corps Incident] (Tokyo: Ketsumeidan Jiken Kōhan Sokki-roku Kankō-kai, 1963), vol. 1, 369.

6. Paul Williams, *Mahāyāna Buddhism: The Doctrinal Foundations*, 2nd ed. (London: Routledge, 1989), 149.

7. See George Tanabe and Willa Jane Tanabe, *The Lotus Sutra in Japanese Culture* (Honolulu: University of Hawai'i Press, 1989), 40.

8. See Philip B. Yampolsky, trans., "Zen Master Hakuin's Letter in Answer to an Old Nun of the Hokke [Nichiren] Sect," in *The Zen Master Hakuin: Selected Writings*, 86–123 (New York: Columbia University Press, 1971).

9. Jacqueline Stone, "Chanting the August Title of the *Lotus Sutra*: *Daimoku* Practices in Classical and Medieval Japan," in *Re-visioning Kamakura Buddhism*, ed. Richard Payne (Honolulu: University of Hawai'i Press, 1998), 130.

10. The three treasures are (1) Buddha, (2) Dharma, and (3) *Sangha*.

11. Quoted in Stone, "Chanting the August Title," 132.

12. Stone, "Chanting the August Title," 138.

13. Stone, "Chanting the August Title," 140.

14. Stone, "Chanting the August Title," 144.

15. See https://en.oxforddictionaries.com/definition/mantra.

16. Quoted in Onuma, *Ketsumeidan Jiken-jōshinsho-gokuchū Shuki* [The Blood Oath Corps Incident–Written Statements–Prison Diaries] (Tokyo: Ketsumeidan Jiken Kōhan Sokki-roku Kankō-kai, 1971), 62–63.

17. Daisetz T. Suzuki, *Zen Buddhism and Its Influence on Japanese Culture* (Kyoto: Eastern Buddhist Society, Otani Buddhist University, 1938), 64.

18. Suzuki, *Zen Buddhism and Its Influence*, 36–37.

19. For details of the Zen school's support of Japanese militarism and totalitarianism, see Brian Victoria, *Zen at War*, 2nd ed. (Lanham, MD: Rowman & Littlefield, 2006), and *Zen War Stories* (London: RoutledgeCurzon, 2003).

20. Shōfukuji, located in Fukuoka city on the island of Kyushu, is the first Zen temple constructed in Japan. It was founded in 1195 by the priest Eisai, who introduced the Rinzai sect of Zen Buddhism from China into Japan.

21. Suzuki, *Zen Buddhism and Its Influence*, 40.

22. *Kwatsu* (aka *Katsu*) is a short, loud shout that is used in Chan and Zen Buddhist dialogues to express the enlightened state of the Zen master or induce an initial enlightenment experience in a student.

23. Suzuki, *Zen Buddhism and Its Influence*, 41.

24. The Mongol invasions of Japan took place in 1274 and 1281.

25. Yampolsky, "Zen Master Hakuin's Letter," 69.

26. Quoted in Suzuki, *Essentials of Zen Buddhism*, 458.

27. From Takuan's *Fudōchi Shinmyō-roku,* as quoted in Ichikawa Hakugen, *Fudōchi Shinmyō-roku/Taia-ki* (Tokyo: Kōdan-sha, 1982), 89–90.

28. Winston L. King, *Zen and the Way of the Sword* (Oxford: Oxford University Press, 1993), 190–91.

29. Quoted in Victoria, *Zen War Stories,* 124. Note that his quotation was included in Sugimoto's memoir, titled *Taigi* (Great Duty), of which more than one hundred thousand copies were printed. These books were distributed throughout the upper grades of the Japanese school system, where "study circles" were established to read, and be inspired by, the book's patriotic content. Thus, the numerous references to Zen's efficacy in warfare had a major impact on encouraging ever larger numbers of Japanese youth to die selflessly on the battlefield, as so many did.

30. See pamphlet titled "Hansen Sōryō Sanba, Jidai ni aragai Buppō ni ikita Hankotsu no Hito," produced by Kyōto-kyōku Yasukuni Mondai Gakushū-kai.

31. Quoted in Garma Chang, *Treasury of Mahāyāna Sutras* (University Park: Pennsylvania State University Press, 1983), 456–57. *Kalpa* is a Sanskrit word referring to a very long period of time in Buddhist cosmology.

32. See, for example, the Dalai Lama speaking on "The Essence of Mahayana Buddhism," http://meridian-trust.org/video/the-essence-of-mahayana-buddhism/.

33. In an interview included in the BBC documentary *The Shadow Circus: The CIA in Tibet,* https://www.youtube.com/watch?v=R_5LOPYzddY&t=2485s.

34. See, for example, the United States government-commissioned film series Why We Fight, specifically the map of China included in the introduction to the 1944 film of this series, "The Battle of China." This film is available at https://en.wikipedia.org/wiki/The_Battle_of_China. Note, too, that the Dalai Lama received personal payments from the CIA in the amount of $180,000 per annum from the late 1950s to the mid 1970s. See https://en.wikipedia.org/wiki/CIA_Tibetan_program.

35. Quoted in Onuma, *Ketsumeidan,* vol. 3, 184.

36. Quoted in Onuma, *Ketsumeidan,* vol. 3, 188.

37. Peter Harvey shared these comments with me in an email dated May 28, 2019.

38. Hugh Byas, *Government by Assassination* (London: Bradford & Dicken, 1943), 57.

39. Byas, *Government by Assassination,* 60.

40. Suzuki, *Zen Buddhism and Its Influence,* 5.

41. Suzuki, *Zen Buddhism and Its Influence,* 34–35.

42. See "Introduction" to *The Lankatavara Sutra,* D. T. Suzuki, trans., 1932, http://lirs.ru/do/lanka_eng/lanka-nondiacritical.htm.

43. Partisans of either the traditional Rinzai form of *zazen* (i.e., using *kōan* as objects of meditation) or *shikantaza* (theme-less meditation) as practiced in Sōtō Zen may claim their form of *zazen* is not susceptible to acts of terrorism, but, as included in the appendices, lay practitioners of both forms of *zazen* have employed their meditative practice in preparation for terrorist acts.

44. See, for example, D. T. Suzuki's uncritical reference to Uesugi Kenshin's use of *samādhi* in battle in *Zen Buddhism and Its Influence,* 56.

45. The Chinese character *mu* literally means "no," "nothing," "naught," or "nullity." However, as an object of meditation in the form of a *kōan,* it is used in the Zen school for the purpose of causing the practitioner to overcome discursive thought. For a more complete explanation, see, for example, Barbara O'Brien's article "What Is 'Mu'?," https://www.learnreligions.com/what-is-mu-in-zen-449929.

46. Yamaji Kazuyoshi, *Zen no Ōyō* [The Practical Use of Zen] (Tokyo: Shūbunkaku Shobo, 1941), 29–30.

47. Quoted in Victoria, *Zen at War*, 125–26.

48. The reference here is to Kusanoki Masashige (1294–1336), a fourteenth-century samurai and devout Buddhist who fought for Emperor Go-Daigo in an attempt to wrest rulership of Japan away from the Kamakura Shogunate. In post–Meiji Restoration Japan, the Japanese government promoted Kusanoki as the ideal of samurai loyalty and a model for all Japanese soldiers. According to legend, when his army was completely surrounded, with only fifty of his original seven hundred horsemen still alive, Kusanoki and his brother pledged to be reborn seven times to serve the emperor.

49. Quoted in Victoria, *Zen at War*, 219.

50. Quoted in Onuma, *Ketsumeidan*, vol. 2, 403.

51. Inoue Nisshō, *Ichinin issatsu* [One Person Kills One Person] (Tokyo: Nihon Shūhō-sha, 1953), 190. Note that repetition of the mantra associated with the Pure Land school of Buddhism, i.e., *Namu Amida Butsu* ("I take refuge in Amida Buddha"), can also be used to induce entrance into *samādhi*. Still further, as Inoue points out in chapter 10, in the hands of a skilled meditator, even the unvoiced, repetitive pasting of envelopes can be similarly used.

52. Suzuki, *Zen Buddhism and Its Influence*, 64.

53. Quoted in Onuma, *Ketsumeidan*, vol. 1, 334–35.

54. Commenting on this passage, Peter Harvey pointed out in an email to me on May 28, 2019, that had Nāgārjuna (c. 150–c. 250 CE), the great Buddhist philosopher, read this passage, he would have undoubtedly told Yamamoto that inasmuch as Japan is empty of "Japanness" he shouldn't be attached to it!

55. Hakuin Ekaku, *Wild Ivy*. A partial translation is available at http://www.naturalthinker.net/trl/texts/Hakuin/wildivy.html.

56. The Five Roots are (1) Root of Faith, (2) Root of Zeal, (3) Root of Mindfulness, (4) Root of Meditation, and (5) Root of Wisdom.

57. *Mahāparnirvāṇa-Sutra*, translated into English in 1973 by Kosho Yamamoto from Dharmakshema's Chinese version (*Taisho Tripitaka*, vol. 12, no. 374), http://nirvanasutra.net/convenient/Mahaparinirvana_Sutra_Yamamoto_Page_2007.pdf.

58. For the war-related 1993 "Statement of Repentance" of the Sōtō Zen sect, see Victoria, *Zen at War*, 153–56. For the war-related 2001 proclamation of the Myōshinji branch of the Rinzai Zen sect, see Victoria, *Zen War Stories*, ix–x.

59. This comment is certainly not meant to deny the historical reality that the greatest purveyors of systematic exploitation and oppression of the world's peoples of color since the sixteenth century were first the Europeans, later joined by the United States in the Philippines and elsewhere. It does suggest, however, that Japanese colonialism and aggression against the peoples of Asia, especially in China, was not fundamentally different, cloaked in the same rhetoric of righteous action.

60. Suzuki, *Zen Buddhism and Its Influence*, 64

61. Suzuki, *Zen Buddhism and Its Influence*, 64.

62. Suzuki, *Zen Buddhism and Its Influence*, 64.

63. Suzuki, *Zen Buddhism and Its Influence*, 35.

64. *Mahāparnirvāṇa-Sūtra*, trans. Kosho Yamamoto.

65. Abhidharma (Pali, *Abhidhamma*) is a category of Buddhist scriptures and the ideas contained in and based on them. It attempts to use Buddhist teachings to develop Buddhist ontology and theories of consciousness within the framework of the theory of salvation.

66. Peter Harvey shared these comments with me in an email dated May 29, 2019. Harvey also noted that in the Theravāda tradition there are various different forms of *samādhi*, i.e., it is not just one state. There are, for example, the four *jhāna/dhyānas*, and the four formless states that go beyond these, as well as *animitta/signless samādhi*.

67. Horner, *Taming the Mind*. Available at http://obo.genaud.net/dhamma-vinaya/pts/mn/mn.108.horn.pts.htm.

68. Quoted in Victoria, *Zen at War*, 87.

69. Mark Tatz, *The Skill in Means (Upāyakauśalya) Sutra* (Delhi: Motilal Banarsidass, 1994), 1.

70. Quoted in an email to me on July 27, 2016.

71. *Kalama Sutta: The Buddha's Charter of Free Inquiry*, translated from the Pali by Ven. Soma Thera, https://www.buddhanet.net/e-learning/kalama1.htm.

CHAPTER 15. TRILOGY CONCLUSION

1. Daisetz T. Suzuki, *Zen Buddhism and Its Influence on Japanese Culture* (Kyoto: Eastern Buddhist Society, Otani Buddhist University, 1938), 120.

2. Quoted in Brian Victoria, *Zen at War*, 2nd ed. (Lanham, MD: Rowman & Littlefield, 2006), 126.

3. Peter Harvey, in a May 29, 2019, email, suggests that this fusion may have been facilitated by "emptiness" being changed from its original meaning, i.e., a lack of essence, into an underlying substance/essence. For further discussion of this issue, see Jamie Hubbard and Paul L. Swanson, eds., *Pruning the Bodhi Tree: The Storm over Critical Buddhism* (Honolulu: University of Hawai'i Press, 1997).

4. Winston L. King, *Zen and the Way of the Sword* (Oxford: Oxford University Press, 1993), 190–91.

5. King, *Zen and the Way of the Sword*, 201.

6. King, *Zen and the Way of the Sword*, 185.

7. Satō Gemmyō Taira's articles are "D. T. Suzuki and the Question of War," *Eastern Buddhist* 39, no. 1: 61–120, and "Brian Victoria and the Question of Scholarship," *Eastern Buddhist* 41, no. 2: 139–66. Both are available at http://www.thezensite.com/MainPages/critical_zen.html. Gary Snyder and Nelson Foster's joint article in defense of D. T. Suzuki is "The Fog of World War II: Setting the Record Straight on D. T. Suzuki," *tricycle*, Summer 2010, https://tricycle.org/magazine/fog-world-war-ii/.

8. D. T. Suzuki, "A Buddhist View of War," *Light of Dharma* 4, no. 2 (July 1904): 179–82, http://www.thezensite.com/ZenEssays/CriticalZen/A-Buddhist-View-of-War.html.

9. Daisetsu Suzuki, *Suzuki Daisetsu Zenshū*, ed. Hisamatsu Shin'ichi, Yamaguchi Susumu, and Furuta Shōkin (Tokyo: Iwanami Shoten, 1999–2003), vol. 36, 247.

10. Soyen Shaku, *Sermons of a Buddhist Abbot*, trans. D. T. Suzuki (La Salle, IL: Open Court, 1906), 203. The entire book is available at http://www.sacred-texts.com/bud/zfa/zfa00.htm. The last three chapters are particularly relevant.

11. Daisetsu Suzuki, *Shin-Bukkyō-to* 13, no. 10: 1005. I am grateful to Takahashi Hara of Tokyo University for bringing the Japanese original of this quotation to my attention.

12. D. T. Suzuki, "Makujiki Kōzen," in Suzuki, *Suzuki Daisetsu Zenshū*, vol. 16, 121–35. Originally published in *Kaikō-sha kiji*, June 1941, 17–26. The phrase, *Makujiki Kōzen*, i.e.,

rush forward without hesitation, is believed to have been part of a conversation between Kamakura Regent Hōjō Tokimune (1251–1284) and his Chinese Zen master, Mugaku Sogen (1226–1286), that took place at the time of the second Mongol invasion of Japan in 1281. These words were an admonition to Tokimune to resolutely face the eminent invasion by rushing forward to engage the enemy without the slightest hesitation. This phrase came to epitomize the fearless mental attitude warriors (or later soldiers) should possess when going into battle. This is also an early example in which the Buddhist precept not to kill is completely ignored. Note, too, that it was a Chinese Zen (Chan) master who first demonstrated the application of Zen to the battlefield.

13. Quoted in Victoria, *Zen at War*, 151–52. Suzuki's voice was, of course, not the only one warning against war with the United States. For example, Navy Admiral Yamamoto Isoroku also opposed it for the same reasons. Nevertheless, being the professional military man and loyal subject that he was, Yamamoto went on to plan and execute the attack on Pearl Harbor.

14. Damien Keown conveyed these comments to me in an email dated February 9, 2019. Peter Harvey, in an email on May 29, 2019, elaborated on Keown's comments by pointing out that in Theravāda Buddhism there are four levels of enlightenment, beginning with "stream-entry" and ending with Arahantship. Significantly even stream-entry involves perfected ethical discipline, for the stream-enterer "possesses the virtues dear to the noble ones (*ariya-kantehi sīlehi*), i.e., unbroken, untorn, unblemished, unmottled, freeing (*bhūjissehi*), praised by the wise, unclung to, leading to concentration (*samādhi-saṃvattanikehi*)" (*Saṃyutta Nikāya* V 343). The first of these virtues is, of course, avoidance of any intentional killing.

15. Inoue Nisshō, *Ichinin issatsu* [One Person Kills One Person] (Tokyo: Nihon Shūhō-sha, 1953), 198.

16. Quoted in Onuma Hiroaki, *Ketsumeidan Jiken Kōhan Sokki-roku* [The Stenographic Record of the Public Trial of the Blood Oath Corps Incident] (Tokyo: Ketsumeidan Jiken Kōhan Sokki-roku Kankō-kai, 1963), vol. 3, 184.

17. Quoted in Onuma, *Ketsumeidan*, vol. 3, 737.

18. Bhikkhu Bodhi, "War and Peace: A Buddhist Perspective," *Inquiring Mind* 30, no. 2 (Spring 2014): 5.

19. "The Victory of Dutthagamani," *Mahāvamsa*, chap. 25, http://www.vipassana.com/resources/mahavamsa/mhv25.php.

20. Quoted in Michael Jerryson and Mark Juergensmeyer, eds., *Buddhist Warfare* (Oxford: Oxford University Press, 2010), 189. Originally, *Māra* was the demon who assaulted Shakyamuni Buddha beneath the *bodhi* tree, using violence, sensory pleasure, and mockery in an attempt to prevent the Buddha from attaining enlightenment. In popular usage, *Māra* represents the personification of Death, the Evil One, the Tempter (the Buddhist counterpart of the Devil or Principle of Destruction).

21. "Sayadaw: Killing Non-Buddhists Is Not a Sin," *Engage Dharma*, November 3, 2017, https://engagedharma.net/2017/11/03/sayadaw-killing-non-buddhists-is-not-a-sin/.

22. "Another Article about Chaplain Malasri," *Buddhist Military Sangha*, August 17, 2007, https://buddhistmilitarysangha.blogspot.com/2007/08/another-article-about-chaplain-malasri.html.

23. "The Dalai Lama's Message to the Armed Forces," *Buddhist Military Sangha*, June 21, 2010, https://buddhistmilitarysangha.blogspot.com/2010/06/dalai-lamas-message-to-armed-forces.html.

24. Quoted in Alan Peto, "The Buddhist Soldier," June 22, 2014, http://www.alanpeto .com/buddhism/buddhist-soldier-military/.

25. Marvin Olasky, "Zen Violence: War and Peace in Buddhism," *World Magazine*, February 2010, https://world.wng.org/2010/01/zen_violence.

26. Matthew 7:3 (New International Version).

27. Paul Johnson, *A History of Christianity* (New York: Atheneum, 1976), 241. While dozens of military-religious orders sprang up during the Crusades in the Holy Land, the three most famous are the Knights Templar, the Knights of St. John of Malta, and the Teutonic Knights.

28. Quoted in George P. Wood, review of Philip Jenkins, *The Great and Holy War: How World War I Became a Religious Crusade* (New York: HarperOne, 2014), https://georgepwood. com/2014/08/21/review-of-the-great-and-holy-war-how-world-war-i- became-a-religious-crusade-by-philip-jenkins/.

29. Quoted in George P. Wood, review of Philip Jenkins, *The Great and Holy War: How World War I Became a Religious Crusade* (New York: HarperOne, 2014), https://georgepwood .com/2014/08/21/review-of-the-great-and-holy-war-how-world-war-i- became-a-religious -crusade-by-philip-jenkins/.

30. Quoted in Heinrich Missalla, *Für Gott, Führer und Vaterland* (Munich: Kösel-Verlag, 1999), 51.

31. Quoted in Norman Cohn, *Warrant for Genocide: The Myth of the Jewish World Conspiracy and the Protocols of the Elders of Zion* (London: Serif, 1998), 187.

32. Daniel Berrigan and Thich Nhat Hanh, *The Raft Is Not the Shore* (Boston: Beacon Press, 1975), 34.

33. Quoted in *Ha'aretz*, April 12, 2001.

34. *New York Times*, August 29, 2004, 8.

35. Lao Tzu, *Tao Te Ching*, chap. 64, http://taoteching.org.uk/chapter64.html.

36. This phrase is often translated as "Work out your salvation with *diligence*." However, Stephan Bachelor suggests "care" is a more accurate translation than "diligence." See Stephan Bachelor, "The Buddha's Last Word: Care," *Insight Journal*, Spring 2005, https://www.bud dhistinquiry.org/article/the-buddhas-last-word-care/.

37. See, for example, Thich Nhat Hanh's contribution to the book *For a Future to be Possible: Commentaries on the Five Wonderful Precepts* (Berkeley: Parallax Press, 1993) or his book *Being Peace* (New York: University of New York Press, 1987).

38. Luke 4:23 (New International Version).

39. David Gordis, "The Essence of Pluralism," http://wisdomofreligion.blogspot .com/2007/02/religious-dialogue-basics.html.

EPILOGUE

1. From a speech delivered on September 17, 2001, titled "President: Today We Mourned, Tomorrow We Work," https://georgewbush-whitehouse.archives.gov/news/releases/ 2001/09/20010916-2.html.

2. Quoted in Peter Ford, "Europe Cringes at Bush 'Crusade' against Terrorists," *Christian Science Monitor*, September 19, 2001, https://www.csmonitor.com/2001/0919/p12s2-woeu.html.

3. Quoted in *Library of Social Science Newsletter*, January 23, 2019, https://www.libraryof socialscience.com/newsletter/posts/2019/2019-01-23-fornari2.html.

4. Franco Fornari, *The Psychoanalysis of War*, trans. Alenka Pfeifer (Bloomington: Indiana University Press, 1975).

5. Quoted in Martha Crenshaw, ed., *Terrorism in Context* (University Park: Pennsylvania State University Press, 1995), 527.

6. Quoted in "Allegations of CIA Assistance to Osama bin Laden," *Wikipedia*, https://en.wikipedia.org/wiki/Allegations_of_CIA_assistance_to_Osama_bin_Laden.

7. Satya Sagar, "Sri Lanka's Sacred Games," Countercurrents.org, April 30, 2019, https://countercurrents.org/2019/04/sri-lankas-sacred-games-satya-sagar.

8. Père Daniel Maes, "The Media Coverage on Syria Is the Biggest Media Lie of Our Time," *Global Research*, January 24, 2017, http://www.globalresearch.ca/the-media-coverage-on-syria-is-the-biggest-media-lie-of-our-time-interview-with-flemish-priest-in-syria/5571199.

9. Max Blumenthal, *The Management of Savagery: How America's National Security State Fueled the Rise of Al Qaeda, ISIS, and Donald Trump* (London: Verso, 2019), 331–32.

10. Quoted in Blumenthal, *Management of Savagery*, 340.

11. Quoted in Blumenthal, *Management of Savagery*, 379–80.

12. Quoted in Blumenthal, *Management of Savagery*, 380.

13. Stephen S. Large, "Nationalist Extremism in Early Showa Japan: Inoue Nissho and the 'Blood-Pledge Corps Incident', 1932," *Modern Asian Studies* 35, no. 3 (2001): 557.

14. Okamura Ao, *Ketsumeidan Jiken* [The Blood Oath Corps Incident] (Tokyo: San-ichi Shobō, 1989), 341.

15. A signature strike is defined as a military attack by a drone or drones in which people are targeted because their activities are believed to fit a particular behavioral profile, though their individual identities are unknown.

16. For example, it is clear that the United States provided arms if not funding to certain terrorist groups in Syria because both the American government and the terrorists oppose the government of Syrian President Bashar al-Assad. For one description, see James Carden, "Why Does the US Continue to Arm Terrorists in Syria?," *Nation*, March 3, 2017, https://www.thenation.com/article/why-does-the-us-continue-to-arm-terrorists-in-syria/.

17. For example, albeit controversially, questions have been raised as to whether one of the reasons the United States chose to kill (rather than capture) Osama bin Laden was to ensure he would not provide damaging revelations about his past connections to the CIA and American government officials.

18. Karen Armstrong, *Fields of Blood: Religion and the History of Violence* (New York: Knopf, 2014), 343–44.

19. For a Buddhist understanding of the importance of a just and equitable society, see Peter Harvey, *An Introduction to Buddhist Ethics* (Cambridge: Cambridge University Press, 2000), 197–203, as well as the *Kūṭadanta Sutta*, e.g., the fourth section, "The Story of King Mahāvijita's Sacrifice," https://suttacentral.net/dn5/en/sujato.

20. Quotation available from http://www.christianity.com/church/church-history/timeline/1601-1700/french-scientist-blaise-pascal-11630138.html. Note, however, the attribution of this quotation to Pascal is contested.

APPENDIX 1. THE ASSASSINATION OF GENERAL NAGATA TETSUZAN

1. The material included in appendices 1 and 2 is an abridged version of material first presented in Brian Victoria, *Zen War Stories* (London: RoutledgeCurzon, 2003), 27–65.

2. Daisetz T. Suzuki, *Zen and Japanese Culture* (Princeton, NJ: Princeton University Press, 1959), 35.

3. This phrase is later quoted by Fukusada Mugai in defense of his disciple, Lt. Col. Aizawa Saburō's actions. It was employed repeatedly by countless Zen masters and other Buddhist leaders during the Asia-Pacific War (and before) to justify their endorsement of Japan's military actions abroad. Its origin can be traced to the famous Chinese Buddhist treatise entitled *Sanlun Xuanyi* written by the Sui Dynasty priest, Jicang (643–712). It forms one of the fundamental tenets of the *Sanlun* school (Three Treatises, J. *Sanron*) based on the Mādhyamika philosophy of Nāgārjuna. However, the "destruction" called for in this school originally had nothing to do with taking the lives of other sentient beings. Instead, it refers to "destroying" the mind of attachment, such "destruction" being in and of itself the establishment of the True [Dharma].

4. For a detailed exposition of the February 26 Incident, see Richard Storry, *The Double Patriots: A Study in Japanese Nationalism* (London: Chatto & Windus, 1957), 177–91, or Hugh Borton, *Japan's Modern Century* (New York: Ronald Press, 1970), 386–89.

5. The incident is described in Meirion Harries and Susie Harries, *Soldiers of the Sun: The Rise and Fall of the Imperial Japanese Army* (New York: Random House, 1992), 181–82.

6. Quoted in David Bergamini, *Japan's Imperial Conspiracy* (New York: William Morrow, 1971), 802. It is also noteworthy that Yamazaki Ekijū, one of those Rinzai Zen masters whom I identified in *Zen at War* (2nd ed., [Lanham, MD: Rowman & Littlefield, 2006], 121–29) as a staunch supporter of Japanese militarism, conducted a memorial service for Maj. Gen. Nagata following his assassination. It can therefore be said that at least in this instance prominent Rinzai and Sōtō Zen masters found themselves on opposite sides of the fence, though both remained, nevertheless, closely connected to the Japanese military. For further discussion of Ekijū's role, see Ichikawa Hakugen, *Nihon Fashizumu ka no shūkyō* [Religion under Japanese Fascism] (Tokyo: NS Shuppan-kai, 1975), 42–44, 81.

7. Quoted in Sugawara Yutaka, *Aizawa Chūsa Jiken no Shinsō* (Tokyo: Keizai Ōrai-sha, 1971), 180–81. Prince Higashikuni was well known for his interest in Buddhism. For details of some of the uses to which he put his Buddhist faith, see Bergamini, *Japan's Imperial Conspiracy*, 813–15, 1374–75. Readers unfamiliar with Bergamini's work, however, are cautioned against accepting at face value the author's always flamboyant and sometimes inaccurate description of events.

8. Sugawara, *Aizawa*, 181.

9. Sugawara, *Aizawa*, 181.

10. Quoted in Yamada Kyōdō, *Mugai-san no Fūkei* [A View of Mugai] (Sendai: Hōbundō, 1991), 191.

11. Sugawara, *Aizawa*, 81.

12. Sugawara, *Aizawa*, 203.

13. Quoted in Katano, *Kongō-hōzan Rinnōji gohyaku-gojū-nen-shi*, 191.

14. Katano Tatsurō, *Kongō-hōzan Rinnōji gohyaku-gojū-nen-shi* [A History of the Five Hundred and Fifty Years of Kongō-hōzan Rinnōji Temple] (Sendai: Kongō-hōzan Rinnōji, 1994), 193.

15. Quoted in Hugh Byas, *Government by Assassination* (London: Bradford & Dicken, 1943), 111.

16. Byas, *Government by Assassination*, 111–12.

17. Byas, *Government by Assassination*, 113.

18. Quoted in James W. Heisig and John C. Maraldo, *Rude Awakenings* (Honolulu: University of Hawai'i Press, 1994), 22.

19. R. H. Blyth, *Zen and Zen Classics*, vol. 4, *Mumonkan* (Tokyo: Hokuseido Press, 1966), 123.

20. Katano, *Kongō-hōzan*, 189.

21. Katano, *Kongō-hōzan*, 190.

22. Katano, *Kongō-hōzan*, 190.

23. Katano, *Kongō-hōzan*, 190.

24. Katano, *Kongō-hōzan*, 193.

25. Quoted in Victoria, *Zen at War*, 37.

26. Suzuki, *Zen and Japanese Culture*, 36–37.

27. Suzuki, *Zen and Japanese Culture*, 36.

28. Suzuki, *Zen and Japanese Culture*, 64.

29. Suzuki, *Zen and Japanese Culture*, 36.

APPENDIX 2. ZEN IN THE FEBRUARY 26, 1936, INCIDENT

1. Dōgen Hosokawa, *Omori Sogen: The Art of a Zen Master* (London: Kegan Paul International, 1999), xi–xiii.

2. For an introduction to Ōmori's connection to Tōyama, see Brian Victoria, *Zen War Stories* (London: RoutledgeCurzon, 2003), 189–90.

3. Quoted in Hosokawa, *Omori Sogen*, 71–72.

4. Quoted in Ōmori Sōgen, *Sanzen Nyūmon* (Tokyo: Kōdan-sha, 1986), 248–49.

5. Quoted in Victoria, *Zen War Stories*, 188.

6. Quoted in Hosokawa, *Omori Sogen*, 28.

7. Quoted in Hori Yukio, *Uha Jiten* (Tokyo: Sanryō Shobō, 1991), 123.

8. Hori, *Uha Jiten*, 125.

9. Hori, *Uha Jiten*, 312.

10. Quoted in Hosokawa, *Omori Sogen*, 41.

11. Hosokawa, *Omori Sogen*, 40.

12. Hori, *Uha Jiten*, 311.

13. See Ben-Ami Shillony, *Revolt in Japan: The Young Officers and the February 26, 1936 Incident* (Princeton, NJ: Princeton University Press, 1973), 42.

14. Arahara Bokusui, *Dai-uha Shi*, 431.

15. Contained in Arahara, *Dai-uha Shi* (Tokyo: Dai-Nippon Issei-kai Shuppan, 1974), 431.

16. Quoted in Hori, *Uha Jiten*, 416.

17. Quoted in Hosokawa, *Omori Sogen*, 43.

18. Quoted in Naimushō Keihō-kyoku, *Shuppan Keisatsu-hō* 73 (September 1934), 166.

19. Arahara, *Dai-uha Shi*, 432.

20. Shillony, *Revolt in Japan*, 112.

21. Quoted in Toyoda Jō, *Kakumeika Kita Ikki* (Tokyo: Kōdan-sha, 1991), 409.

22. Quoted in Hori, *Uha Jiten*, 294.

23. Quoted in Hori, *Uha Jiten*, 294.

24. See Shillony, *Revolt in Japan*, 128.

25. Shillony, *Revolt in Japan*, 132.

26. Quoted in Hosokawa, *Omori Sogen*, 45.

27. Quoted in Shillony, *Revolt in Japan*, 164.
28. Quoted in Shillony, *Revolt in Japan*, 173.
29. Herbert P. Bix, *Hirohito and the Making of Modern Japan* (New York: HarperCollins, 2000), 305.
30. Quoted in Hosokawa, *Omori Sogen*, 45.
31. Quoted in Civil Intelligence Section, General Headquarters, U.S. Far East Command, "The Brocade Banner: The Story of Japanese Nationalism," unpublished report issued September 23, 1946, p. 92.
32. Civil Intelligence Section, "Brocade Banner," 91.
33. Quoted in Hosokawa, *Omori Sogen*, 47.
34. For more on Seki Seisetsu's political views, especially his strong support for the application of the *Bushidō* spirit to Japan's military actions at the time, see Brian Victoria, *Zen at War*, 2nd ed. (Lanham, MD: Rowman & Littlefield), 112–13.
35. Quoted in Hosokawa, *Omori Sogen*, 47.
36. Hosokawa, *Omori Sogen*, 47.
37. Civil Intelligence Section, "Brocade Banner," 129.
38. Quoted in Hosokawa, *Omori Sogen*, 51.
39. Hosokawa, *Omori Sogen*, 49.
40. For further details, see Victoria, *Zen at War*, 190.
41. Hosokawa, *Omori Sogen*, 51.
42. Hosokawa, *Omori Sogen*, 51.
43. As previously noted, Ōmori was closely connected to Tōyama Mitsuru. See Victoria, *Zen at War*, 189.
44. Quoted in Hosokawa, *Omori Sogen*, 51.
45. Hosokawa, *Omori Sogen*, 58.
46. Ōmori, *Yamaoka Tesshū*, 212.
47. Quoted in Hosokawa, *Omori Sogen*, 73.
48. Hosokawa, *Omori Sogen*, 81.
49. Hosokawa, *Omori Sogen*, 95.
50. Hosokawa, *Omori Sogen*, 51.
51. Hosokawa, *Omori Sogen*, 52. Although the term *harakiri* for traditional ritual suicide is better known in the West, the Japanese themselves prefer the term *seppuku*.
52. Quoted in Hori, *Uha Jiten*, 308.
53. Hori, *Uha Jiten*, 308.
54. Hori, *Uha Jiten*, 308.
55. Hori, *Uha Jiten*, 309.
56. Hori, *Uha Jiten*, 234.
57. Quoted in Hosokawa, *Omori Sogen*, 76–77.

APPENDIX 3. HISTORICAL BACKGROUND MATERIALS

1. Quoted in Brian Victoria, *Zen War Stories* (London: RoutledgeCurzon, 2003), 179.
2. Victoria, *Zen War Stories*, 28–29.
3. Quoted in *Japan at War* (New York: Time Life Education, 1980), 18.
4. See "Sadao Araki," https://en.wikipedia.org/wiki/Sadao_Araki. For Emperor Hirohito's role related to Unit 731, see Herbert P. Bix, *Hirohito and the Making of Modern Japan* (New York: HarperCollins, 2000), 362–64.

5. Fukuda Kazuya, *Shōwa Tennō* (*Daisan-bu*) (Tokyo: Bungei Shunjū, 2009), 297–98.

6. Fukuda, *Shōwa Tennō*, 299.

7. Inoue Nisshō, *Ichinin issatsu* [One Person Kills One Person] (Tokyo: Nihon Shūhō-sha, 1953), 324.

8. Margaret Macmillan and Richard Holbrooke, *Paris 1919: Six Months That Changed the World* (New York: Random House, 2007), 487.

9. For further details, see Iris Chang, *The Rape of Nanking* (New York: Basic Books, 2012).

10. Gerhard Weinberg, *The Foreign Policy of Hitler's Germany: Starting World War II, 1937–39* (Chicago: University of Chicago Press, 1980), 176.

11. Translation appears in David C. Earhart, *Certain Victory* (New York: M.E. Sharpe, 2008), 142.

12. Fujita Hisanori, *Jijūchō no kaisō* (Tokyo: Chūō Kōronsha, 1987), 66–67.

13. For an extended discussion of Okawa's mental state, see Eric Jaffe, *A Curious Madness: An American Combat Psychiatrist, a Japanese War Crimes Suspect, and an Unsolved Mystery from World War II* (New York: Scribner, 2014).

14. Nakano Masao, *Kakumei wa Geijutsu nari: Tokugawa Yoshichika no shōgai* (Tokyo: Gakugei Shorin, 1977), 155.

15. One source states that in March 1931 Yoshichika gave a total of two hundred thousand yen to the Sakura-kai (Cherry Blossom Association) in support of a 1931 attempted military coup, which came to be known as the March Incident. A second source claims Yoshichika gave five hundred thousand yen. See https://wiki.samurai-archives.com/index.php?title=Tokugawa_Yoshichika. Whatever the amount, these were sizable sums of money in prewar Japan. Yoshichika is also known to have provided funding for additional coup attempts.

16. Ernst Meunieur, *Völkischer Beobachter* (People's Observer), Munich edition, January 15, 1942.

17. See reference in chap. 10. It is true that Inoue was incarcerated longer than Tōyama expected, but Inoue makes it clear this was due to the intervening Young Officers' Uprising of February 26, 1936.

18. See Bix, *Hirohito and the Making of Modern Japan*, 100.

19. Bix, *Hirohito and the Making of Modern Japan*, 100. For a more detailed description of this incident, see Bix, *Hirohito and the Making of Modern Japan*, 95–101.

20. This phrase originates with Saigō Takamori (1828–1877), one of the leaders of the Meiji Restoration. Later, however, it became closely associated with Tōyama Mitsuru due to his frequent invocation of it.

21. See reference in chap. 7.

22. Takagi Makoto, *Gempō Rōshi* (Tokyo: Daizō Shuppan-sha, 1963), 87.

23. This incident is described in Tamaki Benkichi, *Kaisō—Yamamoto Gempō* [Reminiscences of Yamamoto Gempō] (Tokyo: Shunjū-sha, 1970), 32.

24. Quoted in Tamaki, *Kaisō*, 149.

25. For further details of Asahina Sōgen's right-wing activities, see Brian Victoria, *Zen at War*, 2nd ed. (Lanham, MD: Rowman & Littlefield), 162–66; for those of Harada Sōgaku, see 135–38 in the same book; and for those of Yasutani Haku'un, see chap. 5 of Victoria, *Zen War Stories*, 66–91. Note that Yamada Kōun, as Yasutani's chief Dharma heir, became the administrative and spiritual head (*kanchō*) of the Sanbōkyōdan in 1970. The Sanbōkyōdan (Three Treasures Association) was the name given to what was, in essence, a newly established Zen sect, first registered with the Japanese government in January 1954.

26. For a full introduction to Yasutani's war-related actions and teachings, see Victoria, *Zen War Stories*, 66–91.

27. Quoted in Victoria, *Zen War Stories*, 73.

28. Quoted in Takagi, *Gempō Rōshi*, 84–85.

29. I am grateful to the late Robert Aitken for having shared with me a photocopy of the colophon of this sutra booklet.

30. Quoted in Tamaki, *Kaisō*, 201.

31. Quoted in Tamaki, *Kaisō*, 202.

32. Quoted in Tamaki, *Kaisō*, 202.

33. Quoted in Leonard Mosley, *Hirohito, Emperor of Japan* (London: Prentice-Hall International, 1966), 356.

References

WORKS IN WESTERN LANGUAGES

Armstrong, Karen. *Fields of Blood: Religion and the History of Violence.* New York: Knopf, 2014.

Awaya Kentarō. "The Tokyo Tribunal, War Responsibility and the Japanese People." Translated by Timothy Amos. *Asia-Pacific Journal—Japan Focus* 4, no. 2 (2006). https://apjjf .org/-Awaya-Kentaro/2061/article.html.

Bergamini, David. *Japan's Imperial Conspiracy.* New York: William Morrow, 1971.

Berger, Peter L. *The Social Reality of Religion.* Middlesex, UK: Penguin University Books, 1973.

Behr, Edward. *Hirohito: Behind the Myth.* New York: Vintage Books, 1989.

Beasley, W. G. *The Rise of Modern Japan: Political, Economic, and Social Change since 1850.* 3rd ed. New York: Palgrave Macmillan, 2000.

Berrigan, Daniel, and Thich Nhat Hanh. *The Raft Is Not the Shore.* Boston: Beacon Press, 1975.

Bix, Herbert P. *Hirohito and the Making of Modern Japan.* New York: HarperCollins, 2000.

———. "Symbol Monarchy." *Journal of Japanese Studies* 21, no. 2 (Summer 1995): 319–63.

Blumenthal, Max. *The Management of Savagery: How America's National Security State Fueled the Rise of Al Qaeda, ISIS, and Donald Trump.* London: Verso, 2019.

Blyth, R. H. *Zen and Zen Classics.* Vol. 4, *Mumonkan.* Tokyo: Hokuseido Press, 1966.

Bodhi, Bhikkhu "War and Peace: A Buddhist Perspective." *Inquiring Mind* 30, no. 2 (Spring 2014): 5–7.

Borton, Hugh. *Japan's Modern Century.* New York: Ronald Press, 1970.

Burghardt, Tom. "Drugs, Guns and Nukes: Iran as the New 'Dope, Incorporated.'" Global Research, March 18, 2012. http://www.globalresearch.ca/drugs- guns-and-nukes-iran-as -the-new-dope-incorporated/29839.

Byas, Hugh. *Government by Assassination.* London: Bradford & Dicken, 1943.

Chan, Wing-Tsit. *A Source Book in Chinese Philosophy.* Princeton, NJ: Princeton University Press, 1963.

Chang, Garma, ed. *A Treasury of Mahāyāna Sutras.* University Park: Pennsylvania State University Press, 1983.

Chappell, David W., ed. *Buddhist Peacework: Creating Cultures of Peace.* Boston: Wisdom Publications, 1999.

Civil Intelligence Section, General Headquarters, U.S. Far East Command. "The Brocade Banner: The Story of Japanese Nationalism." Unpublished report issued September 23, 1946.

Cohn, Norman. *Warrant for Genocide: The Myth of the Jewish World Conspiracy and the Protocols of the Elders of Zion.* London: Serif, 1998.

Coomaraswamy, Ananda K. *Buddha and the Gospel of Buddhism.* London: George G. Harrap, 1916.

Crenshaw, Martha, ed. *Terrorism in Context.* University Park: Pennsylvania State University Press, 1995.

Dayal, Har. *The Bodhisattva Doctrine in Buddhist Sanskrit Literature.* London: Routledge & Kegan Paul, 1932.

Demiéville, Paul. "Le bouddhisme et la guerre." In *Choix D'études Bouddhiques.* Leiden: Brill, 1973.

Dower, John W. *War without Mercy.* New York: Pantheon Books, 1986.

Drea, Edward J. *In Service of the Emperor: Essays on the Imperial Japanese Army.* Lincoln: University of Nebraska Press, 1998.

Dumoulin, Heinrich. *Zen Buddhism: A History.* Vol. 1, *India and China.* New York: Macmillan, 1988.

———. *Zen Buddhism: A History.* Vol. 2, *Japan.* New York: Macmillan, 1990.

Earhart, David C. *Certain Victory.* New York: M.E. Sharpe, 2008.

Ehman, Mark A. "The Saddharmapundarika-Sutra." In *Buddhism: A Modern Perspective,* edited by Charles S. Prebish, 102–7. University Park, Pennsylvania State University Press, 1994.

Eliot, Charles. *Japanese Buddhism.* London: Edward Arnold, 1935.

Epsteiner, Fred, ed. *The Path of Compassion: Writings on Socially Engaged Buddhism.* Berkeley CA: Parallar Press, 1985.

Farrell, Brian Padair, and Sandy Hunter, eds. *Sixty Years On: The Fall of Singapore Revisited.* Ann Arbor, MI: Eastern Universities Press, 2002.

Faure, Bernard. *Chan Insights and Oversights.* Princeton, NJ: Princeton University Press, 1993.

———. *The Rhetoric of Immediacy.* Princeton, NJ: Princeton University Press, 1991.

Frank, Richard B. *Downfall: The End of the Imperial Japanese Empire.* New York: Random House, 1999.

Gayn, Mark. *Japan Diary.* New York: William Sloane, 1948.

Harries, Meirion, and Susie Harries. *Soldiers of the Sun: The Rise and Fall of the Imperial Japanese Army.* New York: Random House, 1992.

Harvey, Peter. *An Introduction to Buddhist Ethics.* Cambridge: Cambridge University Press, 2000.

Heisig, James W., and John C. Maraldo, eds. *Rude Awakenings.* Honolulu: University of Hawai'i Press, 1994.

Horner, I. B., trans. *Taming the Mind: Discourses of the Buddha (WH51).* Kandy, Sri Lanka: Buddhist Publication Society, 1983.

Hosokawa, Dōgen. *Omori Sogen: The Art of a Zen Master.* London: Kegan Paul International, 1999.

Hubbard, Jamie, and Paul L. Swanson, eds. *Pruning the Bodhi Tree: The Storm over Critical Buddhism.* Honolulu: University of Hawai'i Press, 1997.

Huffman, James. *Modern Japan: An Encyclopedia of History, Culture and Nationalism.* London: Routledge, 1997.

Ives, Christopher. *Imperial Way Zen.* Honolulu: University of Hawai'i Press, 2009.

———. *Zen Awakening and Society.* Honolulu: University of Hawai'i Press, 1992.

Jaffe, Eric. *A Curious Madness: An American Combat Psychiatrist, a Japanese War Crimes Suspect, and an Unsolved Mystery from World War II.* New York: Scribner, 2014.

Johnson, Paul. *A History of Christianity.* New York: Atheneum, 1979.

King, Winston L. *Zen and the Way of the Sword.* Oxford: Oxford University Press, 1993.

Kisala, Robert. *Prophets of Peace: Pacifism and Cultural Identity in Japan's New Religions.* Honolulu: University of Hawai'i Press, 1999.

Kotler, Arnold, ed. *Engaged Buddhist Reader: Ten Years of Engaged Buddhist Publishing.* Berkeley, CA: Parallax Press, 1996.

Kubota, Jiun. "Apology for What the Founder of the Sanbokyodan, Haku'un Yasutani Roshi, Said and Did during World War II." *Kyōshō* [Awakening Gong] 281 (March–April 2000): 67–69.

Large, Stephan S. "Nationalist Extremism in Early Showa Japan: Inoue Nissho and the 'Blood-Pledge Corps Incident', 1932." *Modern Asian Studies* 35, no. 3 (2001): 553–64.

Lopez, Donald S., Jr., ed. *Buddhism in Practice.* Princeton, NJ: Princeton University Press, 1995.

Lory, Hillis. *Japan's Military Masters: The Army in Japanese Life.* Westport, CT: Greenwood Press, 1973. First published 1943.

Marshall, George N. *Buddha: The Quest for Serenity.* Boston: Beacon Press, 1978.

Marty, Martin E. "An Exuberant Adventure: The Academic Study and Teaching of Religion." *Academe* 82, no. 6 (1996): 14–17.

Maruyama Masao. *Thought and Behaviour in Modern Japanese Politics.* Edited by I. I. Morris. London: Oxford University Press, 1963.

Missalla, Heinrich. *Für Gott, Führer und Vaterland.* Munich: Kösel-Verlag, 1999.

Moore, Charles A., ed. *The Japanese Mind.* Honolulu: University Press of Hawaii, 1967.

Morris, I. I. *Nationalism and the Right Wing in Japan.* London: Oxford University Press, 1960.

———, ed. *Thought and Behavior in Modern Japanese Politics.* London: Oxford University Press, 1963. See also reference under Maruyama Masao above.

Mosley, Leonard. *Hirohito, Emperor of Japan.* London: Prentice-Hall International, 1966.

Nakamura, Hajime. *Ways of Thinking of Eastern Peoples: India–China–Tibet–Japan.* Edited by Philip P. Wiener. Honolulu: East-West Center, 1964.

Nakamura, Masanori. *Japanese Monarchy.* New York: M.E. Sharpe, 1992.

Nhat Hanh, Thich. *The Miracle of Mindfulness.* Boston: Beacon Press, 1976.

Niebuhr, Reinhold. *Moral Man and Immoral Society.* New York: Charles Scribner's Sons, 1932.

Nukariya, Kaiten. *Religion of the Samurai: A Study of Zen Philosphy and Discipline in China and Japan.* Luzac's Oriental Religions 4. London: Luzac, 1913.

Payne, Richard, ed. *Re-visioning Kamakura Buddhism.* Honolulu: University of Hawai'i Press, 1998.

Peattie, Mark R. *Ishiwara Kanji and Japan's Confrontation with the West.* Princeton, NJ: Princeton University Press, 1975.

Queen, Christopher S., ed. *Engaged Buddhism in the West.* Boston: Wisdom Publications, 2000.

Queen, Christopher S., and Sallie B. King, eds. *Engaged Buddhism: Liberation Movements in Asia.* Albany: State University of New York Press, 1996.

Rhys Davids, T. W., and C. A. F. Rhys Davids, eds. *Dialogues of the Buddha.* London: Oxford University Press, 1910.

Saddhatissa, Hammalawa. *Buddhist Ethics.* London: Wisdom Publications, 1987.

Safe, Mike. "Amen." *Australian Magazine,* July 29–30, 22–26.

Sanger, David E. "Mayor Who Faulted Hirohito Is Shot." *New York Times,* January 19, 1990. https://www.nytimes.com/1990/01/19/world/mayor-who-faulted-hirohito-is-shot.html.

Shaku, Soyen. *Sermons of a Buddhist Abbot.* Translated by D. T. Suzuki. La Salle, IL: Open Court, 1906.

Sharf, Robert. "Zen and the Way of the New Religions." *Japanese Journal of Religious Studies* 22, nos. 3–4 (1995): 417–58.

———. "The Zen of Japanese Nationalism." *History of Religions* 33, no. 1 (1993): 1–43.

Shillony, Ben-Ami. *Revolt in Japan: The Young Officers and the February 26, 1936 Incident.* Princeton, NJ: Princeton University Press, 1973.

Silke, Andrew. "Research on Terrorism: A Review of the Impact of 9/11 and the Global War on Terrorism." In *Terrorism Informatics: Knowledge Management and Data Mining for Homeland Security,* edited by Hsinchun Chen, Edna Reid, Joshua Sinai, and Andrew Silke, 27–49. New York: Springer, 2008.

Siniawer, Eiko Maruko. *Ruffians, Yakuza, Nationalists: The Violent Politics of Modern Japan, 1860–1960.* Ithaca, NY: Cornell University Press, 2008.

Smethurst, Richard J. "The Military Reserve Association and the Minobe Crisis of 1935." In *Crisis Politics in Prewar Japan,* edited by George M. Wilson, 1–23. Tokyo: Sophia University, 1970.

Smith, Patrick. *Japan: A Reinterpretation.* New York: Vintage Books, 1998.

Stone, Jacqueline. "Chanting the August Title of the *Lotus Sutra*: *Daimoku* Practices in Classical and Medieval Japan." In *Re-visioning Kamakura Buddhism,* edited by Richard Payne, 116–66. Honolulu: University of Hawai'i Press, 1998.

———. *Original Enlightenment and the Transformation of Medieval Japanese Buddhism.* Honolulu: University of Hawai'i Press, 2003

Storry, Richard. *The Double Patriots: A Study in Japanese Nationalism.* London: Chatto & Windus, 1957.

Suzuki, Daisetz T. *The Essentials of Zen Buddhism.* Westport, CT: Greenwood Press, 1973.

———. *Zen and Japanese Culture.* Princeton, NJ: Princeton University Press, 1959. First published in 1938 as *Zen Buddhism and Its Influence on Japanese Culture* (Kyoto: Eastern Buddhist Society, Otani Buddhist University).

Tanabe, George, and Willa Jane Tanabe. *The Lotus Sutra in Japanese Culture.* Honolulu: University of Hawai'i Press, 1989.

Tatz, Mark, trans. *The Skill in Means (Upāyakauśalya) Sutra.* Delhi: Motilal Banarsidass, 1994.

Titus, David. *Palace and Politics in Prewar Japan.* New York: Studies of the East Asian Institute, Columbia University, 1974.

Twain, Mark. *Autobiography of Mark Twain.* Vol. 2. Berkeley: University of California Press, 2013.

Unno, Taitetsu, trans. *Tannisho: A Shin Buddhist Classic.* Honolulu: Buddhist Studies Center Press, 1984.

Utley, Freda. *Japan's Feet of Clay.* London: Faber & Faber, 1936.

Victoria, Brian. *Zen at War.* 2nd ed. Lanham, MD: Rowman & Littlefield, 2006.

———. *Zen War Stories.* London: RoutledgeCurzon, 2003.

Walshe, Maurice, trans. *Thus Have I Heard: The Long Discourses of the Buddha.* London: Wisdom Publications, 1987.

Wetzler, Peter. *Hirohito and War.* Honolulu: University of Hawai'i Press, 1998.

Williams, Paul. *Mahāyāna Buddhism: The Doctrinal Foundations.* 2nd ed. London: Routledge, 1989.

Wilson, George. "Kita Ikki's Theory of Revolution." *Journal of Asian Studies* 26, no. 1 (November 1966): 89–99.

Wright, Dale S. *Philosophical Meditations on Zen Buddhism.* Cambridge Studies in Religious Traditions 13. Cambridge: Cambridge University Press, 1998.

Yampolsky, Philip B., trans. "Zen Master Hakuin's Letter in Answer to an Old Nun of the Hokke [Nichiren] Sect." In *The Zen Master Hakuin: Selected Writings,* 86–123. New York: Columbia University Press, 1971.

WORKS IN JAPANESE

Akashi Hirotaka and Matsuura Sōzō. *Shōwa Tokkō Dan'atsu-shi 4—Shūkyō-jin ni taisuru Dan'atsu (ge)* [History of Suppression by the Special Higher Police Division—Suppression of Religious Persons (Part Two)]. Tokyo: Taihei Shuppan-sha, 1975.

Arahara Bokusui. *Dai-uha Shi.* Tokyo: Dai-Nippon Issei-kai Shuppan, 1974.

Asahi Shimbun and Tēma Danwa-shitsu, eds. *Nihonjin no Sensō* [The Japanese People's War]. Tokyo: Heibon-sha, 1988.

Chaen Yoshio. *Zusetsu Ni-niroku Jiken.* Tokyo: Nihon Tosho Center, 2001.

Fujita Hisanori. *Jijūchō no kaisō.* Tokyo: Chūō Kōronsha, 1987.

Fukuda Kazuya. *Shōwa Tennō (Daisan-bu).* Tokyo: Bungei Shunjū, 2009.

Hanayama, Shinshō. *Eien e no Michi—Waga Hachijūnen no Shōgai* [The Way to Eternity— My Eighty Years of Life]. Tokyo: Nihon Kōgyō Shimbun-sha, 1982.

Harada, Sogaku. "Nihon Seishin to Daijō Zen" [The Japanese Spirit and Mahayana Zen]. *Chūō Bukkyō,* March 1934, 285–300.

Hori Yukio. *Uha Jiten.* Tokyo: Sanryō Shobō, 1991.

Ichikawa Hakugen. *Fudōchi Shinmyō-roku/Taia-ki.* Tokyo: Kōdan-sha, 1982.

———. *Nihon Fashizumu ka no shūkyō* [Religion under Japanese Fascism]. Tokyo: NS Shuppan-kai, 1975.

Imamura Hitoshi. *Imamura Hitoshi Taishō Kaisō-roku* [Memoirs of General Imamura Hitoshi]. 4 vols. Tokyo: Jiyū Ajia-sha, 1960.

Inoue Nisshō. *Honō no Kyūdō-sha: Inoue Nisshō Gokuchū Nikki jō* [Seeker of Flames: Inoue Nisshō's Prison Dairy]. Vol. 1. Tokyo: Mainichi Shimbunsha, 1979.

———. *Honō no Kyūdō-sha: Inoue Nisshō Gokuchū Nikki jō* [Seeker of Flames: Inoue Nisshō's Prison Dairy]. Vol. 2. Tokyo: Mainichi Shimbunsha, 1979.

———. *Ichinin issatsu* [One Person Kills One Person]. Tokyo: Nihon Shūhō-sha, 1953.

———. "Ketsumeidan Hiwa" [An Unknown Episode of the Blood Oath Corps]. *Bungei Shunjū Magazine* 32, no. 11 (July 1954): 44–49.

———. "'Tamashii no Shi': Azuma Soshin." *Hagakure Kenkyū* 73 (July 2012).

————. *Ume no Mi* [Fruit of the Plum Tree]. In Onuma Hiroaki, *Ketsumeidan Jiken-jōshinsho- gokuchū Shuki* [The Blood Oath Corps Incident–Written Statements–Prison Diaries], 40–131. Tokyo: Ketsumeidan Jiken Kōhan Sokki-roku Kankō-kai, 1971.

Inoue Ryō. "Chichi: Inoue Nisshō ga katatta Nankin to Genbaku" [My Father, Inoue Nisshō, Spoke about the Nanking Incident and the Atomic Bombing]. *Bungei Shunjū Magazine* 85, no. 11 (September 2007): 291–94.

Katano Tatsurō. *Kongō-hōzan Rinnōji gohyaku-gojū-nen-shi* [A History of the Five Hundred and Fifty Years of Kongō-hōzan Rinnōji Temple]. Sendai: Kongō-hōzan Rinnōji, 1994.

Kawabe Masakazu. *Nihon Rikugun Seishin-kyōiku Shi-kō* [Thoughts on the History of Spiritual Education in Japanese Army]. Tokyo: Harashobō, 1980.

Kawano Hitoshi. "Gyokusai no Shisō to Hakuhei Totsugeki" [The Ideology of Death before Dishonour and the Bayonet Charge]. In *Sensō to Guntai*, 154–79. Tokyo: Iwanami Shoten.

Kyōiku-sōkanbu, eds. *Seishin Kyōiku Shiryō* [Materials on Spiritual Education]. Vol. 2. Tokyo: Kaikō-sha, 1941.

Minami Hiroshi. *Nihonjin no Shinri* [Psychology of the Japanese People]. Tokyo: Iwanami Shoten, 1953.

Mutō Tōko. "Dai Tōa Kensetsu to Shōbōgenzō" [The Construction of Greater East Asia and the *Shōbōgenzō*]. *Daihōrin*, January 1942, 16–25.

Naimushō Keihō-kyoku. *Shuppan Keisatsu-hō* 73 (September 1934).

Nakajima Genjō. *Yasoji o Koete* [Beyond Eighty Years]. Numazu, Shizuoka Prefecture: Shōinji, 1998.

Nakajima Takeshi. *Ketsumeidan Jiken* [The Blood Oath Corps Incident]. Tokyo: Bungei Shunjū, 2013.

Nakano Masao. *Kakumei wa geijutsu nari: Tokugawa Yoshichika no shōgai*. Tokyo: Gakugei Shorin, 1977.

Nishida Norimasa, ed. *Izoku Tokuhon* [Reader for Bereaved Families]. Kyoto: Rikugun Juppei-bu, 1941.

Noda Masa'aki. *Sensō to Zaiseki* [War and the Responsibility of the Accused]. Tokyo: Iwanami Shoten, 1998.

Ogata Hiroshi, ed. *Bukkyō to Shakai Undō* [Buddhism and Social Movements]. Tokyo: Ministry of Justice, Bureau of Criminal Affairs, 1939. (*Shisō Kenkyū Shiryō* 52.)

Okamoto Sekiō. "Kokumin Seishin to Muga" [The People's Spirit and the Nonself]. *Sanshō*, June 1935, 206–12.

Okamura Ao. *Ketsumeidan jiken* [The Blood Oath Corps Incident]. Tokyo: San-ichi Shobō, 1989.

Ōki, Michiyoshi. *Bukkyōsha no Sensō Sekinin—Nichiren Shōshū no Rekishi Kaizan o Itou* [The War Responsibility of Buddhists—Questioning the Falsifying of History by Nichiren Shōshū]. Tokyo: Bungei-sha, 1998.

Okuda Kyūji. *Senjinkun to Nihon Seishin* [The Field Service Code and the Spirit of Japan]. Tokyo: Gunji Kyōiku Kenkyū-kai, 1942.

Ōmori Sōgen. *Ken to Zen*. Tokyo: Shunjū-sha, 1966.

————. *Sanzen Nyūmon*. Tokyo: Kōdan-sha, 1986.

————. *Yamaoka Tesshū*. Tokyo: Shunjū-sha, 1983.

Onuma Hiroaki. *Ketsumeidan Jiken-jōshinsho-gokuchū Shuki* [The Blood Oath Corps Incident–Written Statements–Prison Diaries]. Tokyo: Ketsumeidan Jiken Kōhan Sokki-roku Kankō-kai, 1971.

————. *Ketsumeidan Jiken Kōhan Sokki-roku* [The Stenographic Record of the Public Trial of the Blood Oath Corps Incident]. 3 vols. Tokyo: Ketsumeidan Jiken Kōhan Sokki-roku Kankō-kai, 1963.

Onuma Shō. *Issatsu Tashō* [Kill One That Many May Live]. Tokyo: Yomiuri Shimbunsha, 1974.

Ota Beyūji. *Tokugawa Yoshichika no Jūgo-nen Sensō* [Tokugawa Yoshichika's Fifteen-Year War]. Tokyo: Aoki Shoten, 1988.

Satō Gan'ei. *Bushidō.* Tokyo: Senryūdō, 1902.

Sayamoto Yorio, *Sawamoto Yorio Kaigun Jikan Nikki.* Tokyo: Chūo Kōron Magazine, 1998.

Sugawara Yutaka, *Aizawa Chūsa Jiken no Shinsō.* Tokyo: Keizai Ōrai-sha, 1971.

Suzuki Daisetsu [also Daisetz]. *Bukkyō no Tai-i* [An Outline of Buddhism]. Kyoto: Hōzōkan, 1947.

————. "Daijō Bukkyō no Sekaiteki Shimei—Wakaki Hitobito ni yosu" [World Mission of Mahayana Buddhism—Written for Young People]. In *Suzuki Daisetsu Zenshū*, vol. 29, 338–53. Tokyo: Iwanami Shoten, 1970.

————. *Isshinjitsu no Sekai.* Tokyo: Kondō Shoten, 1941.

————. "Jijoden." In *Suzuki Daisetsu Zenshū*, vol. 30, 563–622. Tokyo: Iwanami Shoten, 1970.

————. "Nihonjin no Shōji-kan" [The Japanese View of Life and Death]. In *Suzuki Daisetsu Zenshū*, vol. 29, 29–37. Tokyo: Iwanami Shoten, 1970.

————. *Nihon no Reiseika.* Kyoto: Hōzōkan, 1947.

————. *Nihonteki Reisei* [Japanese Spirituality]. In *Suzuki Daisetsu Zenshū*, vol. 8, 3–233. Tokyo: Iwanami Shoten, 1968.

————. *Reiseiteki Nihon no Kensetsu* [Construction of a Spiritual Japan]. In *Suzuki Daisetsu Zenshū*, vol. 9, 1–258. Tokyo: Iwanami Shoten, 1968.

————. *Shin Shukyō-ron* [Treatise on New Religion]. In *Suzuki Daisetsu Zenshū*, vol. 23, 1–147. Tokyo: Iwanami Shoten, 1969.

————. *Suzuki Daisetsu Zenshū.* New enlarged edition. 40 vols. Edited by Hisamatsu Shin'ichi, Yamaguchi Susumu, and Furuta Shōkin. Tokyo: Iwanami Shoten, 1999–2003.

————. "Tokkō-tai" [Special Attack Forces]. In *Suzuki Daisetsu Zenshū*, vol. 30, 38–43. Tokyo: Iwanami Shoten, 1970.

————. *Tōyōteki Ichi* [Oriental Oneness]. In *Suzuki Daisetsu Zenshū*, vol. 7, 305–442. Tokyo: Iwanami Shoten, 1968.

————. *Zen Hyaku-dai.* Tokyo: Daitō Shuppansha, 1943.

————. "Zenkai Sasshin" [Reform of the Zen World]. In *Suzuki Daisetsu Zenshū*, vol. 30, 410–14. Tokyo: Iwanami Shoten, 1970.

————. "Zen to Bushidō." In *Bushidō no Shinzui*, edited by Handa Shin, 64–78. Tokyo: Teikoku Shoseki Kyōkai, 1941.

Suzuki Nikkyō. "Kun'yu Dai Nijū-go" [Exhortation, Number Twenty-Nine]. *Dai-Nichiren*, January 1942, 1.

————. "Shinkō no Hongi" [The True Meaning of Religious Faith]. *Dai-Nichiren*, April 1942, 11–15.

Takagi Sōgō. *Gempō Rōshi.* Tokyo: Daizō Shuppan-sha, 1963.

Takisawa Makoto. *Gondō Seikyō* [Gondō Seikyō]. Tokyo: Pelikan-sha, 1996.

Tamaki Benkichi. *Kaisō—Yamamoto Gempō* [Reminiscences of Yamamoto Gempō]. Tokyo: Shunjū-sha, 1970.

Tanaka Chigaku, *Shishi-ō Zenshū Daisan-shū* [Complete Works of the Lion King—Part Three]. Vol. 6. Tokyo: Shishi-ō Bunko, 1937.

Tanaka Tadao. *Sawaki Kōdō—Kono Koshin no Hito* [Sawaki Kōdo—Heart of an Ancient Man]. 2 vols. Tokyo: Daihōrin-kaku, 1995.

Terasaki Hidenari. *Shōwa Tennō Dokuhakuroku* [Record of Emperor Hirohito's Monologue]. Tokyo: Bungei Shunjū, 1991.

Toyoda Jō. *Kakumeika Kita Ikki.* Tokyo: Kōdan-sha, 1991.

Tsunemitsu Kōnen. *Meiji no Bukkyō-sha* [Meiji Era Buddhists]. Vol. 1. Tokyo: Shunjū-sha, 1968.

Yamada Kyōdō. *Mugai-san no Fūkei* [A View of Mugai]. Sendai: Hōbundō, 1991.

Yamaji Kazuyoshi. *Zen no Ōyō* [The Practical Use of Zen]. Tokyo: Shūbunkaku Shobo, 1941.

Yasutani Ryōkō (aka Haku'un). *Dōgen Zenji to Shūshōgi* [Zen Master Dōgen and the *Shūshōgi*]. Tokyo: Fuji Shobō, 1943.

Yoshida Yūji. *Tennō Zaibatsu.* Tokyo: Gakkyū, 2011.

Yutaka Yoshida. "Nankin Daigyaku-satsu o dō toraeru ka" [How to Grasp the Great Nanking Massacre]. In *Nankin Daigyaku-satsu to Genbaku*, 120–34. Osaka: Tōhō Shuppan, 1995.

Index

About the Author

Brian Ryōjun (aka Daizen) Victoria holds an M.A. in Buddhist studies from the Sōtō Zen sect–affiliated Komazawa University in Tokyo and a Ph.D. from the Department of Religious Studies at Temple University. He also holds a first-degree black belt in the martial art of *aikidō*.

Brian first came to Japan in 1961 in order to perform his "alternate service duty" as a conscientious objector, promoting international friendship and understanding by teaching English at Aoyama Gakuin University in Tokyo. It was during this period that Brian began his Zen training as a layman at the the Sōtō Zen monastery of Eiheiji in Fukui prefecture. He then formally entered the Sōtō Zen priesthood in 1964 as a disciple of the Venerable Tatsugami Ryōsen, abbot of Reisenji Temple in Fukui prefecture and longtime *Inō* (cantor/discipline master) at Eiheiji.

Following monastic training at Eiheiji, Brian pursued graduate studies in Buddhism at Komazawa University from 1968, during which time he became a disciple of Sōtō Zen scholar-priest Yokoi Kakudō. Following Yokoi's untimely death from cancer, Brian received Dharma transmission from the Venerable Asada Daisen, abbot of Jōkuin Temple in Saitama prefecture, in 1975.

Brian's ordained name is Ryōjun (Penetrating Goodness). His pen name is Daizen (Great Meditation).

In addition to *Zen War Stories* (2003), Brian's writings include *Zen at War* (2nd ed., 2006); an autobiographical work in Japanese titled *Gaijin de ari, Zen bozu de ari* (As a Foreigner, as a Zen Priest) (1971); *Zen Master Dōgen*, coauthored with Prof. Yokoi Yūhō of Aichi-gakuin University (1976); and a translation of *The Zen Life* by Sato Koji (1972).

In the past, legal and nonviolent opposition to U.S. involvement in the Vietnam War, coupled with support for political prisoners throughout Asia, led to Brian's deportation from the Republic of China on Taiwan, the People's Republic of China, South Korea, the former Republic of South Vietnam (on two occasions), and eventual imprisonment and visa cancellation in Japan.

At present, Brian is a senior research fellow of the Oxford Centre for Buddhist Studies, a recognized independent center of the University of Oxford. He is also a special lecturer at the Sōtō Zen–affiliated Hōkyōji Temple in Fukui prefecture, Japan. He is not affiliated with any Zen group in the West.

ASIAN VOICES

An Asia/Pacific/Perspectives Series

Series Editor: Mark Selden